Opportunities
Upper Intermediate

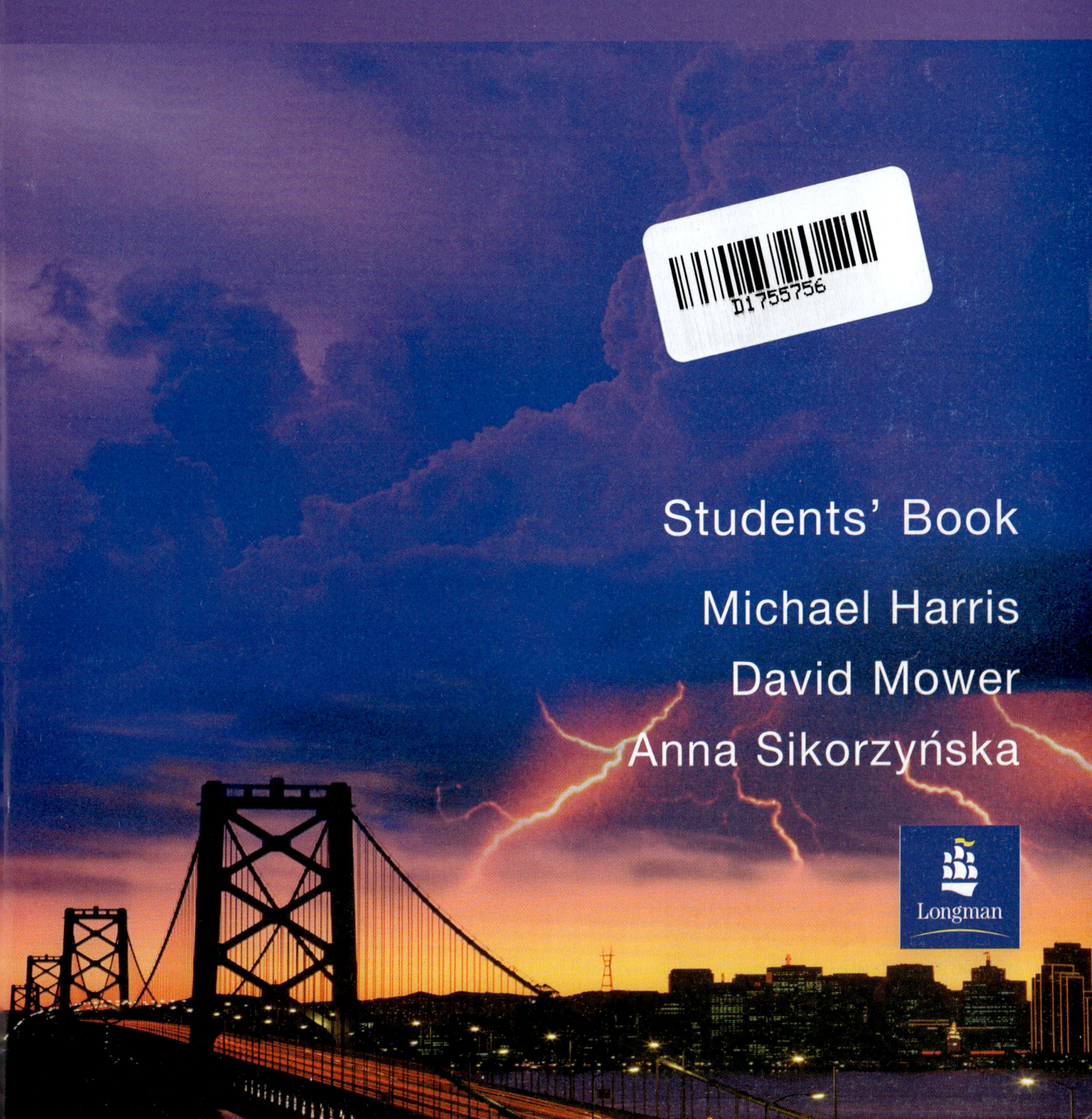

Students' Book

Michael Harris
David Mower
Anna Sikorzyńska

Longman

Contents

LESSON	LANGUAGE	SKILLS
1 IDENTITY		
Warm-up (page 5)	**Vocabulary:** personality adjectives	**Listening:** monologues **Speaking:** describing people
1 Autobiography (pages 6–7)	**Vocabulary:** wordbuilding	**Reading:** biographical extracts **Reading Strategies:** revision
2 Who Are You? (pages 8–9)	**Grammar:** Tenses **Pronunciation:** contractions	**Reading:** handwriting styles
3 National Identity (pages 10–11)	**Function:** preference: colloquial expressions **Vocabulary:** multi-part verbs	**Listening:** a radio phone-in programme; an interview **Listening Strategies:** revision **Speaking:** about own area
Communication Workshop (pages 12–13)	**Writing:** a formal and informal letter **Linking:** revision **Speaking:** a short presentation **Chatroom:** vague language; linking **Speaking Strategies:** revision	
Language Awareness 1 (page 14)	**Grammar:** Reference (1): Determiners	**Reading:** a 'Sherlock Holmes' story
2 LAUGHTER		
Warm-up (page 15)	**Vocabulary:** laughter words and expressions	**Listening:** types of laughter; monologues **Speaking:** talking about humour; personal experiences
4 A Comic Novel (pages 16–17)	**Vocabulary:** collocations	**Reading:** a literature extract **Reading Strategy:** multiple choice **Listening:** a literature extract **Speaking:** personal experiences
5 Crazy But True! (pages 18–19)	**Grammar:** Past Tenses; Past Perfect Continuous	**Reading:** newspaper stories
6 What's So Funny? (pages 20–21)	**Function:** telling jokes **Pronunciation:** emphasis **Vocabulary:** multi-part verbs	**Listening:** a TV programme; jokes **Listening Strategies:** multiple choice **Speaking:** telling a joke
Communication Workshop (pages 22–24)	**Writing:** a personal anecdote **Linking:** sequence linkers; linking with participles **Listening:** an American comedian **Speaking:** a roleplay **Chatroom:** reacting **Speaking Strategies:** preparation	
Language Awareness 2 (page 25)	**Grammar:** Simple and Continuous Tenses	**Reading:** a short story
Review: Modules 1 and 2 (pages 26–27)	Grammar and vocabulary revision	**Pronunciation:** word stress
Culture Corner 1 (page 28)	The History of English	
3 STYLE		
Warm-up (page 29)	**Vocabulary:** opinion adjectives	**Listening:** monologues **Speaking:** a questionnaire
7 Street Art (pages 30–31)	**Vocabulary:** street entertainment; verbs *make, have, get*	**Listening:** musical extracts **Reading:** a magazine article **Reading Strategies:** matching headings and paragraphs **Speaking:** about own area
8 Body Language (pages 32–33)	**Grammar:** Relative and Participle Clauses	**Reading:** a magazine article
9 Branded (pages 34–35)	**Function:** preferences: describing people **Pronunciation:** modifiers **Vocabulary:** multi-part verbs	**Listening:** a conversation; a radio programme **Listening Strategies:** true/false questions **Speaking:** describing a person
Communication Workshop (pages 36–38)	**Writing:** a description of a person and place **Linking:** *so* and *such* **Listening:** a song **Speaking:** discussing a photo **Chatroom:** colloquial expressions **Speaking Strategies:** gaining time	
4 BEAUTY		
Warm-up (page 39)	**Vocabulary:** opinion adjectives	**Listening:** dialogues **Speaking:** about beauty
10 Poetry (pages 40–41)	**Vocabulary:** idiomatic language	**Reading:** a poem **Reading Strategies:** reading poetry **Speaking:** discussing images
11 Wrapped Up (pages 42–43)	**Grammar:** The Passive	**Reading:** an article
12 Music (pages 44–45)	**Vocabulary:** multi-part verbs **Function:** giving opinions: agreeing and disagreeing **Pronunciation:** intonation	**Listening:** film music; a discussion **Listening Strategies:** matching people and opinions **Speaking:** personal tastes in music; reacting to music
Communication Workshop (pages 46–48)	**Writing:** a film review **Linking:** revision; *either ... or, neither ... nor* **Listening:** a conversation **Speaking:** planning an event **Chatroom:** colloquial expressions **Speaking Strategies:** taking turns in group discussions	
Language Awareness 3 (page 49)	**Grammar:** Reference (2): Pronouns	**Reading:** a magazine article
Review: Modules 3 and 4 (pages 50–51)	Grammar and vocabulary revision	**Pronunciation:** /s/ and /z/
Culture Corner 2 (page 52)	English Around the World	

LESSON	LANGUAGE	SKILLS
5 NEW FRONTIERS		
Warm-up (page 53)	**Vocabulary:** scientific words	**Listening:** radio programmes **Speaking:** discussing science today
13 Eureka! (pages 54–55)	**Vocabulary:** compound words	**Reading:** a magazine article **Reading Strategies:** true/false/no information questions **Speaking:** about scientific discoveries
14 Futurology (pages 56–57)	**Grammar:** The Future; Future Perfect; Future Continuous	**Reading:** a magazine article
15 Artificial Intelligence (pages 58–59)	**Function:** clarifying and asking questions **Vocabulary:** multi-part verbs	**Listening:** an interview; a film story **Listening Strategies:** completing notes **Speaking:** explaining how a robot works
Communication Workshop (pages 60–62)	**Writing:** an article **Linking:** reason and purpose **Speaking:** a presentation **Chatroom:** presenting	**Listening:** a song **Speaking Strategies:** giving presentations
6 SOFT MACHINE		
Warm-up (page 63)	**Vocabulary:** parts of the body	**Listening:** a quiz **Speaking:** personal habits and routines
16 Life Savers (pages 64–65)	**Vocabulary:** illness and disease; synonyms	**Reading:** a newspaper article **Reading Strategies:** texts with paragraph gaps **Speaking:** the future of medicine
17 Super Athletes (pages 66–67)	**Grammar:** Conditionals; Mixed Conditionals **Pronunciation:** contractions	**Reading:** a magazine article
18 Brain Power (pages 68–69)	**Function:** giving and asking for advice **Vocabulary:** multi-part verbs	**Listening:** a lecture; a radio phone-in **Listening Strategies:** completing a text **Speaking:** advising a friend
Communication Workshop (pages 70–72)	**Writing:** a discursive essay (1) **Linking:** concession and contrast **Pronunciation:** emphatic stress **Speaking:** a discussion **Chatroom:** colloquial expressions; formal and informal expressions	**Listening:** a TV programme **Speaking Strategies:** avoiding problems
Language Awareness 4 (page 73)	**Grammar:** Modality	**Reading:** a magazine article
Review: Modules 5 and 6 (pages 74–75)	Grammar and vocabulary revision	**Pronunciation:** sounds and spelling
Culture Corner 3 (page 76)	The USA (1): History	
7 JOURNEYS		
Warm-up (page 77)	**Vocabulary:** describing places	**Speaking:** travel preferences **Listening:** travel experiences
19 On The Road (pages 78–79)	**Vocabulary:** wordbuilding	**Reading:** travel literature extracts **Reading Strategies:** sequencing events **Speaking:** about holiday
20 Migrating (pages 80–81)	**Grammar:** Verb Patterns: '-ing' form and infinitive	**Reading:** photo captions
21 Trans-Continental (pages 82–83)	**Vocabulary:** multi-part verbs **Function:** polite requests **Pronunciation:** politeness	**Listening:** an advertisement; dialogues **Listening Strategies:** identifying situations and people **Speaking:** a roleplay **Speaking Strategies:** being polite
Communication Workshop (pages 84–86)	**Writing:** a formal letter **Linking:** condition **Speaking:** a roleplay **Chatroom:** showing sympathy; ellipsis	**Listening:** a song
8 GLOBAL ISSUES		
Warm-up (page 87)	**Vocabulary:** global issues	**Listening:** the news; statistics **Speaking:** discussing global issues
22 Unnatural Disasters (pages 88–89)	**Vocabulary:** disasters; prefixes	**Reading:** a magazine article **Reading Strategies:** completing texts with sentence gaps **Speaking:** disasters and aid
23 Global Warming (pages 90–91)	**Grammar:** Reporting	**Reading:** a newspaper report
24 Rich and Poor (pages 92–93)	**Function:** justifying arguments **Pronunciation:** stress in multi-part verbs **Vocabulary:** solutions to social and environmental problems; multi-part verbs	**Reading:** graphs and statistics **Listening:** a lecture; a dialogue **Listening Strategies:** taking lecture notes **Speaking:** a discussion: problem solving
Communication Workshop (pages 94–96)	**Listening:** a radio programme **Writing:** a report **Speaking:** discussing photos **Chatroom:** giving opinions; impersonal 'you' **Speaking Strategies:** using photos in discussions	**Linking:** formal linkers: a review
Language Awareness 5 (page 97)	**Grammar:** Impersonal Report Structures	**Reading:** a newspaper article
Review: Modules 7 and 8 (pages 98–99)	Grammar and vocabulary revision	**Pronunciation:** word stress
Culture Corner 4 (page 100)	The USA (2): The History of Popular Music	

CONTENTS

LESSON	LANGUAGE	SKILLS
9 SOCIETY		
Warm-up (page 101)	**Vocabulary:** social problems; describing trends	**Listening:** a news report **Speaking:** a discussion
25 Golden Ages (pages 102–103)	**Vocabulary:** rich language	**Reading:** a magazine article **Reading Strategies:** summarising **Writing:** a concluding paragraph
26 Consumer Society (pages 104–105)	**Grammar:** Complex Sentences (1): Persuasion	**Reading:** a newspaper article **Listening:** a dialogue
27 Utopia (pages 106–107)	**Function:** making suggestions **Pronunciation:** strong and tentative suggestions **Vocabulary:** multi-part verbs	**Listening:** a story; a dialogue **Listening Strategies:** understanding cultural references **Speaking:** roleplays
Communication Workshop (pages 108–110)	**Writing:** a discursive essay (2) **Linking:** reason and result **Vocabulary:** crime and punishment **Listening:** a song **Speaking:** problem solving **Chatroom:** exaggeration and understatement; reacting to suggestions **Pronunciation:** assimilation and elision **Speaking Strategies:** preparing for problem solving	
10 CONFLICT		
Warm-up (page 111)	**Vocabulary:** conflict words	**Listening:** TV news **Speaking:** speculating
28 War Memories (pages 112–113)	**Vocabulary:** word families	**Reading:** war memoirs **Reading Strategies:** reading under pressure
29 Neighbours From Hell (pages 114–115)	**Grammar:** Complex Sentences (2): Emphasis	**Reading:** a newspaper story
30 Conflict Resolution (pages 116–117)	**Vocabulary:** multi-part verbs **Function:** arguing **Pronunciation:** mood	**Listening:** a dialogue; a radio programme **Listening Strategies:** identifying mood **Speaking:** roleplays
Communication Workshop (pages 118–120)	**Writing:** a letter of complaint **Linking:** a review **Speaking:** a formal phone conversation **Chatroom:** formal expressions	**Listening:** a filmscript
Language Awareness 6 (page 121)	**Grammar:** Perfective Verb Forms	**Reading:** a letter
Review: Modules 9 and 10 (pages 122–123)	**Grammar and vocabulary revision**	**Pronunciation:** consonant sounds
Literature Spot 1 (pages 124–125)	The Strange Case of Dr Jekyll and Mr Hyde, by Robert Louis Stevenson	
Literature Spot 2 (pages 126–127)	Love Poems: a selection	
Literature Spot 3 (pages 128–129)	The Martian Chronicles, by Ray Bradbury	
Literature Spot 4 (pages 130–131)	The Shepherd Andreas, by Karen Connelly	
Literature Spot 5 (pages 132–133)	No Crime in the Mountains, by Raymond Chandler	

Pairwork / Answer Key (pages 134–136)

Writing Help (pages 137–145)

Grammar Summary (pages 146–150)

Lexicon (pages 151–176)

1 Identify

In this module you...

- **Talk about** different kinds of identity and **give a short presentation about** yourself.
- **Listen to** monologues, a radio programme, an interview and a presentation.
- **Read** extracts from an autobiography, a diary and letters. **Use** listening and reading strategies.
- **Write** a formal or informal letter.
- **Revise** the main tenses in English.

Warm-up

1 Look at the photos of Seb and the people in his life. Listen and identify who is speaking about him.

2 Listen again. Which of the Key Words are used to describe Seb?

KEY WORDS: Personality

ambitious, careless, chatty, cheerful, childish, competitive, considerate, conventional, easy-going, hard-working, idealistic, impatient, individualistic, kind, likeable, moody, outgoing, popular, reckless, reliable, reserved, romantic, selfish, sensible, sensitive, sentimental, shy, sociable, sympathetic

What do you think the good and bad sides of Seb's character are?

Example
good side = cheerful
bad side = impatient with machines

3 Listen and use these words to complete the sentences about Sarah.

deep down, a bit, tends to, not very, seems, can be, rather

1. But she's _____ reserved and shy, maybe because she's too sensitive.
2. Sarah _____ keep to herself a lot and she's _____ sociable.
3. I think she's _____ sentimental.
4. She _____ moody, especially when she's tired.
5. When you first meet Sarah, she _____ a bit unfriendly.
6. But when you get to know her you realise that _____ she's a really good person.

Which of the expressions above do we use to express negative personality traits politely?

4 Choose three different people who know you. Write what they might say about you.

Example This person thinks that I'm nice and kind. She also probably thinks ...

➪ **Lexicon, page 151.**

5 Work in pairs. Read your descriptions to your partner. Guess the people.

A teacher — A close friend — Seb's girlfriend — A team mate — Seb's mother

Module 1

1 Autobiography

Skills Focus

Before you start

1 Think about an important scene in your life that you remember very clearly. Tell the class.

Example A scene I remember very well is when I won a competition at primary school …

Reading

2 Read the Strategies.

> **READING STRATEGIES: Revision**
> - Before reading, look at the title, pictures and the first couple of lines of the text. Look for clues to help you predict what kind of text it is and what it is about.
> - Read the text to get the general idea. Ignore words you don't know.
> - Read the text again. Try to work out the meaning of important new words. Use a dictionary if you can't.
> - Read any comprehension questions and try to think of possible answers. Then find answers to the questions in the text.

Use the Strategies to answer these questions about the texts.

Text 1
1 What time of year do you think it is? Why?
2 Who do you think Peter is? How do you think the diary writer feels about him?
3 How old do you think the writer is? Give your reasons.
4 What do you think is unusual about the writer's situation?

Text 2
1 How was the girl different from other children?
2 Why was her teacher so important for her?
3 How did she learn new words?
4 Why did she feel happy when she understood the meaning of the word 'water'?

What do you think happened later to the writers of the texts? Check your answers on page 135.

Text 1

The weather's been wonderful since yesterday, and I've perked up quite a bit. My writing, the best thing I have, is coming along well. I go to the attic almost every morning to get the stale air out of my lungs. This morning when I went there, Peter was busy cleaning up. He finished quickly and came over to where I was sitting on my favourite spot on the floor. The two of us looked out at the blue sky, the bare chestnut tree glistening with dew, the seagulls and other birds glinting with silver as they swooped through the air, and we were so moved and entranced that we couldn't speak. He stood with his head against a thick beam, while I sat. We breathed in the air, looked outside and both felt that the spell shouldn't be broken with words. We remained like this for a long while, and by the time he had to go to the loft to chop wood, I knew he was a good, decent boy. He climbed the ladder to the loft, and I followed; during the fifteen minutes he was chopping wood, we didn't say a word either. I watched him from where I was standing, and could see he was obviously doing his best to chop the right way and show off his strength. But I also looked out of the open window, letting my eyes roam over a large part of Amsterdam, over the rooftops and on to the horizon, a strip of blue so pale it was almost invisible. 'As long as this exists,' I thought, 'this sunshine and this cloudless sky, and as long as I can enjoy it, how can I be sad?'

………………………

Unless you write yourself, you can't know how wonderful it is; I always used to bemoan the fact that I couldn't draw, but now I'm overjoyed that at least I can write. And if I don't have the talent to write books or newspaper articles, I can always write for myself. But I want to achieve more than that. I can't imagine having to live like Mother, Mrs van Daan and all the women who go about their work and are then forgotten. I need to have something besides a husband and children to devote myself to! I don't want to have lived in vain like most people, even those I've never met. I want to go on living even after my death! And that's why I'm so grateful to God for having given me this gift, which I can use to develop myself and to express all that's inside me!

Identity

Text 2

THE MOST IMPORTANT DAY I remember in all my life is the one on which my teacher, Anne Sullivan, came to me. It was three months before I was seven years old.
On the afternoon of that day, I knew that something was happening. I went outside and waited on the steps of the house. I could feel the sun on my face and I could touch the leaves of the plants. Then I felt someone walking towards me. I thought it was my mother and she picked me up and held me close. This was my teacher who had come to teach all things to me and, above all, to love me.
The next morning, the teacher took me into her room and gave me a doll. When I was playing with it, Miss Sullivan slowly spelled the word 'D-O-L-L' into my hand. I was interested and I imitated the movements with my fingers. I learnt a lot of words like this, but only after my teacher had been with me for several weeks did I understand that everything has a name.
One day I didn't understand the difference between 'mug' and 'water'. I became angry and threw the doll on the floor. In my quiet, dark world I didn't feel sorry for doing it. Then my teacher took me out into the warm sunshine. We walked down to the well where someone was drawing water. My teacher put my hand under the water and spelled the word 'w-a-t-e-r' at the same time in my other hand. Suddenly, I felt an understanding. The mystery of language was revealed to me. I knew then that 'w-a-t-e-r' was the wonderful cool something flowing over my hand. That living word awakened my soul, gave it light, hope, joy, set it free!

Vocabulary: Wordbuilding (Revision)

➡ **Lexicon, page 157.**

3 Use the endings to make adjectives from the words below (a–k). Some groups can have more than one ending.

-y, -ed, -ing, -ful, -(i)ous, -ish, -(i/a)ble, -less, -al, -ic, -istic, -(e/a)nt, -ive

a) mood, stuff, happiness, cloud
b) hope, care, help
c) practice, nature, logic
d) ideal, real, individual
e) decision, create, imagination
f) importance, tolerate, difference
g) mystery, ambition, danger
h) romance, sympathy, science
i) like, rely, sense
j) interest, tire, bore
k) self, child

Make adverbs from the adjectives in a, b and c. Then try to add more adjectives and adverbs to each group. Check spellings.

4 Look at the words in Exercise 3. In which of them is there a change in word stress?

Example
id*ea*l – idealistic

🎧 Listen and check your answers.

5 Put the underlined words in the correct form.

I have some very (1) please memories of my (2) child. We lived in a (3) romance cottage in the country with (4) love views of Lake Windermere. We had a (5) wonder garden with lots of animals. However, I (6) memory one year (7) extreme well. I was eight and one of my (8) favour animals was a goose called Mabel. After coming back from school, I used to (9) food Mabel. With me she was (10) usual very quiet and (11) friend. With everybody else though, Mabel was very nasty and (12) aggression. That winter was very cold and the snow was nearly a metre (13) depth. On Christmas Day we had a (14) tradition lunch – goose and Christmas pudding. I was (15) cheer until I realised that the goose was … Mabel! My (16) happy immediately disappeared and I spent the rest of the meal in tears.

6 Choose another memory from your life. Write notes about these things:

your age, place and time, who you were with, what happened, how you felt, what happened in the end

7 Work in pairs. Tell your partner about your memory.

> QUOTE …. UNQUOTE
> 'To love oneself is the beginning of a lifelong romance.'
> Oscar Wilde

Module 1

2 Who Are You?

Grammar Focus

Before you start

1 Look at the pictures. Which of the things can tell us about ourselves? Write your opinions on a piece of paper.

Example I think that astrology is interesting but I don't believe in horoscopes.

Tell the class.

2 Look at the three pieces of handwriting (1–3). Try to match them with the personality descriptions (a–c).

a) This person is individualistic – someone who likes doing things in their own way. He/She is also a perfectionist who always makes sure that everything is just right.

b) This person is ambitious and idealistic – someone who has strong principles and beliefs. He/She is also very logical.

c) This person is quite conventional – someone who doesn't like to be different. He/She is also rather shy but is a good observer of people.

Check your answers on page 135.

Palm Reading

Graphology – Handwriting Analysis

1 I suppose I am quite a sporty person. (1) I <u>play</u> tennis and badminton quite a lot. (2) I'<u>m</u> also <u>learning</u> judo, though I'm still not very good at it. Unfortunately, I haven't got much time to practise as (3) I'<u>ve been</u> very busy with my exams. Anyway, when (4) I <u>finish</u> school (5) I'm <u>going</u> to do an intensive summer course that they're organising at my local club.

2 Hi Sue
How (6) <u>are</u> you <u>getting on</u>? (7) <u>Has</u> anything <u>happened</u> at home while (8) I'<u>ve been</u> away? (9) <u>Have</u> you <u>been doing</u> anything interesting? (10) We'<u>re getting</u> the boat to Athens and flying back from there on Saturday. The plane (11) <u>leaves</u> quite late, so (12) we'<u>ll</u> probably get home after midnight.
Yesterday, we went to a street market and (13) I <u>bought</u> some really nice things and I bargained a bit! It was fun! By the way, (14) I'<u>ve bought</u> that bracelet you wanted. (15) I'<u>ll see</u> you when (16) we <u>get back</u>.
Love,
Emma

3 One of the worst experiences that (17) <u>has ever happened</u> to me was last year. I was riding my horse Toby in the woods. (18) It <u>had rained</u> a lot the night before and the ground was very wet. (19) We <u>were going down</u> a steep path when (20) I <u>saw</u> a huge snake...

3 Work in pairs. Give your partner the piece of paper with your handwriting on it from Exercise 1. Use the information on page 135 to 'analyse' your partner's handwriting. Tell your partner your analysis. Does your partner agree with it? Let your partner tell the class.

Example
Peter says I'm very ambitious. I don't think that's true!!

Tenses
Revision

4 Look at the <u>underlined</u> verbs in the three texts. What time (past/present/future) do they refer to?

5 Match the examples underlined in the text (1–20) with these tenses and verb forms (a–i).

a) Present Simple
b) Present Continuous
c) Present Perfect
d) Present Perfect Continuous
e) Past Simple
f) Past Continuous
g) Past Perfect
h) 'going to'
i) 'will'

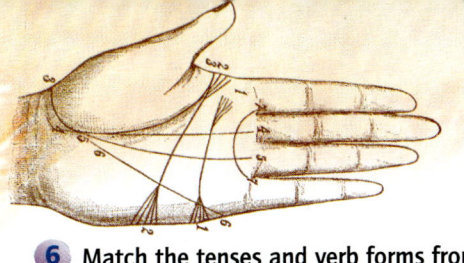

6 Match the tenses and verb forms from Exercise 5 with the uses (1–9).

1 activities going on at the time of speaking/personal arrangements for the future/temporary routines or habits
2 activities that are repeated regularly/future facts
3 intentions for the future
4 actions that happened at a specific time in the past
5 activities that form a background to events in the past
6 events that happened before other past events
7 activities in the past where the time is not important/ states that started in the past and are still true
8 activities that started in the past and continue up to now
9 predictions based on opinion, belief or knowledge/ decisions about the future taken at the moment of speaking

➡ Grammar Summary 1, page 146.

Practice

7 Underline the contractions in these sentences. What auxiliary verbs do they stand for?

a) He's been studying a lot recently.
b) We didn't do it on purpose.
c) I've had problems with my computer lately.
d) We're going out tonight.
e) I'll tell you as soon as I find out.
f) She's planning to study physics.
g) We'd seen the film before.

8 🔊 **Pronunciation.** Listen to the sentences and write down the contractions you hear.

Example 1 = 's (has)

9 Match the sentences (1–7) with the situations (a–g).

1 Have you been playing football in the rain again?
2 I play football every day.
3 I'm playing a football game on the computer.
4 I'm playing in a football match at 10 o'clock.
5 I've already played and won 20 games.
6 I was playing football when I fell badly.
7 I had played 40 games when I was injured for the first time.

a) a professional footballer talking about his job
b) a patient talking to the doctor
c) someone giving an excuse why they can't help someone now
d) someone saying how good they are
e) someone explaining why they can't go shopping the next day
f) a retired footballer looking back on his career
g) a mother to a boy whose clothes are muddy

Tarot

Astrology

10 Complete the text with the appropriate form of the verbs in brackets.

I suppose that, in many ways, I (1) *have been* (be) lucky since the day I was born. I was born two months premature and I was very ill, but somehow I (2) _____ (survive). Then, when I was three, I (3) _____ (fall) into a pond on a farm I (4) _____ (stay) at. My mum (5) _____ (go) into hospital for an operation and some friends (6) _____ (look after) me at the time. Luckily, a man (7) _____ (work) near the pond and he (8) _____ (pull) me out!
Now I'm in my last year at school and all my friends (9) _____ (think) I'm very lucky. For example, I (10) _____ (win) money on the lottery four or five times and I usually (11) _____ (beat) everybody at cards.
I can't say I'm very hard-working, but I (12) _____ (do) well at exams – the right questions always come up. I'm also lucky in love and I (13) _____ (go out) with an amazing girl for the last six months. I hope my luck (14) _____ (continue) in the future.
I (15) _____ (take) my university entrance exams in the summer and as soon as I (16) _____ (finish) them, I (17) _____ (travel) for a couple of months. Then, hopefully, I (18) _____ (study) architecture at university.

11 Look at the questions. In what situations could they be asked? Who could be talking?

Example 1 *people who meet for the first time*

1 What do you do?
2 What have you been doing recently?
3 What are you doing tonight?
4 What are you going to do when you finish school?
5 What were you doing on Sunday evening?
6 What have you done today?

In pairs ask and answer the questions.

12 Take turns to say the sentences about your life using the time expressions below.

Example
I usually play basketball on Tuesday night.

usually, never, now, this weekend, last year, in the future, next year, in 1999, for three weeks, since, at ten o'clock, twice a week, when, while, recently, for a year now

Module 1

3 National Identity

SKILLS FOCUS

Before you start

1 Put the words below into the correct categories in the Key Words box.

animal lovers, advanced, democratic, emotional, friendly, liberal, modern, nature lovers, noisy, outgoing, powerful, violent

KEY WORDS: National Identity

country: developed, developing, historic, innovative, multicultural, wealthy, well-organised
people: class-conscious, communicative, conservative, excitable, family-oriented, law-abiding, nationalistic, polite, proud, religious, reserved, serious, suspicious of foreigners, tolerant, traditional

2 Look at the photos of Britain. Choose eight adjectives or expressions from Exercise 1 that reflect your view of Britain and the British. Tell the class.

Example To me the British seem to be quite traditional.

Listening

3 Read the Strategies.

LISTENING STRATEGIES: Revision
- Before listening, look at the task. Try to guess answers to the questions.
- The first time you listen, answer as many questions as you can.
- The second time, answer the questions you missed.
- Do not worry if you don't understand every word.

Listen to a radio phone-in programme. Use the Strategies to decide if these statements are true (T) or false (F). Then listen again and check your answers.

1 Great Britain is made up of four different nations: England, Northern Ireland, Scotland and Wales.
2 In a poll, British people described themselves as animal lovers and tolerant but suspicious of foreigners and reserved.
3 Eighty-seven percent of British people thought that the British were class-conscious.
4 The first caller thinks Britain is an innovative place.
5 She describes herself as English rather than British.
6 The second caller feels European.
7 The third caller is of Indian origin.
8 She thinks Britain is multicultural but there is an intolerant minority.
9 The last caller thinks Britain is a modern country.
10 He is a Scottish nationalist and doesn't feel British.

Identity

4 🎧 Listen to an interview with Claire. What does she like and dislike about Britain? Where would she like to live for some time?

5 🎧 Listen again and complete the Function File with these words:

'd rather, wouldn't mind, can't stand, 'd prefer, love, hate, don't think I'd want, really into, really like, don't like, really keen on, just love, not keen on myself, 'd love, prefer

Function File

Preferences: Colloquial Expressions

I'm (1) _____ clubbing, you know.
I (2) _____ doing that too.
I mean I (3) _____ the variety.
I'm (4) _____ listening to house and garage.
I (5) _____ rock climbing.
I (6) _____ all the traffic we've got.
I (7) _____ sitting in traffic jams!
Another thing I'm (8) _____ is football.
I (9) _____ all the violence around it.
I (10) _____ watching tennis myself.
I (11) _____ living in Australia, for a while at least.
I (12) _____ to go out there.
But I (13) _____ to live there for ever.
I (14) _____ to go just for a few months.
And I (15) _____ go in their summer.

What is the difference in meaning between 'I love ...' and 'I'd love to ...', 'I prefer ...' and 'I'd prefer to ...'? Make a list of the expressions that are followed by the '–ing' form.

6 Write your answers to these questions.

1 What are you into doing at weekends?
2 What would you like to do this weekend?
3 What sports are you keen on watching?
4 What sports star would you love to meet?
5 What are the things you can't stand doing?
6 What thing would you prefer not to do tomorrow?

Work in pairs. Ask and answer the questions above.

Speaking

7 Make a list of good and bad things about living in your country, town or region.

Example *Good things: rock climbing, sailing, skiing*

Now in pairs, ask and answer the questions below. Use the expressions from the Function File.

Example 1 *I'm really into clubbing.*

1 What kind of things do you like about living in ...?
2 What sort of things do you dislike about living in ...?
3 Where else would you like to live? Why?

Tell the class.

Vocabulary: Multi-part Verbs

➪ **Lexicon, pages 170–176.**

8 Complete the description with these verbs in the correct form.

get at, ring up, get to, take off, get by, put up with, get on with, look forward to, check in

When I am abroad, I always (1) <u>look forward to</u> getting back home. I start feeling homesick as soon as the plane (2) _____ . When I (3) _____ a new place, the first thing I do after I have (4) _____ at the hotel is to (5) _____ my family and have a chat with them. Unfortunately, I have to travel a lot on business and I often go to the States. I (6) _____ the Americans very well – they are always very friendly. I speak good English too, so I can (7) _____ in the States without any problems. I'm not very keen on American food, but I can (8) _____ it. The problem is that I'm a stay-at-home. My sister always (9) _____ me – she says I'm boring and unadventurous. But, as the saying goes, 'home sweet home'.

Comparing Cultures

How would you describe your country or region and the people from it?

QUOTE .... UNQUOTE
'An Englishman is never happy unless he is miserable; a Scotsman is never at home but when he is abroad.'
Anonymous, 19th century

Module 1

Communication Workshop

Writing: A Letter

Before you start

1 Read the two letters and the e-mail. Choose the correct linking words in the letters.

2 Which of the texts is formal? Find formal and informal examples of these things:

greeting, requests, punctuation, grammar, vocabulary, linking words, ending the letter, signing off

Check your answers in the Writing Help, page 137.

Dear Mary,

Let me introduce myself. My name is Patrick Murphy and I've just found out I'm a cousin of yours!
I'm kind of interested in the history of our family (1) <u>so/because</u> I've started doing some research. I've found out that my grandfather, Adam, came over to America in the 1930s (2) <u>when/after</u> leaving Ireland. He was the brother of your grandad (Sam).
(3) <u>Well/However</u>, here's some info about me. I live in Des Moines, Iowa, with my wife (Cheryl) and two kids (Pat 18 and Kim 15). There are about fifty of us altogether here! Here's a picture of some of us at a recent wedding. I'm the one on the far right.
(4) <u>In addition/Anyway</u>, cousin (can I call you that?), can you do me a favor? Can you send me a photo of your family? It'd be great if you could (5) <u>also/too</u> send me any info you have about your folks back in the 'old country'.

I hope to hear from you soon.

Yours,
Patrick Murphy

Hi there Anna,
Don't know if you got my first message. I've been having problems with my computer, so am sending it again.
Look forward to hearing all about you. What kind of music are you into? What sort of things do you do in your free time? What about sport? I'm a football fanatic myself!
Get in touch soon!
All the best,
Mark

Dear Ms Novak,

Thank you for the interest you have shown in our summer courses at Exmoor English College. I enclose a brochure with information about the courses we offer (6) <u>plus/also</u> the accommodation we provide. It lists the trips and activities we organise, (7) <u>as well as/such as</u> canoeing and horseriding.

Exmoor English is a small school. (8) <u>Although/However</u>, we have an excellent teaching staff. (9) <u>Because/In case</u> of the small numbers there is a friendly atmosphere at the school and we can offer our students plenty of individual attention.
(10) <u>In addition/Anyway</u>, I enclose a brochure with local tourist information. (11) <u>Because/Although</u> Dulverton is a small town, there are plenty of things to do here. (12) <u>Despite/As well as</u> being in the national park of Exmoor, Dulverton is near an unspoilt part of the coast.

(13) <u>If/When</u> you are still interested in the course, I would be grateful if you could write us a letter in English (14) <u>because/so that</u> we can judge your level. Could you please tell us about yourself and your experience as a learner of English?

I look forward to hearing from you.

Yours sincerely,

Anne Dutton

Write a reply to one of the letters. Follow the stages below.

Stage 1
Write notes about what information you need to include.

Example *Family – Mum, Dad, Anna and me*

Stage 2
Organise your letter and plan paragraphs.

➪ Writing Help 1 (layout), page 137.

Stage 3
Use your plan to write the letter.

➪ Writing Help 1 (style, useful vocabulary, linking).

Stage 4
Check your letter.

➪ Writing Help 1 (checking).

Talkback
Work in pairs. Read your partner's letter and make suggestions for improving it.

Identity

Speaking: A Short Presentation

Before you start

1 🎧 Listen to Richard's presentation and answer these questions:

1 What are Richard's interests and hobbies?
2 Why does he remember the singing competition so well?
3 What kind of job would he like to do?

Was the presentation formal or informal?

VAGUE LANGUAGE

2 🎧 Listen again. Complete the sentences with these words.

some kind, fortyish or so, that sort of, what's its name?, something like, sort of, about

Sometimes I get up at (1) _____ 6.30.
Next Saturday, we're playing at a club ...
(2) _____ , at Echoes, that's it.
The competition was held in (3) _____ of sports centre.
She was (4) _____ and had a very kind face.
It was made of (5) _____ wood ...
I felt (6) _____ relaxed but excited at the same time.
I think I'd like to be (7) _____ the manager of a sports centre.

LINKING

3 Classify the sentences below (1–7) into the following categories:

a) starting the talk   b) introducing topics
c) adding information d) ending the talk

1 I'm **also** a keen basketball player.
2 **So, to finish off**, my ambitions and plans for the future.
3 **OK, now something else** about me.
4 **I've been asked to** tell you all about myself.
5 **Another thing** I'm really interested in is music.
6 **Well, that's it.** Thanks for listening to me.
7 **First, something about** my interests and lifestyle.

Give a short presentation about yourself. Follow the stages below.

Stage 1
Make notes about these things:
- family
- your lifestyle (interests, hobbies etc.)
- one of the most important experiences in your life
- your ambitions, plans for the future

Think of one or two false things to add.

Stage 2
Read the Strategies.

SPEAKING STRATEGIES: Revision
- When you don't know a word or expression, try not to stop completely.
- Use 'vague language' to explain more or less what you want to say, e.g. *it's a sort of ...*
- Describe things, e.g. *it's a thing you use to ...*

Work in groups. Use your notes and the Strategies to give a short presentation about yourself.

Talkback
Try to guess the false information in the presentation.

Example
I don't think it's true that ...

Language Awareness 1

1 Read the first part of a Sherlock Holmes story. What do you think happens next?

When I called on Sherlock Holmes on the second morning after Christmas, he was lying on the sofa next to some newspapers. On a chair there was a very dirty old hat and a magnifying glass.
'I suppose,' I said, 'that there is a story about that hat which will help you solve another mysterious crime.'
'There's no crime,' said Sherlock Holmes laughing. 'Just a strange little incident. Peterson, the door attendant, found the hat. At about four o'clock in the morning, he was coming back from a party when he saw a tall man carrying a goose. Suddenly, two thugs appeared. One pushed the man and the other thug tried to take the goose. Peterson went to protect the man, but seeing someone in uniform, he dropped the goose and ran away. All the attackers disappeared so Peterson was left with both the goose and the old hat. There was a card with the goose saying 'For Mrs Henry Baker' and the initials 'H.B.' inside the hat, but there are a lot of Henry Bakers in London. Peterson did not know what to do with either the hat or the goose so he brought both to me on Christmas morning. I kept the hat and Peterson had the goose for his Christmas dinner.'
'So can you find any clues about the man from this old hat?'
'What can you see, Watson?'
'Well, it is an ordinary black hat. The lining is made of red silk and there is no elastic. There is some dust on it and several spots. Someone has tried to cover all of the spots with ink. But I can't see any clues.'
'Well, Watson, the hat tells us a lot about the hat's owner. He used to be quite rich but something must have happened to him, probably problems with drink. His wife no longer loves him. He is middle-aged with grey hair - which he has had cut recently. He doesn't do much exercise and he hasn't got gas in his house.'
'You must be joking Holmes. How do you know all that information?'
'Elementary, my dear Watson...'

Find out what happens next in the story and check your guesses to Exercise 1 on page 134.

Reference (1): Determiners

➪ **Grammar Summary, page 149.**

2 Translate the expressions in blue in the text into your language.

3 Match the determiners (1–3) with the situations (a–c).

1 the second   a) there is a choice of only two people or things

2 another   b) it doesn't matter how many people or things there are

3 the other   c) the things or people are clearly ordered

4 Answer these questions.

1 Why does the text say *the sofa* but *a chair* in the description of Holmes's room? (line 2)
2 Could we use *a* instead of *the* in this context? How would the meaning change?
3 The text first mentions *a man* (line 8) and *a goose* (line 9) and later *the man* (line 9) and *the goose* (line 10). Explain why.

5 Cross out the examples in the table which are incorrect. Use the examples in the text to help you.

	Singular countable nouns	Uncountable nouns	Plural nouns
a	a hat	~~a dust~~	~~a men~~
some	some hat	some dust	some men
any	any hat	any dust	any clues
no	no hat	no elastic	no men
several	several spot	several dust	several spots
much	much spot	much exercise	much spots
a lot of	a lot of spot	a lot of exercise	a lot of spots
all (of)	all (of) the spot	all (of) that information	all (of) the spots

☞ Find practice exercises in the Language Powerbook, page 12.

Whoopi Goldberg

1 'Everything is funny as long as it's happening to someone else.'
Will Rogers

Robin Williams

The Marx Brothers

2 'Room service, send me a larger room.'
Groucho Marx

2 Laughter

In this module you...

- **Read** extracts from literature and newspaper articles; **use** reading strategies for answering multiple-choice questions.
- **Talk about** humour and tell jokes and anecdotes.
- **Listen to** a TV programme, jokes, funny stories and a sketch; **learn** listening strategies for answering multiple-choice questions.
- **Practise** using past tenses and **learn** about the Past Perfect Continuous.
- **Write** a personal anecdote.

Warm-up

1 Look at the photos and quotes (1–5) on this page. Which three do you think are the funniest? Tell the class.

2 Look at the Key Words and listen to the different types of laughter. After each one, say in what situation you might hear the laughter.

KEY WORDS: Laughter
burst out laughing, cackle, chuckle, fall about laughing, giggle

Example 1 *Someone might burst out laughing when they understand a joke.*

3 Check you understand the words and expressions below. Then listen to four extracts. In which is someone:

a) telling a joke?
b) pulling someone's leg?
c) being sarcastic?
d) describing an ironic situation?

4 Work in pairs. Ask and answer the questions below.

Example 1 *I remember giggling in a maths exam. I was thinking about ...*

1 Have you ever giggled when everybody else was serious? When?
2 Have you ever fallen about laughing so much that it hurt? When?
3 Do any of your friends make you laugh a lot? Why?
4 Has anyone ever pulled your leg? What happened? How did you feel?
5 Do you know anyone who is often sarcastic?
6 Are you good at telling jokes? Can you tell one in English?

➪ *Lexicon, page 151.*

Laurel and Hardy

3 'Too bad all the people who know how to run the country are busy driving taxi cabs and cutting hair.'
George Burns

4 'I'm not afraid of death I just don't want to be there when it happens.'
Woody Allen

5 'Laugh at yourself first, before anyone else can.'
Elsa Maxwell

Module 2

4 A Comic Novel

Skills Focus

Before you start

1 Which of the Key Words are related to these things?

water, ice, holding people, nervous reactions, noise

> **Key Words**
>
> cling, clutch, drown, emerge, faint, float, grasp, redden, scream, shout, skate, slide, splash, tremble, turn pale

2 Work in pairs. Look at the pictures. Use the Key Words to describe what is happening. Then guess what happens next.

Reading and Listening

3 🎧 Read and listen to the extracts from *The Pickwick Papers* by Charles Dickens. Check your guesses from Exercise 2.

4 Read the Strategies.

> **Reading Strategies:**
> Answering multiple-choice questions
>
> - Read the text to get the general idea. Then read the questions and options.
> - Find parts of the text that are relevant to the questions and read them carefully. Look for synonyms of words in the questions.
> - Be careful – the answer may not be stated explicitly in the text.
> - Choose an option and make sure you can eliminate the others.

Mr Pickwick, his friends and his servant, Sam, visit Mr Wardle in the country at Christmas.

'Now,' said Wardle, after a substantial lunch; 'what do you say to an hour on the ice? We have plenty of time.'
'Capital!' said Mr Benjamin Allen.
'Prime!' exclaimed Mr Bob Sawyer.
'You skate of course, Winkle?' said Wardle.
'Ye-yes; oh yes;' replied Mr Winkle. 'I – I – am rather out of practice.'
'Oh, do skate, Mr Winkle,' said Arabella. 'I like it so much.'
'Oh, it is so graceful,' said another young lady.
A third lady said it was elegant, and a fourth expressed her opinion that it was 'swan-like'.
'I should be very happy, I'm sure,' said Mr Winkle, reddening; 'but I have no skates.'
When someone announced that there were plenty of skates, Mr Winkle expressed exquisite delight, and looked exquisitely uncomfortable.

Everyone went outside to the frozen pond and Bob Sawyer started skating brilliantly.

All this time, Mr Winkle, with his face and hands blue with the cold, had been putting his skates on. At last, with the assistance of Sam, Winkle was raised to his feet.
'Now, then, Sir,' said Sam, 'off with you, and show 'em how to do it.'
'Stop, Sam, stop,' said Mr Winkle trembling violently, and clutching hold of Sam's arms with the grasp of a drowning man. 'How slippery it is, Sam!'

5 Use the Strategies to choose the best alternatives according to the text, a, b, c or d.

1 When someone suggested going ice skating, Mr Winkle was
 a) happy b) embarrassed c) enthusiastic d) bored
2 When someone said there were skates for everyone, Mr Winkle was
 a) excited b) depressed c) anxious d) overjoyed
3 Sam had to help Winkle to his feet because
 a) Winkle was very cold b) Winkle was tired
 c) Winkle couldn't skate d) Winkle was very nervous
4 When Sam said it was 'not uncommon' for ice to be slippery, he was being
 a) sarcastic b) helpful c) impatient d) observant
5 Winkle offered Sam the coats and the money because
 a) he was being generous b) he wanted Sam to stay with him to help him skate c) he was making conversation d) Sam was helping him
6 Winkle crashed into Bob Sawyer because
 a) Sam pushed him deliberately b) he wasn't looking c) he was jealous of Sawyer's skating skills d) he couldn't stop
7 It was … to get Mr Pickwick out of the water.
 a) difficult b) not necessary c) easy d) impossible

'Not an uncommon thing upon ice, Sir,' replied Sam.
'Now, Mr Winkle,' cried Mr Pickwick, quite unconscious that there was anything the matter. 'Come: the ladies are all waiting.'
'Yes, yes,' replied Mr Winkle with a ghastly smile. 'I'm coming.'
'Now, Sir, start off,' said Sam.
'Stop a moment, Sam,' gasped Mr Winkle, clinging most affectionately to Sam. 'I've got a couple of coats at home that I don't want, Sam. You may have them, Sam.'
'Thank'ee, Sir,' replied Sam.
'You needn't take your hand away,' said Mr Winkle quickly. 'I meant to give you five shillings this morning for Christmas. I'll give it to you this afternoon, Sam.'
'You're very good, Sir,' replied Sam.
'Just hold me at first, Sam, will you?' said Mr Winkle. 'There – that's right. Not too fast, Sam, not too fast.'
At that moment Mr Pickwick innocently shouted 'Sam! Here, I want you.'
'Let go, Sir,' said Sam. 'Don't you hear Mr Pickwick calling? Let go, Sir.'
With a violent effort, Sam moved away; and in doing so gave a considerable push to the unhappy Mr Winkle. That unfortunate gentleman went quickly towards the centre of the ice where Mr Bob Sawyer was skating beautifully. Mr Winkle hit him and with a loud crash they both fell heavily down.'

After this incident, some of the people started to slide on the ice without skates.

'Do you slide?' asked Wardle to Mr Pickwick.
'I used to do it, when I was a boy,' replied Mr Pickwick.
'Try it now,' said Wardle.
'Oh do, please, Mr Pickwick,' cried all the ladies.
Mr Pickwick pulled off his gloves, and put them in his hat, took two or three short runs and then stopped. At last, he took another run and went slowly down the slide, to the shouts of all the spectators who soon joined in.
The sport was at its height, the sliding was at the quickest, the laughter was at the loudest, when a crack was heard. A large piece of ice disappeared and Mr Pickwick's hat and gloves were floating on the surface; this was all of Mr Pickwick that anybody could see.
The males turned pale and the ladies fainted. Mr Tupman ran off as fast as possible, screaming 'Fire!'
At that very moment a face, head and shoulders emerged from beneath the water, and disclosed the features and spectacles of Mr Pickwick. After a lot of splashing and struggling, Mr Pickwick was finally rescued and stood on dry land.

Laughter

Vocabulary: Collocations

▷ *Lexicon, pages 160–161.*

6 Match the words from the text that go together.

1 out of   a) an opinion
2 turn   b) practice
3 dry   c) pale
4 express   d) heavily
5 fall down   e) land

Classify the collocations above into the following categories:

a) verb + adverb
b) adjective + noun
c) prepositions + noun
d) verb + adjective
e) verb + noun

7 Use the collocations below to write six sentences.

out of breath, out of order,
out of this world, out of control
turn red, turn cold, turn nasty
dry clothes, a dry climate,
a dry sense of humour
express thanks, express concern,
express horror
rain heavily, spend heavily, sleep heavily

Speaking

8 Work in pairs. Ask and answer these questions.

1 Have you ever been in a situation like Mr Winkle when you lied about your abilities? What happened?
2 What, if anything, did you find funny in the main text?
3 Have you ever chuckled to yourself while reading a book? Which book?
4 Who are some of the comic writers in your language?

5 Crazy But True!

GRAMMAR FOCUS

Before you start

1 Match the headlines with the pictures (1–3) and the newspaper extracts (a–c).

Eating Humble Pie

On Thin Ice

Out to Grass

A Erica Glendale, at 20 years old, is one of the oldest cows in Britain. Erica has delivered 238,000 pints of milk in her life and used to be a champion dairy cow. 'She won prizes every year when she was in her prime and we would always celebrate together,' said farmer Bob Maxwell. Erica has retired from competitions but last week, after he had finished work, Bob took Erica for a birthday treat to the Red Lion Inn for a slice of cake and a drink. 'If you work with an animal for 20 years you get pretty attached to it,' said Bob. 'All the regulars love Erica,' said one customer. 'But I think the Red Lion ought to think about getting a new carpet.'

B Mrs Janet Williams, of Wrexham, had a nasty shock last weekend. She was driving her car in Chester, when she noticed people were waving at her as she passed by. She started to get the feeling that something was wrong. It was! She had taken a wrong turn and was driving on a frozen canal! She managed to get out of the car just before it sank through the ice.

C Mrs Merrick, 70, had just come back from Bodmin, where she had been shopping, when she was attacked by Billy, a runaway bull. When Mrs Merrick bravely tried to defend herself, Billy knocked her over and started eating the contents of her shopping bag. The pensioner was finally rescued by a man who had been working in a nearby garage. 'The farmer sent her a lovely steak and kidney pie,' said one neighbour. 'But he didn't say whether Billy was in it.'

2 Headlines in British newspapers often 'play' with words. Match the headlines with these references (a–c).

a) an expression meaning to be in a dangerous position
b) saying you are sorry or wrong
c) an expression meaning to be retired

Which of the stories did you like most? Why?

PAST TENSES Revision

3 Read sentences 1–5 from extracts A and B. Match the tenses and verb forms with their uses (a–e).

1 We **would** always **celebrate** together.
2 She **used to be** a champion.
3 He **took** Erica for a birthday treat.
4 People **were waving** at her.
5 She **had taken** a wrong turn.

a) a situation that continued for some time in the past but is no longer true
b) a regularly repeated action in the past
c) an event that occurred before other past events
d) a single event in the past
e) a longer activity around an event in the past

4 Put these events from extract B in the order in which they actually happened. Some events may have happened at the same time.

a) Janet got out of the car.
b) People waved at Janet.
c) Janet took a wrong turn.
d) Janet noticed the people.
e) The car sank.
f) Janet drove on a frozen canal.
g) Janet felt something was wrong.

Past Perfect Continuous
Presentation

5 Read the sentence below from extract C.

Mrs Merrick, 70, had just come back from Bodmin, where she <u>had been shopping</u>, when she was attacked by Billy.

Does the <u>underlined</u> verb form describe:

a) an event before other events in the past?
b) a longer activity that happened before the main event?

6 Match the sentences with the timelines.

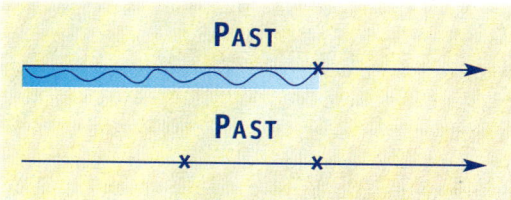

1 After he **had finished** work, Bob **took** Erica for a birthday treat.
2 The pensioner **was rescued** by a man who **had been working** in a nearby garage.

➡ Grammar Summary 2, page 146.

Practice

7 Use the cues in brackets and the Past Perfect Continuous to explain the situations.

Example 1 *His arms were sunburnt because he had been sitting in the sun all day.*

1 His arms were sunburnt. (sit in the sun all day)
2 She was very tired. (work for hours without a break)
3 Their clothes were muddy. (play football)
4 She was fired. (not come to work on time)
5 She was very angry. (wait for her boyfriend for half an hour)
6 His ear ached. (talk on the phone for hours)
7 He was covered in oil. (repair his car all afternoon)
8 She was scared stiff. (watch a thriller on TV)

8 Write two explanations for each situation (1–5), one in the Past Perfect, and one in the Past Perfect Continuous.

Example 1 *She had been eating too many sweets. She had dropped her keep-fit classes.*

1 Sharon put on five pounds.
2 Steve was feeling down.
3 Jack's shirt was torn.
4 Ann failed her final exam.
5 Emily and Tessa were very excited.

9 Put the verbs in brackets in the Past Perfect or the Past Perfect Continuous.

1 We couldn't open the door because it _____ (snow) heavily all night.
2 She looked shocked and she said she _____ (see) a UFO.
3 Billy had a black eye and Joe's lip was cut – they _____ (fight).
4 John decided to complain as his neighbours _____ (have) parties every day for two weeks.
5 Jill looked great – she _____ (lose) a few pounds and _____ (put on) a smart evening dress.
6 Sheila's eyes were red and swollen as if she _____ (cry) all night.

10 Complete the text with appropriate past tenses of the verbs in brackets.

Ken Coates (1) <u>was enjoying</u> (enjoy) his 52nd birthday at the King's Arms in Aston. He (2) _____ (play) in a local pool championship in a room at the back of the pub. Ken (3) _____ (play) well for half an hour and (4) _____ (win) three of the first five games. He (5) _____ (put) down the glass he (6) _____ (drink) from and (7) _____ (get) ready to pot the black to win the final game when his false teeth (8) _____ (drop out). Unfortunately, instead of potting the ball, he (9) _____ (pot) his own false teeth! Ken's wife, Alice, who (10) _____ (watch) the championship all night, immediately (11) _____ (rush) to help her husband. She (12) _____ (put) her hand in the pocket to fish out the false teeth when disaster (13) _____ (strike). Alice's hand got stuck in the pocket and she (14) _____ (can not) get it out again. Finally, after Ken (15) _____ (make) an emergency phone call, the fire officers (16) _____ (arrive) on the scene. With the help of a power saw and some washing-up liquid, they (17) _____ (free) Alice's hand. 'Poor Ken, he (18) _____ (try) to win the championship for years,' said a friend. 'In the replay, Ken (19) _____ (play) terribly. I think he (20) _____ (worry) about his teeth again.'

11 Work in pairs. Use the cues and the past tenses to write about a disastrous day trip.

- Mr and Mrs Smith never (be) abroad so (decide) to go on a 'no passport' day trip to France
- they (go) through the Channel Tunnel and (arrive) in Boulogne – first (go) shopping then sightseeing – in the afternoon they (decide) to visit some friends in Lille – they (go) to the station
- (not learn) French at school so (not understand) the announcements at the station – (get) on the wrong train
- while they (have) a nap on the train, it (cross) the border with Germany
- German police (ask) for their passports – they (say) they (leave) them at home – the police (put) them on a train back to Boulogne

Module 2

6 What's So Funny?

SKILLS FOCUS

Before you start

Vocabulary: Multi-part Verbs

➪ Lexicon, pages 170–176.

1 Look at the quiz. Try to work out the meaning of the underlined verbs. Then answer the quiz.

Comedy Quiz

Can you think of a comedian who

- <u>goes in for</u> imitating famous people?
- <u>puts on</u> different voices?
- <u>gets into</u> trouble and then <u>gets out of</u> it?
- <u>makes out</u> that he/she is not very bright?
- <u>dresses up</u> as different people?
- <u>makes up</u> good original sketches and jokes?
- has <u>got on</u> because he/she is so witty?
- really <u>cracks</u> you <u>up</u>?
- really <u>turns</u> you <u>off</u>?
- you used to like but you've <u>gone off</u> him/her?

Work in pairs. Compare your answers to the quiz.

Listening

2 Read the Strategies.

> **LISTENING STRATEGIES:** Answering multiple-choice questions
> - Before you listen, read the questions and options.
> - Use your own knowledge to predict the most likely answers.
> - Look at the options and think of possible synonyms, e.g. loud = noisy; in work situations = at work / when working.
> - The first time you listen, try to get the general idea and circle possible options.
> - The second time you listen, try to answer all the questions.
> - Even if you don't know an answer, always guess!

3 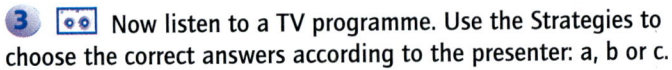 Now listen to a TV programme. Use the Strategies to choose the correct answers according to the presenter: a, b or c.

1 How do many foreigners see British people?
 a) loud b) quiet c) badly behaved

2 Foreigners might find it strange that British people use humour
 a) in silly situations b) in work situations
 c) in formal situations

3 Many jokes in English are hard to understand because
 a) they contain cultural references
 b) they are political c) they are about history

4 Jokes in English often depend on
 a) knowledge of grammar b) being difficult for foreigners
 c) words with double meanings

5 People like Charlie Chaplin and Mr Bean have been successful internationally because
 a) they have funny expressions
 b) their humour is visual c) they are famous

Laughter

4 Work in pairs. Look at the drawings above and decide what the joke is about. Tell another pair.

Example
We think the parents go away for the weekend and …

5 🎧 Listen to the joke and compare it with your version.

6 🎧 Listen to the joke again and complete the Function File with these words.

And then, guess what, there are, just can't, just before, Have you heard the one about, Luckily, right, or somewhere like that, So, eventually, Well

Function File

Telling Jokes

(1) _____ the two brothers and their dad's car?
Well, (2) _____ these two brothers.
One's just passed his driving test and the other's a bit younger, (3) _____?
And one weekend, their parents decide to go away to London, (4) _____ .
(5) _____, the parents go off to the airport …
(6) _____, they meet some friends and go out to a club.
When they get back home it's about five in the morning. (7) _____ …
When they get up, they go to the garage, and (8) _____ .
(9) _____, one of their friends works in a garage.
He (10) _____ comes and does the car, (11) _____ their parents come back home.
I (12) _____ believe it!

What tenses do we use to tell jokes? What is the difference between the meaning of *just* in numbers 11 and 12?

Pronunciation

7 🎧 Listen to the sentences. Write down the words which are emphasised to make the story more interesting. Then listen again and repeat the sentences.

Example 1 *promise / not*

Speaking

8 Work in pairs. Student A turns to page 134 and Student B to page 136. Practise telling the joke to yourself. Add words (e.g. articles and pronouns) and words and expressions from the Function File. You can add more information to make it more interesting.

9 Take turns to tell your joke to your partner. Listen to your partner's joke actively.

Example
A: *This old couple go into a cafe, right? They sit down near the window and guess who walks in.*
B: *Who?*

Comparing Cultures

Work in pairs. Discuss these questions.

1 Do jokes in your language sometimes 'play with words'? Can you think of an example?
2 In what situations do people use humour in your country? Are they the same as in Britain?
3 Do you have similar expressions for telling jokes in your language?
4 What do people tell jokes about in your country?
5 Do people where you live tell jokes about other nationalities or regions? Why? Is it fair?

Communication Workshop

Writing: A Personal Anecdote

Before you start

1 Read the story and match the headings (1–6) with the paragraphs (A–E). There is one extra heading.

1. Meeting Rusty Charley
2. The dice game
3. Some tough guys
4. High blood pressure
5. Back to normal
6. At Charley's place

2 Complete the story with these linking words.

suddenly, following, then, when, all of a sudden, in the end, before, at last, until, after (x2), as soon as, immediately, eventually

3 Find words and expressions in the text which mean the same as the words below (paragraphs in brackets).

very high (A), to die (A), hard men (C), house (D), woman (D), to hit (D), friend (D)

What style is the story 'Blood Pressure' told in: formal, neutral or informal?

'Blood Pressure' is a short story by the American writer Damon Runyan. It is set in the shady underworld of New York in the 1920s.

A I had never heard of my blood pressure (1) _____ I went around to see Doc Brennan about my stomach. Having examined me, he told me that my blood pressure was higher than a cat's back. I should be careful to avoid excitement, or I may pop off (2) _____ .
'A nervous man such as you must live quietly,' Doc Brennan said. 'Ten bucks, please.'

B (3) _____ leaving Doc Brennan's, I was standing in the street (4) _____ I saw Rusty Charley in front of me. I did not want anything to do with him for he was a hard guy indeed. He was known to carry a gun and sometimes shoot people if he did not like the way they wore their hats – and Rusty Charley was very critical of hats.
'Hello, Rusty,' I said, very pleasantly.
'Let's go to Nathan Detroit's dice game and win some money,' said Rusty.
Of course, I had no desire to go to the dice game with Rusty Charley. As well as that, I remembered what Doc Brennan had told me and I knew there was likely to be excitement at the dice game if Rusty Charley went there. But, naturally, I was not going to argue with Charley, so we went to the game.

C It was in a room full of smoke and there were some very tough guys around the table. I knew this was a very bad place for my blood pressure. (5) _____ we entered, all the guys looked around and (6) _____ there was a space at the table for us. Charley took the dice and bet Louie 1,000 dollars that he couldn't get a ten.
(7) _____ throwing the dice into a hat, he said, 'Ten'. He didn't let anybody else look in the hat, but nobody was going to doubt that Charley had thrown a ten. (8) _____ Louie handed him over a fat note, very, very slowly.

D Having left the game, Charley said, 'Let us go to my joint and have my wife make us some breakfast.' (9) _____, we got to his place and this red-headed doll opened the door.
(10) _____, she picked up a baseball bat and smacked Charley on the head.
'Wait a minute, honey, this is a pal who's here for some breakfast.'
She gave me a look I will always remember and said, 'So you are the one who keeps my husband out all night, are you?'
(11) _____ getting to the door, something hit me on the head and the roof caved in on me.
(12) _____, I woke up on the street somewhere.

E The (13) _____ day I went to Doc Brennan's. I had a lump on my head so big he thought it was a tumour. 'But,' Doc Brennan said, having taken my blood pressure, '(14) _____, your pressure is down below normal. It only goes to show what a little bit of quiet living will do for a guy,' he said. 'Ten bucks, please.'

Laughter

4 Find examples of these structures in the text.

| 1 After leaving the doctor's, | I bought a |
| 2 Having left the doctors, | newspaper. |

Use the structures to link these sentences.

1 finish my English homework – walk to the post office to post a letter
2 post the letter – meet a friend in the street and go for a coffee
3 have coffee – go to the cinema together
4 watch a really bad film – go to play table tennis at the local club
5 lose three games – I go back home again

Write a personal anecdote. Follow the stages.

Stage 1

Decide what situation you are going to write about. Here are some suggestions.

1 a day when everything went wrong
2 a disastrous school outing
3 a terrible night out

Think about the other people who were involved. Were they funny, tough, nervous?

Stage 2

Draw a timeline and write notes about the main events.

Stage 3

Divide your notes into four or five paragraphs.

➪ *Writing Help 2 (layout), page 138.*

Stage 4

Write your story in sentences.

➪ *Writing Help 2 (useful vocabulary, linking).*

Stage 5

Check your story for mistakes.

➪ *Writing Help 2 (checking).*

Talkback

In groups, read each other's anecdotes. Choose the most amusing one and tell the class.

Listening: An American Comedian

Before you start

1 Match the words (1–6) with their meanings (a–f).

1 shell	a) a book of instructions
2 tick	b) a bomb or explosive
3 manual	c) a tool used to put in or take out screws
4 screwdriver	d) metal cable used for electrical connections
5 coin	e) to make a noise like a watch or clock
6 wire	f) a piece of money made of metal

Which word can also mean 'the hard covering of a sea animal' – the sort of thing you find on the beach?

Listen to a comedy sketch and answer the questions.

2 Choose the best answer for the questions, a, b or c.

1 When police officer Willard telephones to say that he has found a bomb, the lieutenant
 a) is frightened b) misunderstands him c) ignores him

2 When the lieutenant tells Willard the bomb is 'live', Willard
 a) hangs up b) panics c) laughs

3 When Willard asks the lieutenant to come down, the lieutenant
 a) makes an excuse not to leave the office
 b) offers to bring the manual down
 c) asks Willard to bring the bomb to the office

4 Willard opens the bomb with
 a) a screwdriver b) a plate c) a coin

5 When Willard turns the wheel, the bomb
 a) ticks more slowly b) stops ticking
 c) ticks faster

6 The lieutenant can't speak to the small boy because
 a) the bomb explodes b) the boy runs away
 c) it's too noisy

7 The lieutenant is relieved in the end because the bomb
 a) was only a toy b) exploded without causing damage c) is the coastguards' responsibility

Communication Workshop

Speaking: A Roleplay

Before you start

1 🎧 Listen to the conversation in the train. Complete the notes about the man. Which three things are obviously not true?

from – the USA
family – (1) _____ children
possessions – a palace in (2) _____ and a castle in (3) _____
previous jobs – in the (4) _____ and in the US Marines
experience – lost in mountains for (5) _____ weeks
had to eat (6) _____ and worms
the snow was (7) _____ deep
the temperature was (8) _____ °C
famous people met – went (9) _____ with George W. Bush
went out with (10) _____
children – son is an (11) _____ and daughter is the new 'Madonna'

 **Chatroom**

REACTING

2 🎧 **Pronunciation.** Listen to the sounds and words in the box. What do they express? Then listen again and repeat the sounds and words.

sympathy, surprise, showing that you are listening, agreement

| Mmm   Really?   I'm sorry.   Were you?   That's right. |
| Did you?   How awful!   Have you?   You didn't!   Yeah   Uhuh |

Act out a roleplay. Follow the stages.

Stage 1
Read the Strategies.

SPEAKING STRATEGIES:
Preparation

- Before speaking activities, think about what you are going to say.
- Write notes, but do not write out what you are going to say in full. Use Key Word boxes from the module and the Lexicon to help you.
- Look at the Function File and Chatroom sections from the module for useful expressions.
- Practise saying useful expressions on your own.

Now make up lots of things about yourself. Exaggerate! Use the notes in Exercise 1 to help you.

Stage 2
Practise talking about yourself.

Example
Of course there are a lot of famous people in my family. Russell Crowe is a cousin of mine and …

Stage 3
Work in pairs. One person talks about himself/herself. The other listens and reacts using expressions from Exercise 2.

Talkback
What was obviously not true about your partner? Tell the class.

Example
Adam said he was a scientist from Canada. He said he invented the mobile phone!

Language Awareness 2

1 Read the story and answer these questions.

1. What kind of problems had the man been having?
2. How had he been feeling?
3. What physical problems did the man have?
4. Why was the doctor's suggestion not very helpful?

This story is about a middle-aged man who was feeling very down. Everything had been going wrong for him. He had had problems at work and his wife had left him to go off with a lion tamer. So, when he had been feeling depressed for over a month, he decided to go to the doctor.

He had to wait for what seemed ages in the doctor's surgery. The man next to him was looking at his watch nervously, a woman was coughing badly and a baby was screaming. Finally, after he had been waiting for about half an hour, he was called in.

The doctor was writing a note at her desk when he came in. 'Just a moment, I'm just finishing something. I'm afraid we've been very busy this morning.' She then turned to the man. 'So what's the problem?' asked the doctor.

'Well, I've been having a bit of a crisis. You know, lots of problems,' replied the man. 'And I've been doing a lot of work.'

'Mmm, you're looking very pale.' The doctor started to examine him.

'Well, everything is working OK,' she announced afterwards. 'You have slightly high blood pressure and you are breathing quite heavily, but otherwise everything's fine.'

'So what can I do?' asked the man. 'I am going on a trip soon. I am working in the States for three months. This time next week, I'll be arriving in New York.'

The doctor thought for a while. 'I think what you need is a good laugh. That would do you a lot of good. A circus is performing in town. Why don't you go along to it? I hear there's an amazing clown in town, who'll make you really laugh. His name's Grock.'

'I am Grock,' replied the man sadly.

Continuous and Simple Tenses

➡ *Grammar Summary, page 149.*

2 Find all the examples of continuous tenses in the text. Identify the tenses.

3 Which sentence in each pair below describes a finished action and which describes an unfinished action?

a) The doctor **was writing** a note at her desk.
b) The doctor **wrote** a note at her desk.

a) I've **been doing** a lot of work.
b) I've **done** a lot of work.

4 Which sentence in each pair below suggests something permanent and which suggests something temporary?

a) You **are breathing** quite heavily.
b) You **breathe** quite heavily.

a) A circus **is performing** in town.
b) A circus **performs** in town.

5 Which sentence in each pair below describes a prolonged or repeated activity and which describes a single event?

a) The man next to him **was looking** at his watch nervously.
b) The man next to him **looked** at his watch nervously.

a) I've **been having** a bit of a crisis.
b) I've **had** a bit of a crisis.

6 Match the activities (a–f) with the correct tense type: continuous or simple.

a) temporary activity   d) unfinished activity
b) permanent activity   e) single event
c) finished activity   f) repeated or prolonged event

7 Read the two sentences. Can you change the verbs in bold into continous?

I **think** what you **need** is a good laugh.
I **hear** there's an amazing clown in town.

8 Which of the verbs in the list cannot be used in the continuous tenses and which can but with a different meaning?

know, look, like, have, see, understand, think, belong, resemble, realize, taste, feel

☞ Find practice exercises in the Language Powerbook, page 26.

Review Modules 1 and 2

Grammar

1 Complete the profile of Rowan Atkinson with the verbs in brackets in the correct past tense.

'**Rowan** (1) <u>used to be</u> (be) shy with a rubbery face, just like the one he has now,' says his former headmaster. 'The other boys (2) _____ (make) him pull funny faces. I'm sure they (3) _____ (be) imitations of me and my colleagues,' adds headmaster Grove.

Rowan was born in 1955, the youngest of three sons. By the time he was thirteen, he (4) _____ (win) a scholarship to a private school. After he (5) _____ (study) there for a while, he got involved in acting. By the time he was seventeen, he (6) _____ (already act) in a play at the Edinburgh Festival. His teachers (7) _____ (predict) a future in acting, but despite this, Rowan still (8) _____ (not plan) a career in entertainment.

He eventually (9) _____ (go) to Oxford to do a science degree. He (10) _____ (previously study) electronic engineering at Newcastle University and (11) _____ (believe) that was where his future lay. But while he (12) _____ (study) at Oxford, he met a group of friends who are his partners to this day.

A happy accident finally unlocked Rowan's talents while he (13) _____ (practise) a script in 1976. He (14) _____ (play) around pulling faces for ten minutes in front of a mirror when he realised what he (15) _____ (do). 'I discovered my face,' he said later. John Lloyd, a BBC producer, says, 'It was one of those things which happen very rarely in your life, when you realise you are in the presence of genius. I (16) _____ (convince) he would be more famous than Chaplin.'

2 Choose the correct form of the verbs: simple or continuous.

1 I *have read/have been reading* a lot recently. I *have read/been reading* ten books in the last week.
2 A lorry *went past/was going past* and splashed me when I *stood/was standing* on the side of the road.
3 When she arrived I *washed/was washing* the car. After she left, I *finished/was finishing* the job.
4 He was attacked by a man who *had hid/had been hiding* in the bushes and who *had put/had been putting* on a mask.
5 I hardly slept all night because the dogs *barked/were barking* all the time. Every time I fell asleep, one of them *barked/was barking* and woke me up.
6 I *have/am having* a lot of problems with my computer because of a programme I installed recently. I think it *has/is having* some kind of computer virus.
7 His clothes *got/were getting* very dirty because he *had worked/had been working* in the garden.
8 Pandas *live/are living* in bamboo forests in China but their numbers *go down/are going down* very rapidly because people *destroy/are destroying* the forests.
9 The birds *sang/were singing* and the *sun shone/was shining*. It was a lovely day.
10 I *had finished/had been finishing* cooking when she arrived.
11 I *had worked/had been working* for a few minutes when I *looked/was looking* out of the window and saw the two men. They *broke/were breaking* into my car!
12 He *has worked/has been working* on that book for a long time. It will be the third book he *has written/has been writing*.
13 I *stay/am staying* with my brother because my flat *is painted/is being painted*.

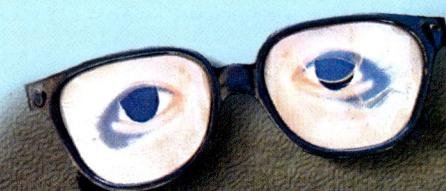

26

Laughter

Vocabulary

3 Complete the story with a suitable word in each gap.

Example 1 = nasty / terrible

I had a (1) _____ shock the other day. I was riding my (2) _____ new motorbike and I was in a very (3) _____ mood. The night before there had been (4) _____ rain, so the roads were slippery and I was rather (5) _____ practice. I took a (6) _____ turn and went down a very steep road. I very nearly (7) _____ into a parked car and (8) _____ a tree. Luckily, I was (9) _____ but my bike was badly (10) _____ . Unfortunately, I left my bike in the middle of the road. A van came down the road, tried to avoid the bike and nearly went (11) _____ of control. The van driver, who was fortyish or (12) _____ , was very angry. I (13) _____ terrible. In the end, the driver (14) _____ sorry for me and took me and my bike back home.

4 Make adjectives from these words.

Example *affectionate*

affection, sympathy, sense, self, fun, nerve, reserve, convention, practice, decision, sentiment, child, ambition

Use the words to write sentences about somebody you know.

Example
My cousin is very affectionate – she's got a warm personality.

5 Complete the sentences with multi-part verbs using the verbs in brackets.

1 I don't _____ (get) one of the people in my class. She's always being sarcastic and _____ (get) me.
2 I am really _____ (look) the end of term party. It's going to be great and I just love _____ (dress) in my best clothes.
3 She _____ (take) her mother. Not only do they both look very similar, but they both _____ (go) the same kind of clothes.
4 He _____ (make) that he didn't understand what they were saying to him, but I know he speaks French well.
5 A bomb _____ (go) in the shopping centre but luckily no one was hurt.
6 I don't know how you can _____ (put) it. I couldn't stand living next to such a busy road.

Pronunciation

6 Say the words below to yourself. Classify them according to word stress.

1st syllable	2nd syllable	3rd syllable from the end	penultimate syllable
scientist	pedestrian	responsibility	sentimental

institution, temperature, imaginative, information, conservative, practical, scientific, ability, spectator, nationalistic, communicative, embarrassment, deliberate, article, enthusiastic, comfortable, democracy, interesting, organisation, national, affectionate, business, restaurant, nationality, democratic, electricity

In which four words are some letters 'silent'?

Example *vegetable*

🎧 Listen and check your answers.

7 Can you say this proverb? Use the phonetic chart on the inside back cover to help you.

/hi huː lɑːfs lɑːst lɑːfs ˈlɒŋɡəst/

What do you think the proverb means?

Check Your Progress

Look back at the Module Objectives on pages 5 and 15.
- Which activities did you enjoy most?
- Which activities did you have the most problems with?
- Which grammar area do you need to practise more?

Culture Corner 1

THE HISTORY OF ENGLISH

CAXTON INTRODUCES THE PRINTING PRESS

SAMUEL JOHNSON

ST AUGUSTINE INTRODUCES CHRISTIANITY

1 Try to put these events in order.

a) Caxton introduces the printing press.
b) Norman invasion of England.
c) Samuel Johnson's dictionary.
d) Germanic invasions of Roman Britain.
e) Viking raids and Danish invasions.
f) English is used at court again.
g) St Augustine introduces Christianity.

2 Listen to the lecture and check your answers. Write down the dates.

Example: *Germanic invasions – around 449 AD*

3 Listen again and choose the best answer.

1 Why are there so few Celtic words in English?
   a) the Saxon invasion took a long time
   b) the Celts and Saxons did not mix
   c) the two languages were too similar

2 What impact did Christianity have on English?
   a) it changed the grammar
   b) it introduced new words
   c) it influenced pronunciation

3 Why is it difficult to understand old Anglo-Saxon?
   a) most of the words were different
   b) the spelling was different
   c) the grammar was unusual

4 Why did the Danish invasions influence English grammar?
   a) Danish grammar was different from Anglo-Saxon
   b) the two languages were similar so they mixed and simplified
   c) new Danish endings appeared on some words

5 What happened after the Norman Conquest?
   a) English disappeared for a long time
   b) French became the most important language
   c) English was the language of culture

6 Why did English become the official language again in the 15th century?
   a) because of great writers like Chaucer
   b) because of the printing press
   c) because it was used by their ruling classes

7 What changed in the 16th and 17th centuries?
   a) English pronunciation
   b) English grammar
   c) English vocabulary

8 In which way is English different from other European languages?
   a) it was standardised a lot later
   b) it has a lot of scientific words
   c) it does not have an official academy

9 What has been the most important influence on English in the last few years?
   a) the old empire (e.g. India/Australia)
   b) the United States
   c) Europe (e.g. France)

4 Listen to eight people talking. Try to identify their accents. Use the clues in the text to help you.

Accents: Standard English, Scottish, Welsh, Irish, London (cockney), Manchester, Birmingham, West Country (SW England)

5 Work in pairs. Answer these questions.

1 How has your language changed in the last few years?
2 What differences are there between the dialects of different cities and regions?
3 How do you think your language will change in the future?

Discuss your answers with the class.

3 Style

In this module you...

- **Read** magazine articles and a description. **Use** reading strategies for matching.
- **Listen to** descriptions, dialogues, a radio programme and a song. **Use** listening strategies for answering 'true/false' questions.
- **Talk about** people, fashion and places.
- **Write** a description of a person and a place.
- **Learn about** defining and non-defining relative clauses and participle clauses.

Warm-up

1 Match these captions with the pictures.

- A room in surrealist *style* by Salvador Dalí.
- The latest *style* on the catwalk.
- An unconventional *hairstyle*.
- Eating out in *style*.

2 👓 Listen and match the speakers with the pictures.

3 👓 Listen again. Which Key Words do the people use to describe the pictures?

KEY WORDS: Opinion Adjectives

cheap, chic, classy, contemporary, dated, elegant, fashionable, old-fashioned, smart, sophisticated, stylish, tacky, tasteless, trendy, unfashionable, up-to-date

4 Put the Key Words into four groups with similar meanings.

1 elegant   2 fashionable   3 tasteless   4 dated

➡ *Lexicon, page 152.*

5 Work in pairs. Give your opinions about the styles in the pictures.

Example   A: *I think the dress is very stylish.*
          B: *Yes, but I would never wear it.*

6 Work in pairs. Answer the questionnaire.

How important is 'style' for you?

1 How would you define your own style in clothes?
   a) 'cool' – I like the latest gear.
   b) 'smart' – I like classy things.
   c) 'independent' – I wear what I like.

2 How much do you know about the latest fashions?
   a) I'm well-informed.
   b) I know something.
   c) I haven't got a clue!

3 How do you usually find out about the latest trends in clothes and music?
   a) from the TV
   b) from your friends
   c) from the Net
   d) from magazines

4 What do you do when you hear about a new craze or fad?
   a) go straight out to the shops
   b) think about it first
   c) usually ignore it

5 Is it important to spend a lot of money to be 'stylish'?
   a) not at all
   b) quite important
   c) extremely important

Decide how 'style-conscious' your partner is.

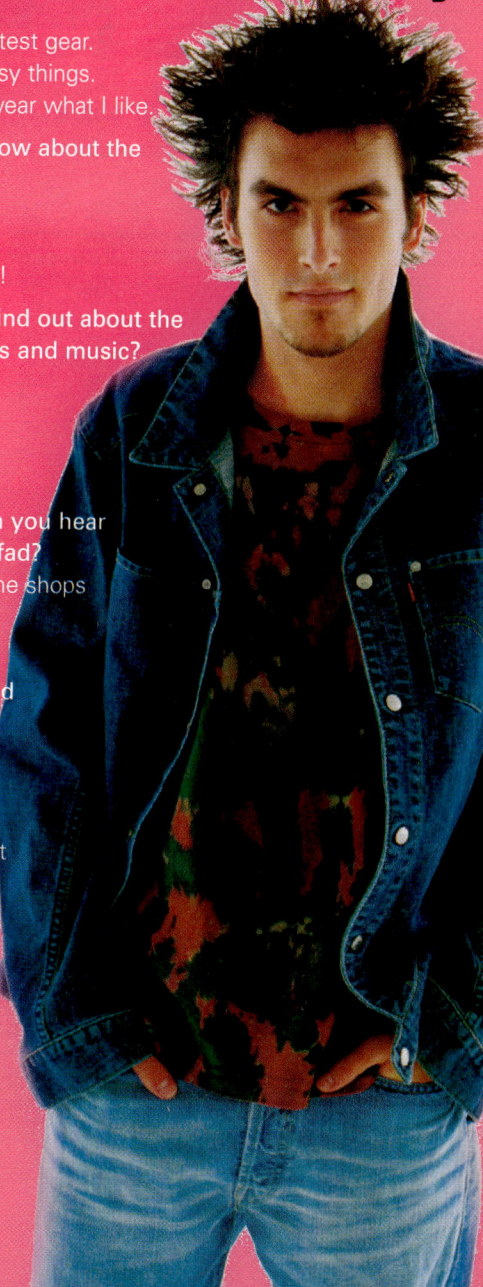

Module 3

7 Street Art

SKILLS FOCUS

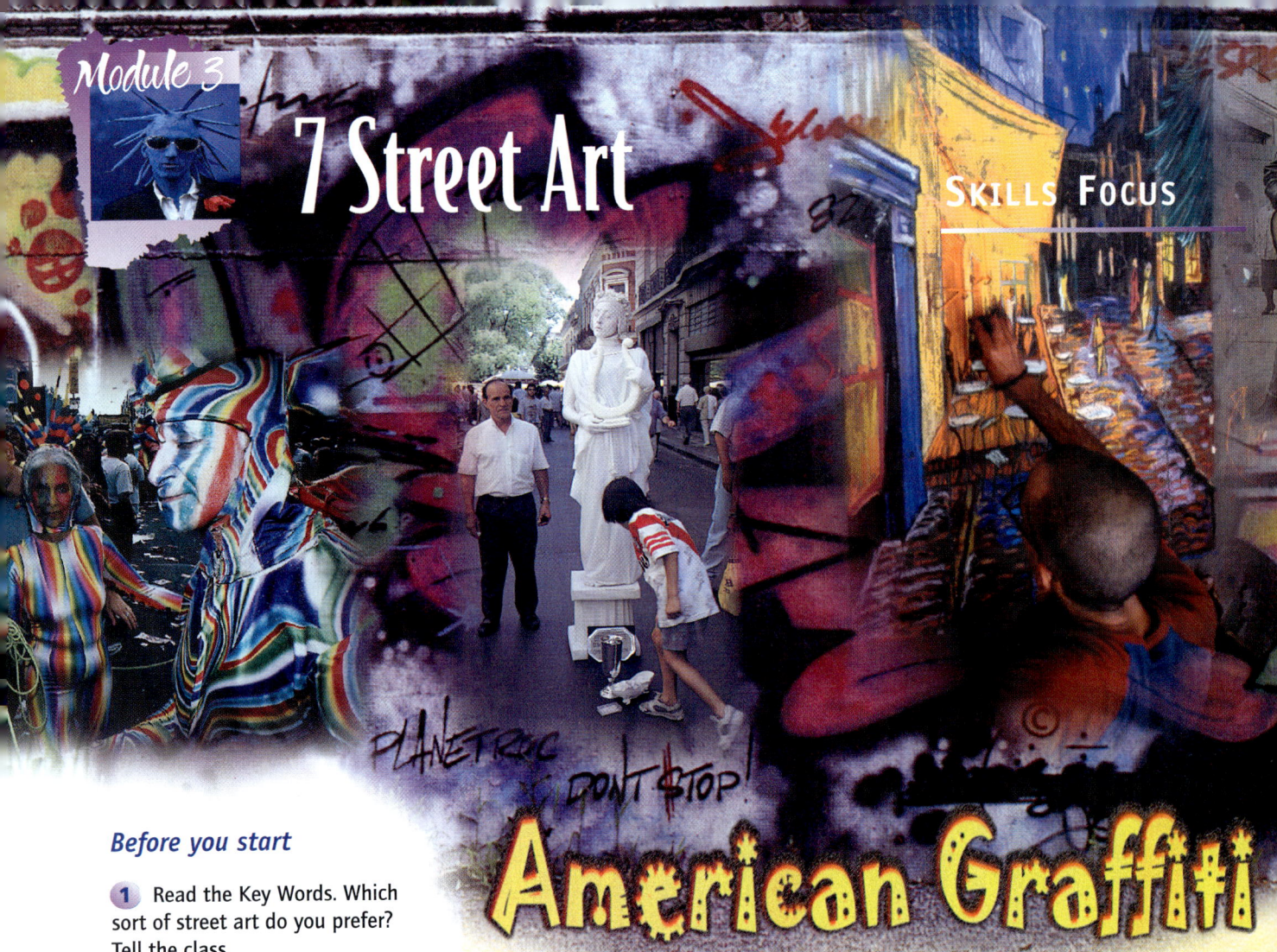

Before you start

1 Read the Key Words. Which sort of street art do you prefer? Tell the class.

> **KEY WORDS**
>
> advertising billboards, buskers, clowns, drama groups, fireworks, graffiti, 'live statues', musicians, open-air concerts, pavement artists, sculptures, statues

2 🎧 Listen to some music. What style of music is it?

- rock and roll • jazz
- hip-hop/rap • folk

Which of these things do you associate with this music?

- young or middle-aged people?
- Europe or the USA?
- black or white culture?
- rural or urban culture?

Reading

3 Read the article and check your answers to Exercise 2.

American Graffiti

UNTIL RELATIVELY RECENTLY, GRAFFITI WAS CONSIDERED TO BE AN EXAMPLE OF ANTI-SOCIAL BEHAVIOUR, THE WORK OF VANDALS. NOWADAYS, MANY OF THOSE 'VANDALS' ARE TREATED AS RESPECTED ARTISTS, AND SOME OF THEM HAVE MADE IT IN THE WORLD OF BUSINESS. SUE CLARKE REPORTS.

① New Yorkers used to see the graffiti on the walls of poor neighbourhoods and subway trains as something menacing and an example of urban decay. The scrawled names and slogans were seen as unsightly and aggressive, the work of vandals seeking to express their identities or even make a political point. Up to the 1970s, most New Yorkers hated graffiti, considering it as an eyesore that was illegal and punishable by fines.

② Since those days, graffiti has changed a lot and it is no longer found only in the subway and the poor ghetto areas of the city. Nowadays, it has the status of 'street art' and you get graffiti in places where you wouldn't expect to – in advertisements, on clothes, on toys, and even on the Wall Street Journal's official website! In the early 1980s, there was a real craze for graffiti art and the sophisticated Manhattan art world had displays of street art in its galleries. The trend was short-lived – until the arrival of hip-hop music in the late 80s.

③ In her book, *Subway Art*, Martha Cooper says "Graffiti came back with hip-hop music and people are now appreciating it for its style, which they couldn't back then, because they couldn't get beyond the vandalism thing." Hip-hop was originally black ghetto music, sung by young African Americans from the poor, run-down districts of American cities. When it suddenly got to the top of the American music charts, hip-hop culture was spread, bringing graffiti with it.

④ Today companies are starting to realise the appeal of graffiti in advertising. Kel Rodriguez, who used to spray New York subway trains, was the artist chosen to design the Wall Street Journal's website and it is obviously done in graffiti-style. "Some of that graffiti feeling, that energy, sort of got in there," Rodriguez explained.

5 Many of this new wave of artists give lectures on developments in their art. Lee Quinones is having a lot of success in Europe and feels that European galleries and museums are more open to his art form. "They want to support an artist as he develops," comments Quinones, who can get up to $10,000 for his paintings. Indeed, the Groninger Museum in Holland is one of the few museums in the world that displays and recognises graffiti as an art form.

6 Another artist, Blade, has his own website devoted only to the world of graffiti. This website has a 'merchandise page' where Blade sells things with his own original designs all over the world – everything from baseball caps to yo-yos! Leonard McGurr, a street artist for 25 years, went from painting subway trains to designing and marketing graffiti-inspired clothes for young people. "Graffiti has been a story of survival," he says. "There's a way to benefit from your work without spoiling public property."

4 Read the Strategies.

READING STRATEGIES:
Matching headings and paragraphs

- Read each paragraph carefully. Underline 3–5 of the most important words.
- Be careful – the first sentence in a paragraph often introduces the main idea – but not always!
- Read the headings and match them with the paragraphs. They often contain a word or a synonym of a word from the paragraph.
- Check that the extra heading does not match any of the paragraphs.

Use the Strategies to match the headings (a–g) with paragraphs 1–6. There is one extra heading.

a) Spoiled Cities
b) Transatlantic Success
c) Wall Street Art!
d) Ghetto Culture
e) Tasteless Comics
f) Graffiti Products
g) Big Change

5 Find synonyms in the text for these words and expressions. Paragraph numbers are in brackets.

1 threatening (1)
2 ugly (1)
3 fad (2)
4 classy (2)
5 damage to property (3)
6 depressed area (3)
7 receptive (5)
8 acknowledges (5)
9 products (6)
10 advertising and selling (6)

6 Answer these questions about the text. Use words from Exercise 5.

1 Why did New Yorkers consider graffiti the work of vandals?
2 Why did graffiti artists suddenly become respectable in New York?
3 What influence did music have on the popularity of graffiti artists?
4 In what way does Europe take graffiti art more seriously than the USA?
5 How do some graffiti artists make money?

Vocabulary: *make, get, have*

➔ Lexicon, page 162.

7 Find these expressions (1–8) in the text. Then match the underlined parts of the expressions with their meanings (a–h).

1 *make it* in business (line 4)
2 *make* a point (9)
3 *get* graffiti (14)
4 *have* a display (17)
5 *get beyond* something (21)
6 *get to* the top (23)
7 *get in* somewhere (28)
8 *get* up to $10,000 (35)

a) put on
b) find
c) succeed
d) enter
e) see further than
f) demonstrate
g) receive
h) reach

8 Match the verbs *make*, *get* and *have* with the words below. Add your own examples.

a dream, an effect, fed up, an influence, in touch, a look, lost, a mess, a mistake, money, a phone call, a promotion

9 Use the words in Exercise 8 to write as many sentences as you can in five minutes.

Example *I made a lot of mistakes in my last English essay.*

Work in groups. Take turns to read out your sentences.

Comparing Cultures

What 'street art' do you see or hear in your town or area? Give examples.

Module 3

8 Body Language

Grammar Focus

Before you start

1 What can people have done to their body? Match the Key Words with these parts of the body.

arm, ears, eyebrows, hair, nails, navel, nose, tongue

> **Key Words**
> dyed, pierced, shaved, tattooed, varnished

Would you consider having any of these things done? Tell the class.

Example
I might have my hair dyed one day. But I would never have my eyebrows pierced.

2 Read the text and answer these questions.

1. Why do some body piercers give the profession a 'bad name'?
2. How can body piercing 'go wrong'?
3. Is body piercing expensive?

Relative and Participle Clauses

Presentation

3 Read these sentences from the text.

a) Mick Shannon, *who is a qualified body piercer*, took me to his salon.
b) I've also known people *who have got diseases*.

What word(s) in the sentences above do the clauses (in *italics*) refer to?

Which clause in *italics*, a or b, gives:

- information that we need to identify the person/object we're talking about? (**defining clause**)
- extra information which is not necessary to identify the person/object we're talking about and can be left out? (**non-defining clause**)

Which type of clause uses commas?

Lisa West went to meet a professional body piercer and asked

What is the Point?

Everywhere you look these days, you can see people that have got rings – hanging from ears and pushed through noses, lips and eyebrows. And they are in lots of other places that you can't see, too!

Mick Shannon, who is a qualified body piercer, took me to his salon. I was looking at the walls, covered with photos of clients showing off their rings and jewellery and Mick pointed out his certificate, which was on the wall. "Some people give our profession a bad name," he said. "They don't clean their equipment, which shows they don't know what they're doing. I've known people who have got diseases like hepatitis from cheap ear-piercing guns. I only pierce young people whose parent or guardian is with them. And they have to be over fifteen to have their navel done and over eighteen for their tongue."

Is it an expensive fashion? "That depends. Ears, costing $8, are cheap, eyebrows are about $35, and the tongue over $100. Anything else I have to negotiate!"

I watched Mick pierce a girl's navel. First he marked the area where he had disinfected the skin, then he pushed a needle through. He finished by giving the girl advice on how to help the skin get better, which was a nice professional touch.

I asked the girl why she had wanted her navel pierced. "I don't know. I just like the idea. It'll be a little secret that I won't share with anyone!" Did she think it was a way of rebelling? "No," she laughed, "but I don't suppose my mother will like it ... if she ever finds out!"

Style

4 Read these sentences and complete the table with the relative pronouns: *who, whose, which, that* and *where.*

1. You can see people **that** have got rings.
2. Mick pointed out his certificate, **which** was on the wall.
3. I've also known people **who** have got diseases.
4. I only pierce young people **whose** parent or guardian is with them.
5. He marked the area **where** he had disinfected the skin.
6. It'll be a little secret **that** I won't share with anyone.

	Relative pronouns
people	
things	
places	
possessive	

5 Read the sentences below. Which participle clause in *italics* tells us:

a) what the person/thing underlined is doing?
b) what is done to the person/thing underlined?

1. I was looking at the <u>walls</u>, *covered with photos of clients.*
2. You can see <u>rings</u> *hanging from ears.*

What verb form is used for a) and b)?

6 Read sentences 1 and 2 from the text. What is the function of the clauses in *italics*, a, b or c?

a) help to identify a person or thing
b) give extra information about a person or thing
c) comment on the situation described in the first part of the sentence, before the comma

1. They don't clean their equipment, *which shows they don't know what they're doing.*
2. He finished by giving the girl advice on how to help the skin get better, *which was a nice professional touch.*

➪ *Grammar Summary 3, page 146.*

Practice

7 Underline the relative clauses in these sentences and decide if they are defining (D) or non-defining (N–D). Add commas where necessary.

Example 1 *Barbara, <u>who is a hairdresser</u>, has her own beauty salon.* (N–D)

1. Barbara who is a hairdresser has her own beauty salon.
2. Body piercing which has become very popular is not a very expensive fashion.
3. Most people like wearing things that make them look slim.
4. People who have a degree in architecture have numerous career opportunities.
5. We stayed in a hotel whose windows overlooked the sea.
6. St Petersburg which is sometimes called the 'Paris of the north' is going to be extensively renovated.
7. I need a suntan lotion that will protect me from the tropical sun.

8 Join the sentences using a suitable relative pronoun to form defining and non-defining clauses.

Example
1 *He put the ring, which was made of gold, through her nose.*

1. He put the ring through her nose. It was made of gold.
2. I know somebody. Her father has got a tattoo on his back.
3. I read a leaflet. It said body piercing was dangerous.
4. I went to a salon. They did body piercing there.
5. My sister dyed her hair pink. I find it an attractive colour.
6. I saw a girl. She had each part of her face pierced.
7. They opened a beauty salon in St George's Square. There used to be a perfume shop there.

9 Expand the sentences by adding participle clauses after the nouns in *italics*.

Example 1 *The car <u>speeding down the road</u> ran over a bike <u>left in the middle of the road</u>.*

1. *The car* ran over *a bike.*
2. *The portrait* shows *my grandmother.*
3. *The committee* accepted *the solution.*
4. *The singer* has already recorded six *CDs.*
5. *The shark* had attacked *two surfers.*
6. *The accident* was reported in *a TV programme.*

10 Add a comment to each of these statements. Then tell the class.

Example *Some men would prefer to wear skirts, which is understandable especially in summer.*

1. A lot of young people have tattoos on their bodies, which …
2. Young people like wearing expensive designer clothes, which …
3. Some people spend a lot of money on cosmetics, which …
4. The computer is becoming an essential part of every household, which …
5. Some schools insist on their students wearing uniforms, which …
6. There is more and more violence on TV, which …

9 Branded

Before you start

1 Work in pairs and answer the questions.

1 What is the connection between the two photos and the title of this lesson?
2 How many designer labels or brands (e.g. Nike) can you think of?
3 Why do some people think designer labels are important? Are they important for you?

2 Work in pairs. Take turns to describe the man in the photo.

Listening

3 🎧 Listen to a conversation. Find differences between the photo and the girl's description of the man.

4 🎧 Listen to the description again. Complete the Function File with these words.

ancient, attractive, dark, different, good (x2), nice, quick, scatty, seriously, shy, tall, thin, useless, younger

Preferences: Describing People

Well, he's **very** (1) _____ .
He's **a bit too** (2) _____ maybe! And he's **a bit** on the (3) _____ side.
But he's got a **rather** (4) _____ smile.
And he's **quite** (5) _____ .
George Clooney? He's **absolutely** (6) _____ !
Of course, Ben's **much** (7) _____ .
He comes across as **slightly** (8) _____ and serious at first.
He takes his studies **fairly** (9) _____ .
He's **completely** (10) _____ .
He's got a **really** (11) _____ sense of humour.
He's got **pretty** (12) _____ taste in clothes, too.
No, he's just **extremely** (13) _____ and witty.
He's **totally** (14) _____ when it comes to remembering times and dates.
And he's **a bit** (15) _____ and tends to lose things all the time!

SKILLS FOCUS

Pronunciation

5 Stress and intonation can change the meaning of a sentence.

Example
Alice is <u>quite</u> nice = she is nice but not <u>very</u> nice
Alice is quite <u>nice</u> = she is very nice

🎧 Now listen to the description of a girl. Underline the words in *italics* that are stressed.

Alice is (1) *quite nice*. She's (2) *rather tall* and she's got (3) *fairly long* hair. She's got a (4) *rather nice* smile and she's (5) *quite friendly*. She's (6) *pretty good* at telling jokes and she's (7) *quite witty*. She's (8) *fairly bright* and the school she goes to is (9) *quite good*. But she's (10) *pretty scatty* and absent-minded!

In the description, which modifiers (*quite, rather, fairly, pretty*) could you replace with *very*?

6 Look at the modifying expressions in bold in the Function File. Which of them make a comment:

1 stronger? 2 weaker? 3 either stronger or weaker, depending on the intonation?

Style

Speaking

7 Imagine you have just met someone. Write notes about him/her. Use the expressions from the Function File. Think about these things:

- age • appearance • personality • interests • abilities

➡ *Lexicon, pages 151 and 152.*

8 Work in pairs. Have a conversation about the people you have met.

Example
A So what is she like?
B Well, she's very outgoing and …

Vocabulary: Multi-part Verbs

➡ *Lexicon, pages 170–176.*

9 Match the sentences (1–8) with the replies (a–h).

1 Tell us about this new guy you're **going out with**.
2 He's **getting on** a bit.
3 I've **gone off** him.
4 We **get on** really well.
5 He **comes across** as slightly shy.
6 I don't **go for** guys with earrings.
7 He **goes in for** telling lots of jokes.
8 He **takes after** his mum.

a) Yes, he must be in his fifties.
b) Well, you have a lot in common.
c) I do. I think they're really attractive.
d) He's quite shy, really.
e) Yes, they're both a bit scatty!
f) Me too. I don't like him anymore.
g) But apparently he's really funny when you get to know him.
h) Yes, and he's always pulling my leg!

10 Write sentences about yourself and people you know. Use the multi-part verbs in Exercise 9.

Example
I'd like to go out with Jennifer Lopez!

11 Work in pairs. Say your sentences and reply to them.

Example
A: I really go for guys with short hair.
B: Yes, me too, but not guys with shaved heads.

Listening

12 Read the Strategies.

> **LISTENING STRATEGIES:**
> Answering true/false questions
>
> - Read the statements. Use your knowledge of the world to guess if they are true or false.
> - Look for important words in the statements, e.g. 1 = *protest*, *multinationals*. Try to think of their synonyms, e.g. *protest – complaint*, *multinational – big global company*.
> - Listen the first time to get the general idea.
> - Listen the second time for the important words in the statements; or synonyms for them.
> - Decide which statements are true and which are false.
> - After listening, make guesses about the statements you are still not sure about.

Now listen twice to the radio programme about a book by Naomi Klein. Use the Strategies to decide if these statements are true (T) or false (F).

1 The book is a sort of protest against multinationals.
2 'Logos' are words in a new international language.
3 Most people in the world can recognise the most famous logos.
4 There will never be advertisements in space.
5 The workers who work in brand name factories have good working conditions.
6 A company once paid one sports star more than all its workers' salaries put together.
7 The number of protests against the policies of global companies is falling.
8 The author thinks we should worry about who we *are* and not about what we *have got*.

Do you agree with Naomi Klein's ideas? Why or why not?

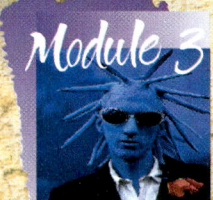

Communication Workshop

Writing: A Description of a Person and Place

Before you start

1 Read the text and complete the gaps (1–10) with the following:

such lovely, such as, too big, so that, a lot bigger, so untidy, as big as, biggest, such a big, big enough

2 Read the text again and match the paragraphs (A–D) with these headings.

- focus on one important room
- introduction to the person and place
- general description of the house
- comment on the person

A Pamela is my cousin. She is in her mid-thirties and has got short, red hair, green eyes and a warm, friendly face. She dresses casually, usually in a sweater and jeans. She is a journalist. In her free time she listens to classical music, mainly Romantic composers like Chopin, Brahms and Liszt. One of her (1) _____ interests is gardening, which is one reason why she moved house. She has just moved into a big house in the country with a huge garden. It's (2) _____ than her previous house. In fact, my mother says it's (3) _____ for one person and Pamela won't be able to afford it, but Pamela has always been reckless, particularly with her money!

B The house is on the edge of a village. It is quite old and has got three spacious bedrooms, all with (4) _____ views of the countryside that it is a really relaxing place to be. There is also an enormous kitchen, (5) _____ to eat in, with an old-fashioned stove. Pamela spends a lot of time there when she is not working. The living room is also huge, with wooden floors and an open fireplace. The walls are covered with oil paintings. Pamela is outgoing and sociable and there always seem to be people around – fortunately it is (6) _____ house that she has lots of room for parties.

C Pamela writes for fashion magazines, (7) _____ Vogue, and works in another fair-sized room which she calls her 'office'. It has got a very relaxed atmosphere and has a marvellous view of the fields and hills, though it's not (8) _____ the other rooms. She works at a massive desk near the window (9) _____ she has lots of light, and it's usually cluttered with all sorts of things like papers and old coffee cups, with books everywhere as she loves reading. Her desk is (10) _____ that she often can't find her computer mouse! It's a cosy room, and you can often find Pamela listening to music here, sitting in her favourite comfortable armchair. She is not very keen on the red and green wallpaper, though, which is rather strong! She says it's completely tasteless, and wants to change it.

D I admire my cousin Pamela because she is very independent. She is one of the most likeable people I know and she is always very cheerful.

Photo A

3 Find five synonyms of the word 'big' in the text.

4 Complete the second sentence so that it has a similar meaning to the first sentence, using the word given.

Example
She is so hard-working that she works at weekends.
such
She is <u>such a hard-working person</u> that she works at weekends.

1 It's such a big house that she has lots of room for parties.
so
The house is _____ that she has lots of room for parties.

2 Her desk is so untidy that she often can't find her computer mouse!
such
It's _____ desk that she often can't find her computer mouse.

3 The wallpaper is so tasteless that she wants to change it.
such
It is _____ wallpaper that she wants to change it.

4 She listens to Romantic composers like Chopin.
such
She listens to Romantic composers _____ Chopin.

5 She works near the window to get a lot of light.
so that
She works near the window _____ a lot of light.

Write a description of a person you know and where they live. Follow the stages.

Stage 1

Think of a person you know, e.g. someone in your family, a friend or a neighbour. Write down some adjectives that describe their character, and examples of their behaviour that show their character.

Example
outgoing – likes parties, going out with friends
musical – plays the guitar, likes all kinds of music

Now think about where they live and write down some features of the place.

Example
small flat, near park, huge CD collection

⇨ *Writing Help 3 (useful vocabulary), page 139.*

Stage 2

Write notes for four paragraphs.

⇨ *Writing Help 3 (layout).*

Stage 3

Use your notes to write your composition. Try to include:

- words from the Function File in Lesson 9, e.g. *a bit, quite, rather*
- examples of relative clauses (see Lesson 8), e.g. *She works in a room which she calls her office.*
- structures using *so* or *such* (see 'Before you start')

Stage 4

Check your work.

⇨ *Writing Help 3 (checking).*

Talkback

Work in groups. Read your descriptions. Which person would you like to meet? Why?

Listening: A Song

Dedicated Follower of Fashion

1 Listen to a song about a man in London in the 1960s and complete these lines.

1 His clothes are _____ but never _____ .
2 Eagerly pursuing all the latest _____ and trends.
3 He thinks he is a _____ to be looked at.
4 There's one thing that he loves and that is _____ .
5 His world is built round _____ and _____ .
6 He flits from shop to shop just like a _____ .

2 Which of the following words and expressions would you use to describe the man in the song?

conventional, fashionable, hard-working, pleasure-seeking, reserved, vain

Communication Workshop

Speaking: Discussing A Photo

Photo B

Before you start

1 🎧 Listen to two people discussing the room in Photo A in the Writing Workshop. What sort of person do they think lives there? Does it match the description of Pamela?

Chatroom

COLLOQUIAL EXPRESSIONS

2 Find words in Paragraph C of the text in the Writing Workshop to match these colloquial words from the conversation.

Example
relaxed = laid-back

1. must be **a big reader**
2. books **all over the place**
3. really **laid-back**
4. a bit too **messy** for me
5. the **great big** desk
6. **loads** of light
7. that armchair looks really **comfy**
8. I'm not **dead keen** on the wallpaper
9. it's **a bit over the top**
10. it's quite **tacky**

Discuss the room in Photo B. Decide what sort of person might live there. Follow the stages.

Stage 1

Look at Photo B above and quickly write down words (nouns and adjectives) you could use to describe the room.

➪ *Lexicon, pages 152 and 161.*

Stage 2

Think about what sort of person might live there. Do things in the room suggest a particular personality?

➪ *Lexicon, page 151.*

Stage 3

Read the Strategies.

> **SPEAKING STRATEGIES:** Gaining time
>
> When you are speaking, you need time to think:
> - Try not to leave long pauses without saying anything.
> - Use hesitation words, e.g. *right, well, you know*.
> - Use 'vague' language, e.g. *kind of, sort of*.
> - Use fixed expressions, e.g. *let me think for a second, I know what you mean, that's very true*.

Work in pairs. Talk about the room and decide what sort of person lives there. Do not just describe the room. Use the Strategies above.

Talkback

Tell the class about what you decided. Did the others have similar ideas?

4 Beauty

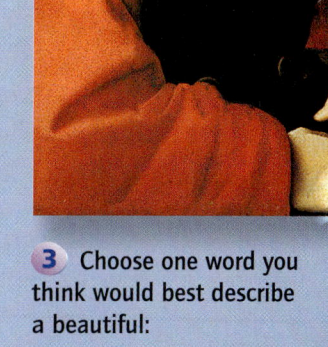

In this module you...

- **Read** poems, a newspaper article and a film review. **Use** reading strategies for answering true/false questions.
- **Talk about** people, literature, music and films.
- **Listen to** music and dialogues. **Use** listening strategies for matching people and opinions.
- **Write** a film review.
- **Revise** and **learn more about** passive structures.

Warm-up

1 🎧 Listen to three dialogues about beauty and match them with the photos.

2 🎧 Listen again. Put the Key Words into the five groups in the table.

KEY WORDS: Describing Beauty

attractive, beautiful, breathtaking, brilliant, effortless, elegant, glamorous, good-looking, gorgeous, graceful, handsome, impressive, lovely, magnificent, a real masterpiece, perfect, picturesque, powerful, pretty, scenic, striking, stunning, a thing of great beauty

3 Choose one word you think would best describe a beautiful:

- area of countryside
- sunset • painting • dancer
- building • film star

Men	Women	Places	Objects	Movement
attractive				

Which of these words can you *not* use with all the categories above?

beautiful, lovely, nice, pretty

4 Work in pairs. Talk about beautiful people, places and objects.

Example
A: *The views in the Lake District are really stunning.*
B: *I've never been there, but I've heard it's very picturesque.*

➪ *Lexicon, page 152.*

10 Poetry

Module 4

SKILLS FOCUS

Before you start

1 Look at the picture of the jaguar. Which of the Key Words do you associate with the animal?

KEY WORDS: Description

Verbs: to hurry, to lie still, to run, to shriek, to stare, to stroll, to strut, to stride, to yawn
Adjectives: bored, enraged, fatigued, fierce, graceful, indolent, lovely, powerful, striking, wild

Reading

2 Read the poem. List the Key Words the poet uses to describe the jaguar.

The Jaguar, by Ted Hughes

The apes yawn and adore their fleas in the sun.
The parrots shriek as if they were on fire, or strut
Like cheap tarts to attract the stroller with the nut.
Fatigued with indolence, tiger and lion

Lie still as the sun. The boa-constrictor's coil
Is a fossil. Cage after cage seems empty, or
Stinks of sleepers from the breathing straw.
It might be painted on a nursery wall.

But who runs like the rest past these arrives
At a cage where the crowd stands, stares, mesmerized,
As a child at a dream, at a jaguar hurrying enraged
Through prison darkness after the drills of his eyes

On a short fierce fuse. Not in boredom -
The eye satisfied to be blind in fire,
By the bang of blood in the brain deaf the ear -
He spins from the bars, but there's no cage to him

More than to the visionary his cell:
His stride is wildernesses of freedom:
The world rolls under the long thrust of his heel.
Over the cage floor the horizons come.

3 Read the Strategies.

READING STRATEGIES: Reading poetry
- Read a poem first to get the general feeling. Don't worry if you only understand a little.
- Read the poem again more slowly. Think about the subject, the actions and the feelings.
- Identify parts of the poem you still don't understand. Read them again using a dictionary to help you. Remember word order is often very different in poems, e.g. *By the bang of blood in the brain deaf the ear.* = The noise of the blood in its brain makes it deaf in the ear.
- Identify the images that the poem provokes, e.g. *shrieking parrots on fire.* Try to work out what they mean, e.g. they are screaming extremely loudly and painfully.

4 Use the Strategies. Decide if these statements about the poem are true (T) or false (F).

1 The apes are extremely active.
2 The parrots are screaming because it is so hot.
3 The parrots are trying to get food from the visitors.
4 The boa-constrictor looks dead.
5 It is in the middle of a hot summer's day.
6 People show little interest in the jaguar.
7 The jaguar's cage is large and spacious.
8 The jaguar is trying to escape.
9 The jaguar is pacing his cage.
10 The jaguar is imagining a world of freedom.

Beauty

5 Look at these two ways of describing the same thing.

Metaphor	Simile
The *burning* parrots shriek.	The parrots shriek *as if they were on fire.*
The boa-constrictor's coil *is a fossil.*	The boa-constrictor's coil is *like a fossil.*

Match the parts of the sentences in *italics* (1–6) with the meanings (a–f).

1 The parrots *strut like cheap tarts*.
2 Tiger and lion *lie still as the sun*.
3 The crowd are *as a child at a dream*.
4 The jaguar hurries through *prison darkness*.
5 The jaguar is *on a short fierce fuse*.
6 *The world rolls* underneath his feet.

a) are motionless
b) a cage
c) everything is in continual movement
d) walk proudly looking for attention
e) about to explode
f) hypnotised by something

6 Match the situations (1–5) with the images (a–e). Do you think they are good images?

1 a firework display
2 an astronaut on a spacewalk
3 a child crying in its cot
4 an old man walking
5 a crowd entering a stadium

a) a parrot shrieking in its cage
b) a multi-coloured spider's web
c) a baby and its umbilical cord
d) ants going into their nest
e) a tortoise moving

7 Work in pairs. Write suitable images for these situations.

Example
a ship in a storm = a leaf in the wind

- a ship in a storm
- a baby trying to walk
- a fashion parade
- trees in winter
- people at a party

Tell the class your images. Choose the best ones.

Vocabulary: Idiomatic Language

▷ *Lexicon, page 164.*

8 Match the expressions with the pictures. Try to work out the meaning of each. Then complete the sentences below with the expressions.

fish out of water, bee in her bonnet, rat race, bookworm, let the cat out of the bag, fly on the wall, black sheep

1 She's always got her head in a novel – she's a real _____ .
2 I can't get used to this situation. I feel like a _____ .
3 I'd love to be a _____ when those two have an argument!
4 We tried to keep the party a secret. But then someone _____ .
5 Modern life is such a _____ – it's so competitive and stressful.
6 She's got a _____ about litter – she's obsessed by it.
7 All the brothers were respectable, except James – he was the _____ of the family.

9 Write five of your own sentences using the expressions.

Comparing Cultures

Work in pairs. Discuss these questions.

- Who are the most famous poets in your language? Who is your favourite?
- Are there any similar idiomatic expressions in your language like the ones in Exercise 8?

QUOTE .... UNQUOTE
'Most people ignore most poetry because most poetry ignores most people.'

Adrian Mitchell, British poet.

Module 4

11 Wrapped Up

GRAMMAR FOCUS

Before you start

1 Look at the photos. What is *your* reaction to these works of art?

2 Guess the answers to these questions about the photos.

1 How long do you think it took to make them?
2 What materials are they made of?
3 How popular were they?
4 Why do you think they were made?

3 Read the article and check your guesses in Exercise 2.

THE PASSIVE

Revision

4 Complete the table with examples of passives from the text.

People, bridges, buildings, rivers, valleys, even entire coastlines and islands, have all been wrapped up by the Bulgarian artist, Christo, his French wife, Jeanne-Claude, and their team of helpers. Stephen Treasure reports.

One of their most spectacular projects was called Surrounded Islands. Eleven islands on the coast near Miami were surrounded by over six thousand square metres of pink plastic! Another project was wrapping up the German Parliament building which couldn't have been done before the fall of the Berlin Wall. Many people thought that permission wouldn't be given, and some thought the project should never have been allowed. However, when the wrapping of the Reichstag in golden fabric had finally been completed, the glowing building received international acclaim, and Christo loved being appreciated.

Two or three new projects are currently being developed by Christo and his team. One of them is in Colorado in the USA where the Arkansas River will be covered by 10 kilometres of luminous, translucent fabric. The fabric is going to be suspended above the river so that the work of art can be seen from both above and below. Thousands of people will be needed to complete this feat of engineering. Christo manages to do all this without being given any money – his projects are financed completely by the sale of his drawings through galleries and over the Internet.

Christo's works of art are dismantled after only two or three weeks, but hundreds of visitors manage to see them. When The Reichstag was being displayed it attracted huge numbers of visitors from around the world. However, his work still tends to be criticised. 'What's the point of it all? Why bother when it takes so long?' Christo replies that their work is a kind of architecture and they use space, light and texture to make beautiful things.

Present Simple	Works of art are dismantled after only 2 or 3 weeks.
Present Continuous	
Present Perfect	
Past Simple	
Past Continuous	
Past Perfect	
be going to + infinitive	
modal + infinitive	
modal + perfect infinitive	

Presentation

5 Match the underlined verb forms in the sentences below (1–3) with the names (a–c).

1 The project should never <u>have been allowed</u>.
2 Christo loved <u>being appreciated</u>.
3 His work still tends <u>to be criticised</u>.

a) passive gerund
b) passive infinitive
c) passive perfect infinitive

Find one more example of each verb form in the text.

Beauty

9 Change the sentences into passive. Use 'by …' only if necessary.

1. Gustav Eiffel designed the Eiffel Tower in Paris.
2. Athens will organise the next European year of culture.
3. People expected Ted Hughes to win the Nobel Prize for literature.
4. The police were transporting a Van Gogh painting from Amsterdam to London when the rain damaged it.
5. Someone has stolen a Picasso from The Louvre.
6. United Artists are making a new Harry Potter film.
7. An artist is going to cover the Kremlin in red fabric.
8. Someone should have supported Mozart financially so that he could write more music.

10 Change the verb in brackets into the passive infinitive, passive perfect infinitive or passive gerund.

Example
1. I hate **being treated** like a child.

1. I hate _____ (treat) like a child.
2. It's nice _____ (give) something you've always wanted to have.
3. J.F. Kennedy may _____ (assassinate) by a madman.
4. It's hard to play football without _____ (kick) by other players.
5. Everybody wants _____ (like) and _____ (respect).
6. Seat belts must _____ (fasten) during take-off and landing.
7. _____ (praise) in public can be quite embarrassing.
8. There is a suspicion that the 'Mona Lisa' may not _____ (paint) by Leonardo da Vinci.

6 Match the reasons for using the passive (a–c) with the sentences (1–3) from the text.

a) to focus on the action rather than the doer
b) to put special emphasis on the doer
c) to avoid having a long subject in an active sentence

1. People, bridges, buildings, rivers and valleys, have all been wrapped up by the Bulgarian artist, Christo.
2. The fabric is going to be suspended above the river.
3. His projects are financed completely by the sale of his drawings through galleries and over the Internet.

7 Where are you more likely to see or hear passive sentences?

- newspapers • informal letters • scientific articles
- conversations

➪ Grammar Summary 4, page 147.

Practice

8 Rewrite the dialogue and the newspaper story below so that they sound natural. Change the passive into active in the dialogue and the active into passive in the newspaper story.

A: How was your weekend?
B: OK. Football was played by me and the game was lost by our team. What about you?
A: I was met by a friend in the street and a film was seen by us at the cinema.
B: Was it enjoyed by you?
A: Yes, the ending was really loved by me and my friend.

The police arrested three men today. The police chased them for twenty minutes and the police caught them when a lorry hit their car. The police took the men to Scotland Yard for questioning.

11 Rewrite this newspaper report using passive structures when they are more suitable.

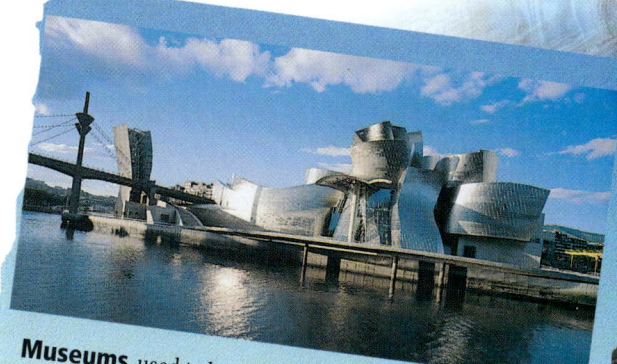

Museums used to be dull and dusty places. Then along came a man called Frank Gehry. They awarded Frank Gehry, the architect of the Guggenheim Museum in Bilbao, the Royal Gold Medal for Architecture last week. People have called him a 17th century Baroque architect of the 21st century. His latest building is the Experience Music Project in Seattle. He designed it to look like an electric guitar that someone had melted. Not surprisingly, when they opened the building, someone labelled him the King of Baroque 'n' Roll.

43

Module 4

12 Music

SKILLS FOCUS

Before you start

1 🎧 Listen to the extracts from film music and match them to the photos. Which music do you like most? Why?

2 🎧 Listen again. Which of the Key Words would you use to describe the music?

> **KEY WORDS: Describing Music**
>
> catchy, dramatic, exciting, haunting, lively, monotonous, moving, romantic, sad, scary, sentimental, sinister, soothing, soppy, tear-jerking, tedious, terrifying, thoughtful

Listening

3 Read the Strategies.

> **LISTENING STRATEGIES:**
> Matching people and opinions
> - Underline the 'topic' word in each opinion and important opinion words (usually adjectives).
> - Decide if the opinions are positive or negative.
> - As you listen, identify the 'topic' words and write down any opinion words you hear.
> - Decide if the opinion words are synonyms or opposites of the words you underlined.
> - Pay attention to the intonation used when agreeing and disagreeing.

4 🎧 You will hear two people talking about music. Use the Strategies to decide who has these opinions – write M (man), W (woman) or B (both) next to each sentence (1–10).

    topic   opinion   topic
    ↓   ↓   ↓

1. David Gray's a wonderful singer.
2. David Gray's music is rather superficial.
3. Rap music is boring and the lyrics are disgusting.
4. Rap is strong stuff.
5. Techno music is quite good.
6. Some of the new rock bands are not bad.
7. Beck puts on a great performance.
8. Some of the old rock bands are not bad at all.
9. Jimi Hendrix was a fantastic guitarist.
10. The Stones were better than the Beatles.

Do you agree or disagree with any of the opinions above?

5 Look at the Function File. Which expressions are used:

- to introduce an opinion?
- to ask for agreement?
- to show disagreement?
- to ask another person's opinion?
- to show agreement?

Function File

Giving Opinions; Agreeing and Disagreeing

1) **I think** it's really great, **don't you?**
2) **Personally**, I'm **not that keen on** that sort of music.
3) You know, **it's not really my thing**. **Don't you think** it's a bit soppy and sentimental?
4) Oh, **I don't think** that's fair!
5) Well, **if you ask me**, rap's horrible.
6) And, **to be honest**, the music's just boring. It's nearly always the same, **isn't it?**
7) **That's not the point**.
8) **Do you like** techno music?
9) **Me too**. I like the faster stuff.
10) **So do I**.
11) **That's true**. That guy Beck's pretty hot. **Do you think** he's good?
12) Yeah, **I'm not sure**.
13) But **don't you like** the Stones?
14) **I have to admit** some of their music is good.
15) But **wouldn't you agree** that the Beatles were better?
16) No, **I wouldn't!**

6 Listen to the conversation again and check your answers.

7 Match these questions (1–4) with their meanings (a–d).

1 Don't you like the Stones?
2 Do you think their concerts are good?
3 Do you like the Stones?
4 Don't you think their concerts are good?

a) Are the Stones one of your favourite groups?
b) I like the Stones, don't you?
c) Are their concerts any good?
d) Their concerts are great, aren't they?

Pronunciation

8 Listen to the sounds, words, expressions and the intonation. Which of these do they express? Then listen again and repeat the expressions.

a) strong agreement
b) agreement
c) hesitant agreement
d) indecision
e) hesitant disagreement
f) strong disagreement

Speaking

9 Work in pairs. Tell your partner about your tastes in music. Agree or disagree with your partner.

Example
A: I think U2 are really great!
B: Do you? If you ask me, they're ancient. I like rap groups.
A: I'm not keen on rap music.
B: Don't you like Eminem?
A: No, not really.

10 Work in groups. Listen to some musical extracts. After each piece of music, take turns to give your opinions about it.

Vocabulary: Multi-part Verbs with 'turn'

➩ Lexicon, pages 170–176.

11 Complete the sentences with the particles *down, up, off,* or *on.*

1 He turned _____ an hour late for the meeting!
2 The dog suddenly turned _____ me and bit me on the leg.
3 She turned _____ the job offer because she wanted more money.
4 He turned _____ his collar to keep his neck warm.
5 Just after the lights, turn _____ the main road into our street.
6 I quite liked him, but I was turned _____ by the ring through his nose.

QUOTE .... UNQUOTE
'Music can name the unnamable and communicate the unknowable.'
Leonard Bernstein, American composer.

Communication Workshop

Writing: A Film Review

Before you start

1 Read the film review and match paragraphs A–D with the following headings.

- good and bad points
- basic information about the film
- conclusion and recommendation
- brief summary of the plot

OUR 100 GREATEST FILMS

Beauty and the Beast (1946)

No 9

A 'Beauty and the Beast' was directed by Jean Cocteau. It is based on the fairy tale by Madame Le Prince de Beaumont and it stars Jean Marais as the Beast and Josette Day as Beauty.

B Beauty is one of three daughters of a French merchant. Her sisters, Felicie and Adelaide, are mean and treat Beauty as a servant. (1) _____ Beauty's father gets lost in the forest, but finds a strange castle, (2) _____ he enters, looking for help. The owner of the castle is a repulsive monster, half-man, half-beast, (3) _____ threatens the merchant – either one of his daughters replaces him as a prisoner in the castle or he will die. Beauty offers to replace her father and goes to live in the castle. (4) _____, she discovers the Beast is not as hideous and inhuman as he seems, but a handsome prince.

C The film deals with the theme of appearances in very interesting and clever ways. In one memorable scene, Beauty looks in the mirror and her face is transformed into the Beast's. For its time (1946), the film uses some clever special effects, (5) _____ when Beauty is striding up and down waiting for the Beast to visit her room – behind her, a statue's head follows her movements! (6) _____, the whispering furniture is as frightening as anything in modern films. The film does, (7) _____, have its weak points. The Beast's voice is rather squeaky, and the lovers flying at the end is a bit corny! (8) _____, though, it must be one of the most beautiful films ever made. (9) _____ it is in black and white, the striking use of light makes it seem at times like a moving painting. The music is also magnificent.

D Beauty and the Beast is a fairy tale with an obvious message – you shouldn't judge a book by its cover. (10) _____, it has neither the cute characters nor the Hollywood songs of the Disney version; it speaks to people of all ages. I recommend it for all the family.

46

Beauty

2 Linking. Complete the gaps in the text with these words.

all things considered, although, however, in the end, moreover, of course, one day, such as, which, who

3 Look at these examples from the text for talking about two alternatives.

- ... **either** one of his daughters replaces him as a prisoner in the castle **or** he will die.
- ... it has **neither** the cute characters **nor** the Hollywood songs of the Disney version.

Now use the cues to write sentences using *either ... or* and *neither ... nor*.

Example
The film was set in either the 1920s or the 1930s.

1 film / set in 1920s (?) / 1930s (?)
2 directed / Steven Spielberg (?) / George Lucas (?)
3 film / romantic (X) / funny (X)
4 star / Julia Roberts (?) / Sandra Bullock (?)
5 film / good special effects (X) / good music (X)

Write a film review about one of your favourite films. Follow the stages.

Stage 1
Use the headings in Exercise 1 to make notes about the film.

▷ *Writing Help 4 (layout, useful vocabulary), page 139.*

Stage 2
Write your review in four paragraphs.

▷ *Writing Help 4 (style, linking).*

Stage 3
Check your writing.

▷ *Writing Help 4 (checking).*

Talkback
Work in groups. Read each other's film reviews. Which sounds like the best film?

Listening: A Conversation

Before you start

1 Look at the photo. What do you think they're talking about? Which of the people do you think is doing most of the talking?

Listen to the conversation and answer the questions.

2 🎧 Listen and find out the subject of their conversation. Who interrupts other people most: Richard, Sue or Kate?

3 🎧 Listen again. Answer the questions by writing R (Richard), S (Sue) or K (Kate) in the boxes.

1 Who suggests having a disco? ☐
2 Who doesn't like the idea of a disco? ☐
3 Who likes the suggestion of having a folk group? ☐
4 Who reluctantly accepts the suggestion of a folk group? ☐
5 Whose idea for the art exhibition is accepted? ☐
6 Who would like to have two films about the same subject? ☐
7 Who can't stand spy films? ☐
8 Who really loves old black and white silent films? ☐
9 Who is in charge of looking for films? ☐
10 Who suggests ending the conversation? ☐

47

Communication Workshop

Speaking: Planning An Event

Before you start

1 🎧 Listen to extracts from the conversation in the Listening Workshop. Classify the way in which the people interrupt each other.

a) a polite interruption
b) a rude/abrupt interruption
c) a failed interruption

Chatroom

COLLOQUIAL EXPRESSIONS

2 Match these colloquial expressions (1–8) with their meanings (a–h).

1 I'm **sick and tired** of discos.
2 We're all **bored to death** with school discos.
3 We've had **loads and loads** of them.
4 I won't make a **song and dance** about it.
5 **Hang on a second.**
6 No, they're **really corny**.
7 They're **right up your street**.
8 Just a few **bits and pieces**.

a) a great deal
b) wait a moment
c) fed up
d) exactly what you like
e) old-fashioned and uninteresting
f) extremely bored
g) small items
h) a fuss

Plan an 'Arts Week' for your school or university. Follow the stages.

Stage 1

Individually, decide what sort of things you would like to have. Choose from this list or think of others.

- a play • a poetry reading • a classical concert
- a photo competition • old 'silent' films

Stage 2

Work in pairs. Discuss your ideas. Try to use expressions from the Function File in Lesson 12 and the Chatroom.

Example
A: *Don't you think we should have ...*
B: *No, I don't. They're really corny!*

Stage 3

Read the Strategies.

> **SPEAKING STRATEGIES:**
> Taking turns in group discussions
> - Don't dominate a discussion. Give your opinions and ask the others what they think.
> - Show interest in what the others are saying. Use words like 'right', 'absolutely' and 'exactly' and sounds like 'mm'.
> - If you really need to interrupt, interrupt politely! Wait for the other person to pause first.

Stage 4

Work in groups of three or four. Decide the events for your Arts Week and finally choose a celebrity to open it.

Talkback

Tell the class what your group decided.

Language Awareness 3

1 Think of a place in your country that you know well and think is beautiful. Say why.

2 Read the information about an area of England. Would you like to visit it? Why? Why not? What things would you like to do there?

Looking for **somewhere** to go away for a long weekend? At this time of year, there is **nowhere** better than the unspoilt countryside of South Shropshire. On the borders of England and Wales, **it** is full of beauty, with high hills, wooded countryside and picturesque towns and villages, all of which means that it is an ideal place to visit.

It is probably sensible to base yourselves in Ludlow, which is the biggest town in the district. As the well-known local historian, David Lloyd, has said, 'there are few towns like **ours** in Britain with such fine architecture.' **It** has a breathtaking castle and a church tower that one can see from miles and miles away. Cross the medieval bridge over the River Teme and enter the town through a gate in the old town walls. You will find **yourself** in Broad Street with **its** impressive 18th century houses. Architecturally, **this** is one of the most famous streets in England. Other places worth a visit are the castle, **which** defended the town against the Welsh, and St Laurence's, a spectacular medieval church. **These** are just some of the things that make Ludlow a very special town.

As well as seeing these sights, there are plenty of others to visit in the area such as the historic towns of Cleobury Mortimer and Bishops Castle. If **you** like castles, it's a good idea to visit picturesque Stokesay Castle or the ruins of Wigmore Castle, the seat of the powerful Mortimer family. **They** are amongst the scores of castles in the area.

There are also plenty of things to do for **those who** like the outdoor life. Go canoeing on the river Teme or hang gliding from Clee Hill. South Shropshire is also a walkers' paradise, with Mortimer's Trail **that** goes from Ludlow through Mortimer's Forest to the Welsh border. If you have children, drop in to The Secret Hills Discovery Centre in Craven Arms where **they** can learn all about the area and enjoy **themselves** at the same time.

There are plenty of good hotels and restaurants in Ludlow and **their** food has an excellent reputation. Three restaurants hold the famous Michelin star, **which** is really quite surprising when you think that there are only several of **them** in the whole country. In addition, Ludlow is only 150 miles from London, which makes it a great place for a weekend.

Reference (2): Pronouns

➪ *Grammar Summary, page 149.*

3 Look at the words in red and underline the parts of the text that they refer to.

4 Underline the parts of the sentences that *which* refers to in each case.

1 ... it is full of beauty, with high hills, wooded countryside and picturesque towns and villages, all of **which** makes it an ideal place to visit.
2 ... base yourself in Ludlow, **which** is the biggest town in the area.
3 Other places worth a visit are the castle, **which** defended the town against the Welsh.
4 Ludlow is only 150 miles from London, **which** makes it a great place for a weekend.

5 Among the words in bold in the text find:

a) two personal pronouns (subject and object)
b) two reflexive pronouns
c) two indefinite pronouns
d) a possessive pronoun
e) a possessive adjective
f) three relative pronouns
g) a demonstrative pronoun

6 Which of these words do not express the same meaning as *one* in the sentence below?

a) you   b) everyone   c) anyone
d) this person

Ludlow has a church tower that **one** can see from miles and miles away.

☞ Find practice exercises in the Language Powerbook, page 52.

Review Modules 3 and 4

Grammar

1 Complete each gap with the best answer: a, b, c or d.

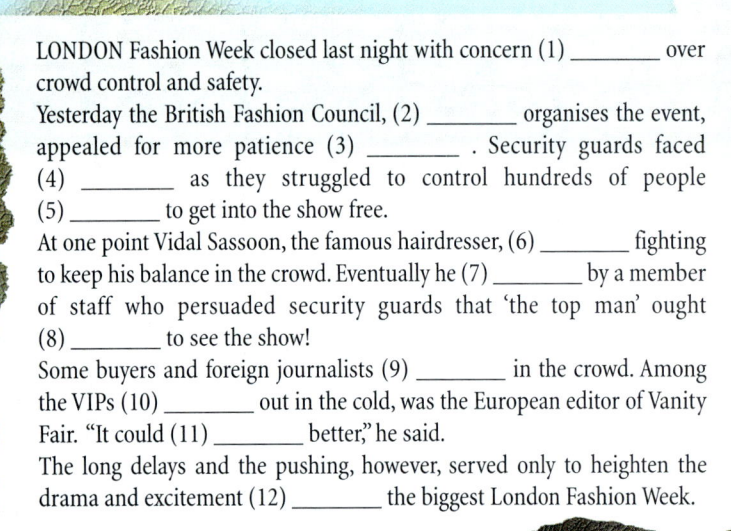

LONDON Fashion Week closed last night with concern (1) _____ over crowd control and safety.

Yesterday the British Fashion Council, (2) _____ organises the event, appealed for more patience (3) _____ . Security guards faced (4) _____ as they struggled to control hundreds of people (5) _____ to get into the show free.

At one point Vidal Sassoon, the famous hairdresser, (6) _____ fighting to keep his balance in the crowd. Eventually he (7) _____ by a member of staff who persuaded security guards that 'the top man' ought (8) _____ to see the show!

Some buyers and foreign journalists (9) _____ in the crowd. Among the VIPs (10) _____ out in the cold, was the European editor of Vanity Fair. "It could (11) _____ better," he said.

The long delays and the pushing, however, served only to heighten the drama and excitement (12) _____ the biggest London Fashion Week.

1 a) expressing   b) being expressed   c) was expressed   d) to express
2 a) who   b) what   c) which   d) that
3 a) showing   b) being shown   c) to be shown   d) shown
4 a) being hurt   b) hurting   c) hurt   d) to be hurt
5 a) trying   b) tried   c) to try   d) to have tried
6 a) left   b) was leaving   c) was left   d) leaving
7 a) recognised   b) be recognised   c) was recognising   d) was recognised
8 a) allow   b) to allow   c) be allowed   d) to be allowed
9 a) trapped   b) was trapped   c) were trapped   d) to be trapped
10 a) left   b) was left   c) leaving   d) was leaving
11 a) have been organised b) be organised   c) organise   d) was organised
12 a) to surround   b) being surrounded   c) surrounding   d) have been surrounded

2 Join these sentences using defining and non-defining relative clauses.

Example
1 *Street artists, who are respected more in Europe, can get thousands of dollars for their paintings.*

1 Street artists are respected more in Europe. They can get thousands of dollars for their paintings.
2 My sister is sixteen. She had her eyebrows pierced yesterday.
3 People spray paint on walls. They are spoiling the environment.
4 Merchandise is sold on the Internet. It has an enormous market.
5 Pamela bought a big desk. She put it near the window.
6 I went to an art gallery. There was an avant-garde exhibition there.
7 Jeans used to be considered working clothes. They became fashionable among young people.
8 Tom's father plays the cello. Tom wants to be a musician.
9 Some graffiti artists have moved into designing products. They can make a lot of money.
10 He marked the area near her navel. He had disinfected her there.

Beauty

3 Expand the sentences by adding participle clauses after the underlined nouns.

Example
'Blade' designs T-shirts, using special computer software.

1 'Blade' designs T-shirts.
2 'Surrounded Islands' was a work of art.
3 The jaguar stared straight ahead.
4 I think graffiti is an eyesore.
5 The music was very moving.
6 The Beast told Beauty he loved her.

4 Complete the text with the verbs in brackets in a suitable form, active or passive.

Virtual Reality Art

Examples of the new 'virtual reality art' (1) _____ (show) at the Inter Communication centre in Tokyo. "The Cave" (2) _____ (build) at a cost of over $1 million. The viewer (3) _____ (put on) special glasses and (4) _____ (confront) by a wooden puppet. If the puppet (5) _____ (move), the three dimensional world (6) _____ (twist) and (7) _____ (turn). This moving world (8) _____ (accompany) by music and sounds. A similar exhibit (9) _____ (build) in the USA. Computer graphics (10) _____ (combine) with 3-D images which (11) _____ (project) on the walls and ceiling, and the viewer (12) _____ (take) on a tour of what seems like another dimension. As one expert (13) _____ (point out) recently, the rise of the 'Nintendo generation' (14) _____ (cause) art and game cultures (15) _____ (merge).

Vocabulary

5 Complete these sentences with the correct form of *get*, *have* or *make*.

Yesterday we (1) _____ a meeting and (2) _____ a look at the figures. Sally (3) _____ a good point. She thought that the Internet (4) _____ a big effect on sales. She thought we were (5) _____ a big mistake if we didn't (6) _____ our own website. She thinks that if you want to (7) _____ it in business and (8) _____ to the top these days, you need one. Mind you, she's only interested in (9) _____ money and (10) _____ a promotion.

6 Complete the sentences with these words.

anti-social, eyesore, graffiti, respected, vandals

1 _____ is very difficult to clean off walls.
2 That new sculpture near the station is horrible; it's a real _____ .
3 Playing loud music late at night is just one example of his _____ behaviour.
4 The phone box was broken by _____ .
5 He is a _____ and well-liked member of society.

7 Complete the sentences with *down*, *from*, *off*, or *up*.

1 You can't seem to get away _____ graffiti nowadays.
2 She turned _____ late, as usual!
3 He turned _____ the offer of a job abroad.
4 He turned _____ the road just before the station.
5 Foreign players make _____ about half the team.

Pronunciation

8 Put these verbs into two groups according to how you pronounce the letter 's' – /s/ or /z/.

advertise, advise, compose, design, discover, display, escape, inspire, practise, recognise, suspend, visit

Group 1: /s/ discover, ...
Group 2: /z/ advertise, ...

🎧 Listen and check your answers. Repeat the words.

9 🎧 Listen and repeat these sentences.

1 She strode along the catwalk in a stunning dress.
2 Modern lifestyles can be stressful.
3 That striking design was inspired by graffiti.
4 I think that sprayed slogans on walls are an eyesore.
5 We stared at the breathtaking sunset.

10 Can you say this proverb? Use the phonetic chart on the inside back cover to help you. What does it mean?

/ˈbjuːti ɪz ɪn ði aɪ əv ðə brɪˈhəʊldər/

Check Your Progress

Look back at the Module Objectives on pages 29 and 39.
• Which activities did you enjoy most?
• Which activities did you have the most problems with?
• Which grammar area do you need to practise more?

Culture Corner 2

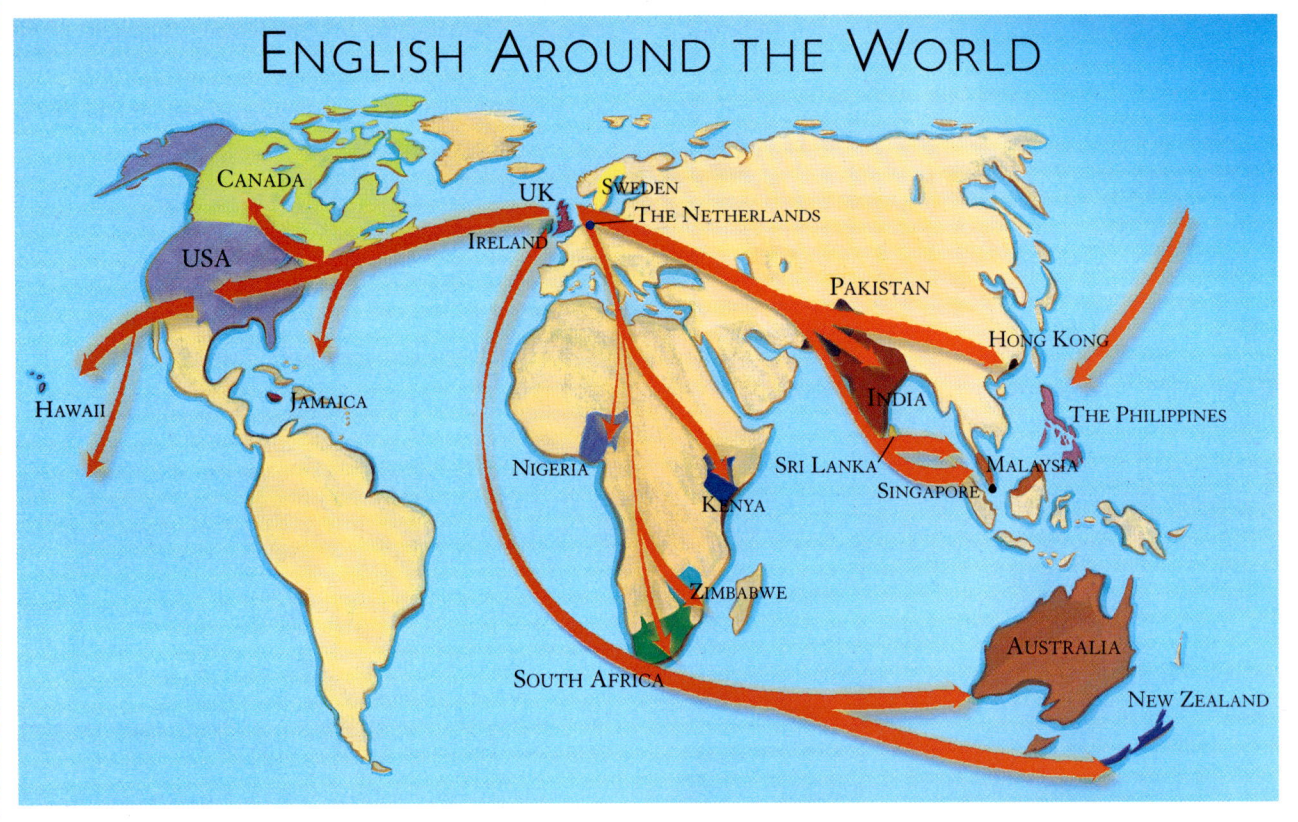

ENGLISH AROUND THE WORLD

1 Look at the map and classify the countries according to the following groups.

- English spoken as a first language
- English spoken as a second language – it is used in schools and universities and as a lingua franca
- English spoken widely as a foreign language

2 Listen to the first part of a lecture and check your answers to Exercise 1.

3 Listen to the second part of the lecture. Match these dates with the events below.

1788, 1806, 1782, 1840, 1607, 1848

1 _____ the first British colony in Virginia
2 _____ British loyalists move north into Canada
3 _____ the first prison colony in Australia
4 _____ Webster's Dictionary of American English
5 _____ the treaty between the British and the Maoris in New Zealand
6 _____ the start of massive emigration from Central Europe to the USA

4 Listen again. Are these sentences true or false?

1 At the time of the independence of the US there were thirty states.
2 American English borrowed words from Native American languages.
3 Noah Webster changed the spelling of many English words.
4 Canadians do not use American words.
5 Australian English has similarities with a London 'cockney' accent.
6 New Zealand English sounds very different from Australian English.

5 Listen to six people talking. Use the clues to identify their accents.

American, Australian, New Zealand, Canadian, Jamaican, South African

6 Listen again and answer these questions.

1 Which of the varieties of English sound very similar?
2 Which do you find most difficult to understand?
3 Which do you find the easiest?

7 Work in pairs. Discuss these questions.

1 What are the positive aspects of English being a global language?
2 What are the negative aspects?

4 A Microchip
2 An Atom
1 A Radio Telescope
3 A Microscope

5 New Frontiers

In this module you...

- **Read** magazine and newspaper articles. **Use** reading strategies for true/false questions.
- **Talk about** science and the future and **give a presentation**.
- **Listen to** dialogues, film extracts, an interview and a presentation. **Use** listening strategies for completing notes.
- **Write** an article.
- **Revise** future tenses and **study** the Future Perfect and Future Continuous.

3 👓 Listen to four extracts and identify these different programmes.

• documentary • quiz • news • interview

4 Think about the answers to these questions.

1 How has science affected our lives in the last two hundred years? Think of:

communication, entertainment, housing, medicine, transport, war, work.

2 Which of the changes in our lives have not been beneficial? Why?
3 In what areas do you think we need to do more research?

Work in pairs. Discuss the questions.

Warm-up

1 Match the branches of science with the numbered objects.

- biology
- information technology
- physics
- astronomy/cosmology

Can you think of any other areas of science?

Example
geology (the study of rocks)

Which areas of science do you think are the most interesting? Why?

5 A DNA Molecule

2 Match the Key Words with the four branches of science in Exercise 1. Add more words.

KEY WORDS: Science

antibiotics, artificial intelligence, atom, bacteria, black hole, data processing, deep space, DNA molecule, electric current, energy, equation, galaxy, gene, gravity, human genome, light year, mass, microchip, microscope, online, radioactivity, radio telescope, search engine, solar system

⇨ *Lexicon, page 153.*

Module 5

13 Eureka!

SKILLS FOCUS

LANDMARKS OF SCIENCE
THE 20TH

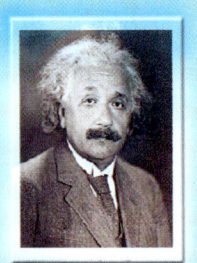

Before you start

1 Try to match the discoveries (1–5) with how they were discovered (a–e).

1) the equation e = mc²
2) Hubble's law
3) penicillin
4) the first computer
5) the model of DNA

a) scientists worked together as a team
b) there was a lucky accident
c) a scientist observed something very carefully
d) a scientist had a moment of inspiration
e) scientists were competing to make a discovery

Reading

2 Read the text and check your guesses from Exercise 1.

3 Read the Strategies.

READING STRATEGIES: Answering true/false/no information questions

- First, read the text to get the general idea.
- Then read the questions/statements and identify important words.
- Find the relevant part of the text and identify the important words.
- Decide if the important words in the question/statement and text express the same ideas.
- To decide if there is no information, make sure that the answer (true/false) cannot be inferred from the text. Also make sure that you base your decision only on the information in the text.

In the summer of 1905, a young man was sitting at home after a day's work. While rocking his one-year-old baby, he thought something over. Suddenly, it came to him! The equation 'e = mc²' was born, an equation which would change our understanding of the universe but would help to create the nuclear bomb. Albert Einstein was aware of recent developments, such as Marie Curie's research into radioactivity, but he had been working on his own. His mould-breaking equation showed how a small piece of mass could produce an unbelievable amount of energy. Einstein then demonstrated in his 'theory of relativity' that not even time, mass or length are constant – they vary according to our perspective of them. For example, if we could see people moving at the speed of light, they would appear much heavier and larger and would seem to move in slow motion.

By the time Einstein had become world-famous, a young ex-lawyer returning from the First World War started work at the Mount Wilson Observatory in California. Using the most high-powered telescope of its time, he began a painstakingly slow observation of nebulae, small patches of light that appeared outside our galaxy. Edwin Hubble was on the brink of making the greatest astronomical breakthrough of the century. He discovered that these nebulae were in fact galaxies like our own, millions of light years away from us, which proved that the universe was vastly larger than had previously been thought. Then, Hubble proved that the universe is actually expanding and that the further away galaxies are the faster they move.

Just before Hubble's Law was published in 1929, another far-reaching finding was made by the son of a Scottish shepherd. Before going on holiday, he left a dish with bacteria near the window of his laboratory. When he came back, he was just about to throw the dish away when he noticed something out of the ordinary. He double-checked and saw a blue mould in the dish around which the bacteria had been destroyed. This blue mould was in fact the natural form of penicillin which Fleming realised was an effective way of killing bacteria. A few years later, penicillin was being mass-produced and helping to save the lives of millions. Despite the outcome of his discovery, Fleming remained modest and unassuming. 'Nature makes penicillin,' he said, 'I just found it.'

During the Second World War when penicillin was first being used, the US Navy were looking for ways of improving the accuracy of their artillery shells, but this involved incredibly complex calculations. The navy turned to Eckert, an engineer, and Mauchly, a physicist to produce a machine to do the job. Although they and their team did not finish the machine until after the war, in February 1946, it did not matter. They had produced the world's first computer. Eniac (Electronic Numerical Integrator and Computer) was huge, measuring 100 feet long by over 10 feet high and weighing over 30 tons. It contained 18,000 tubes and had more than 6,000 switches.

CENTURY

It consumed so much energy that when it was turned on, the lights in the local town went dim. However, it worked and it was the first programmable computer.

The computer arrived too late to help in the next ground-breaking find. From the mid 1940s, biologists knew about a molecule that had an important role in passing on genetic information for all living things. However, they did not know how it worked and the race to find this out had begun. Then, two young scientists at Cambridge University saw the results of some studies by Rosalind Franklin. The last piece of the jigsaw puzzle had fallen into place. In 1953, Watson and Crick published their model of the DNA molecule. As a result, in 2000, after years of time-consuming and expensive research using computerised data processing and despite many setbacks, the so-called 'genome' for human beings was discovered. The four chemicals in our DNA combine to produce a code that would fill over 500,000 pages of a telephone directory and that contains information about our 100,000 genes. Already, this has helped doctors to cure some hereditary illnesses and the outlook for the future seems promising.

4 Are these statements true (T) or false (F) according to the text or is there no information (NI)? Use the Strategies to help you.

1 Einstein was at work when he thought of the formula '$e = mc^2$'.
2 Einstein participated in the programme that developed the nuclear bomb.
3 Einstein observed changes in time, size and mass.
4 Hubble studied the nebulae for over twenty years.
5 Hubble discovered that our galaxy is bigger than we thought it was.
6 Fleming had been studying bacteria in his laboratory when the discovery happened.
7 There was a blue mould around the bacteria in the dish.
8 Fleming developed the process for manufacturing penicillin.
9 The Eniac project failed to meet its original objective.
10 The Eniac computer was extremely difficult to program.
11 The code for a DNA molecule has over half a million letters in it.
12 The process of decoding the human genome was long and costly.

New Frontiers

Vocabulary: Compound Words

➡ *Lexicon, page 159.*

5 Match the categories (a–e) with the examples from the text (1–5). Then add examples of your own.

a) compound noun (noun + noun)
b) compound noun (verb + preposition)
c) compound noun (adjective + noun)
d) compound verb
e) compound adjective

1 one-year-old; ground-breaking; time-consuming; far-reaching; high-powered
2 telephone directory; human being; data processing; jigsaw puzzle; CD player
3 slow motion; nuclear bomb
4 breakthrough; setback; outcome; outlook
5 mass-produce; double-check

6 Make the plural of the compound nouns in Exercise 5 (e.g. *human beings*). Which two nouns can you not make plural? Why not?

Speaking

7 Work in pairs. Discuss these questions with your partner.

1 Which of the discoveries mentioned in the text has been the most important so far? Why?
2 Which discovery will have the most important consequences in the future? Why?
3 Which of the scientists in the text do you admire most? Why?
4 Which of the discoveries is the most difficult to understand?

8 A Science Quiz. Work in pairs. Student A turns to page 134 and Student B to page 136. Ask and answer the questions.

QUOTE .... UNQUOTE
'Creativity in science could be described as the act of putting two and two together to make five.'
Arthur Koestler (1905–1983), British author

Module 5

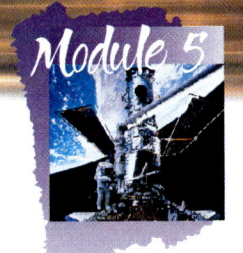

14 Futurology

GRAMMAR FOCUS

Before you start

1 Look at the headlines below. What do you think they mean?

- From Astrology to Futurology
- The Future Business
- Tomorrow's World
- A Perfect Future?

Read the article and choose the best title for it.

2 Which of the predictions would you like or not like to come true? Why?

THE FUTURE

Revision

3 Match the sentences from the text (1–8) with the uses (a–g).

1 I *might get* a pleasant surprise one day.
2 This weekend hundreds of futurologists *are meeting* at Newcastle University.
3 The conference *starts* on Thursday.
4 All of us *are going to use* our voices to give instructions to computers.
5 Tiny robots *may be sent* around our bodies.
6 I'm sure you*'ll agree*.
7 I*'m going to give up* astrology.
8 I*'ll be* there in Newcastle this weekend.

a) an arrangement for the future
b) a future fact
c) a firm prediction based on speaker's/writer's opinion
d) a weak prediction (x2)
e) an intention
f) a spontaneous decision
g) a prediction based on observable evidence

4 Which of the predictions expressed in the text:

a) are definitely **going to** happen (we can see evidence now)?
b) **will** probably happen (this is your opinion)?
c) **may** happen in your lifetime (there is a chance they will happen)?
d) **might** happen in your lifetime (there is a small chance that they will happen)?

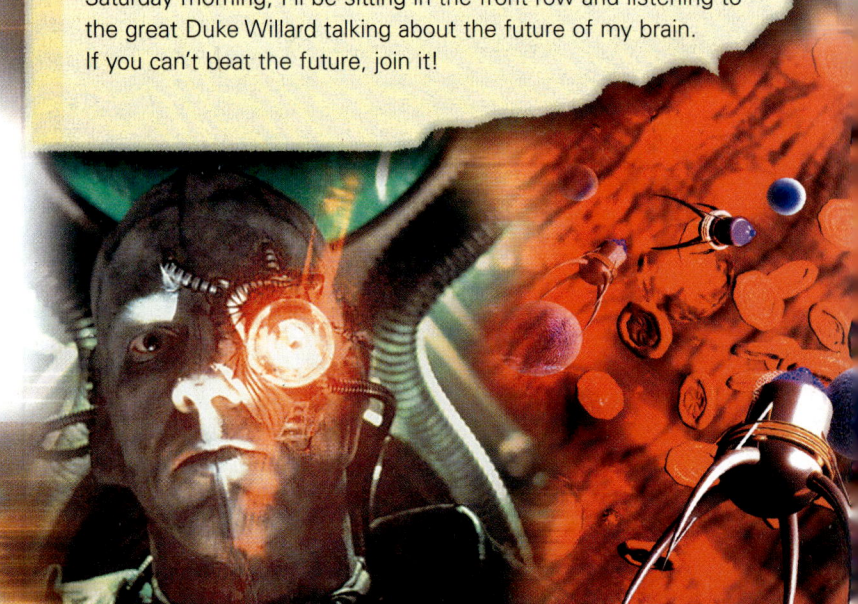

Hannah Jones gazes into the future of futurology.

I confess I am obsessed with the future – and I am not the only one. Over the centuries, people have used the stars, cards, crystal balls and even tea-leaves to look into the future. I still read my horoscope every day: 'When you get home on Friday, you will receive some very good news.' or 'At the weekend, after you've done the shopping, you will have a pleasant surprise.' I never do have a pleasant surprise in the supermarket car park, but who knows? One day I might!
This weekend, however, we will get a surprise because hundreds of futurologists are meeting at Newcastle University. The conference starts on Thursday and the experts will be discussing the impact of technology on the future. The future is now big business. I logged on to the websites of some professional futurologists and found these predictions:

- The technology already exists, so very soon all of us are going to use our voices to give instructions to computers.
- In the next few years, we will be communicating with our friends around the world using life-sized video images on large screens in our living rooms.
- By the year 2020, computers will already have become more efficient and powerful than the human brain both in terms of intelligence and the amount of information they can store.
- By the year 2030, genetic engineering and nanotechnology will enable us to live for at least 150 years. Using nanotechnology, tiny, insect-like robots may be sent around our bodies to carry out repairs and keep us healthy.
- By the middle of the century, computers, millions of times smarter than us, will have been developed. By this time, we will be linking our brains with 'ultra-smart' computers. A new species might have developed – 'Homo Cyberneticus'.
- By the end of the century, we will have colonised our solar system and will be looking for ways to colonise deep space.

Much more interesting than horoscopes, I am sure you will agree! I've decided I'm going to give up astrology and take up futurology – I'll be there in Newcastle this weekend. At nine o'clock on Saturday morning, I'll be sitting in the front row and listening to the great Duke Willard talking about the future of my brain. If you can't beat the future, join it!

56

New Frontiers

Presentation

5 In which of these sentences do we emphasise that the underlined activity must be finished before the other one happens?

1 When you <u>get home</u> on Friday, you'll receive good news.
2 After you<u>'ve done the shopping</u>, you'll have a pleasant surprise.

6 Which of the tenses below refers to:

a) something that will finish before a certain time in the future?
b) something that will be in progress at a certain time in the future?

Future Perfect
By the end of the century, we **will have colonised** our solar system.

Future Continuous
At nine o'clock on Saturday morning, I'll **be sitting** in the front row and **listening** to the great Duke Willard.

Find more examples of the tenses in the text.

➪ *Grammar Summary 5, page 147.*

Practice

7 Complete the sentences using the Present Perfect.

1 I'll help you as soon as I _____ .
2 She can't buy a computer until she _____ .
3 You can leave the exam room only after you _____ .
4 I'll phone you when I _____ .
5 We'll let you know as soon as _____ .
6 Your telephone line will be activated only after _____ .

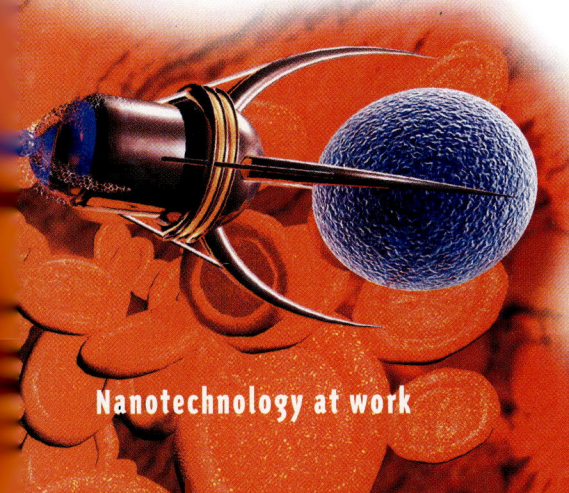

8 Complete these predictions about the world in 2020 by putting the verbs in brackets either in the Future Perfect or the Future Continuous.

1 people (use) solar energy extensively
2 people (use) up all natural resources of oil
3 people (travel) into space on a regular basis
4 people (eat) only genetically engineered food
5 traditional farms (disappear)
6 many new galaxies (discover)
7 Mars and Venus (investigate) and (describe) in detail
8 scientists (study) chances of people settling down in other galaxies

9 Look at the programme of the futurologists' conference and the cues below (1–7). Write full sentences using the Future Perfect or the Future Continuous.

Example 7 p.m. on Friday – the participants attend a panel discussion
At 7 p.m. on Friday the participants will be attending a panel discussion.

Friday	
4 – 5.30 p.m.	Prof Howard Green: Alternative Sources of Energy – New Perspectives
6 – 7.30 p.m.	Panel discussion: Love and Friendship in the 21st century
8 p.m.	Reception
Saturday	
9 – 11.30 a.m.	Prof Duke Willard: The Future of the Human Brain
12 – 1.30 p.m.	Dr B. A. Lorry: Vehicles of the Future
2 – 3.00 p.m.	Lunch
4 – 5.30 p.m.	Prof Stella Spacek: Exploration of Mars and Venus
6 – 7.30 p.m.	Dr D.N.A. Gene: Genetics – Hope or Threat?
8 p.m.	Reception
Sunday	
9 – 11.30 a.m.	Panel discussion: Earth in 2050
12.00 a.m.	Closing ceremony

1 5 p.m. on Friday – Prof Howard Green gives a lecture on alternative sources of energy
2 Saturday lunchtime – the participants listen to three lectures
3 2.30 p.m. on Saturday – everyone has lunch
4 Saturday night – the participants have a reception
5 Sunday morning – the participants attend two receptions
6 Sunday noon – they identify a few problems of the future
7 the end of the conference – the futurologists discuss many important issues

10 Work in pairs. Make predictions about each other in ten years' time. Say what you think about your partner's predictions.

Example A: *I think that in 10 years' time you'll be working as a vet.*
B: *I hope so!*

1 Will he/she be living here or abroad? Where?
2 How many jobs will he/she have had by that time?
3 What will he/she have achieved?
4 Will he/she be married? For how long?
5 Will he/she have any children?

Nanotechnology at work

Module 5

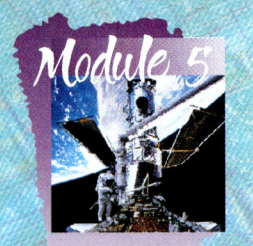

15 Artificial Intelligence

SKILLS FOCUS

Before you start

1 Look at the pictures. Work in pairs and discuss these questions.

1. What science fiction films have you seen that have intelligent robots or androids?
2. How did the robots behave towards humans?
3. Which of these things can robots and computers do now?

work in factories, play football, control cars and planes, beat us at chess, compose music, give us the news, speak to us, have a real conversation with us, have feelings

Check your answers to number 3 on page 135.

Listening

2 🎧 Listen to the interview with Ananova and answer the questions.

1. Where can you see and hear her? What does she do?
2. Does Ananova really exist? Can she really talk?
3. Why are there no photos of her as a child?
4. How does she find news stories?
5. What are her plans for the future?

Do you think Ananova is intelligent? Why/Why not?

3 🎧 Listen to the interview again. Complete the Function File with these expressions.

In other words, Is that clear?, What I don't quite understand, To put it another way, what I mean is, What that means, So does that mean, Could you explain how, What I'm trying to say, What I'm getting at, that's a programme which, I mean

Function File

Clarifying and asking questions

And tonight she's in the studio for an interview with us, well, (1) _____ , she's here on screen, of course, because she's not real, she's a virtual character – just an image.
(2) _____
It's not a real interview. (3) _____ is that we sent the questions to her programmers beforehand.
(4) _____ your creators decided what you should look like?
(5) _____ , they only receive what they want to know.
(6) _____ , I have no childhood.
(7) _____ is how you are so quick.
(8) _____ is how do you gather the news so quickly?
I also have a 'Web Spider' – (9) _____ searches the Internet...
(10) _____ they tell you whether to smile or read in a serious voice?
So what next? (11) _____ what are the plans for Ananova?
(12) _____ is I will deliver the latest stories that you're interested in wherever you are.

Speaking

4 Work in pairs. Student A turns to page 134 and Student B to page 136. Read the notes about the robots. Add your own information.

5 Explain your robot to your partner using expressions from the Function File. Ask questions about your partner's robot.

Example
A: It's quite fast. What that means is that it goes at about 40 kph.
B: What I don't quite understand is how it moves.
A: Well, it's got wheels.
B: So could you explain how it goes up stairs?

Listening

6 Read the Strategies.

> **LISTENING STRATEGIES:**
> Completing notes
> - Look at the notes and decide what kind of information you need, e.g. a date, a number, an adjective, etc.
> - Don't worry if you don't understand everything – just listen for the important words.
> - Complete the notes with one word or a short phrase.

Listen to the woman talking about her favourite film and complete the notes.

2001: Space Odyssey was first released in (1) _____.
Some people's reaction was to walk out of (2) _____.
It's not a typical science fiction film because there is not much (3) _____.
Two of the best things about the film are the (4) _____.
The first scene is set on Earth (5) _____.
Some ape-men find a black monolith, a machine sent by (6) _____.
The next part of the film is set on (7) _____.
The third part of film is about a journey to (8) _____.
Only the intelligent computer HAL knows the (9) _____.

Vocabulary: Multi-part Verbs

➡ **Lexicon, pages 170–176.**

7 Match these verbs with those in bold in the text.

take over, walked out, get across, give away, get on fine, is to do with, makes up for, came out, make out, got a lot out of

The woman (1) **enjoyed** the film, even though it (2) **was released** a long time ago. She explains that when it was first shown, some people couldn't (3) **understand** what it was about and (4) **left**. In her opinion, the director (5) **compensates for** the lack of plot by using visual effects and employs music to (6) **communicate** the mood of the film. The woman talks about the plot of the film but she does not (7) **reveal** the ending. Among other things, the film (8) **is about** intelligent machines. In the story, some astronauts and a computer (9) **have a good relationship**, but then the computer tries to (10) **take control**.

Listening

8 Listen to the story of HAL and answer the questions.

1. How many astronauts are there on the ship? How many are in 'hibernation'?
2. Why do Frank and Dave talk about disconnecting HAL?
3. Why does HAL start killing the astronauts?
4. Why does HAL refuse to let Dave back into the spaceship?
5. What emotions does HAL feel when he is being disconnected?
6. Why does HAL sing a song before he 'dies'?

Comparing Cultures

Work in pairs. Discuss these questions.

1. Do you think technology and the media have made cultures around the world more similar? How?
2. Will different cultures and languages disappear in the future? How can cultures and languages be protected?

QUOTE .... UNQUOTE
'Men have become the tools of their tools.'
H.D. Thoreau, American writer (1817–1862)

Communication Workshop

Module 5

The International Space Station

Writing: An Article

Before you start

1 Read the article. Match these headings with the paragraphs (A–E).

- Life on Mars • The Space Race
- The Last Frontier
- Globetrotters • Into Deep Space

2 Find sentences in the text that mean the same as these colloquial sentences. Paragraph letters are in brackets.

1 The space age kicked off when they sent up Sputnik 1. (B)
2 But they carried on sending out robot ships to have a look round. (B)
3 Space exploration is in again because of that new telescope. (C)
4 It's so good that it's found loads of new planets. (C)
5 They're going to launch robot ships to find places like Earth. (D)

The Hubble Telescope

Space: The Big Frontier

A 'What's beyond that hill?' 'What's on the other side of that river?' Curiosity and the desire to explore have been with us since our ancestors left Africa (1) <u>to</u> spread out over the world. By the beginning of the 21st century, virtually all of Planet Earth has been visited, photoed, described, mapped. We have left our mark (and our rubbish) in the four corners of the globe. Now only one frontier remains to explore – space.

B The age of space exploration began in 1957, when Sputnik 1 was launched by the Soviet Union. The first successful manned flight took place in 1961, when Yuri Gagarin was shot into space. This triggered the 'space race' between the USA and the USSR, culminating in the moon landing in 1969. After this, there was something of an anticlimax and the number of manned missions dropped off, largely (2) <u>due to</u> the end of the space race. Nevertheless, space probes like Pioneer and Voyager continued to be sent out (3) <u>in order to</u> explore the neighbouring planets such as Mars and Venus. The American shuttle and the Russian *Mir Space Station* were also ground-breaking, (4) <u>as</u> they developed the practicalities of space travel.

C Recently, there has been another burst of interest in space (5) <u>as a result of</u> the Hubble Telescope. It was launched in 1990 (6) <u>so that</u> astronomers could observe space without interference from the Earth's atmosphere. The Hubble has provided views of such phenomena as distant galaxies, dying stars and black holes. (7) <u>Because of</u> its precision, over fifty new planets have been located beyond our solar system. Other exciting developments have been the Prospector and Pathfinder probes (8) <u>for</u> exploring our solar system, looking for water on the Moon and primitive life on Mars.

D The International Space Station is now being built in the Earth's orbit and soon will be working as a permanently manned scientific base, (9) <u>so as to</u> research life in space and provide a stepping stone (10) <u>in case</u> future manned missions are sent out. Further space probes, such as *Deep Space*, will be sent out (11) <u>in order that</u> they might detect small Earth-like planets where there might be life. A permanent base will probably be established on the Moon in the next twenty years and a manned mission to Mars might take place some time after. Later in the century, some scientists believe we may develop the technology (12) <u>so as to</u> be able to begin interstellar exploration, starting with our nearest star, Proxima Centauri, four light years away.

E In conclusion, space exploration is still in its infancy and is restricted by many technical problems but the possibilities are incredible. While humankind's innate curiosity remains, we will keep exploring. The sky is no longer the limit.

New Frontiers

3 Match these words with the idiomatic expressions from the text (1–6) in *italics*.

just beginning, all over the world,
a stage on the way, the possibilities are endless,
started off, shown we've been

1 We have *left our mark* everywhere.
2 *The four corners of the globe.*
3 It *triggered* the space race.
4 It's *a stepping stone.*
5 It's *in its infancy.*
6 *The sky's the limit.*

4 Classify the linking words underlined in the text.

a) reason (explains the cause of an action)
b) purpose (shows the aim of an action)

Example 1 purpose

Which of the linkers are followed by modal verbs?

5 Complete the second sentence so that it has a similar meaning to the first sentence.

1 Take an umbrella because it might rain.
   Take an umbrella in case _____ .
2 Bring your costume to swim in the river.
   Bring your costume so that _____ .
3 It's foggy so you can't drive fast.
   You can't drive fast due to _____ .
4 If you leave your telephone number, we will contact you.
   Leave your telephone number in order that _____ .
5 My aunt's coming so don't come round.
   Don't come round because of _____ .
6 Check if he's in by giving him a ring.
   Ring him up first in order to _____ .
7 Wear warm clothes as the nights can be very cold.
   Wear warm clothes in case _____ .
8 You might spill it if you fill the jug too much.
   Don't fill the jug too much so as to _____ .

> Write an article for a local magazine about a subject you are interested in. Follow the stages.

Stage 1
Choose a subject that interests you, e.g. contemporary ballet, computers, the Olympics. Make a list of places where you can get information about it.

Example
- websites – www.ballet.com
- magazines – Dance Today
- books – The History of Ballet
- radio – arts programmes
- television – Come Dancing

Stage 2
Find information. Write notes and organise them into five paragraphs.

⇨ Writing Help 5 (layout), page 140.

Stage 3
Use your plan to write the article.

⇨ Writing Help 5 (style, useful vocabulary, linking).

Stage 4
Check your article.

⇨ Writing Help 5 (checking).

Talkback

Work in pairs. Read each other's articles. Then tell your partner:

- what (for you) is the most interesting information in his/her article
- what information is not so interesting for you
- if any part of the article is not very clear or difficult to understand

Listening: A Song

In the year 2525 (by Zager and Evans)

1 Listen to the song about the future. Which years are mentioned?

2929, 3535, 4545, 5555, 6565, 7575, 8585, 9595

2 Listen again. Which of these things are predicted?

intelligent machines, pills that control you, test-tube babies, machines for doing everything, an invasion by aliens, changes in our bodies, a nuclear war, space travel to other stars, the end of humankind

Communication Workshop

Speaking: A Presentation

Before you start

1 🎧 Listen to a class presentation about Mars and complete the notes.

- The gravity on Mars is (1) _____ .
- Canyons and valleys show that in the past there was (2) _____ .
- The astronomer Schiaparelli observed (3) _____ .
- In H.G. Wells' book, Martians had (4) _____ .
- Mariner 4 flew past the planet in (5) _____ .
- Pathfinder was a success because it (6) _____ .
- NASA claimed that a meteorite proved (7) _____ .
- A study of the meteorite in 2001 found (8) _____ .
- A manned mission to Mars would take about (9) _____ .

Chatroom

PRESENTING

2 Match the expressions from the presentation (1–9) with why we use them (a–g).

1. Today I'm going to talk about …
2. As you can see in this photo …
3. Well, first I'd like to talk about …
4. What about the history of …?
5. Right, now let's look at …
6. Another area of great interest …
7. So what is the future of …?
8. To sum up, …
9. That's all. Thank you.

a) to refer to a drawing or photo
b) to start off the presentation
c) to finish the presentation
d) to start the conclusion
e) to introduce the first topic
f) to introduce a new topic with a question (x2)
g) to introduce a new topic (x2)

3 Read the Strategies. Which of them do you think are the most useful?

SPEAKING STRATEGIES: Giving presentations

- First, make sure you understand the subject and have collected enough information.
- To prepare, choose the most interesting information. Then write notes about what you want to say. Do not write out your presentation.
- Find visual aids to help you: slides, photos, diagrams, etc.
- Practise giving your presentation to yourself. Go through it again just before you give it.
- If you get very nervous beforehand, breathe in and out deeply a few times.
- At the start, state clearly what you are going to talk about.
- If you make a mistake or forget something, don't worry – continue talking.
- Finish your presentation with a summary of the main points and then ask for any questions.

Give a five-minute presentation to the rest of the class (about the topic of your article from the Writing Workshop). Follow the stages.

Stage 1
Look at your notes from Stage 2 of the Writing Workshop. Add notes for your objectives (beginning) and for a summary (at the end). Underline information to help you remember it.

Stage 2
Look at the expressions in the Function File in Lesson 15 and in the Chatroom in this lesson. Practise giving your talk to yourself.

Stage 3
Give your presentation to the rest of the class. When listening to other people, take notes about their talk.

Talkback

Work in pairs. Discuss these things:

1. Which was the most interesting presentation? Why?
2. Which subject would you like to find more about?
3. Which of the Speaking Strategies were the most useful?
4. What were the biggest problems you had?

6 Soft Machine

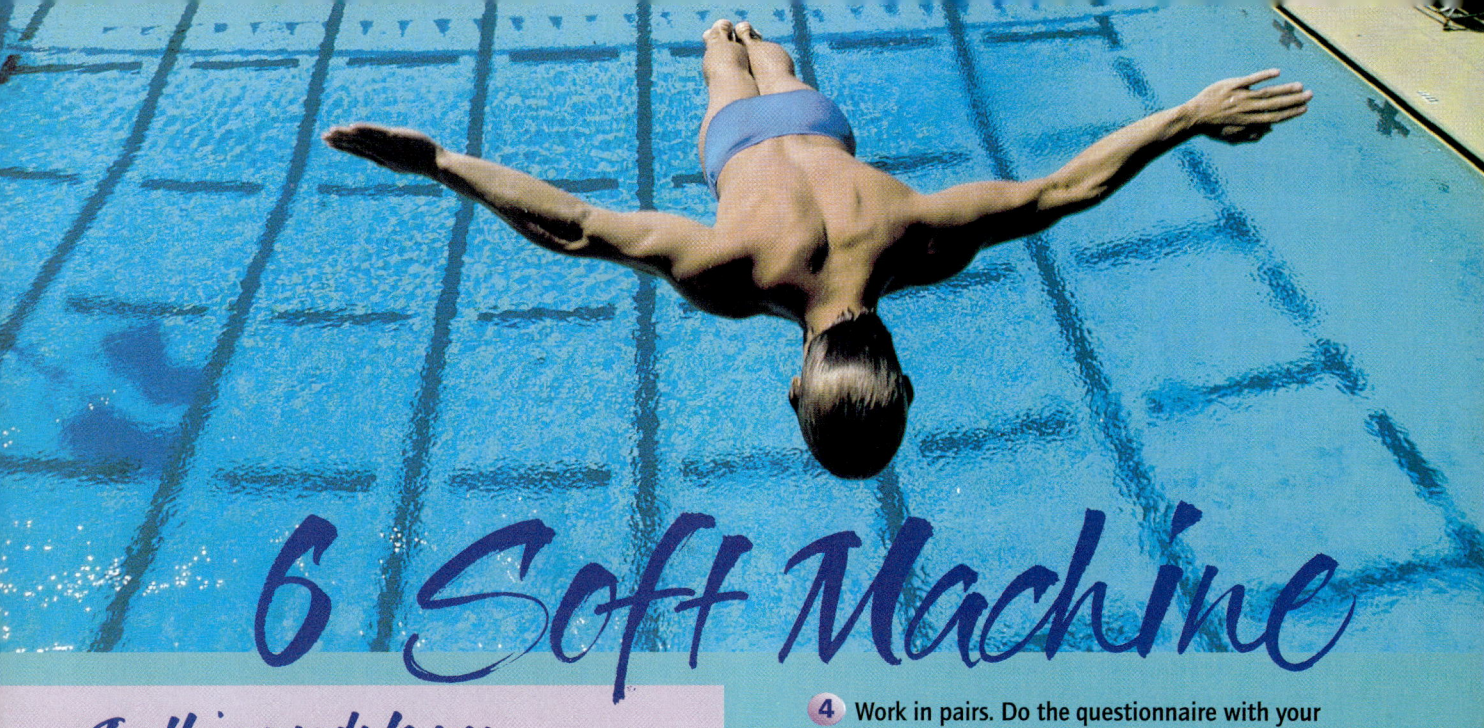

In this module you...

- **Read** newspaper and magazine articles and **use** reading strategies to complete texts with paragraph gaps.
- **Talk about** issues related to health and medical advances.
- **Listen to** monologues, dialogues, a lesson, a radio phone-in, a TV programme and **use** listening strategies for completing gaps in texts.
- **Write** a discursive essay.
- **Revise** and **learn** more about conditional sentences.

Warm-up

1 Find six Key Words to label the parts of the body in the diagram.

KEY WORDS: The Body
ankle, brain, eye, heart, kidneys, knee, liver, lungs, muscle, ribs, skin, spine, stomach, wrist

▷ *Lexicon, page 153.*

2 Listen and guess which parts of the body are being described. Which words helped you decide?

3 Work in pairs and test your body 'machine'.

Test Your Body Machine

Memory. Write down five telephone numbers and give them to your partner to look at for 30 seconds. How many can he/she remember?
Hearing. Everybody in the class sits in silence for 30 seconds. Write down every sound you can hear. Compare your list with your partner's.
Heart. Find the pulse on your partner's wrist. How many times does his/her heart beat in one minute? Is he/she more or less relaxed than you?

4 Work in pairs. Do the questionnaire with your partner.

Do You Look After Yourself?

1 How many hours per night do you sleep?
a) under 6 hours b) about 7 or 8 hours
c) more than 9 hours

2 How often do you clean your teeth?
a) once a day b) twice a day
c) after every meal

3 How often do you do physical exercise, enough to make you out of breath?
a) never b) once a week
c) two or three times a week

4 How often do you eat sweets or chocolate?
a) never b) occasionally
c) quite a lot

5 How many pieces of fresh fruit do you eat per day?
a) one or two
b) more than two
c) none

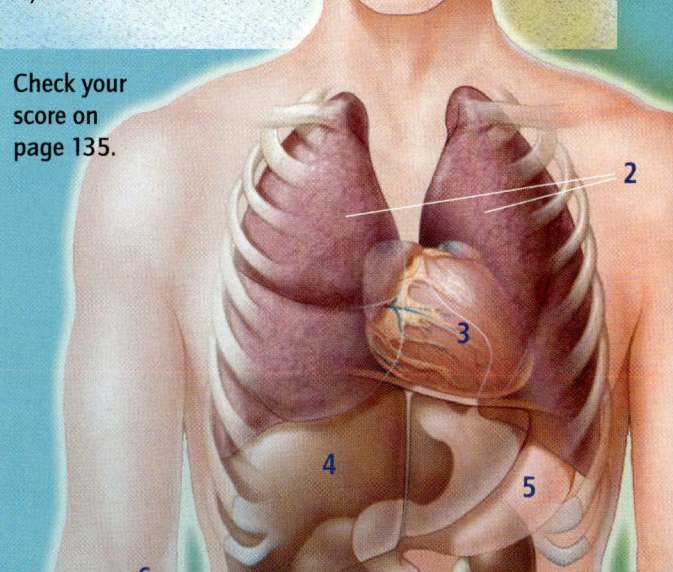

Check your score on page 135.

Module 6

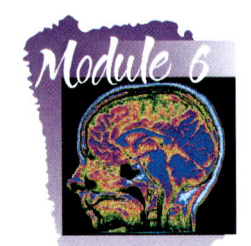

16 Life Savers

SKILLS FOCUS

Before you start

1 Look at the Key Words. For which of the diseases is there a vaccine to prevent the illness?

> **KEY WORDS**
>
> Aids, bronchitis, cancer, diarrhoea, 'flu (= influenza), heart disease, malaria, measles, pneumonia, polio, tetanus, TB (= tuberculosis)

2 Work in pairs. Do you think these statements are true (T) or false (F)?

1. Measles, diarrhoea and pneumonia kill an estimated seven million children a year.
2. Each year 600,000 babies pick up tetanus bacteria and die – even though there is a vaccine.
3. Many children still suffer from polio; every year the disease disables 140,000 children.
4. Over two million people a year get malaria and die, mostly in Africa.
5. Nearly one-third of the world's population is infected with tuberculosis, which kills almost three million people per year.
6. By the year 2000, more than 20 million people had contracted and died of Aids since the outbreak of the epidemic.

Check your answers on page 135.

3 Read the Strategies.

> **READING STRATEGIES:**
> Texts with paragraph gaps
>
> - Read the text with gaps to get the general idea and see how it develops, e.g. *The X-factor* on page 65.
> - Read the sentences before and after the gaps to give you an idea of what the beginning or end of the missing paragraph might refer to, e.g. paragraph 2 might begin with a reference to a history-making event or end with a reference to the 'little boy'.
> - Read the missing paragraphs and look for these references.
> - If a paragraph doesn't seem to fit, you may have made a mistake *or* it may be 'the extra paragraph'.

Now use the Strategies to match five out of six paragraphs (A–F) with gaps 2, 4, 6, 8 and 11 in the text. There is one extra paragraph.

A Three months after the infusion, his astonished parents were told they could take him home. There he remains, a normal, healthy two-year-old boy.

B For the first time, doctors had used their knowledge of the genes involved in a fatal disease to cure it. After years of experiments, gene therapy's promise to correct nature's flaws was being realised. Now that our genetic code has been cracked, more and more of those flaws will come within reach of repair.

C Dr Cavazzana-Calvo agrees that there has not been enough time to claim that it's a definitive treatment. "Nevertheless, the importance of this work is that it has proved this strategy can work. It has been a breath of fresh air for gene therapy."

D In every person's bone marrow is a group of cells known as 'stem' cells. When they receive the right chemical signals, they multiply to become red and white blood cells.

E Adrian Thrasher, a consultant in child immunology at a London hospital, announced: "This is the first time we can say, unequivocally, that gene therapy is effective on its own. Patients have not received any other treatment, yet have got better."

F Meanwhile, doctors Alain Fischer, Marina Cavazzana-Calvo and Salima Hacein-Bey took out a few million of his bone marrow cells and managed to insert a healthy gene in them. Then they put them back – a single, simple infusion of 20 to 30 millilitres of fluid. It took half an hour to give the boy what they hope will be a lifetime of normal immunity.

The X-factor

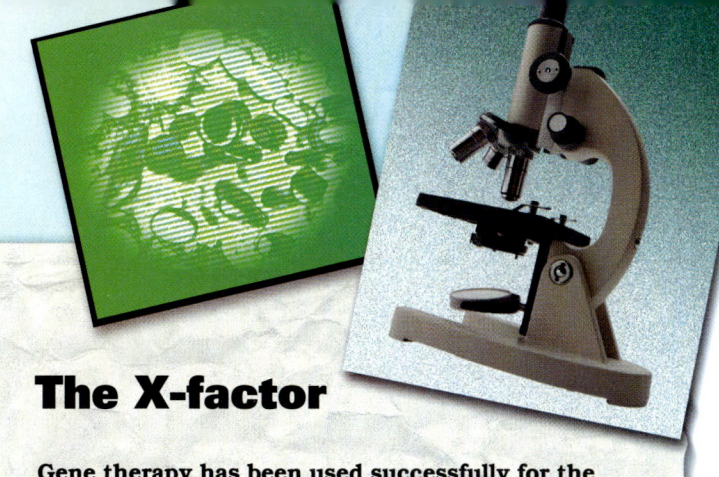

Gene therapy has been used successfully for the first time. James Meek looks at how this was achieved.

1 Last February, there was an air of euphoria in the corridors of the Necker Hospital for Sick Children in Paris. An incredible transformation was happening to an 11-month-old baby boy in an airtight bubble. In fact, history was being made there.

2 ...

3 When the little boy was admitted to hospital, he was facing death from a rare inherited disorder called 'X-linked SCID', a disease that causes children to be born without a working immune system. The slightest infection can be deadly. For several days, the boy lay in his bubble and his only direct contact with his mother, father and nurse was through plastic gloves.

4 ...

5 Within 15 days, doctors knew from tests that the new gene was working. But the marvel for the parents was watching the change in their sickly, underweight boy. Before their eyes, he began to get better. The ugly red blotches on his skin faded away, his diarrhoea disappeared, he put on weight and his breathing became easier.

6 ...

7 "Afterwards, we lived through three months of euphoria," said Cavazzana-Calvo. "Everyone was so happy then." Since then, treatment of three other children in the Necker Hospital has also turned out well. A fifth boy has done less well, because the disease had already caused serious complications, but the Necker is pressing ahead with further trials later this year, and similar gene therapy is to be carried out in London.

8 ...

9 Despite the initial optimism, this first achievement of gene therapy will have to be further proved over time, as it might not be so successful in treating other genetic diseases. Nevertheless, it is a major step forward in gene therapy.

10 Dr Jennifer Puck, a leading genetics researcher, underlines the importance of this breakthrough. "Although these children had no immunity when they were born, now they're exactly as good as any babies of their age. However, the immune system is not totally mature until they're three or four years of age. So the question is, is this going to last a lifetime?"

11 ...

4 Complete these sentences about the text in your own words.

1 The baby had to be kept in an airtight bubble because ...
2 The parents were allowed to take the boy home because ...
3 Adrian Thrasher believed gene therapy could work because ...
4 Doctors are careful not to be too optimistic about the operations because ...
5 Doctors should be able to cure more illnesses in the future because ...

5 How did you feel after reading the article? Tell the class.

Vocabulary: Synonyms

6 Match the words from the first four paragraphs (1–10) with their meanings (a–j).

1 euphoria   a) treatment
2 transformation b) uncommon
3 fatal   c) great happiness
4 therapy   d) put in
5 flaw   e) weakness
6 rare   f) deadly
7 disorder   g) liquid
8 insert   h) disease
9 fluid   i) protection
10 immunity   j) change

7 Find idiomatic words or expressions in the text which mean the same as these.

1 feeling of happiness (paragraph 1)
2 deciphered (paragraph 2)
3 be in our capacity (paragraph 2)
4 nearly dying (paragraph 3)
5 very quickly (paragraph 5)
6 continuing (paragraph 7)
7 important advance (paragraph 9)
8 a great encouragement (paragraph 11)

Speaking

8 Work in pairs. Which of these things do you think will happen within the next 25 years?

1 Genetic therapy will cure cancer.
2 New drugs will help people to live for 150 years.
3 Malaria will disappear in the developing world.
4 Manipulating genes will cause new illnesses.

Module 6

17 Super Athletes

Grammar Focus

Before you start

1 What champion athletes can you name? What were their achievements?

Example
Michael Johnson – world record in 400m

2 Read the article and answer the questions.

1 What reasons are given for improved performance?
2 How did drugs distort world records in the 1980s?
3 What would the effect of 'gene-doping' be?
4 What was the original 'Olympic spirit'?

Conditionals Revision

3 Match the conditional sentences in *italics* in the text with the following types:

- zero conditional
- 1st conditional
- 2nd conditional
- 3rd conditional

Which of the sentences in *italics* talk about the past, the present and the future?

Practice

4 🔊 **Pronunciation**. Listen to the sentences and write down the contractions you hear. Then listen again and repeat the sentences.

Example 1 'd've (would have) / 'd (had)

5 Make conditional sentences about these situations (1–6).

Example
1 *If he hadn't taken drugs, he wouldn't have been banned.*

1 Ben Johnson took drugs ➔ he was banned from sport
2 athletes earn a lot of money ➔ they train hard
3 someone will run 100 metres in 9.3 seconds ➔ nobody will believe it
4 Gabriela Szabo is very fit ➔ it's easy for her to run long distances
5 an athlete will win four gold medals in athletics ➔ they will be a record breaker
6 in 1980 the Olympic Games were organised in Moscow ➔ the USA didn't take part

THE 100 METRES IN 8 SECONDS?

Many contemporary amateur athletes and swimmers *would have broken world records if they had taken part in the first Olympic Games.* Since then, records have tumbled in track, field and swimming events as performance has improved dramatically.
If records fall, it is usually due to better equipment, training and diet but recently improvements have begun to slow down. In Sydney, only three runners achieved Olympic bests with no world records. Some experts predict a ceiling for many events, such as 9.5 seconds for the 100 metres – Maurice Greene's current record is 9.79 seconds.
However, past predictions are nearly always wrong. All the levels of performance predicted in the 1930s had been reached by the 1970s. Ron Maughan, from Aberdeen University, believes that if more people around the world took part in organised sport, more records would have fallen.
One factor is the use of performance-enhancing drugs, or 'doping'. Ben Johnson would still be the 100 metres world record holder if he had not been caught taking drugs. Other records remain dubious, like Florence Griffith's 100 metres record back in 1988. Did she take drugs? If current Olympic champion, Marion Jones, took such drugs, she would probably have broken that world record more than once.
Unless we are careful, 'gene-doping' will be the next big threat.
For medical purposes, scientists have already found ways to build muscle and increase stamina through gene therapy. *If gene therapy were used now, it would be almost impossible to detect.* In the future, genetically-modified athletes might be able to run the 100 metres in 8 seconds or the marathon in under two hours. However, *if a generation of genetic monsters were created, it would show that the whole point of sport has been lost.*
It would be much better to forget the records and return to the original Olympic spirit – taking part is more important than winning.

Worldbeater Gabriela Szabo wins Olympic gold.

MIXED CONDITIONALS
Presentation

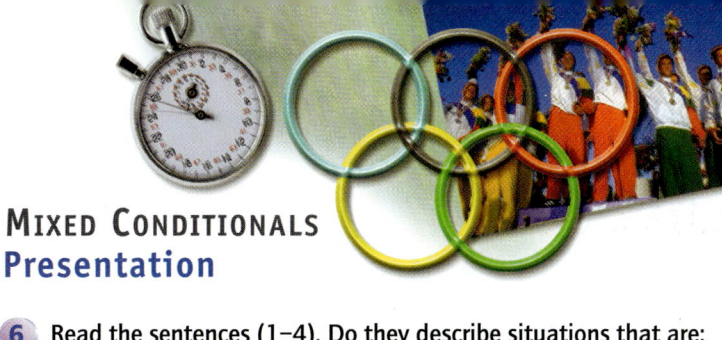

6 Read the sentences (1–4). Do they describe situations that are:

a) true or could possibly happen?
b) imaginary, unreal or contrary to facts?

1 <u>If current Olympic champion Marion Jones took such drugs</u>, she would probably have broken that world record more than once.
2 <u>If Peter was a more skilful player</u>, he would have scored more points.
3 Ben Johnson would still be the 100 metres world record holder, <u>if he had not been caught</u>.
4 <u>If he had broken that record</u>, he would be a world-famous runner now.

7 What time does each condition (<u>underlined</u>) in the sentences in Exercise 6 refer to: past or present? What tense is used? Complete the table.

Condition	Time reference	Verb form
1	the present	Past Simple
2		
3		
4		

What time does the result in the sentences in Exercise 6 refer to: past or present? What verb form is used? Complete the table.

Result	Time reference	Verb form
1	the past	would + perfect infinitive
2		
3		
4		

➪ *Grammar Summary 6, page 147.*

Practice

8 Write answers to the questions.

1 What would the situation be now:
a) if performance–enhancing drugs hadn't been developed?
b) if penicillin hadn't been discovered?
c) if the computer hadn't been invented?
d) if the Second World War had never broken out?

2 What would or would not have happened in the past:
a) if football was a less popular sport?
b) if the Americas and Europe were one continent?
c) if people didn't like travelling?
d) if the sun was closer to the Earth?

Compare your answers with your partner's.

9 Use the cues to write mixed conditional sentences.

Example
If John weren't so tall, he wouldn't have had to have the doors in his house changed.

1 John is seven foot tall ➔ he had to have the doors in his house changed
 ➔ he joined a basketball team at school
 ➔ he had problems finding a date for a school disco
2 Jessica has been a world-class gymnast since she was 11 ➔ she suffers from spine problems
 ➔ she is a famous person now
 ➔ she is able to support her family financially

10 Choose one adjective from each pair that reflects your personality.

a) lazy/hardworking
b) sociable/shy
c) well organised/disorganised

Write three conditional sentences about some events in your life that these personality traits contributed to.

Example
If I was more hardworking, I would have studied harder and passed the last chemistry test.

11 Write about three things that you did or didn't do, or that happened or didn't happen to you in the past and what the present consequences are. Use mixed conditional sentences.

Example
If I had started to play tennis when I was ten, I could be a champion now.

Tell the class.

Module 6

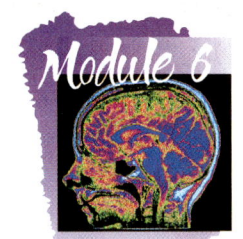

18 Brain Power

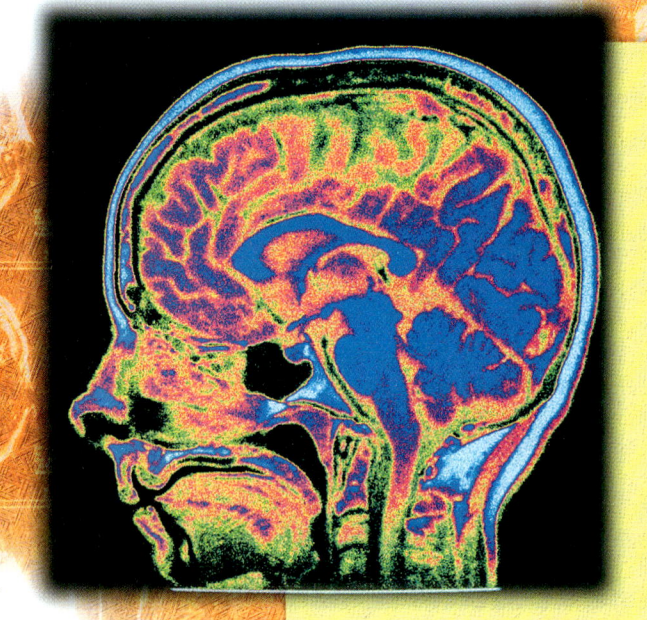

SKILLS FOCUS

Before you start

1 Match the Key Words with the definitions (1–5).

KEY WORDS

atom, billion, cell, neuron, organ

1 one thousand million
2 a part of the body that has a particular purpose, e.g. the heart, the liver
3 the smallest piece of a substance that can exist alone
4 a nerve cell
5 a unit of structure of living matter

Listening

2 Read the Strategies.

LISTENING STRATEGIES: Completing a text

- Before you listen, read the text and predict what kind of information you need, e.g. the first gap in Exercise 3 is probably a colour. Remember, you may need more than one word.
- Underline some important words in the text before each gap, e.g. *consists of*, *weighs*.
- While you are listening, listen for these important words – the information you need should follow them.
- You can complete the gaps using abbreviations at first – this saves time. Then write them in full.

3 Listen to a science lesson. Use the Strategies to complete the gaps in this summary.

The brain consists of grey and [1] _____ matter. It weighs [2] _____. It uses [3] _____ of the body's energy. It contains over [4] _____ which make up neurons. These neurons are connected by electrical impulses. There are more possible connections in one brain than there are [5] _____. Neuroscientists have mapped different areas of the brain which are responsible for [6] _____.
The areas of the brain related to controlling [7] _____ could be compared to miniature film studios. Our eyes and ears send signals [8] _____, and it is our brain that interprets these signals and builds up a picture of the outside world. Scientists have also identified areas responsible for different emotions, such as [9] _____, love and laughter. There are also different areas for different types of thinking, such as learning your own language and learning a [10] _____ language.

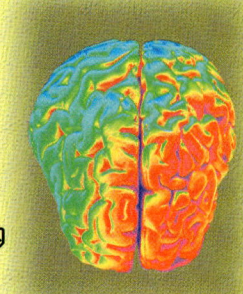

4 Listen to the lesson again and answer these questions.

1 How do you think the teacher feels about his subject?
2 What example does he use to explain the way the brain controls different parts of the body?
3 What does he compare to a film studio?

5 Listen to a student phone-in programme about revising for exams. Who said these things (1–6): Dan, Charlie or Mohammed? Write D, C or M in the boxes.

1 You need to get some exercise in the fresh air to keep your brain working well. ☐
2 Keep yourself motivated by rewarding yourself. ☐
3 Get organised with a revision timetable. ☐
4 Prioritise – study the important things first. ☐
5 Leave some time to relax. ☐
6 Don't drink lots of coffee. ☐

Which piece of advice do you think is the most useful? Why?

6 🎧 Listen again and complete the Function File with these words.

must, mustn't, ought to, should, shouldn't, advise, need to, If I were you, have got to, Could, There's no point in, it's important to, What tips, can be counter-productive, What

Giving and Asking for Advice

(1) _____ have you got for me and our listeners?
I think (2) _____ plan your revision.
I think you (3) _____ make a list of all the things you've got to study.
You (4) _____ work out what the priorities are.
(5) _____ do you think I should do?
(6) _____ , I'd make sure that I got some exercise.
You (7) _____ get out of the house and get some fresh air.
I think spending hours and hours in the library without a break (8) _____ .
You (9) _____ drink lots and lots of coffee.
(10) _____ you give me some advice?
You (11) _____ give yourself rewards.
And you (12) _____ give yourself a break.
You (13) _____ just think about the exam all the time.
(14) _____ doing that.
I'd (15) _____ people to watch a good film.

Speaking

7 Work in pairs. Read your role cards and invent more details for each situation.

STUDENT A
You find it hard to study for exams at home (*why?*). You think you are going to fail but don't want to speak to your teacher (*why not?*). You don't know what to do.

STUDENT B
Some friends have invited you on a camping holiday in the summer (*where?*). You want to go. They are very sporty types and will want to do lots of activities (*such as?*). You are not very sporty, but you want to get fit for the summer. What should you do?

STUDENT A
Your parents are going on holiday soon (*where?*) but you don't want to go with them (*why not?*). Your parents are worried about leaving you at home. What should you do?

STUDENT B
A friend is always copying your homework and ideas (*how?*), but your friend always seems to get better marks (*which subject?*)! You are sure the teacher thinks you copy from your friend and not the other way round. What should you do?

Vocabulary: Multi-part Verbs

➡ **Lexicon, pages 170–176.**

8 Match the words and expressions below with the verbs in the text (1–11).

Example 1 *postpone*

appear, discover, learn from, look at in detail (x2), make a note of, mention, pass, postpone, start, understand

Last month, I had an important English exam. I decided not to (1) **put off** studying (as I normally do!) and got up early every morning to (2) **get down to** work straight away. I'm a 'morning person' and I (3) **got a lot out of** my revision sessions. I always began by (4) **going over** a practice test I had done – checking my answers and (5) **finding out** what things I'd got wrong. I also tried to (6) **work out** why I'd made mistakes. If I didn't understand something, I'd (7) **write** it **down** and then (8) **bring** it **up** in class with my teacher. She was very helpful and she (9) **went through** all of the things that would probably (10) **come up** in the exam. In the end, the exam wasn't so bad after all and I think I (11) **got through** it. Mind you, I still haven't had my results yet!

9 Work in pairs. Discuss these questions.

1 What new information have you found out about brains?
2 Which school subject do you get most out of?
3 Do you try to work out your English mistakes yourself before you ask the teacher?
4 Do you write down vocabulary lists or just try to remember everything?
5 Do you put off studying for an exam or a test until the night before?
6 Have you ever got through an exam or a test you thought you'd failed?

QUOTE .... UNQUOTE
'The brain is a wonderful organ; it starts working the moment you get up in the morning and doesn't stop until you get into the office.'
Robert Frost, American poet (1874–1963)

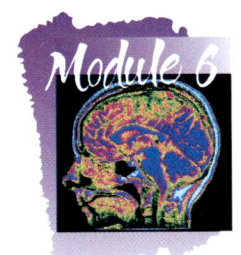

Communication Workshop

Writing: A Discursive Essay (1)

Before you start

1 Rewrite the information below using these words and expressions to join the two sentences.

although, despite, even though, however, in spite of, on the other hand, whereas

Some people find the idea of cloning a whole person repulsive. They don't mind the cloning of human organs for transplant operations.

Example
***Although** some people find the idea of cloning a whole person repulsive, they don't mind the idea of cloning human organs for transplant operations.*

2 Read the article. Match these headings with the paragraphs A–D.

- conclusion (your opinion)
- arguments against cloning
- introduction of the topic
- arguments for cloning

3 Complete the text with these linking words.

although, despite, even though, however, in spite of, on the other hand, whereas

---

Every week we invite a well-known personality to speak about an issue in the news. This week, Sophie Maclean looks at cloning and asks …

Does Mother Nature Know Best?

A **Cloning** – using genetic engineering to make exact copies of living plants and animals – has been in science fiction for years. Since 1997, with the cloning of a sheep, Dolly, it has become part of real life and the subject of public debate.

B For some people, human cloning is acceptable in medicine (1) _____ the criticism that it is unnatural. For example, human tissue can be cloned for use in organ replacement or gene therapy. Also, organs could be provided by human clones. When a child is suffering from a fatal disease and needs an organ donor, its parents could have a younger cloned brother or sister – effectively an identical twin. This would provide 100% donor compatibility (2) _____ an organ donated from another brother or sister would only stand a 25% chance of being successful. Moreover, couples who can't have children may wish to clone a child from themselves. Finally, endangered animals could be cloned to increase their numbers.

C (3) _____ , there are many arguments against cloning. (4) _____ many people saw the cloning of Dolly as a major breakthrough, it is just another step towards 'playing with nature'. Firstly, (5) _____ what they say, scientists have no idea of the long-term effects of genetic engineering. More and more genetically altered plants are being produced, and cloned farm animals are next. (6) _____ , creating 'perfect' plants and animals could eliminate the great variety of species on our planet. Furthermore, some scientists say we could transplant organs from cloned animals into humans, (7) _____ the risks to health are enormous and many people find the idea repulsive.

D All things considered, I am against cloning. It is clear that we need to regulate genetic engineering and stop experiments now, before it is too late!

Write an essay with the title: 'Should Smoking Be Banned?' Follow the stages.

Stage 1

Work in pairs to brainstorm ideas. List as many arguments as you can – both for and against banning smoking.

Example

For	Against
Government would save money on medical treatment.	Government would lose money from tax on cigarettes.

Stage 2

Work individually. Decide what your opinion is. Write notes for four paragraphs.

▷ *Writing Help 6 (layout), page 141.*

Stage 3

Use your notes to write the essay.

▷ *Writing Help 6 (useful vocabulary, linking).*

Stage 4

Check your essay.

▷ *Writing Help 6 (checking).*

Talkback

Work in pairs. Read each other's essays and assess them:
a) a good argument but I don't agree
b) totally convincing!
c) not a very convincing argument

Listening: A TV Programme

Before you start

1 Look at the picture. What kind of programme do you think it is?

a chat show, a documentary, a panel discussion, a game show

2 Listen and check your answers to Exercise 1. Then put these topics in the order they are mentioned.

- freezing dead bodies
- genetic engineering
- long life

Listen to a doctor taking part in a TV programme. Answer the questions.

3 Listen again. Complete each statement from Dr Cartwright with a few words.

1 Our knowledge of the human genome will radically change medicine _____ .
2 There's no doubt that it will help us _____ .
3 We have already identified a lot of genes that _____ .
4 We know that many common diseases, like certain kinds of _____ .
5 We can manipulate processes, but _____ .
6 We may be able to freeze certain body parts which _____ .
7 By the year 2020, over 20 percent of the population _____ .

Pronunciation

4 Listen to three sentences. Choose the correct meaning, a, b or c, according to the way each sentence is stressed.

1 The man at the back in the blue jacket.
   a) not the woman b) not the front c) not the green jacket
2 There is no doubt that it will help us to cure all sorts of illnesses.
   a) not some doubt b) not identify c) not diseases
3 By the year 2020, over 20 percent of the population will be over eighty.
   a) not the year 2010 b) not 30 percent c) not over 90

Work in pairs. Practise saying the same sentences but with a different stress to show the other meanings.

Communication Workshop

Speaking: A Discussion

Discuss issues related to health and medical advances. Follow the stages.

Stage 1
Read the Strategies.

> **SPEAKING STRATEGIES:**
> Avoiding problems
> - Try to avoid difficult subjects with vocabulary you don't know.
> - Don't pretend you know about topics when you don't!
> - If you don't have a clear opinion about something, be honest, e.g. *To be honest, I haven't really thought about that.*

Which of these subjects below would you avoid?

1. Should we genetically modify plants and animals?
2. What problems would occur if people lived to be over 100?
3. Should the government ban smoking?
4. Should women over fifty be allowed to take fertility drugs to help them have a baby?
5. What do you think about inserting computer chips in the brain to increase brain power?
6. Do you think teenagers in your country are becoming more unhealthy?

Stage 2
Write a few notes about the topics above that you can talk about.

Stage 3
Look at the expressions in the Chatroom and in the Function File on page 45 (Lesson 12). Practise saying your opinions to yourself.

Stage 4
Work in groups. Discuss some of the issues above.

Talkback
Tell the class some of the opinions of the people in your group.

Before you start

1 🔊 Listen to two people discussing genetic engineering. How would you describe Tom's and Jan's opinions on the subject:

- strongly in favour? • strongly against?
- in favour but with reservations?

Chatroom

COLLOQUIAL EXPRESSIONS

2 🔊 Listen again and match these words with the colloquial expressions.

are not at all interested, I disagree, am sure, not in any circumstances, completely unacceptable or absurd, from the beginning

1. **From the word go**
2. They **don't care two hoots** about ...
3. I **bet** you would ...
4. I **wouldn't touch it with a bargepole!**
5. It's **totally off the map!**
6. **Come off it!**

⇨ *Lexicon, page 164.*

FORMAL AND INFORMAL EXPRESSIONS

3 Match the formal expressions (1–5) from the TV programme in the Listening Workshop with the informal expressions (a–e) from Tom and Jan's discussion.

1. The first thing I'd like to say is ...
2. The important thing is to ...
3. I'd like to point out that ...
4. There's no doubt that ...
5. In my opinion ...

a) We've got to ...
b) Let's face it ...
c) For starters, I think ...
d) I reckon ...
e) Just look at ...

Language Awareness 4

1 Read the article about Lance Armstrong. What have been his two major achievements?

THE COURAGE OF A WINNER

Many people will know about Lance Armstrong's three wins in the Tour de France, but fewer people will have heard of his battle with cancer.

In the summer of 1996, everything must have been going perfectly for the twenty-five-year-old Texan cyclist. He had just won a major race and was ranked 7th in the world. He had been offered contracts by big sporting companies, such as Nike, and did not need to worry about money. His future looked bright.

Then, in September 1996, Armstrong went to the doctor with a pain. He should have gone earlier, but he had ignored the pain so that he could continue racing. When he went to the doctor that day, he could not have known what was about to happen to him. Within two hours, he had been diagnosed as having cancer which had spread to his lungs. There was a 60% chance he would survive and a 40% chance he might die.

Lance put his head on the doctor's desk in despair. However, when he looked up he said with determination: 'Let's get started. Let's kill this stuff.' In the next few months, he had to have two operations and to undergo chemotherapy treatment. He lost weight and felt so tired that he had to sleep twelve hours a day. But throughout his battle with cancer, Armstrong was determined not to let it beat him.

After months of suffering, Armstrong recovered enough to start his next battle: to win the Tour de France. During periods when he did not have to have chemotherapy, he rode his bike 30 to 50 miles a day. By the summer of 1999, he did not need to take any more medication and, according to his doctors, was 98% 'home' in his battle against cancer.

Many people doubted Armstrong's ability to become a top cyclist again but they need not have worried. In 1999 and 2000, he won the Tour de France, and then in 2001, he rode triumphantly up the Champs Elysees a third time!

Lance Armstrong is now a sporting superstar. He does not have to worry about proving himself any more. However, we must not forget that he is different from other stars. Money and success do not seem to interest him and he must have a different kind of motivation: 'Every year I come back and try to win the Tour is another year without illness.'

In his autobiography, Armstrong gives advice to young men between the ages of 20–34 who should be aware of the disease he suffered. 'I never thought I'd get cancer,' he says. 'But young, strong men must realise that this can happen to them, too.'

(Lance Armstrong has written an autobiography, 'It's Not About The Bike.')

2 How do you think Armstrong must have felt at these times:

- before he went to the doctor?
- when he received the diagnosis?
- during chemotherapy?
- when he was training for the Tour de France?
- when he won the Tour de France the first time?

Modality

➪ *Grammar Summary, page 150.*

3 Look at the sentences with *must* in the text. When does *must* express:

a) obligation?   b) speculation?   c) prohibition?

4 Look at the expressions in red. Which of them say that someone:

a) did something although it wasn't necessary
b) didn't do something because it wasn't necessary

5 Read these sentences from the text. Does *will* express:

a) future?   b) speculation?   c) obligation?

1 Many people **will know** about Lance Armstrong's three wins in the Tour de France.
2 Fewer people **will have heard** of his battle with cancer.

What time does each sentence talk about?

6 Which of the modal verbs and expressions in blue express:

a) obligation?   b) lack of obligation?
c) speculation?   d) prediction?
e) possibility/ability?

Which of them talk about:

a) present?   b) past?   c) future?
d) future in the past?

☛ Find practice exercises in the Language Powerbook, page 78.

73

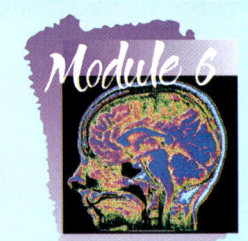

Review Modules 5 and 6

Grammar

1 Complete the conditional sentences using a suitable form of the verbs in brackets.

1. If Fleming _____ (not leave) bacteria in a dish, he wouldn't have discovered penicillin.
2. Have you seen your horoscope? I _____ (not go) out this afternoon if I were you!
3. If you _____ (not go out) in the rain, you wouldn't have caught a cold.
4. Many athletes _____ (not break) records if they hadn't used drugs.
5. Unless we control 'doping', the original spirit of the Olympics _____ (disappear).
6. If you laid out flat the grey matter of a human brain, it _____ (cover) an office desk!
7. If you have a headache, why _____ you _____ (not take) an aspirin?
8. If farmers used the new types of plants, they _____ (have) crops that can resist disease.
9. If plants were engineered in the right way, they _____ (have) the taste and consistency of meat – good news for vegetarians!
10. If we had not bred from the wolf, the astonishing range of dogs _____ (not exist).

2 Write sentences about what life would be like now if these things had not been invented or discovered. Use mixed conditional sentences.

electric lightbulbs, a vaccine for cholera, printing, penicillin, the atomic bomb, computers, guns, the wheel, cloning, cars

Example
If electric lightbulbs hadn't been invented, we would still have to use candles.

3 Complete these sentences saying what things would have happened in the past if the world was different. Use mixed conditionals.

Example
1 *If the Earth was covered by sea, humans would not have evolved.*

1. If the Earth was covered by sea, …
2. If humans had small brains, …
3. If spaceships could travel at the speed of light, …
4. If humans lived 200 years, …
5. If there were intelligent robots, …

4 Look at some of the ideas from NASA. Write predictions about them.

Example
Personally, I don't think that in fifty years' time we'll have developed a …

NIAC: the Nasa Institute for Advanced Concepts
- a lift to take us into space
- 'astrotels' – space rockets like hotels going between the Earth, the moon and Mars
- the perfect telescope to observe the universe
- plants we can program and give commands to, e.g. 'start growing', 'produce fruit'
- using plants for producing atmospheres on other planets, like Venus or Mars
- using robots to explore other planets
- using robot 'fish' to explore the oceans of Europa, Jupiter's second moon

5 Write predictions about your own life. What do you think:

- you will be doing in five years' time?
- you will be doing in ten years' time?
- you will have achieved by the time you are thirty-five?

6 Complete the second sentence so that it has a similar meaning to the first one. Use the word given and up to four more words.

1. I doubt if winning the marathon was easy for her.
   must
   Winning the marathon _____ for her.
2. We should give them a ring in case they think we've had an accident.
   will
   We should give them a ring _____ had an accident.
3. It was very kind of you to come and collect me but it wasn't necessary.
   need
   It was very kind of you, but you _____ and collected me.
4. I cut my hand but luckily stitches weren't necessary.
   need
   I cut my hand but I _____ .
5. She's probably feeling a bit depressed after getting her exam results.
   can't
   She _____ after getting her exam results.

Vocabulary

7 Complete the sentences with these words.

off, out (x3), out of, over (x2), up (x2)

1 I always put _____ tidying my room as long as possible!
2 I picked _____ a 'flu bug while I was away. It took me two weeks to get _____ it.
3 You shouldn't give _____ so easily – keep trying!
4 It took us a long time to carry _____ the research, but we got a lot _____ the project.
5 I used the Internet to find _____ about genetically modified food, but I still can't work _____ exactly how they do it.
6 Some people think computers are taking _____ our lives.

8 Complete the compound words in these sentences.

1 The nearest star to our solar _____ is over four light _____ away.
2 Are you sure that's correct? Can you double-_____ it?
3 In the museum there are life-_____ models of dinosaurs.
4 Many things are mass-_____ in factories nowadays.
5 They showed a slow _____ replay of the goal.
6 I am against genetic _____ of plants and animals.
7 She is a record-_____ athlete, but has been under suspicion of taking performance-_____ drugs.
8 After several set _____ and years of time-_____ experiments, the scientists finally made a major break _____ in the field of artificial _____ .
9 British-_____ , fifteen-_____-_____ Jon Kaspar is a software engineer.
10 Neuro _____ have first _____ knowledge of the data _____ abilities of the brain through studying its electrical impulses.

9 Complete the sentences with the words below.

'flu, malaria, measles, pneumonia, polio, tetanus, TB

1 Phil has a pain in his lungs and finds it difficult to breathe. He could have _____ or _____ .
2 Sonia has a very bad cold and a high temperature. She may develop _____ .
3 Mary has a temperature and small red spots on her skin. She might have caught _____ .
4 Stewart is in the tropics and has got a very high temperature. He could be suffering from _____ .
5 Ian contracted _____ when he was a child; it affected the nerves in his spine and now he can't move the muscles in one of his legs.
6 I cut my hand recently and now I can't move my jaw. Do you think I may have picked up _____ ?

Pronunciation

10 Listen to the sounds in these words:

1 /uː/ y**ou** 2 /ɔː/ s**or**t 3 /əʊ/ g**o**
4 /ɒ/ **o**ff 5 /ʌ/ st**u**ff

Now match the sounds with the words below.

Example *fought* = 2

fought, though, through, cough, thought, ought, enough, although, rough, tough, bought

Listen and check your answers. Then listen again and repeat the words.

11 Listen and repeat these sentences. How many different sounds for 'ou' can you identify?

1 The young couple bought a new house.
2 Although he was wounded, the tough boxer fought another round.
3 You were unconscious for about four hours.

12 Can you say this proverb? Use the phonetic chart on the inside back cover to help you.

/ɔːl wɜːk ənd nəʊ pleɪ meɪks jæk ə dʌl bɔɪ/

What do you think the proverb means?

Check Your Progress

Look back at the Module Objectives on pages 53 and 63.

- Which activities did you enjoy most?
- Which activities did you have the most problems with?
- Which grammar area do you need to practise more?

Culture Corner 3

THE USA
PART 1: HISTORY

1773	Boston Tea Party
____	Declaration of Independence
1775 – 1783	War of Independence
1812 – 1814	War with Britain
____	Californian Gold Rush
____ – ____	Civil War between the North and South
____	First trans-continental railway
1876	US Army defeated in battle by Native Americans
____	Native Americans massacred at Wounded Knee
1920 – 1933	'Prohibition' – alcohol banned
____	Wall Street Crash – collapse of stock exchange
____	Two nuclear bombs dropped on Japan
____	President Kennedy assassinated
____	Martin Luther King, Jr, assassinated
____	First person on the moon
1973	Last US troops leave Vietnam

1 Look at the timeline. Can you add any of the dates?

2 🎧 Listen to the history programme and complete the dates on the timeline.

3 🎧 Listen again and complete the gaps in each statement with *one* word.

1. The Declaration of Independence was signed by _____ British colonies.
2. The Americans had to pay _____ to the British government.
3. Abraham Lincoln was against _____ .
4. During the prohibition, people were not allowed to _____ or _____ alcohol.
5. After the Wall Street Crash, many people were _____ and _____ .
6. The USA was about to take its place on the world _____ .
7. The US government realised it was _____ to win the war in Vietnam.
8. John Kennedy was _____ when he became president.
9. Who really killed president Kennedy remains a _____ .

4 **A Quiz.** Match the people with what they said.

1 Abraham Lincoln, 2 Chief Seattle,
3 President Kennedy, 4 Martin Luther King,
5 Neil Armstrong

Answers on page 135.

a) 'Let us never negotiate out of fear. But let us never fear to negotiate.'
b) 'That's one small step for a man. One giant leap for mankind.'
c) 'The white man's God cannot love his red children or he would protect them.'
d) 'In giving freedom to the slave, we assure freedom to the free.'
e) 'Our scientific power has outrun our spiritual power. We have guided missiles and misguided men.'

7 Journeys

In this module you...

- **Read** a travel story and an advert. **Use** reading strategies for sequencing events.
- **Listen to** monologues, dialogues, a TV advert and a song. **Use** listening strategies for identifying situations.
- **Talk about** travel experiences and do a **roleplay**.
- **Write** a formal letter.
- **Learn about** verb patterns and expressions using 'ing' forms and infinitives.

Warm-up

1 Match the photos with three places from the list of the National Geographic's best 'places of a lifetime'.

CITIES
Barcelona, Hong Kong, Istanbul, London, New York, Paris, Rio de Janeiro, San Francisco, Venice

WORLD WONDERS
The Acropolis in Athens, The Giza Pyramids, The Great Wall of China, Machu Picchu, The Taj Mahal in India

WILD PLACES
Antarctica, The Amazon Rainforest, The Canadian Rockies, The Galapagos Islands, The Grand Canyon, The Sahara Desert, The Serengeti Game Park

2 Listen to four people talking about journeys they have made. Which of the places in Exercise 1 do they mention?

3 Listen again and write the number of the speaker next to what happened (a–e). There is one extra event. Which person:

a) didn't go as far as planned?
b) took too much luggage?
c) bumped into a friend?
d) had the holiday of a lifetime?
e) spent the night in an airport?

4 Choose five of the places in Exercise 1 that you would like to go to. Use the Key Words to help you write brief notes about them.

KEY WORDS: Describing Places
breathtaking views, bustling streets, cultural melting-pot, delicious food, dramatic scenery, elegant architecture, exotic animals, historic buildings, ideal for adventure sports, interesting flora and fauna, lively nightlife, romantic atmosphere, snow-capped mountains, spectacular buildings, teeming wildlife, unspoilt forests, wide open spaces, world-class art galleries

5 Think of the disadvantages of going to some of the 'places of a lifetime'. Think about crowds, dangers, climate, lack of comfort, etc.

➪ *Lexicon, page 154.*

6 Work in pairs. Talk about the advantages and disadvantages of the places you chose.

Module 7

19 On The Road

SKILLS FOCUS

TWENTY-TWO-YEAR-OLD TOBY GREEN TRAVELLED 6,000 KILOMETRES ON HORSEBACK AND FOOT, FOLLOWING THE STEPS OF THE SCIENTIST CHARLES DARWIN IN SOUTH AMERICA.

1 Starting off in Uruguay

The time came for us to leave, and Gustavo helped us to saddle up. He looked at our baggage in bafflement.
'Poor horse.'
We had far too many things. We had foolishly tried to bring enough of everything for a year: books, razors, toothpaste, clothes, maps ... However hard we squeezed and swore at the saddle bags, it couldn't all fit in. So we tied the sleeping bags and a cavernous holdall on top. Now we were really a travelling circus ...
I was riding ahead of Emily, when she called out:
'Watch out, Toby! The bags ...'
At this point the entire pack, including the saddle, slid right off Chimango's back ...
We had gone 200 metres.
'We're just going to have to throw things out,' Emily said. Gustavo said nothing. We squatted down on the track, then and there, and went through everything. Naturally, the first bag I turned out was my wash bag. Cleanliness would not be playing a major part in my journey. We also dumped books, clothes, spare sets of shoes and rucksacks ...
We rode down to the end of the drive, followed by Gustavo, Rosana and their children in the jeep. They followed us a little of the way along the dirty road beyond. Then they turned back and we rode alone into our journey.

2 Walking in Chile

Now that I was walking, the character of my days changed. People still stared, since they rarely saw a grubby gringo trudging along the coastal highway with a hole-ridden bag slung over his shoulder, but they did not stare as much as when I had passed on horseback. Sometimes, when I reached a town, people would look at me limping and feeling sorry for myself. Often, they sidled up to me and asked what on earth I was doing. I remember one man, in the small town of El Quisco:
'Where are you going, *amigo*?'
'North,' I said unhelpfully, and then added: 'On foot.'
'I can see that!' he laughed.
'How?'
'Look at yourself! No one limps like a dog unless they're walking. Why are you walking?'
'It's a long story.'
'That's OK. I've got time.'
So I told him, over a couple of beers, the story of the last year.
'and then, these bloody floods came along. I was going to go on, but it seemed like it would be difficult with things like this.'
'Just a bit! You know that Viña del Mar is still flooded out. And it's even worse further north. We were lucky here, really.'
'Yes. So I sold my horse, and now I've just got my bag and myself.'
'Aren't you afraid of dying?'
'I can't imagine myself doing anything else just now. I've been wandering for so long, it seems normal. Nothing's happened to me really.'
'Nothing!' he exclaimed, uproariously. 'You're funny. You started out with three horses and a girlfriend. Now you haven't got any horse and you haven't got a girlfriend. And you tell me that nothing's happened!'

Before you start

1 Look at the map and the photo. Which of the objects in the Key Words would you take on such a trip on horseback? What else would you take?

KEY WORDS: Baggage
holdall, pack, rucksack, saddle, saddle bag, sleeping bag, spare clothes, tent, wash bag

Reading

2 Read the first extract from a travel book. What problems did Toby have with his baggage? What did he decide not to take?

3 Journey's end in the Galapagos

I was strolling through the town on my first day there, wondering how I could reach Alcedo and see the tortoises. The only recognised tour guide had told me that it was impossible to reach Alcedo, that the only accessible volcano was Sierra Negra. But I was determined to give it a try, and as I walked through a dusty street I bumped into Juan …
'Alcedo,' he said, and laughed. 'That's a long way, *amigo*.'
'Is it possible?'
'Oh, we can walk there,' he said. 'It's just that it'll take us a while.'
'Juan,' I said, as we went. 'You've lived with a lot of tourists.'
'Yes.'
'Am I very disorganised?'
'Yes,' he said, and then after a pause: 'Disorganised, and very dirty.'
We both roared with laughter, since neither of us cared.
'I'm not sure that your family will recognise you when you return,' he said.
'I don't know. It will be very difficult to be the same person there as I am here,' I said. 'I change my character with my language; I think we all do that.'
As we walked up the steepest slope of all, which culminated in a plunge into one of the most cavernous craters I had seen, a rainbow began to form, colours spirited from the mists by the magic of the Galapagos: a perfect, complete rainbow, curving in a complete arc from the highest crater down to the lava fields.
'Look,' I said to Juan, and gestured at the dallying film of light.
'Oh yes,' said Juan. 'That's the most beautiful rainbow I've ever seen. It's very special. A sign from God. Scientists will say that it's caused by light refracting through the water, by this and that and the other – but it's a sign from God, Tobías.'
I didn't know what to think anymore.

3 Read the Strategies.

READING STRATEGIES:
Sequencing events

- Read the whole text carefully to get the general idea before reading the list of events.
- Remember that events in the text are not always mentioned in strict order. They can refer to what has happened before the time of the story.
- Read the text again and start to sequence the events. Pay attention to linking words and tenses (e.g. Past Perfect) that describe events that had happened previously.
- Finally, read through the order you have decided on and check it with the text.

4 Use the Strategies to sequence these events from the story.

a) Toby started off the journey with three horses.
b) The bags fell off the horse and they had to throw out a lot of things.
c) Toby and his girlfriend split up.
d) He met someone to take him to the volcano.
e) He and his girlfriend brought lots of things for the journey.
f) He sold his horse because of the floods.
g) He saw a beautiful rainbow.
h) He travelled to the Galapagos Islands.
i) He had to start walking along the coast.

5 Read the story again and answer these questions.

1 How can you tell that Toby was an inexperienced traveller when he set off?
2 How do you think he felt when walking on his own in Chile?
3 Why do you think he and his girlfriend split up?
4 How did the people mentioned in the extracts react to Toby?
5 What do you think Toby is like as a person?
6 Why will he be different when he gets home?
7 How do you think his attitudes to religion and science might have changed?

Vocabulary: Wordbuilding

➪ Lexicon, page 156.

6 Match the prefixes with the words to make the opposites.

Example *to disappear, uncomfortable*

prefixes	dis, il, ir, im, in, mis, un
verbs	appear, believe, do, dress, pack, qualify, understand, wrap
adjectives	comfortable, convenient, correct, crowded, efficient, friendly, helpful, honest, interesting, legal, loyal, lucky, patient, possible, reliable, responsible, sensitive, similar, spoilt, tolerant

Speaking

7 Work in pairs. Imagine you are on holiday together and talk about these things. Use prefixes to contradict your partner.

hotel, beaches, local people, countryside, tour guide, waiters, food, local buses

Example
A: *I like the hotel we are staying at. It's quite comfortable.*
B: *I disagree. I think it's really uncomfortable!*

QUOTE .... UNQUOTE
'Like all great travellers, I have seen more than I remember, and remember more than I have seen.'
Benjamin Disraeli (1804–1881) British Prime Minister

Module 7

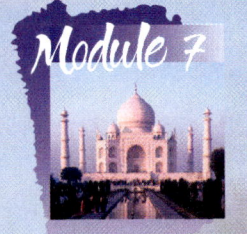

20 Migrating

GRAMMAR FOCUS

Before you start

1 Read about the animals. Why do they migrate?

2 🎧 Listen to a woman talking about travel. Which of the animals has she seen?

Monarch butterflies live in North America but can't survive being there during the hard winters. In the autumn, they fly 3,000 km south to California or Mexico where they semi-hibernate. Most survive the trip – birds avoid going near them because of their bright wings. They don't want to risk eating the butterflies as bright colours often indicate that an animal is poisonous.

Green turtles migrate all the way from the coast of Brazil to breed on the small island of Ascension, some 3,340 km out in the Atlantic! They are an endangered species and ecologists expect them to have been made extinct by hunting by the end of the century.

Salmon live most of their life in the sea but each generation has a very strong instinct to migrate. They swim hundreds of miles up rivers and streams to lay their eggs in exactly the same place where they were born.

In winter, **reindeer** migrate, looking for the warmer forests of Scandinavia and Russia. They get together in groups numbering several hundred – and they don't mind walking 500 km and back!

Blue whales eat tons of plankton in the polar seas but in the winter the sea freezes over. By migrating to temperate or tropical zones, the whales are able to survive the winter, but often without eating anything for months!

VERB PATTERNS: '-ING' FORM AND INFINITIVE

Revision

3 Look at the examples from the listening text. Try to choose the correct verb forms in *italics*.

1 I've always enjoyed *to travel/travelling*.
2 It's no use *to complain/complaining*.
3 What about *to go/going* abroad?
4 We decided *to see/seeing* the world.
5 I refuse *to stand/standing* still.
6 There's no point in *sit/sitting* around.
7 I can't stand *to do/doing* nothing!
8 I put off *to go/going* abroad all my life.
9 It's worth *to spend/spending* my savings.
10 I expect *to live/living* for a few more years.
11 I've always been interested in *to look/looking* at nature.
12 By *find/finding* holiday bargains we've managed *to travel/travelling* ...
13 It's amazing *to see/seeing* ...
14 It'd be a good idea *to do/doing* that soon.
15 We're planning *to go/going* to Mexico next year.
16 I'm looking forward to *watch/watching* ...

🎧 Listen to the woman again and check your answers.

4 Put the verbs and expressions from Exercise 3 in the correct column in the table. Add more items to each column.

Verbs and expressions followed by '-ing' form	Verbs and expressions followed by infinitive
enjoy	decide

5 What verb form always follows a preposition: an '-ing' form or infinitive?

6 Choose the correct meaning (a or b) for the verbs in bold in each sentence.

1 I **remember having** a great time.
   a) not to forget an obligation b) to recall a past situation
2 I **regretted not having** been abroad.
   a) to feel sorry about something from the past
   b) to feel sorry about something you have to do
3 I **stopped working** and retired.
   a) to give up the activity b) to interrupt an activity in order to do something else
4 Salmon **were trying to fight** their way up.
   a) to make an effort to do something
   b) to do something in order to see the results

Journeys

Practice

7 Put the verbs in brackets in an '-ing' form or infinitive.

A: How was the party?
B: Horrible, I regret (1) _____ (go) there.

A: Good morning, Mr Jackson. Have you corrected our tests?
B: Yes, I have and I regret (2) _____ (tell) you that you've all failed.

A: I can't open this jar of honey.
B: Try (3) _____ (put) it in hot water for a few minutes.

A: It looks like our video has broken down.
B: Why don't we try (4) _____ (look) at the manual?

A: Are you sure you locked the door?
B: I clearly remember (5) _____ (turn) the key in the lock.

A: Did you remember (6) _____ (buy) a present for granny?
B: Yes, I did. And I remembered (7) _____ (get) her flowers, too.

A: I could do with a drink of water or juice.
B: I'm quite thirsty myself. Let's stop (8) _____ (get) a drink.

A: Would you like some chocolate?
B: No, thanks, I stopped (9) _____ (eat) sweets ages ago.

8 Imagine you are in a big city in a foreign country. You have just lost your passport and your money. In pairs, discuss ideas for contacting home, getting money, finding somewhere to stay, finding food, getting back home. Use the expressions in the box.

Example
A: It'd be a good idea to find the police station.
B: Yes, but first it's worth …

> What about, It'd be a good idea to,
> It's worth, There's no point in,
> It's no use, We can't risk,
> I can't stand, I don't mind

Presentation

9 Which of the sentences below say that somebody saw:

a) the action in progress?
b) the completed action?

1 I saw herds of reindeer **trekking** south.
2 I saw a blue whale **come** to the surface.
3 We watched them **swimming** off the coast in Patagonia.
4 I watched it **dive** with its tail in the air.

10 Match the expressions in bold in the sentences (1–3) with their meaning (a–c).

1 We **used to** go camping a lot.
2 I'm **used to** doing things.
3 We've **got used to** being abroad.

a) a habit in the past
b) the process of becoming more accustomed to something
c) the state of being very familiar with something

Which of the expressions are followed by an infinitive and which are followed by an '-ing' form?

⇨ **Grammar Summary 7, page 147.**

Practice

11 Match the sentences with the pictures.

1 I saw him get off the train.
2 I saw him getting off the train.
3 I watched the man climbing the mountain.
4 I watched the man climb the mountain.

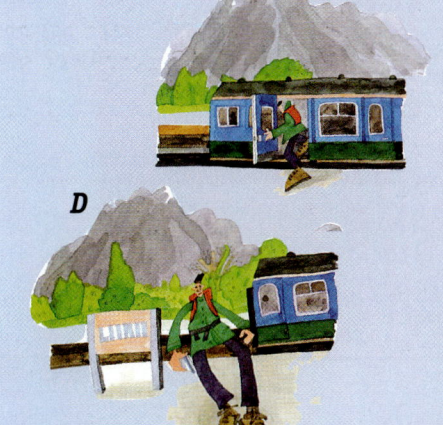

12 Complete the sentences with *be used to*, *get used to* or *used to* in the appropriate form.

1 Wild animals in the Serengeti _____ the sight of people taking photos of them.
2 Dinosaurs _____ be the most intelligent creatures on Earth.
3 When I lived in Africa, I gradually _____ sleeping under a mosquito net.
4 A hundred years ago people in Europe _____ eat less fruit and vegetables.
5 We haven't been able to _____ all that travelling yet.
6 Travellers _____ living in different climates and conditions.

21 Trans-Continental

Module 7

SKILLS FOCUS

Before you start

1 Work in pairs. Ask and answer the questions. Check you understand the words in *italics*.

1. What do you like and dislike about *travel*?
2. What is the longest *journey* you've been on?
3. What was the best *trip* you've ever been on?
4. What was the last *school outing* you went on?
5. Have you ever been on a *package tour* or on an *excursion* while on holiday?
6. Would you like to go on a *cruise*?
7. Would you like to go on a long sea *voyage*?

Listening

2 🎧 Listen and complete the sentences with one or two words. Would you like to go on the trip? Why or why not?

GREAT RAIL JOURNEYS – TRANS CANADA

1. The company offers a holiday that lasts for _____ .
2. You can sleep in a _____ compartment or a private bedroom.
3. You can have your food in your room or in the _____ .
4. The observation dome is the best place for _____ .
5. The company organises _____ trips every year.
6. Prices range from £_____ to £_____ .
7. The holiday includes the flight from _____ to Canada and _____ .
8. You also get _____ in Toronto and Vancouver.
9. For a free brochure, phone _____ .
10. The name of the company's website is _____ .

3 Read the Strategies.

LISTENING STRATEGIES:
Identifying situations and people

- Before you listen, look at the alternatives in the questions. Think about what they are going to talk about.
- What are the important words you hear? These can help you identify the situation.
- Sound effects also often help you identify the situation.
- Is the language formal or informal? This can help you decide relationships between the people.
- Listen to the intonation of the people to identify their moods.

🎧 Listen to the Canadian travel dialogues. Use the Strategies to choose the correct alternative for each dialogue. There is one extra answer.

1. Where are the people?
   a) in a tourist information office
   b) in a hotel   c) at the observation dome
   d) at the travel agent's
2. Who is talking?
   a) a tourist and a trainee   b) a receptionist and a hotel guest   c) a passenger and the Tour Manager   d) two passengers
3. What are they talking about?
   a) a tour around the city   b) a delay
   c) stopping off somewhere
   d) the city's buildings
4. How do the tourists feel?
   a) nervous   b) frustrated
   c) happy   d) tired

Journeys

4 🎧 Listen again and use these expressions to complete the Function File.

Would it be possible, Could you, I'm sorry but, I was wondering if, Do you think I could, Will you be, I'd prefer not, I'm afraid, Is it all right if, If you'd like, Could you possibly, I wonder if

Function File

Polite Requests

1 _____ to fill in this form here, please.
2 I know this is unusual, but after the long flight _____ to go on with the group.
3 _____ I just go off on my own a bit later?
4 _____ she won't be here till about ten o'clock.
5 _____ having lunch in the hotel, sir?
6 _____ give me a map of the city, please?
7 _____ you could give me information about visits to some of the buildings in Toronto, please?
8 _____ have something about the modern buildings, please?
9 _____ ask someone else, please?
10 _____ I could ask you something?
11 _____ to stay over an extra night in Winnipeg?
12 _____ we have to keep to the timetable, sir.

Are the expressions in the Function File direct and not very polite or indirect and polite?

5 🎧 **Pronunciation.** Listen and think about language and intonation. Which requests are:

a) polite and indirect?
b) too direct and possibly rude?

🎧 Now listen and repeat six polite requests.

Vocabulary: Multi-part Verbs

➡ *Lexicon, pages 170–176.*

6 Complete the requests with these verbs.

keep to, stop off, stay over, set off, get in touch with, go off, pick me up, catch up with

1 Could you _____ outside the hotel in ten minutes, please?
2 Is it all right if I just _____ on my own?
3 When can I _____ the tour guide, please?
4 Do you think we could _____ at the shops for a couple of minutes?
5 Would it be possible to _____ an extra night in Winnipeg and _____ the train later?
6 Could you possibly be here at ten, please, as we have to _____ the timetable?
7 Could you please tell me what time we _____ tomorrow?

Speaking

7 Read the Strategies.

SPEAKING STRATEGIES: Being polite

- For requests in all situations, always use 'please' and 'thank you'.
- In formal situations, use more indirect expressions (see Function File).
- Try to use polite intonation.
- When refusing a request, give a reason, e.g. *I'm sorry but ...*, *I'm afraid that ...*
- Try to look friendly and smile at the person you are talking to.

Work in pairs. Student A turns to page 134 and Student B to page 136.

Comparing Cultures

Is your language more or less direct than English? Think of examples.

QUOTE .... UNQUOTE
'Good breeding consists of concealing how much we think of ourselves and how little we think of the other person.'
Mark Twain (1835–1910)

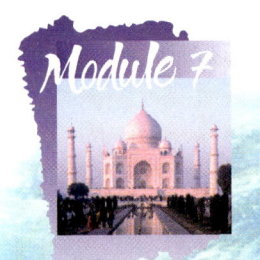

Module 7
Communication Workshop

Writing:
A Formal Letter

Before you start

ORBITAL TOURS
THE EXPERIENCE OF A LIFETIME!

FROM TODAY, reservations are being taken for the first sightseeing trip into space which we hope to offer from 2007 onwards. For around £75,000, astro-tourists can book a week's trip into a low orbit 60 miles above the Earth, staying in comfortable accommodation on our space hotel. The price includes:
- full physical training
- a made-to-measure space suit
- preparations for zero-gravity
- space walks

A team of ex-Nasa scientists and astronauts are involved in the project. The flight to the space hotel from Cape Canaveral lasts three hours. Then orbit the Earth once every three or four hours for breathtaking views of home!

1 Read the advertisement and the letter to Orbital Tours. Which of these things is the letter writer worried about?

training, space suit, weight limit for baggage, health insurance, accommodation, flights, space walks, the price

2 Find mistakes of style in the letter.

1 (line 1) 2 (line 4) 3 (line 7)
4 (line 9) 5 (line 10)
6 (line 11) 7 (line 15)
8 (line 20) 9 (line 21)
10 (line 22)

Example 1 = Hi there

3 Replace the mistakes with these formal words and expressions:

can be guaranteed, would prefer not, Dear Sir/Madam, if possible, I look forward to hearing from you, to reserve, would like, I would be grateful if you could, Yours faithfully, Could you please tell me

---

Hi there,
   I am writing to ask for more information about the 'Orbital Tours' holiday which I saw advertised in The Times. I am very interested in the holiday, but I want some details.
   Firstly, it is not clear whether your company only arranges flights from the USA. I would like to fly from Europe, if that's all right with you.
   Secondly, I would be grateful if you could tell me about what kind of accommodation is available. I would like you to save me a place, provided that the safety of the trip is OK. Does the hotel have single or double rooms? I really don't want to share a room unless there is no alternative.
   Thirdly, you say the price includes full training at your special space centre. Does this mean the actual holiday is less than one week? Just tell me what the training involves exactly.
   Finally, your advertisement also mentions NASA experts and space walks. The idea of space walks sounds very interesting, as long as I am not expected to do any work for NASA on the outside of the hotel.
   Send me more details about the dates and prices.
Write soon.
All the best,
Michael Davidson

Journeys

4 Look at the sentences below. Replace the underlined words with these words:

as long as, except if, if

It is not clear <u>whether</u> your company only arranges flights from the USA.
I would like you to reserve me a place, <u>provided that</u> the safety of the trip can be guaranteed.
I would prefer not to share a room <u>unless</u> I have to.

Now choose the correct words from the brackets.

1 I like going to the beach (as long as / unless) it isn't too crowded.
2 I won't go (provided that / unless) the room has a shower.
3 I don't know (unless / whether) I would enjoy a balloon flight.
4 The Arctic cruise sounds great (provided that / unless) it isn't too cold!
5 I don't like sightseeing (unless / whether) I have a guide.
6 The submarine holiday sounds fine, (as long as / whether) it's safe.
7 I am not sure (if / provided that) it's such a good idea.
8 I'd love to stay (unless / provided that) there are en suite bathrooms.

> Write a letter replying to a magazine advertisement by a holiday company. Follow the stages below.

Stage 1

Choose a type of holiday, e.g. Antarctic cruise, African safari, ballooning across Europe, deep-sea diving in the Indian Ocean. Decide who you are going with, e.g. friends, family, and when you want to go. Then write a list of things you want to find out.

- price – how much? what does it include? are there any extras?
- accommodation – tent? cabin? hotel? single or double room?
- food – what kind? are meals included in the price?
- baggage – any weight limit?
- clothes – what clothes are suitable?
- equipment – is it provided?
- health and accident insurance – how safe is it?
- language – do guides speak English?

⇨ *Writing Help 7 (useful vocabulary), page 142.*

Stage 2

Plan your paragraphs.

⇨ *Writing Help 7 (layout).*

Stage 3

Write your letter. Remember to write in a formal style. Try to include examples of *unless, whether, as long as* and *provided that*.

⇨ *Writing Help 7 (style, linking).*

Stage 4

Check your letter.

⇨ *Writing Help 7 (checking).*

Talkback

Work in pairs. Read your partner's letter. Then imagine you are a travel agent. Answer the questions from his/her letter.

Listening: A Song
'Daniel' by Elton John

1 Look at the lyrics. Try to guess the missing words. For the final word of each line think about words that rhyme with the previous line (e.g. *cry/my*).

Daniel is travelling (1) _____ on a plane
I can see the red tail lights heading for (2) _____
Oh and I can see Daniel waving goodbye
God it looks like Daniel, must be the clouds in my (3) _____

They say (4) _____ is pretty though I've never been
Well Daniel says it's the best place that he's ever (5) _____
Oh and he should know, he's been there enough
Lord I miss Daniel, oh I miss him so much

Daniel my brother you are (6) _____ than me
Do you still feel the (7) _____ of the scars that won't heal
Your eyes have died but you see more than I
Daniel you're a star in the face of the (8) _____

2 Now listen to the song and check your guesses. Answer these questions about the song.

1 How does the singer feel about the brother?
2 Why do you think Daniel is going away?
3 What do you think might have happened in the family?

Communication Workshop

Speaking: A Roleplay

Before you start

1 🔊 Listen to two travellers talking about their journeys. Complete the table.

	from	places visited	places going to	good experiences	bad experiences
Girl:	Ireland				
Boy:					

What request does the girl make?

Chatroom

SHOWING SYMPATHY

2 🔊 Listen to the conversation again. Which of the expressions below are used to sympathise?

1 Me too.
2 Me neither.
3 Really?
4 Sounds good fun.
5 What a drag.
6 I bet you were.
7 Oh no!
8 That's terrible!
9 What a shame!

3 Which two of these expressions introduces a request?

1 Do you think you could …?
2 Will you be staying …?
3 It'd be great if you could …
4 Can you …, please?
5 Could you do me a favour?

How are the requests above different from the requests in the Function File in Lesson 21?

ELLIPSIS

4 In spoken English, people often miss out words. What words are missing from these extracts from the dialogue?

Example 1 *Have you been here long?*

1 Been here long?
2 Yeah, been waiting ages.
3 Tried hitchhiking?
4 No, wouldn't risk it.
5 Oh, all over.
6 Anything interesting happen?
7 A real mess!
8 Sounds good fun.
9 No, never is, is it?
10 Had to sit around for five hours!
11 Missed a big rock festival that was on.

Imagine you have been travelling for a few weeks. Talk about your experiences to someone you meet. Follow the stages.

Stage 1

Look at the table in Exercise 1 and use it to make notes.

Example *good experiences – fantastic week in Uruguay, met someone special*

Stage 2

Think of questions to ask your partner and a request to make.

Example
Anything interesting happen? Can I have a look at your guidebook, please?

Stage 3

Work in pairs. You meet your partner at a station. Talk about your experiences and make a request. Show interest and sympathy in your partner's experiences.

Example
A: *Hi. Where are you from?*
B: *I'm from Slovakia. I've been travelling around Europe for a month. And you?*

Talkback

Tell the class about one of your good or bad experiences.

Women still underpaid

Villages cut off by floods

1.5 billion more people by 2020

World warms up
Deviation from 1961-1990 average temperature (°C)

Destruction of natural habitats puts some animals on the brink of extinction

8 Global Issues

In this module you...

- **Read** a magazine page, a newspaper article and a report. **Use** reading strategies for doing sentence gap activities.
- **Listen to** the news, a lecture, a radio programme and dialogues. **Use** listening strategies for taking lecture notes.
- **Talk about** important human and environmental issues in the world today.
- **Write** a report.
- **Learn more about** reported speech.

Warm-up

1 Match the Key Words with the photos, graphs and headlines.

KEY WORDS: Global Issues

deforestation, the destruction of habitats, endangered species, the exploitation of women, famine, flooding, global warming, the greenhouse effect, malnutrition, natural disasters, overpopulation, poverty

Which of these issues are 'environmental' and which are 'human'? Which are both?

2 🎧 Listen to four news stories and identify the issues.

CO₂ levels climb
Concentration in the atmosphere (ppm)

3 🎧 Listen again. What do these figures refer to?

Example
1 = temperature increase in the 20th century

| 1 | 0.6°C | 2 | 6°C | 3 | 5,000 | 4 | 11,000 |
| 5 | 6 billion | 6 | 40% | 7 | 9 billion | 8 | 12 cm |

4 Work in pairs. Talk about the global issues on this page. Which issue do you think is the most important for the 21st century?

Example
A: *I think famine is a very important issue. I think ...*

Tell the class what you agreed.

➪ *Lexicon, page 154.*

Aid workers under pressure

Module 8
22 Unnatural Disasters

SKILLS FOCUS

Hell and High Water

The last few years have been the worst period on record for environmental disasters and experts are predicting far worse to come. Tim Radford reports.

A Here is how to become a disaster statistic. Move to a shanty town on an unstable hillside near a tropical coast. Crowd together as more and more people arrive. Wait for the world to get a little warmer. More evaporation means more rain, which means the slopes will get progressively more waterlogged. One day, the land will turn to mud, and the neighbourhood will begin to go downhill. Literally. And if the slope is steep enough, the landslide will accelerate to more than 200 miles an hour. Peter Walker, of the international federation of Red Cross and Red Crescent societies, has seen it all too often. "First, your house has been washed away. Second, the land that you farmed has disappeared. (1) _____"

B In the last decade, floods, droughts, windstorms, earthquakes, avalanches, volcanic eruptions and forest fires have become increasingly common. There has been disastrous flooding in Asia, Africa, Central and South America and Oceania. (2) _____ Storms have been getting worse everywhere too, with a growing number of hurricanes hitting the US, the Caribbean and Central America. Drought has affected large areas of Sub-Saharan Africa for years and many other zones are becoming drier. (3) _____ A number of nations have already been in armed conflict over water, and drought in the West of the US has resulted in enormous forest fires.

C Volcanic eruptions and earthquakes have always been a threat in certain parts of the world. A volcanic eruption virtually wiped out the small Caribbean island of Montserrat in 1997 and there have been serious earthquakes in Greece, Turkey and El Salvador. The quake that rocked the small Central American country of El Salvador in 2001 came as the people were still rebuilding their houses and recovering from 1998's Hurricane Mitch.

Before you start

1 Which of the disasters in the Key Words do you think are:
- caused by people?
- made worse by people?
- natural?

KEY WORDS: Disasters
avalanches, cyclones, droughts, earthquakes, floods, forest fires, hurricanes, landslides, volcanic eruptions, windstorms

Reading

2 Read the article and check your answers to Exercise 1.

3 Read the Strategies.

READING STRATEGIES:
Completing texts with sentence gaps
- Read the text to get the general idea.
- Read a paragraph with a sentence gap and identify the topic, e.g. disasters.
- Read the sentences before and after the gap and look for clues about the missing sentence, e.g. is it an example of what is mentioned before?
- Certain words may help you: time references (*then*), pronoun references (*it, that*), linking words (*however*).
- Decide which sentence goes in the gap. Check that it fits the sentences before and after it.

4 Now use the Strategies to complete the gaps in the text (1–6) with these sentences (a–g). There is one extra sentence you do not need.

a) But geological evidence shows that 73,000 years ago there was a much greater eruption.
b) Even prosperous Europe has suffered and large areas of France, Britain and Germany have all been under water.
c) That is probably not the most important factor either.
d) Third, the other bits of land you might have been able to farm are now useless.
e) On top of all that, add climate change and the spectre of global warming.
f) For example, the Yellow River, once notorious for flooding the Chinese landscape, failed to reach the sea at all on 226 days in 1997.
g) One answer is overpopulation.

D So why is nature beginning to turn on us? (4) _____ The population of the world is growing at the rate of 10,000 people an hour, 240,000 every day, nearly 90 million a year, with most of the growth in the developing world. People in agricultural areas, unemployed and sometimes undernourished, move to the cities, and then set up homes on poor soil, crowded into substandard buildings. (5) _____ This has mainly been caused by the mismanagement of the world's resources: carbon emissions from rich countries; the activities of the big multinational companies; the deforestation of the world's forests. As a result, a hotter ocean breeds fiercer cyclones and hurricanes. It surrenders greater quantities of water as evaporation, and more powerful winds dump this water against mountainsides with increasing fury. Atlantic hurricanes, for instance, are 40% more intense now than they were 30 years ago.

E Volcanoes and earthquakes are even more dangerous than in the past as around half the world's population now lives in cities. There are more than 500 active and semi-active volcanoes, about fifty of which erupt each year, and more than 500 million people now live within range of a volcanic eruption. An even greater number live at risk, in some degree, from earthquakes which have taken a toll of more than 1.6 million lives in the last hundred years.

F All the betting from the disaster professionals is that things will get worse. Professor McGuire, of University College London, is a volcanologist who has been warning for years that the world has not seen the worst nature can do. The worst eruption in human history was probably Mt Tambora in 1815, in Indonesia. It pumped so much dust into the stratosphere that it effectively cancelled the following summer in Europe and America. (6) _____ "It reduced temperatures by maybe 6°C in some places and the whole planet was plunged into winter for years. And there are about two of these events every 100,000 years …"

5 Read the text again and answer these questions.

1 What is the attitude of the journalist towards the future?
2 Who is most likely to be a victim of natural disasters?
3 Why are there now more hurricanes, floods and droughts?
4 Why are volcanoes and earthquakes more dangerous now?
5 What could be the biggest threat to the planet in the future?
6 What effects might this threat have?

Vocabulary: Prefixes

➪ *Lexicon, page 156.*

6 Look at the words from the text (1–10) and the other examples in brackets. Match the prefixes with the meanings (a–j).

1 **over**population (overgrown, oversleep)
2 **sub**standard (subway, submarine)
3 **de**forestation (defuse, dehydration)
4 **down**hill (downstream, downgrade)
5 **under**nourished (underpaid, undercooked)
6 **re**build (replace, rewind)
7 **un**stable (unusual, uncommon)
8 **semi**-active (semi-circle, semi-final)
9 **multi**national (multi-purpose, multi-racial)
10 **mis**management (misunderstand, misplace)

a) again
b) badly
c) below
d) too much
e) many
f) opposite of an action
g) not enough
h) downwards
i) opposite of an adjective
j) partly / half

7 Complete the sentences with words from Exercise 6 in a suitable form.

1 After the storm they had to _____ hundreds of houses which had been damaged.
2 Many people in the developing world suffer from diseases because they are _____ .
3 Our team was knocked out in the _____ of the competition.
4 The bomb was about to go off but the experts managed to _____ it.
5 I _____ the question and failed the exam.
6 I _____ yesterday and arrived an hour late for class.
7 A lot of houses collapsed in the earthquake because of _____ construction.
8 Floods are not _____ these days; they happen more and more often.

Speaking

8 Work in pairs. Discuss these questions.

1 What natural disasters have happened in the last few months?
2 What do you think governments can do to prevent natural disasters?
3 What organisations do you know that provide aid after disasters or work for the environment?
4 What can we do as individuals to improve the environment and help victims of natural disasters?

Tell the class some of your answers.

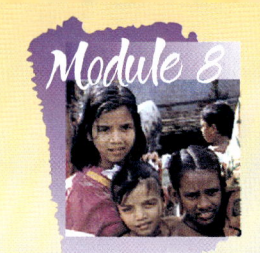

23 Global Warming

Module 8

GRAMMAR FOCUS

Before you start

1 Look at the map and answer these questions.

1 Which countries produce the most CO_2?
   a) developed countries
   b) developing countries
   c) both
2 How many tonnes of CO_2 are produced per person in your country?

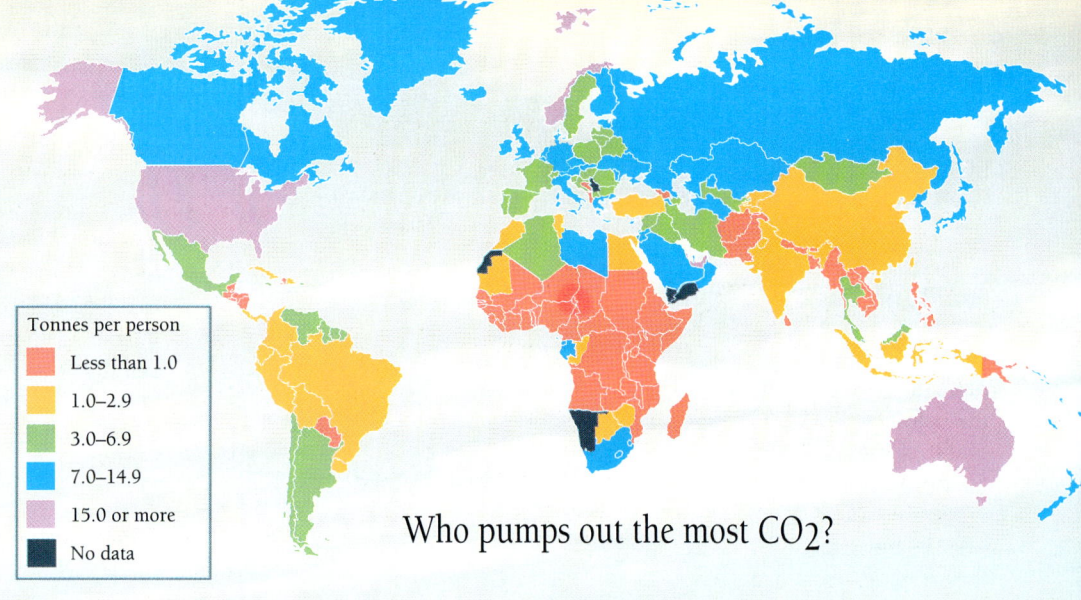

Tonnes per person
- Less than 1.0
- 1.0–2.9
- 3.0–6.9
- 7.0–14.9
- 15.0 or more
- No data

Who pumps out the most CO_2?

2 Work in pairs. Decide if these statements are true (T) or false (F).

1 The 'greenhouse effect' is caused by the release of carbon-based gases. ☐
2 Britain's coal industry is producing more and more carbon-based gases. ☐
3 The USA produces more harmful gases than any other country in the world. ☐
4 All experts agree that global warming is part of a natural weather cycle. ☐
5 Only the industrially developed countries are responsible for global warming. ☐

Now read the text and check your guesses.

REPORTING

Revision

3 What were the original sentences reported in the text?

In the text	Original sentence
1 Ministers told the world's press they had failed to reach an agreement.	'We _____ _____ _____ !'
2 The USA asked why the targets were so unrealistic.	'Why _____ _____ ?'
3 Governments promised that they would reduce emissions of carbon-based gases below 1990 levels.	'We _____ _____ _____ _____ !'

Climate conference collapses

By Bob Roberts

Ministers at the conference in The Hague today told the world's press that they had failed to reach an agreement on 'greenhouse gas' emissions, which raise the Earth's temperature. Scientists warned that this would mean more pollution and a greater risk of disasters across the globe. A United Nations representative said the conference had been organised to reach agreements on reducing emissions. It was a follow-up to the 1997 conference in Kyoto, Japan, when governments promised they would reduce emissions of carbon-based gases below 1990 levels by 2012. In Kyoto, the European Union agreed to cut emissions by 8%, Japan 6%, and the USA 7%. At the conference in The Hague, Britain declared that it was one of the few countries to have reduced its emissions, but critics asked if this was due to government policy or the decline in the coal industry. The EU reminded the USA (the world's biggest polluter producing 24% of the world's emissions) that it had not met its targets. The USA firmly denied it was making excuses and asked why the targets were so unrealistic.
Some environmentalists at the conference claimed that the world is warming faster than at any time in the last 10,000 years. However, other experts suggested that it is part of natural weather cycles. In 1995 the Intergovernmental Panel on Climate Change (IPCC) announced that there was a definite human influence on climate change. Some government ministers reluctantly admitted that they may need to cut global emissions by up to 60% in the long-term. However, many developing countries have refused to sign any pollution agreements; they say it would harm their economic growth and insist that the developed countries lead the way and show it is possible to break the link between economic growth and rising emissions.

(Adapted from *The Telegraph*)

Global Issues

Presentation

4 What verbs are used in the text to report these statements?

Example 1 = *to warn that*

1 We're afraid that this lack of agreement will mean more pollution.
2 OK, we'll cut emissions by 8%.
3 We are one of the few countries to have reduced their emissions.
4 Remember you have not met the targets.
5 We're not making excuses.
6 The world is warming faster than at any time in the last 10,000 years.
7 It's probably part of natural weather cycles.
8 There is definite human influence on climate change.
9 Well, we may need to cut global emissions by up to 60%.
10 We will not sign any pollution agreements.
11 The developed countries lead the way.

5 Read the sentences below (1–3). Why has the tense of the underlined verb not been changed? Match the sentences with the explanations (a–c).

a) because the reporting verb is in the present
b) because we report something which is still true
c) because we report something that hasn't happened yet

1 Galileo said that the Earth <u>is</u> round.
2 Futurologists believe that the world's future <u>doesn't look</u> very bright.
3 Most experts claimed that a lot of areas <u>will be flooded</u> due to global warming.

➡ **Grammar Summary 8, page 148.**

Practice

6 Which of the sentences below (1–6):

a) says that the country exports nuclear waste?
b) suggests that the country exports nuclear waste?
c) suggests that the country opposes the idea of exporting nuclear waste?
d) reports the minister's reaction to an accusation?
e) reports the minister's declarations about future actions?
f) reports a warning?

1 The minister denied that his country exported nuclear waste.
2 The minister warned that his country could export nuclear waste.
3 The minister admitted that his country exported nuclear waste.
4 The minister insisted that his country didn't export nuclear waste.
5 The minister accused his country of exporting nuclear waste.
6 The minister promised that his country would not export nuclear waste.

7 Match the sentences with appropriate reporting verbs from the list. Then write the reported sentences.

admit, boast, forbid, inquire, invite, order, suggest, threaten

1 We'll close credit lines if you don't reduce carbon dioxide emission.
2 OK, you're right, some poisonous chemicals did escape into the atmosphere.
3 Why don't you drop in tonight?
4 Stand up immediately!
5 I'm the best student in this school!
6 You can't use your dictionaries during the test.
7 Shall we have a cup of tea?
8 Is the bus service running according to the timetable today?

8 Use the following verbs to report the two dialogues.

a) admit, advise, promise, warn

Tom: I don't think you should play the game today, John.
John: You're right. I'm still a little bit ill, but I promise I won't overdo it.
Tom: Be careful, if you run around too much in this weather you may get another attack of 'flu.

b) accuse, beg, complain, deny, explain, refuse

Daughter: Mum, please, will you buy me this CD? I've always wanted it.
Mother: Sarah, you know I can't afford it. Why do you always ask me to buy you expensive things?
Daughter: That's not true. You just never buy me things that I want, only those that you like!

9 Report the following statements that you heard at 7 a.m. this morning. Do you need to change the tense?

1 "Women live longer than men."
  I heard that …
2 "I'm hungry."
  Claire said that …
3 "Our galaxy contains several thousand million stars."
  An astronomer announced that …
4 "The 2012 Olympics will be organised in Africa."
  A sports expert said that …
5 "This coffee is too hot."
  Jonathan complained that …

91

Module 8

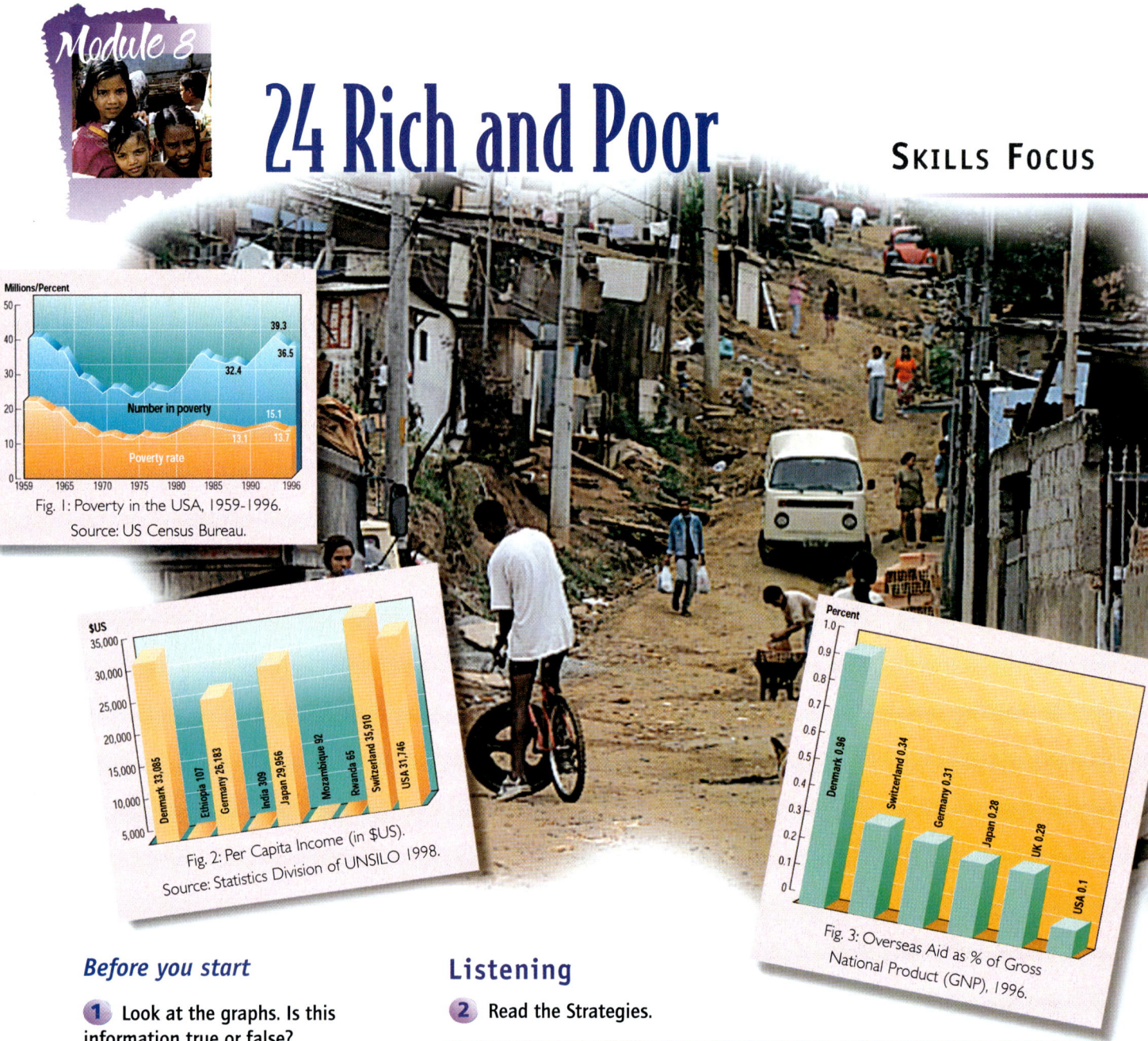

24 Rich and Poor

SKILLS FOCUS

Fig. 1: Poverty in the USA, 1959-1996.
Source: US Census Bureau.

Fig. 2: Per Capita Income (in $US).
Source: Statistics Division of UNSILO 1998.

Fig. 3: Overseas Aid as % of Gross National Product (GNP), 1996.

Before you start

1 Look at the graphs. Is this information true or false?

1. There were less poor people in the USA in the 1990s than in the 1980s.
2. The percentage of poor people in the USA was highest in the late 1950s.
3. In 1998 Denmark had the highest average income per capita (per person).
4. The country with the highest per capita income gives the highest percentage of its GNP in foreign aid.
5. Denmark gives the highest percentage of its GNP in foreign aid.

What are your opinions about the statistics in the graphs?

Listening

2 Read the Strategies.

> **LISTENING STRATEGIES:** Taking lecture notes
> - Listen for 'topic' words, e.g. *poverty, number, poor people*. These words are usually stressed and the facts are often repeated, e.g. *increasing, going up, growing*.
> - List your main points using numbers or an asterisk (*). This makes your notes easier to read when you look at them later.
> - Don't try to write down everything; select important information.
> - Use abbreviations and your own shorthand (see example below).

Listen to the lecture. Use the Strategies to write some notes.

Example
* Poverty
– increasing – 1/3 world pop.
– rich/poor gap – growing

3 Work in pairs. Use your notes and take turns to say sentences.

Example
A: *Poverty is increasing.*
B: *Yes, about one-third of the world ...*

Compare your notes. Are your partner's notes easy to follow? Tell the class the most important information that you got from the lecture.

Global Issues

Vocabulary: Multi-part Verbs

➡ *Lexicon, pages 170–176.*

4 Complete the last part of the lecture with these verbs.

come, cut, get, put, set, take

In 1996, the United Nations asked the world's richest countries to (1) _____ aside 0.7 percent of their GNP, that's their gross national product, for aid to developing countries. Only a few countries met that target and some even (2) _____ down on aid programmes! However, governments must (3) _____ up the challenge and (4) _____ up with solutions. They should (5) _____ up new, realistic aid programmes to (6) _____ rid of poverty once and for all, not just in the Third World, but everywhere.

Pronunciation

5 🎧 Listen and check your answers to Exercise 4. Mark the stress on the multi-part verbs.

Example
1 = put aside

6 🎧 Listen to the dialogue and complete the Function File with these expressions.

so that, That's why, basically, because of that,
One reason, to, That's the real reason why,
A lot of it's to do with

Function File

Justifying Arguments

Don't you think rich countries should give more aid (1) _____ help develop poorer countries?
I mean, (2) _____ , some countries will never be able to pay back the interest on the money they borrowed, will they?
And I think, (3) _____ , we should just forget what they owe us.
(4) _____ they're poor is the changing climate anyway.
(5) _____ there are a lot of these disasters, isn't it?
And poverty's often related to discrimination.
(6) _____ job opportunities.
(7) _____ in our country women and blacks are often the poorest.
The government should create more jobs
(8) _____ poor people have more of a chance.

Speaking

7 Read the factfile about an imaginary country.

Population: 10 million
GNP per capita: $100
Unemployment: 30%
Agriculture: poor soil – some production of bananas
Industry: very little – a chemical factory in the capital
Communications: most roads muddy – problems in the wet season; airport in need of repair; very few telephones
Education: only 40% literacy rate; very few secondary schools
Health: only 2 hospitals (100 hospital beds); poor sanitation – malaria is common
Housing: many houses badly damaged in recent floods
Natural disasters: bad floods in central river valley; danger of earthquakes
Environment: several endangered species (including a rare kind of bear); main river and lake polluted by the chemical factory

Imagine you are planning an aid programme. Decide on your priorities and think of solutions to the problems. Use these Key Words for ideas.

KEY WORDS:

education programme (building schools and training teachers), health programme (building hospitals, training doctors and nurses, vaccinating children), housing programme, modernised farming, recycling of materials, road building programme, renewable energy (solar and hydro-electric power)

8 Work in groups. Discuss the problems and your solutions using expressions from the Function File and multi-part verbs from Exercise 4. Try to agree on the two most important things.

Example
A: *I think we should set up an education programme. The main reason is that we should be thinking about the long-term future.*
B: *That's a good idea. The country needs ...*

Tell the class what your group decided.

QUOTE .... UNQUOTE
'You cannot feed the hungry on statistics.'
David Lloyd George (1863-1945), British politician

93

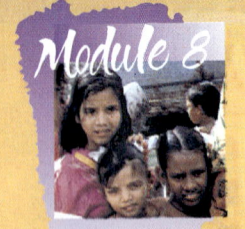

Communication Workshop

Listening: A Radio Interview

Before you start

1 Look at the photos. What do you think are the most serious problems for women around the world?

Listen to a radio programme about the status of women in the world. Answer the questions.

2 Read these statements. Use the Strategies in Lesson 15 to predict the kind of information that is missing. Then listen and complete the notes with one or two words.

1 There are 1.3 billion people living in poverty and nearly _____ of these are women.
2 More than _____ of the world's women do unpaid work.
3 In developed countries, women do _____ as much unpaid work as men.
4 On average, women earn only _____ of the pay of men.
5 Unemployment among women is _____ than that of men.
6 A lot of women have much less job _____ than men.
7 Nearly _____ of the world's children who don't go to school are female.
8 Two thirds of the world's _____ illiterate adults are women.
9 Only _____ of the world's politicians are women.
10 _____ towards women happens on a big scale.

3 Listen to the second part of the radio programme. Use the Strategies in Lesson 24 and take your own notes on the following:

- improvements in the situation for women
- what still needs to be done

Work in pairs and compare your notes. Did you miss any important information?

Subject: Business Opportunities for Women in the UK and the USA.
Date: 23.03.02

A This report aims to assess the opportunities for women in top jobs in the world of business. It will examine statistics from the UK and the USA.

B In many ways, the present situation is not very positive for women in the workplace.
a) The number of women directors with companies in the UK has fallen since 1999, and fewer than 3% of directors in public companies are female.
(1) _____ , if you are a woman and want to get on, it helps to have a title.
(2) _____ a recent survey, about one-third of female directors are women with titles such as lady, professor or doctor.
b) Many women feel let down by the world of big business. They believe their work is not regarded as valuable as the work of male colleagues.
(3) _____ , they perceive they need to work harder than men in the same job to get a top position in a company. (4) _____ , women with young children often feel unsupported by company policies.

Writing: A Report

Before you start

1 Read the report quickly and match sections A–D with these headings.

positive comments, conclusion and recommendations, negative facts, aim of the report

2 Complete the report with these linking words and expressions.

according to, also, although, as a result, for example, furthermore, however, in addition, moreover, on the other hand, in this way, to sum up

Global Issues

Write a report. Follow the stages.

Stage 1

Choose one of these subjects for your report.

- the status of women in the world
- the environment (in your country or the world)
- global warming and natural disasters
- animals in danger of extinction
- rich and poor in the world
- refugees and immigration

Stage 2

Find out statistics and information about the topic of your report. Useful sources might be:

- lessons in this module
- notes you have made from this module
- a library
- the Internet (e.g. www.newscientist.com, www.britannica.com, www.discovery.com, www.un.org, www.greenpeace.org)
- encyclopaedias (books or CDs)
- magazine articles (e.g. *National Geographic*, *New Scientist*)
- television and radio documentaries
- friends and relatives (they may have relevant books or magazines)

Stage 3

Plan your report. Decide if the statistics should be included in the positive or negative facts. Think of one or two recommendations for the conclusion.

➪ *Writing Help 8 (layout), page 143.*

Stage 4

Write your report. Try to avoid repeating words and expressions.

➪ *Writing Help 8 (useful vocabulary, linking).*

Stage 5

Check your report.

➪ *Writing Help 8 (checking).*

Talkback

Work in groups. Read each report and the recommendations. Talk about them and say if you agree or disagree.

(Adapted from an article in *The Times*)

For example, a lot of companies are inflexible and make no allowance for the responsibilities of mothers (or fathers).
c) The Internet, with a few notable exceptions, is still a male-dominated world. (5) _____ , only 8% of computer engineers are women. The statistics are more encouraging for computer analysts and programmers, where 20% are female. (6) _____ , another estimate puts women working in information technology at 24% – much lower than the figures in 1994.

C (7) _____ , the future is not all gloomy.
a) More women are beginning to use e-mail and new technology to develop their own businesses from home. (8) _____ they can avoid the discrimination of a traditional workplace and the big companies' lack of flexibility. (9) _____ , they can balance work and family responsibilities.
b) In the USA, 70% of new jobs are being set up in the small business sector where women predominate.

D (10) _____ , there are some positive developments, (11) _____ the world of business is still dominated by men. Governments should encourage more girls in the education system to follow courses in business or computer studies. (12) _____ , companies need to be more flexible with working timetables for women with family responsibilities.

3 You can avoid repetition in a report by using synonyms. Find words and expressions which are similar to these.

women directors, the world of business, men, company, feel, figures

4 Rewrite this paragraph. Do not repeat the words *job* or *company* (underlined). Instead use:

firm, profession, business, post, work, corporation, multinational, employment, occupation

When people ask me about my job I say that I have two; my job is a lawyer but I am also a poet. I love my job as a lawyer but I write poetry in my spare time. My first job was for a big company with offices all over the world. However, I don't like big companies, they are too impersonal. So I left and started my own small company. It is not a very big company but it provides jobs for ten people and the company is not doing badly.

95

Communication Workshop

Speaking:
Discussing
Photos

Before you start

1 🎧 Listen to two people discussing an article from the newspaper. Who has these opinions – the man (M), the woman (W) or both (B)?

1 Feels sorry for tigers.
2 Finds the article very depressing.
3 Is very worried about climate change.
4 Is not sure about climate change.
5 Thinks we should change our lifestyles.
6 Thinks we produce too much pollution.

Chatroom

GIVING OPINIONS

2 Which of the expressions from the dialogue (in bold) are used to:

a) give you time to think? b) express an opinion?

1 **What I don't understand is** why people want to kill them.
2 **What's really worrying is** all this stuff about climate change.
3 **I'm not sure. I haven't thought about it much.**
4 **What's ridiculous is** that they say the climate isn't changing …
5 **That's a good question.**
6 **What we should do is** start using renewable sources of energy.

IMPERSONAL 'YOU'

3 Look at the use of 'you' in the conversation. Which of the examples (1–5):

a) refer to a particular person?
b) refer to people in general?

1 Have **you** seen this article on the environment?
2 It depresses **you** just to think about it, doesn't it?
3 Don't **you** think so?
4 The problem is, **you** don't want to just give up your car and central heating, do **you**?
5 **You** don't want to go back to the Stone Age.

Discuss the photos. Follow the stages.

Stage 1

Look at the photos and think about:
• the global issue each photo represents
• the causes of the problem
• your opinions and possible solutions

Stage 2

Look at the expressions in the Function File in Lesson 24 and the Chatroom. Practise giving your opinions about the issues in the photos.

Stage 3

Read the Strategies.

> **SPEAKING STRATEGIES:**
> Using photos in discussions
> • Do not just describe the photo in detail. Avoid saying things like: *I can see …* or *On the left there is …*
> • Speculate about what is in the photo – what is happening, what has happened, what is going to happen.
> • You can describe the photo indirectly as you speculate and give your opinions, e.g. *The man is probably driving to or from his work. The nervous expression on his face shows he is stressed.*
> • Don't forget to involve your partner(s). Use expressions like *Don't you agree?* or *What do you think?*

Work in pairs. Discuss the photos.

Talkback

Tell the class what your group agreed.

Language Awareness 5

1 Read the article and match the headings (1–4) with the paragraphs (a–c). There is one extra title.

1 Indifferent Lover 2 Mid-Life Crisis 3 Fame!
4 Falling Numbers

Lonesome Male of the Galapagos

Jo Tuckman on the Galapagos Islands

A   Celebrity is not usually a characteristic associated with middle-aged giant tortoises from the Galapagos Islands. However, few have been so influenced by humanity as Lonesome George. Fame came to George in 1971 when he was discovered on the tiny uninhabited island of Pinta. He is known to be the last surviving member of his sub-species but it is hoped that George will pass on his genes to a new generation.

B   The numbers of Galapagos tortoises are said to have begun their decline when it was realised that they could supply excellent fresh meat for passing ships, because they were known to be able to survive for six months without food and water. Nevertheless, it was the effect of the goats introduced to the Galapagos by the early settlers that are understood to have destroyed the ecological balance on the islands and the livelihood of George's clan. Recently, there was another threat when the tanker Jessica ran aground near the islands. It is believed to have leaked almost a million litres of oil into the sea. At first, it was feared that the islands' many unique species would be damaged, but the archipelago is expected to make a full recovery.

C   By the time George was discovered, breeding programmes were known to be increasing the numbers of other tortoise sub-species, but it was acknowledged that his case was different. Unless a mate could be found, his group faced extinction. George was taken to the Charles Darwin Research Centre on Santa Cruz island and provided with a harem from related sub-species, but was said to have been uninterested. Thirty years later the last *Geochelone elephantopus abingdoni* is as lonesome as ever.

2 Are you optimistic about the future of the Galapagos Tortoises? Give your reasons.

Impersonal Report Structures

➪ *Grammar Summary, page 150.*

3 Look at the sentences in blue in the text. Do they express:
a) a general opinion/experience?
b) the opinion/experience of a particular person?

4 Read these two sentences. Which of them talks about:
a) a present belief? b) a belief held in the past?

1 **It is hoped** that George will pass on his genes to a new generation.
2 **It was realised** that they could supply excellent fresh meat for passing ships.

5 Find the sentences in the text which express the same as:

1 Scientists know that he is the last surviving member of his sub-species.
2 Everybody understands that the goats introduced by the early settlers destroyed the ecological balance on the islands and the livelihood of George's clan.
3 People expect that the archipelago will make a full recovery.

Now answer these questions about the three sentences above.

1 What is the form of the verbs *expect, know* and *understand*?
2 Are the opinions held in the present or past?
3 Which sentences express an opinion about:
 a) the past   b) the present   c) the future?
4 What is the form of the verbs in red in the text? How does the form depend on the time the verb refers to?

6 Which of these sentences below expresses:

a) a past belief about an earlier situation or event?
b) a past belief about a situation or event that was parallel in time?

1 The tortoises were **known to be able** to survive for six months without food and water.
2 George **was said to have been** uninterested.

7 Find sentences in the text similar to the ones in exercises 5 and 6. Rewrite them, beginning with '*It is/was said/believed that*'.

Example   The archipelago is expected to make a full recovery.
It is expected that the archipelago will make a full recovery.

8 Look at the two sentences from the text. Does *it* refer to something specific in the text? If so, what?

1 **It** is believed to have leaked almost a million litres of oil into the sea.
2 **It** was feared that the islands' many unique species would be damaged.

☛ Find practice exercises in the Language Powerbook, page 104.

Review Modules 7 and 8

Grammar

1 Complete the texts with the correct form of the verbs in brackets: '-ing' form or infinitive.

Our readers tell us about their ...

Dream Destinations

"I went to the States last year with a friend. We're used to (1) _____ (travel) around on our own without (2) _____ (spend) too much money, so we didn't mind (3) _____ (take) buses everywhere. We avoided (4) _____ (hitchhike) because we didn't want to risk (5) _____ (be mugged) – but we saw someone (6) _____ (be mugged) outside a bus station! Apart from that, it was a great holiday. The Grand Canyon was the most breathtaking sight I've ever seen."

"I'd always wanted (7) _____ (go) to Italy and visit Rome, the Vatican, Florence, and see all the magnificent art there – and I wasn't disappointed! It's worth (8) _____ (learn) (9) _____ (speak) a bit of Italian before you go. I managed (10) _____ (see) quite a lot, but there was so much to see, and so many tourists! I can't stand (11) _____ (queue) and some places were impossible – you must have seen the crowds (12) _____ (be pushed) through places like cattle. But, as I say, it was my dream destination and it was marvellous. I'd planned (13) _____ (go) to Venice, too, but didn't have time in the end."

"My brother emigrated to Australia twenty years ago. We'd always kept in touch and I'd seen his wife and kids (14) _____ (sit) in their garden on video, but I'd promised (15) _____ (visit) them, and so I did, last Christmas. Before that I'd always refused (16) _____ (fly), but there's no point in (17) _____ (worry) too much at my age, is there? And it was the best Christmas I've ever had!"

"Every Muslim who is healthy and has enough money is expected (18) _____ (visit) Mecca once in his or her lifetime. I'd put off (19) _____ (go) for years – I just couldn't afford (20) _____ (go). But then, last year, I decided (21) _____ (make) a real effort and go. It was amazing. I had seen the crowds (22) _____ (walk) round on TV before, but the place was really bustling. I really enjoyed (23) _____ (meet) people from so many different countries."

2 Report this conversation between two travellers, using *ask*, *exclaim*, *guess*, *reply* and *say*.

Example
Elsa asked Banu where she was from. She replied that ...

Elsa: So, where do you come from?
Banu: I'm from a small town on the Aegean coast, in Turkey, called Bodrum.
Elsa: Really? What a coincidence! I spent a few days there last summer.
Banu: Did you have a good time?
Elsa: Well, I was having a great time until I was bitten by a scorpion.
Banu: How terrible!
Elsa: And while I was in hospital, my boyfriend met an American girl from Nevada. They're getting married next month.
Banu: Oh, no!
Elsa: But then I met this fantastic Turkish boy called Kemal. Would you like to see a photo of him? He's very handsome.
Banu: I don't believe it! That's my brother. You must be Elsa!
Elsa: Yes! We've got a lot to talk about! Come on, let's go to the dining car.

3 Rewrite what the government minister said at a meeting, using the verbs in brackets.

1 (claim): 'Unemployment is going down at a steady rate.'
2 (insist): 'The problem started with the previous government.'
3 (announce): 'We will create 100,000 more jobs by next year.'
4 (admit): 'There were more than 1,000 new cases of Aids last year.'
5 (warn): 'The number is likely to rise by 20 percent in the next two years.'
6 (promise): 'We will end poverty.'
7 (deny): 'The government has done something about it.'
8 (remind the public): 'We have spent over £500 million on new houses.'
9 (agree): 'Yes, I'll answer questions at the end of the meeting.'
10 (refuse): 'I'm sorry, I won't answer questions about my personal life.'

Bodrum, Turkey

Global Issues

6 Make the opposite of these words.

Example visible / invisible

Adjectives: believable, correct, crowded, efficient, happy, interesting, legal, patient, popular, similar, spoilt, successful, tidy, tolerant, usual, visible
Verbs: agree, appear, believe, dress, pack, trust, wrap

Now write six sentences using the opposites you have made.

4 Complete the second sentence so that it has a similar meaning to the first sentence. Use the word given and up to four more words.

1 Climate change is now an accepted fact.
  known
  It _____ the climate is changing.
2 They are optimistic about the patient's chances of recovery.
  expected
  The patient _____ .
3 They say that the burglars got in by using a helicopter.
  said
  The burglars _____ used a helicopter.
4 There are probably no survivors from the shipwreck.
  feared
  It _____ from the shipwreck.
5 According to experts, Neanderthal Man could speak in a limited way.
  believed
  Neanderthal Man _____ able to speak in a limited way.
6 Doctors now recognise that malaria is transmitted by the Anopheles mosquito.
  acknowledged
  It _____ is transmitted by the Anopheles mosquito.

7 Complete the sentences with a suitable word.

1 He picked me _____ at about six and dropped me _____ at the station.
2 We set _____ early and stopped _____ at a couple of places on the way.
3 The price of petrol has gone _____ a lot, so I have to cut _____ on my use of the car.
4 He has to pay _____ a big loan from the bank so he puts _____ some money every week.
5 She came _____ _____ a great idea for the fancy dress party.
6 Why doesn't the government take _____ the challenge of homelessness?

Pronunciation

8 🔊 Mark the main stress in these words. Then listen and check your answers.

1 exploit / exploitation
2 communicate / communication
3 relax / relaxation
4 celebrate / celebration
5 discriminate / discrimination
6 industry / industrial
7 environment / environmental
8 politics / political
9 geography / geographical
10 history / historical

9 Can you say this proverb? Use the phonetic chart on the inside back cover to help you. What does it mean?

/ə ˈhʌŋgri mæn ɪz ən ˈæŋgri mæn/

Vocabulary

5 Complete each sentence with a word beginning with the prefix.

1 A lot of people in the Third World are *under*_____ .
2 Many countries like China and India are *over*_____ .
3 She has been *un*_____ since the factory closed last year.
4 That company has had to close because of *mis*_____ .
5 A lot of the housing there is *sub*_____ .
6 After the earthquake they had to start *re*_____ the city.
7 The forests have been cut down by big logging *multi*_____ .
8 The audience stood around the live statue in a *semi*-_____ .

Check Your Progress

Look back at the Module Objectives on pages 77 and 87.
• Which activities did you enjoy most?
• Which activities did you have the most problems with?
• Which grammar area do you need to practise more?

Culture Corner 4

THE USA
PART 2: THE HISTORY OF POPULAR MUSIC

1 Try to match the photos (a–f) with these captions.

1. One of the greatest jazz singers
2. *Rhapsody in Blue* (1924) fused jazz and classical
3. His *West Side Story* is one of Hollywood's best musicals
4. The king of rock and roll
5. From folk revival to folk-rock
6. A great jazz trumpet player

2 🎧 Listen to the radio programme and check your answers to Exercise 1. Which of the musical extracts did you like most?

blues, rock and roll, jazz trumpet

3 🎧 Listen again. Are these statements true or false according to the programme or is there no information? Write T, F or NI.

☐ 1 Some people became rich from songwriting.
☐ 2 Blues and country and western songs had nothing in common.
☐ 3 Jazz was highly developed by the 1920s.
☐ 4 Musicals often began on the stage before being adapted for the cinema.
☐ 5 Shakespeare was Leonard Bernstein's favourite writer.
☐ 6 Rock and roll had its roots in southern white music.
☐ 7 Elvis Presley was from the south of the USA.
☐ 8 Bob Dylan changed the face of popular songwriting.
☐ 9 The Beatles owed nothing to American popular music.

4 **A Music Quiz**. Can you say which of the following performers are American? What nationalities are the others?

1. Madonna
2. Eric Clapton
3. Robbie Williams
4. Britney Spears
5. Ricky Martin
6. Enrique Iglesias
7. Cher
8. George Michael
9. Laura Pausini
10. Jon Bon Jovi

Check your answers on page 135.

9 Society

In this module you...

- **Discuss** social issues, **talk about** society in the past and **make** suggestions.
- **Listen to** a radio news report, a story, dialogues and a song.
  Use listening strategies for dealing with cultural references.
- **Read** magazine articles and letters to a newspaper.
  Use reading strategies for summarising.
- **Write** a discursive essay.
- **Learn about** complex sentences used for persuasion.

Warm-up

1 What are the biggest problems in your country or area? Put them in order of importance.

KEY WORDS: SOCIAL PROBLEMS

begging, discrimination, domestic violence, drugs, homelessness, inequality, poverty, racism, unemployment, vandalism, violent crime

Tell the class your opinions.

2 Listen to a radio news report about changes in British society. Match the topics with the graphs below.

a) percent of households with cars
b) percent of households with computers
c) percent of women in work
d) percent of 16–18 year olds in full-time education

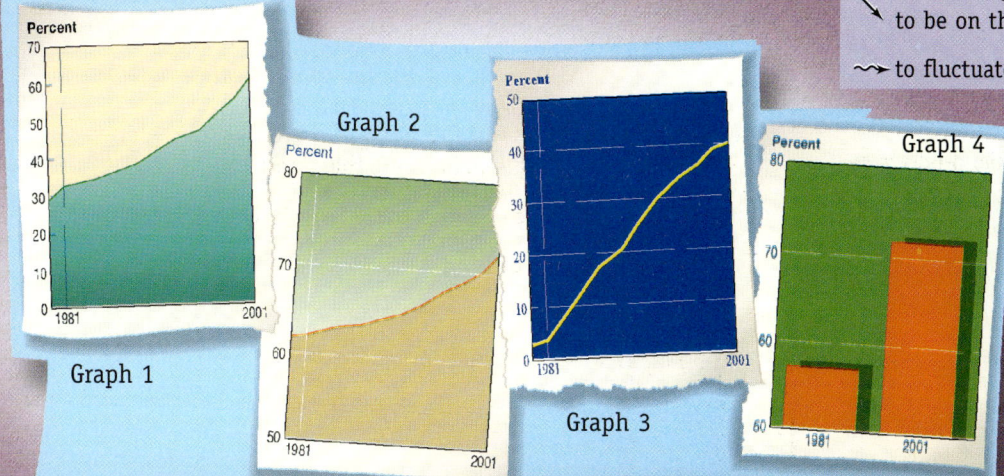

3 Listen again and complete the table.

	1981	2001
average income of British family per week	£326	
life expectancy for men and women		
unemployment	1.7 million	
numbers in full-time further education		
number of crimes (England and Wales)		

4 Work in pairs. Use the Key Words to say true or false sentences about trends in British society.

Example
A: *The number of crimes has gone down over the last twenty years.*
B: *False. It has gone up by ...*

KEY WORDS: DESCRIBING TRENDS

↗ to rise, to climb, to go up, to rocket, to double/triple, to be on the increase

↘ to fall, to go down, to decline, to be on the decrease

∼ to fluctuate, to go up and down

➪ *Lexicon, page 155.*

Graph 1
Graph 2
Graph 3
Graph 4

Module 9

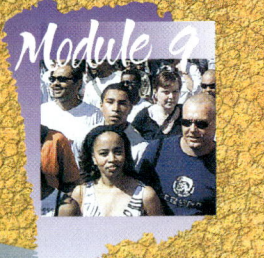

25 Golden Ages

SKILLS FOCUS

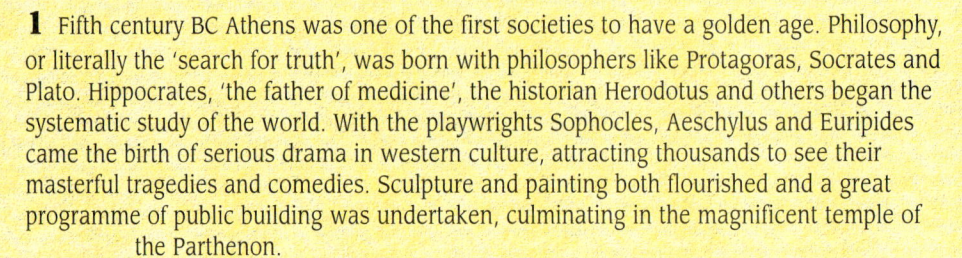

1 Fifth century BC Athens was one of the first societies to have a golden age. Philosophy, or literally the 'search for truth', was born with philosophers like Protagoras, Socrates and Plato. Hippocrates, 'the father of medicine', the historian Herodotus and others began the systematic study of the world. With the playwrights Sophocles, Aeschylus and Euripides came the birth of serious drama in western culture, attracting thousands to see their masterful tragedies and comedies. Sculpture and painting both flourished and a great programme of public building was undertaken, culminating in the magnificent temple of the Parthenon.

Why did this all happen in Athens and not somewhere else? To start with, Athens could afford it. The city state of Athens was the greatest trading centre in the Mediterranean with an empire which provided plentiful food and other goods. Rich Athenian citizens had plenty of time for leisure and culture as most of the work in the city was done by slaves and much of the business and trade conducted by 'metics' or foreigners. Many of these foreigners, such as Herodotus, were drawn to the cultural magnet of Athens and played a vital role in the cultural life of the city.

Socially, Athens was in a period of transition between a conservative, aristocratic society and an urban, commercial society in which citizens were equal by law. Athens became the first direct democracy in history where major political decisions were taken by large numbers of citizens. At the same time, Athenian society was moving away from the old beliefs in the gods and ancient myths towards values based on rationality and a belief in human nature.

Before you start

1 Match the cities with their golden ages – their periods of greatest cultural or technological achievement.

a) Los Angeles   1   1760–1830 (the industrial revolution)
b) Rome   2   1950–2000 (the information revolution)
c) San Francisco   3   1870–1910 (a revolution in painting)
d) Manchester   4   1910–1950 (the golden age of Hollywood)
e) Paris   5   50 BC–150 AD (the imperial capital)

Check your answers on page 135.

Reading

2 Read the Strategies.

> **READING STRATEGIES: Summarising**
> - Read the text to get the general idea and identify paragraph topics.
> - Underline the key sentence in each paragraph (often at the beginning). Then find information that backs it up.
> - Write notes of the main points and the key information. Use your own words.

Work in groups of three. Each student reads one of the texts (1–3) and uses the Strategies to summarise the main information.

Speaking

3 Work in your group. Use your notes from Exercise 2 to tell each other about your city. Use your own words.

Example
The greatest time for art and culture in Athens was …

Writing

4 Work in your group. Use the information you have collected to write a paragraph (about 75 words) about the reasons for the three golden ages. Begin like this:

So what was the key to the creative outbursts in these three cities? First of all, …

Compare your paragraph to the one on page 135.

5 Individually, read about the other two cities. Which of the cities in the article would you like to have visited? Why?

Example
I'd like to have gone to Athens because …

2 In the 15th century, the Italian city state of Florence was to undergo a frenzy of creativity as the cradle of the Renaissance. Outstanding painters and sculptors like Botticelli, Donatello and later Michelangelo and Leonardo da Vinci rediscovered classical traditions. They aimed, like the Greeks before them, to create an ideal form of beauty based on nature. Brunelleschi's breathtaking cathedral dome is just one example of the architectural splendour of Florence during this period.
Why did this happen in Florence and not in other Italian cities like Milan, Genoa or Venice? One reason was that Florence was able to build on the cultural achievements of the previous century. The fourteenth century had not only produced great writers such as Petrarch and Dante but also gifted painters like Giotto. Another reason was that Florence was simply the richest city; its central position made it a major trading and industrial city. Florence was also the scene of a commercial revolution which saw the development of modern banking and accounting.
As a result, Florentine society was in a state of flux between the old, stable medieval world and a new dynamic commercial world. There was greater social mobility than before with many opportunities for individuals to go up (and down) socially. The new merchants and bankers had money to spend and they were not afraid of showing off their new wealth by building magnificent palaces and filling them with superb works of art. Finally, there was an open and tolerant climate for artists to work in, helped by an increase in the number of schools and an improved literacy rate.

3 In the late 16th and early 17th centuries, there was a sudden creative flowering of all forms of literature in London. There were poets such as Donne and Spenser but the main explosion of creativity was centred around the theatre. The building of London's first theatre in 1576 changed drama from an amateur recreation into a professional art. Within a few years, a dozen theatres employed increasing numbers of professional actors and attracted large but not always well-behaved audiences. There was an insatiable demand for new plays and well over 800 plays were written and performed in London between 1570 and 1620. Brilliant playwrights emerged, like Marlowe, Jonson, Webster and of course Shakespeare.
What caused this burst of literary activity to take place? At this time, London was undergoing dramatic changes. It was growing rapidly, attracting thousands from the countryside, such as the young William Shakespeare from Stratford. The city was also undergoing an economic revolution as a centre of commerce with ships from London going all over the world. London was the home of the English court and the aristocracy, but traditional society was being revolutionised by the new money from trade. London was a place where fortunes could be made or lost. A new class was emerging, ready to spend to show their new status and looking for ways of enjoying themselves. Theatres like the Globe grew up outside the city to satisfy the demand for entertainment for both rich and poor. The London theatre was big business with companies of actors and playwrights like Shakespeare or Jonson who were celebrities in their time.

Vocabulary: Rich Language

6 Match the words and expressions from the text (in the box) with the expressions (a–d).

a) a great time for art and culture
b) changing a lot
c) really good
d) it was the start of …

Example a = an explosion of creativity

an explosion of creativity, outstanding, in a period of transition, a golden age, undergoing dramatic changes, masterful, the birth of …, living through major changes, breathtaking, a frenzy of creativity, a creative flowering, … was born, in a state of flux, a burst of literary activity, being revolutionised, magnificent, was the cradle of…, sculpture and painting flourished, was emerging, bursting with new ideas

In which of these types of text would you expect to see 'rich' language?

popular newspapers, quality newspapers, history books, novels, books about art

7 Complete the paragraph with words from the texts.

In the late 19th century, Paris went through a (1) _____ age. Great programmes of public building were (2) _____ and many artists were (3) _____ to the cultural magnet of the city from all over Europe. The Impressionist painters were inspired by (4) _____ innovations such as photography and their works satisfied the (5) _____ demand for art of the wealthy middle classes. The city was (6) _____ economic changes and there was greater (7) _____ mobility than before. Fortunes were (8) _____ in industry and trade and one way of (9) _____ wealth was through buying paintings. In this way, the Paris art market (10) _____ an important role in the (11) _____ of creativity that (12) _____ in this period.

Comparing Cultures

What 'golden ages' have there been in the history of your country? Use expressions from the texts to write sentences about them.

26 Consumer Society

GRAMMAR FOCUS

Spend, Spend, Spend

Many of us in developed societies are in a vicious circle. We work hard so that we can earn more money. When we have more money, we spend more. Because we spend more, we have to work even harder. The circle goes round and round. The result is not increased happiness, but more stress and less free time to be ourselves and be with our families and friends.

However, there is growing resistance to this consumer society, especially from young people. Protest groups are insisting that some of our money be redistributed to the third world. Trade unions demand that the Prime Minister reduce the working week. They are also suggesting that people should share work and thus reduce unemployment.

As a society, it's high time that we took these issues more seriously. We should insist that advertising is more controlled, especially advertising aimed at children. We should also make sure that there are constructive ways for young people to use their free time apart from spending money. On a personal level, we ought to visit the shops less and worry less about our image. Above all, we should remember that 'being' and 'doing' are much more important than 'having'.

Before you start

1 Look at the photos and the title of the article. Which three of these things do you think will not be mentioned in the article?

global trade, stress and lack of time, crime and violence, reductions in the working week, work sharing, advertising, opportunities for leisure, drugs

2 Read the article and check your guesses.

3 Which of the writer's views do you agree and disagree with?

COMPLEX SENTENCES (1): PERSUASION

Presentation 1: Written English

4 In the text underline all sentences with the following verbs and expressions.

should, ought to, insist, demand, suggest, it's high time

5 Look at the sentences you underlined in the text. Now form the rules by matching 1–4 with a–e.

After:	we use:
1 should	a) (that) + subject + should do something
2 ought to	b) (that) + subject + subjunctive (same form as infinitive, e.g. 'I suggest he go.')
3 insist, demand, suggest	c) (that) + subject + present tense
	d) (that) + subject + past tense
4 it's high time	e) infinitive without 'to'

➪ *Grammar Summary 9, page 148.*

Society

Presentation 2: Spoken English

6 🎧 Listen to the dialogue between Grant and Lucy. Answer these questions.

1 Which of them buys second-hand clothes?
2 Which of them spends a lot of money on clothes?
3 Which of them has an evening job?
4 Which of them is a vegetarian?
5 Which of them suggests going to a film?

7 🎧 Listen to the dialogue again and complete the sentences. What are the verb forms used after the expressions in bold?

*** **It's about time you** _____ going there.
* **If I were you, I** _____ buying all those expensive clothes.
*** **I'd (= I would) rather you** _____ that.
** **I think you ought to** _____ that job.
** **I think you should** _____ meat yourself.
**** **You'd (= you had) better** _____ going.

Note: 1–2 stars = weak and polite expressions; 3–4 stars = strong expressions/criticism

➪ **Grammar Summary 9, page 148.**

Practice

8 Complete the sentences with the words in the list. You do not need all of them.

should, ought, suggest, rather, would, insist, better, time, had

1 If I were you, I _____ start saving now.
2 You'd _____ get a part-time job.
3 His boss _____ that he work longer hours.
4 I think you _____ to spend more time at home.
5 You _____ better avoid carrying heavy weights.
6 It's _____ you started thinking about your future.
7 I'd _____ you didn't buy so many gadgets.
8 I _____ that she open her own bank account.

9 Use the words in brackets to paraphrase the sentences.

1 I suggest that he should change his career plans.
He _____ his career plans. (better)
2 Please don't play music late at night.
I'd _____ music late at night. (rather)
3 The committee should manage the funds more carefully.
We _____ the funds more carefully. (insist)
4 I think it's a good idea to study economics nowadays.
If _____ economics. (were)
5 I think he should start looking for a job.
It's about _____ for a job. (time)
6 Her teachers made her wear longer skirts.
Her teachers _____ longer skirts. (demand)
7 I'd prefer you to dress more smartly for work.
I _____ more smartly for work. (rather)
8 Jim should see a doctor before it gets any worse.
Jim _____ a doctor before it gets any worse. (had)

10 Read the situations. What would the people in brackets say? Use the stronger expressions (three or four stars) from Exercise 7.

1 Mark spends all his pocket money on the lottery.
(Mark's father)
2 Peter spends all his free time playing computer games.
(Peter's mother)
3 Jenny is always borrowing her older sister's clothes without asking.
(Jenny's older sister)
4 Elaine watches TV until late at night and can never get up in the morning.
(Elaine's parents)
5 Ian has got an exam next month and he hasn't done any revision yet.
(Ian's teacher)

11 Work in pairs. Talk about your problems and give each other advice. Use the weaker expressions (one or two stars) from Exercise 7.

Student A:
- you are dreaming about a holiday abroad but you have no money
- you don't know how to get to know the boy/girl you're interested in
- you can never find anything in your room because it is always in a mess

Student B:
- you don't know what to buy your best friend for his/her birthday
- you are very unfit and always feel tired
- you've lost your friend's favourite CD

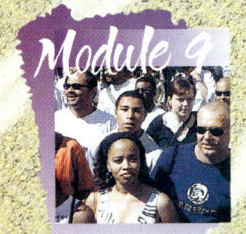

27 Utopia

SKILLS FOCUS

Before you start

1 Look at the picture of the ideal society of Utopia. Guess the answers to some of these questions.

1 Are there any differences between rich and poor people?
2 What leisure activities are there?
3 How democratic is the society?
4 What punishments are there?

Listening

2 🎧 Listen to Sir Thomas More's story about Utopia. Check your answers to Exercise 1.

3 🎧 Listen to the story again. List two things you would like about Utopia and two things you would hate. Would you like to live in More's Utopia? Why or why not?

4 Read the Strategies.

> **LISTENING STRATEGIES:**
> Understanding cultural references
>
> - When listening to English you will often hear cultural references (e.g. to people, places, objects, TV programmes, measurements) which you are not familiar with.
> - Use the context of the conversation to try to guess what they refer to.

🎧 Listen to the conversation. Guess what these things refer to.

Example 1 = *a street*

1 The Broadway
2 Rotherham
3 the number 23
4 a season ticket
5 Jaguars
6 EastEnders
7 mini-London Eye
8 Scunthorpe
9 the Barbican/the South Bank
10 The Ministry of Sound
11 scones

5 🎧 Listen again and complete the Function File with these words and phrases.

let's, It's time, I'd charge, Why don't they, I think they should, what would be really great is if, I wish they'd, They ought to, It's about time, There could be, What about, It'd be a good idea if, I think it'd be good if they, What we need

Function File

Making Suggestions

Tentative suggestions

1 _____ they stopped traffic going into the centre.
2 _____ lots more pedestrian streets ...
3 _____ doing something about public transport?
And 6 _____ they were free.
8 _____ people more for bringing cars into the centre.
10 _____ spent money on things for young people to do.
13 _____ start a decent club.

Stronger suggestions

4 _____ we had more buses.
5 _____ put buses every fifteen minutes.
7 _____ are some big changes in this place.
9 _____ make a decent park?
11 _____ build a decent sports centre ...
12 _____ they set up a cultural centre.
And 14 _____ have some more scones.

Pronunciation

6 🎧 Listen to eight more suggestions. Which of them sound tentative (T) and which sound stronger (S)? Then listen again and repeat the suggestions.

Example 1 = S

Speaking

7 Work in pairs. Use the rolecards to make suggestions about how to improve a town. Use suggestions from the Function File (! = strong; ? = tentative).

Example
A: It's about time they cleaned up the river!
B: That's true. And it'd be a good idea if ...

Student A
- clean up the river (!)
- make public transport free (?)
- make pedestrian streets (!)
- charge more for parking (?)
- do up the main square (?)
- build a sports centre (!)
- create a venue for concerts (?)

Student B
- make more parks (?)
- increase the number of buses (!)
- build more car parks (!)
- do up the old houses in the centre (?)
- build a new hospital (!)
- set up an Internet café (?)
- start a new library (?)

8 Think about ways of improving your local community. Write notes about these things.

traffic and transport, historic buildings, parks and gardens, pollution and the environment, recreation facilities for young people (sport/socialising/culture), health services, care for the elderly/poor/homeless

9 Work in pairs. Discuss your suggestions with your partner.

Example
A: It's about time we started to look after the historic buildings in our city.
B: That's true but I think it'd be better to spend money on ...

Tell the class about some of your ideas.

Example
Both of us think it'd be a good thing to build a new outdoor swimming pool.

Vocabulary: Multi-part Verbs with *up*

➪ *Lexicon, pages 170–176.*

10 Complete the sentences with these verbs in the correct form.

go, turn, set, brighten, make, give, dress, pick, hold, take, clean, do

1 Why don't they _____ up the river and _____ up that old house next to the bridge? It's nearly falling down.
2 It would be a good idea to _____ up a theatre group. It would _____ things up a bit in this town. I love _____ up and I'd like to _____ up acting.
3 I was _____ up for twenty minutes in a traffic jam and _____ up late for class. But the teacher thought I _____ up an excuse.
4 The cost of tickets keeps _____ up, so I _____ up taking the bus and started walking to college. Though sometimes my neighbour _____ me up in the morning and takes me there in her car.

QUOTE .... UNQUOTE
'Man is by nature a political animal.'
Aristotle

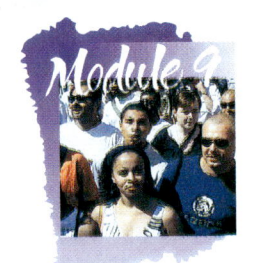

Communication Workshop

Writing: A Discursive Essay (2)

Before you start

1 Look at the Key Words. Which of the crimes are the biggest problem in your society now? What punishments would *you* give for the crimes?

> **KEY WORDS: CRIME AND PUNISHMENT**
> *Crime:* burglary, drug dealing, mugging, murder, rape, shoplifting, theft
> *Punishment:* the death penalty (capital punishment), fine, prison sentence, soft/hard sentences, life sentence

2 Read the two letters. Which do you agree with most?

Crime and Punishment

June 14

Polly Filler's article last week was excellent as she condemns the 'soft' sentences given to criminals in this country. My brother works as a police officer and he tells me that drug dealers, muggers and burglars can be out on the streets only a few weeks or months after committing their crimes or even let off with fines. What is even more scandalous is the fact that some rapists and even murderers are let out of prison after three or four years. (1) _____ this, many people are losing faith in the British system of justice.

I think we should bring back much harder sentences in this country, (2) _____ criminals are made to pay for what they have done. I totally agree with the American idea of 'three strikes and out' – that after committing three crimes criminals are locked up for life. That is the only way of protecting society and deterring young people from a life of crime.
(3) _____ money is spent on prisons that they have become like luxury hotels with televisions and gyms. Prisoners should be made to work and not treated as residents at a holiday camp.
I also believe we should restore capital punishment in this country as in the States. When a person has killed somebody they don't deserve to live. We also need to think about the wishes of the families and friends of murder victims who demand that justice be done.

RJ Butcher
Kingham, Oxfordshire

June 20

I was horrified to read RJ Butcher's letter in this newspaper last week. He/She sees punishment as an opportunity for revenge. In my opinion, the primary objective of punishment should be to reform the person who has committed the crime. We need to help and reform convicted criminals (4) _____ make them into useful members of the community. We also need to eliminate the social problems, like drugs and poverty, that often lead to crime.

I am totally against harder sentences on principle. The only time that life sentences should be given is when a person is so dangerous that the community is at risk if he or she is let out of prison. Mr/Ms Butcher's suggestion that we bring back the death penalty is even worse. Let's face it, capital punishment is judicial murder and no better than any other murder (5) _____ it is committed by the state. It is a savage form of punishment which is against human dignity. Besides, it is highly unfair (6) _____ judicial mistakes. In the USA in the last 100 years 23 men have been executed wrongly and there are doubts about 400 other executions. The death penalty also affects some sections of the community much more than others. (7) _____, in the USA the death penalty is not as likely if the victim is black and the murderer white as the other way around.

Paul Mason
York

3 Match the sentences listing arguments from a discursive essay (1–8) with personal opinions in the two letters.

1 Many people feel that harder sentences should be brought back.
2 The American system of 'three strikes and out' has supporters in Britain.
3 Moreover, some people say that conditions in prisons are too soft.
4 There are arguments for the restoration of the death penalty.
5 The wishes of victims' family and friends possibly need to be taken into account.
6 There are arguments against harder sentences and capital punishment.
7 It is strongly felt by many people that capital punishment is the equivalent of judicial murder.
8 Furthermore, the death penalty is seen as savage and an affront to human dignity.

4 Read the letters again and complete the gaps with these linking words (reason/result).

consequently so, due to, so much, just because, so that, as a result of, in order to

> Write an essay discussing this statement:
> 'The only way to cut crime in our country is to make punishment more severe.'
> Follow the stages below.

Stage 1
Look at the two letters. List the arguments 'for' and 'against':

a) the death penalty and hard sentences
b) punishment as reform

Add other arguments and reasons backing them up (e.g. from your country).

Stage 2
Use your notes to write a plan of your essay.

➪ Writing Help 9 (layout), page 144.

Stage 3
Use your plan to write the essay.

➪ Writing Help 9 (style, useful vocabulary, linking).

Stage 4
Check your essay.

➪ Writing Help 9 (checking).

Talkback
Work in pairs. Give your essay to your partner to read. Comment on the arguments.

Listening: A Song
'Father and Son' by Cat Stevens

1 What differences are there between your generation and your parents' generation in your society? Think about these things:

a) tastes in music/clothes
b) attitudes to work and money
c) attitudes to marriage

2 Listen to the song. Who do you think said these things, the father or the son?

1 It's not time to make a change.
2 You're still young, that's your fault.
3 Find a girl, settle down.
4 But take your time, think a lot.
5 For you will still be here tomorrow, but your dreams may not.
6 How can I explain, when I do he turns away again.
7 From the moment I could talk I was ordered to listen.
8 Now there's a way and I know that I have to go away.
9 Just relax, take it easy.
10 There's so much you have to know.
11 If you want you can marry.
12 Look at me, I am old but I am happy.
13 If they were right, I'd agree, but it's them you know, not me.
14 I know I have to go.

3 Listen again. Answer these questions.

1 What do you think the situation is? Why do you think the son wants to go away?
2 What is the father's advice?
3 How do you think both of them feel?

Communication Workshop

Speaking: Problem Solving

Before you start

1 Look at the photo. If you had to spend two weeks in a wood without any of the comforts, what would you miss most?

Example hot water

2 Which of these would be the biggest survival problems for you?

making a fire, finding food, making a shelter, first aid, finding water, cooking

3 🎧 Listen to three people on a survival course. Which of the problems in Exercise 2 are mentioned?

Chatroom

EXAGGERATION AND UNDERSTATEMENT

4 🎧 Listen again and match the expressions.

1 It's freezing.
2 My feet are blocks of ice.
3 I'm dying for a cup of coffee.
4 There are a few stones around …
5 It's huge.
6 It would take ages …
7 It's quite muddy …
8 I'm getting a bit peckish.

a) It's knee-deep in mud.
b) It's not what you'd call tropical.
c) Mine are a bit cold.
d) I'm starving!
e) It would take a while.
f) There are millions.
g) It's quite big.
h) I wouldn't mind one.

Which of the expressions involve exaggeration and which understatement? Do you use these a lot in your language?

REACTING TO SUGGESTIONS

5 Look at the reactions to people's suggestions. Which are negative?

1 That's a good idea.
2 Surely, it'd be better to explore a bit.
3 OK, let's do that.
4 It's quite big, but I don't see why we have to build it here.
5 Don't you think it would be better near the stream?
6 How come?
7 Right. I'll collect the stones …
8 OK. Why don't we both do that?
9 Surely, we can do that when it's finished.

6 🎧 **Pronunciation.** Listen to the words said slowly and then said fast. Which of these sounds disappear or are added: /t/, /d/, /r/, /v/?

1 start getting 2 Let's start. 3 explore a bit 4 best place
5 for a cup 6 cup of coffee 7 could build 8 need people
9 some of them 10 before it 11 bit peckish

Make group decisions about how to survive in the wild. Follow the stages below.

Stage 1
Read the Strategies.

> **SPEAKING STRATEGIES:**
> Preparing for problem solving
>
> • First, read the information. Don't worry if you don't know all the vocabulary.
> • Identify the most important problems.
> • Write simple notes with suggestions/ solutions. Give reasons for them.
> • Think of what you would volunteer to do.

Use the Strategies to prepare for the task.

Task – survive two weeks in a forest in groups of three
Temperature – maximum 25°C – minimum 8°C
Equipment – knife, fish hooks, torch, flint, first aid kit, cooking pot, water bottle, food for one day

Stage 2
Look at the expressions in the Function File on page 107 and the Chatroom. Practise making and reacting to suggestions.

Stage 3
Work in groups of three. Discuss your survival plans. Decide what you are going to do and who is going to do different jobs.

Talkback
Tell the class how you plan to survive. Which of the groups in the class do you think has the best chances of surviving?

'Richard III'

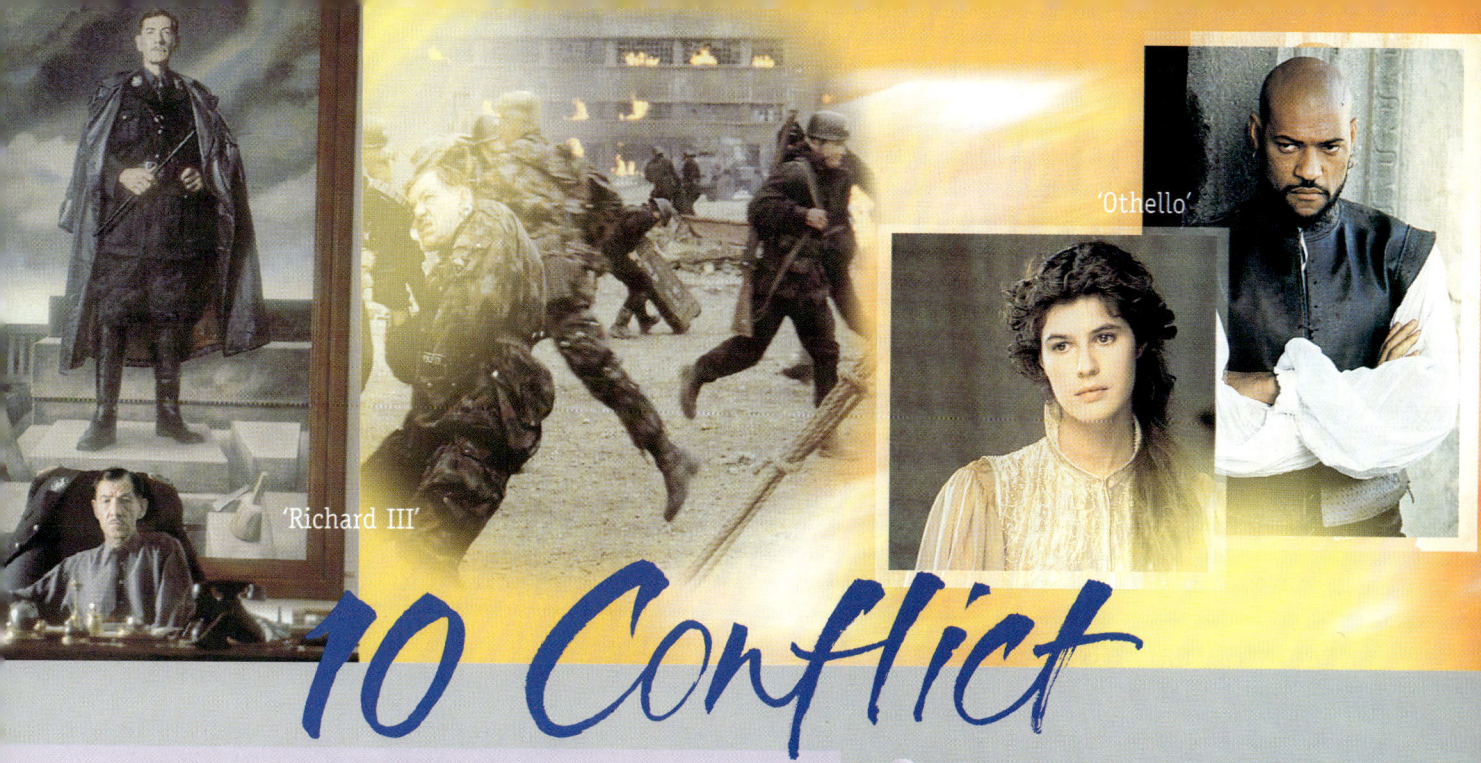

'Othello'

10 Conflict

In this module you ...

- **Talk about**, act out and resolve different kinds of conflict.
- **Listen to** TV news reports, dialogues, a radio documentary and a radio play. **Use** listening strategies for identifying mood and sequencing events.
- **Read** war memories, a newspaper article and a formal letter. **Use** reading strategies for reading under pressure.
- **Write** a formal letter of complaint.
- **Learn about** complex sentence structure for emphasis.

Warm-up

1 🎧 Listen to the imaginary TV news stories and match them with the plays.

2 🎧 Listen again. Complete the expressions with the Key Words.

KEY WORDS: Conflict
argument, battle, clash, feud, fight, friction, gang, quarrel, row, violence, war, warfare

1 civil _____
2 decisive _____
3 heavy _____
4 street _____
5 rival _____
6 long-standing _____
7 family _____
8 gang _____
9 family _____
10 domestic _____
11 have a _____
12 petty _____

3 Work in pairs. Discuss the newspaper headlines below. Use the Key Words to help you.

- What do you think the story is about?
- What do you think caused the conflict?

KEY WORDS: Motives
ambition, fear, greed, hatred, intolerance, jealousy, revenge

➪ **Lexicon, page 155.**

Example
A: For number one, I think a woman has been robbed in the street.
B: Yes. And the robber took five dollars. I don't think greed was the motive.
A: No, maybe the robber needed money for ...

1 Woman mugged for $5
2 'TV breeds copycat violence' claims minister
3 Rebel leader replaces President
4 Police investigate increased attacks on immigrants
5 Boyfriend admits he was 'out of control'

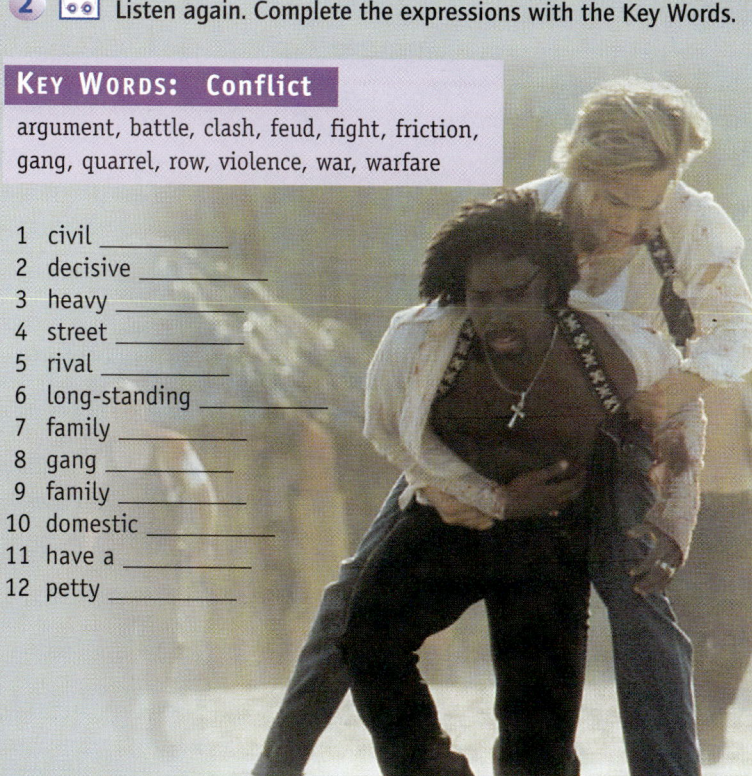

'Romeo and Juliet'

Module 10

28 War Memories

SKILLS FOCUS

Before you start

1 **A Quiz.** Work in pairs and do the quiz on page 136.

Reading

2 Read the Strategies.

> **READING STRATEGIES:**
> **Reading under pressure**
> - Decide how long you need to spend on each task.
> - Read the questions and decide what strategies you need to answer them.
> - If you have difficulty with a question, don't spend too long on it. Move on to the next one – you can always go back to it later.
> - Don't leave a question unanswered – guess the answer!

Now use the Strategies to read the texts and answer the questions in Exercises 3–5. You have 20 minutes.

3 Match these titles with the extracts. There is one extra title.

- A Brave Patient
- Village Nightmare
- A Decisive Battle
- Feeling Helpless
- No More Fighting

4 Complete the gaps in Text B with these sentences. There is one extra sentence.

a) Just before midnight we all decided not to start firing before they did.
b) We told him he wasn't the only one who was fed up with it.
c) The enemy had stuck up a similar one.
d) The noise of the guns was incredible.
e) Then we all got out of the trench.

A Do Chuc is a gnarled, forty-eight-year-old Vietnamese peasant whose two daughters and an aunt were killed by GIs in My Lai that day. He and his family were eating breakfast when the GIs entered the village and ordered them from their homes. Together with other villagers they were marched a few hundred meters into the plaza, where they were told to squat. "Still we had no reason to be afraid," Chuc recalled. "Everyone was calm. We'd seen it all before." He watched as the GIs set up a machine gun. The calm ended. The people began crying and begging. One monk showed his identification papers to a soldier, but the American simply said, "Sorry." Then the shooting started. Chuc was wounded in the leg, but he was covered by dead bodies and thus spared. After waiting an hour, he fled the village.
(From *My Lai* by Seymour Hersh)

B On Christmas morning we stuck up a board with "A Merry Christmas" on it. (1) _____ Two of our men then threw their equipment off and staggered out of the trench with their hands above their heads. Two of the Germans did the same and they met and shook hands. (2) _____ 'Buffalo Bill' (our officer) tried to prevent it but it was too late so he and the other officers climbed out too and strolled over. We and the Germans trudged through the mud and met in the middle of no-man's-land.
We mucked in all day with one another. Some of them could speak English. By the look of them, their trenches were in as bad a state as our own. One of their men, speaking in English, mentioned that he had worked in Brighton for some years and that he was fed up to the neck with this damned war and would be glad when it was over.
(3) _____ The German commander asked Buffalo Bill if we would like a couple of barrels of beer and they brought them over to us. The officers came to an understanding that the unofficial truce would end at midnight.
(4) _____ During the whole of Boxing Day we never fired a shot and they the same; each side seemed to be waiting for the other to set the ball rolling. One of their men shouted across in English and inquired how we had enjoyed the beer. We replied that we were very grateful and spent the whole day chatting with them. That evening we were replaced by another battalion.
(From *Old Soldiers Never Die* by Frank Richards)

Conflict

C I got a phone call from the chief nurse, saying, "You've got a patient there that is going to get an award. Make sure that the ward looks good." This really turned me off to begin with: 'Let's clean up the ward because we've got VIPs coming in.' Well, the VIPs happened to be the general of the 25th Infantry Division and an entourage of about twelve people. This was this patient's second visit to us, this time with both his legs blown off – he was all of about twenty years old. When he was waking up from his anesthesia he whispered: "Don't you remember me, ma'am?" I said, "Oh yeah!" But really I didn't because there were so many of them.

The entourage was coming to give him the award because he happened to be number twenty thousand to come through this hospital. They had this little ceremony, gave him a Purple Heart and a watch. As the general handed him the watch, "from the 25th Infantry Division, as a token of our appreciation," the kid more or less flung the watch back at him. He said something like, "I can't accept this, sir; it's not going to help me walk." After this little incident, I went over and just put my arms around him and hugged him. If I remember correctly, I started crying and I think he was crying too. I really admired him for that. That was one time I let somebody see what I felt. It took a lot for him to do that, and it sort of said what this war was all about to me.
(From *A Piece of My Heart* by Keith Walker)

D ME AND A BUDDY WERE WALKING behind an English pub once, going back to our Canadian base, and we saw one of our planes come over heading for an American base just across the valley. One of its engines was on fire and we saw it hit the ground. We didn't know if it still had its bombs aboard or if it was coming back from Germany, so we didn't dare go near it. I tried to phone the American base, but I couldn't get through. The line just didn't work. Fire brigades came from all over, but nobody dared go near the plane because it was on fire and we couldn't find out if it still had its bombs and tanks full of petrol. The crew couldn't get out and we could hear the men screaming and shouting and there was nothing we could do because of the bombs. They died, five of them. Then we found out later it was on a training mission.
(From *Six War Years* by Barry Broadfoot)

5 Choose the best alternative to complete each sentence, a, b, c or d.

1 The Vietnamese villagers were calm at first because
 a) they knew the American soldiers.
 b) this was a normal procedure.
 c) they had identification papers.
 d) they didn't understand English.

2 The troops got together on Christmas Day because
 a) they had planned it beforehand.
 b) they all knew each other.
 c) they were tired of the war.
 d) the officers declared a truce.

3 The nurse wasn't enthusiastic about the award ceremony from the start because
 a) she had to clean up the ward.
 b) she didn't like her boss's attitude to the VIPs.
 c) the patient had been badly wounded.
 d) the patient started to cry.

4 The Canadian airmen did not go near the plane because
 a) there was danger of an explosion.
 b) it had full tanks.
 c) it was on a bombing mission.
 d) they had no permission.

Vocabulary: Word Families

➪ *Lexicon, page 163.*

6 Classify these words from the text.

beg, chat, inquire, march, mention, recall, reply, shout, stagger, stroll, trudge, whisper

WALK *stagger*
SPEAK / SAY / TELL *chat*
ASK *inquire*

Speaking

7 Would you fight in a war? Why? Why not?

29 Neighbours From Hell

GRAMMAR FOCUS

Before you start

1 What usually causes conflict between neighbours? Have you ever had problems with your neighbours?

2 Listen to some traditional Scottish bagpipe music. Do you like it?

3 Read about the dispute between two neighbours. Whose side are you on, the bagpiper's or his neighbours'? Why?

Neighbours Call the Tune

Fergus Maclean, a professional piper, has packed his bags. Not only has he decided to move house, but he is emigrating to America after his neighbours in Dundee made several complaints about noise pollution.
Never has he known anything like it. What Mr Maclean feels upset about is the fact that people call his music 'noise pollution'. 'It's this that really gets to me,' fumes Mr Maclean. 'I mean, the pipes are our national instrument, aren't they? It's not surprising that a lot of our best pipers go to live abroad.'
Seldom have bagpipes caused such conflict. Mr Maclean's neighbours claimed that they were literally being driven mad by the noise. Had they known that their neighbour was a piper, one couple said, they wouldn't have moved into the street. 'All we want to do is forget the sound of bagpipes!' they said. No sooner had they moved in than the noise began to drive them mad. Mr Maclean practised for five hours a day and rarely did they get a chance to have a lie-in in the morning. Neither could they read a book at home without wearing earplugs!
In the end, the local council took action. 'It was only after careful consideration that we gave Mr Maclean a warning,' a council spokesman said. 'What counts as noise pollution is not clearly defined – there is no difference between someone playing the bagpipes and loud rock music.'

COMPLEX SENTENCES (2): EMPHASIS

Presentation

4 Compare the sentences in the table. Which of the statements below (a–c) are true about the formal sentences? Only one statement is false.

a) they begin with a word that has a negative meaning
b) they have the word order of a question (inversion)
c) they sound less emphatic

Find more examples of formal sentences in the text. Make a list of negative words and expressions that these sentences begin with.

Formal Written Language	Neutral Language
Never has he known anything like it.	**He has never known** anything like it.
Seldom have bagpipes caused such conflict.	**Bagpipes have hardly ever caused** such conflict.
Neither could they read a book at home without wearing earplugs!	**They couldn't read** a book at home without wearing earplugs **either**.

5 Paraphrase these conditional sentences so that they sound less emphatic and less formal.

Had I known that my neighbour was a piper, I wouldn't have moved in in the first place.
I would have felt terrible at the ceremony, **had my friends not been** there with me.

6 How are these neutral statements (1–3) reported in the text?

1 I'm moving house. In fact, I'm going to America.
2 We'd only just moved in when the noise began to drive us mad.
3 We hardly ever get a chance to have a lie-in.

7 Find sentences in the text which mean almost the same as the sentences below.

1 Mr Maclean feels upset about the fact that people call his music 'noise pollution'.
2 This really gets to me.
3 We want to forget the sound of bagpipes.
4 We gave Mr Maclean a warning after careful consideration.

Underline the parts of the sentences (1–4) which are emphasised in the text.

Example
Mr Maclean feels upset about the fact that people call his music 'noise pollution'.

➡ Grammar Summary 10, page 149.

Practice

8 Using the beginnings provided, rewrite the sentences to make them more emphatic and more formal.

1 They will never admit their mistakes.
  Never _____ .
2 If she had come, she would've learned the truth.
  Had _____ .
3 He didn't only sing in the choir, he played in the school band as well.
  Not only _____ .
4 We can hardly ever listen to such powerful performances.
  Seldom _____ .
5 Politicians hardly ever experience what war really feels like.
  Rarely _____ .
6 I don't argue with people and I have never been in a real fight either.
  I don't argue with people and neither _____ .

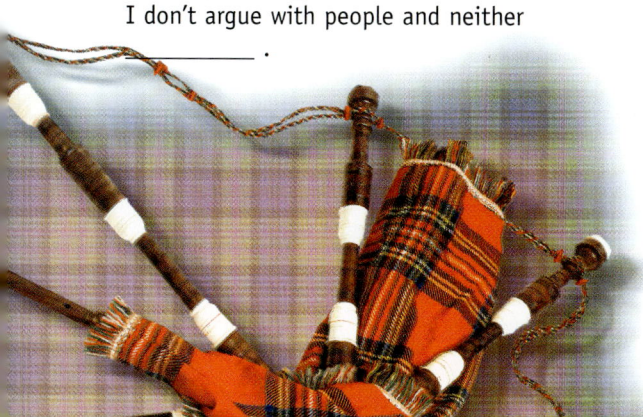

9 Complete the sentences using the beginnings and the cues provided.

Example
The flight was a nightmare. (take off / it turn out that the engine was on fire)
No sooner had we taken off **than** it turned out that the engine was on fire.

1 People spend too much money nowadays.
  Not only … (they buy things they don't really need / go on expensive holidays)
2 British football fans are the most violent in Europe.
  Seldom … (it is quiet after the match)
3 The sunset at the seaside is an extraordinary sight.
  Rarely … (one see anything so beautiful)
4 The evacuation of the building was completed just in time.
  No sooner … (than) … (the last person had left / the fire broke out)
5 The press conference generated enormous interest.
  Never before … (there had been such a great turnout of reporters and journalists)

10 Rewrite the sentences below so the emphasis is on the underlined phrase. Start each sentence with It … .

Example
We enjoyed the wine, but not the food.
It was the wine that we enjoyed, not the food.

1 Jenny wrote a letter of complaint to the manager.
2 I'm allergic to dairy products, not wheat.
3 They offered us financial compensation only after we threatened to take them to court.
4 She is constantly arguing with her mother, not her father.
5 Tim took part in the competition because of the attractive prizes.

11 Complete the sentences.

Example
I don't watch a lot of TV. All I watch is the news.

1 I don't eat much. All I …
2 He didn't come to see me. It was …
3 I don't enjoy talking about politics. What I …
4 I didn't order spaghetti bolognese. It was …
5 We didn't do anything exciting in Greece. All we …
6 I don't really mind people being late. What I …

12 In pairs ask and answer the questions. Always start your answers with All I … or What I … .

1 How do you like spending your free time?
2 Do you do a lot of sport?
3 What do you usually do together with your friends?
4 Do you watch television a lot?
5 How much water do you drink a day?
6 What do you usually have for breakfast?
7 How do you spend your holidays?

What can you say about your partner's lifestyle?

Module 10

30 Conflict Resolution

SKILLS FOCUS

Before you start

Vocabulary: Multi-part Verbs

➪ *Lexicon, pages 170–176.*

1 Match the verbs below with those underlined in the questionnaire.

criticise, discuss, get revenge, irritate, make, return, say OK, stop liking, suggest, take, tolerate

HOW ASSERTIVE ARE YOU?

1 You're angry with your neighbours because they wake you up early on Sunday mornings. Do you:

  a) <u>talk</u> it <u>over</u> with them and <u>put forward</u> a solution?
  b) <u>get your own back</u> by making a lot of noise late at night?
  c) put cotton wool in your ears when you go to bed?

2 Your sister is always <u>going off with</u> your things and never giving them back. She comes to your room and asks to borrow your best T-shirt for a party. Do you:

  a) refuse to give it to her and explain why?
  b) say no and tell her to get out and never ask for anything again?
  c) <u>give in</u> and lend it, but tell her to <u>give it back</u>?

3 A shop assistant is rude to you. Do you:

  a) calmly explain that you are a customer and so you expect good manners?
  b) <u>kick up a fuss</u> and ask to see the manager?
  c) <u>put up with</u> it but never go back there again?

4 A friend is always <u>getting at</u> you about the clothes you wear. Do you:

  a) tell him/her in private that it is really <u>getting to</u> you?
  b) make fun of his/her clothes in front of everyone?
  c) say nothing but <u>go off</u> him/her?

2 How would *you* react in the situations? Answer the questionnaire in Exercise 1. Then check your answers on page 136 to see how assertive you are.

Listening

3 Read the Strategies.

> **LISTENING STRATEGIES:** Identifying mood
> - Listen for expressions that are positive (e.g. *I'm really pleased*.) or negative (e.g. *Stop getting at me!*).
> - Pay attention to intonation to help you identify people's moods (e.g. *happy, angry, nervous, upset*).
> - Be careful with sarcasm. Sometimes people say something positive but with a falling intonation so that it means the opposite.

4 🎧 Listen to the argument between a brother and sister. Use the Strategies to decide if these statements are true (T) or false (F).

1. Lucy is not happy about her history essay. ☐
2. Pete is interested in hearing about her result. ☐
3. Lucy is upset by his reaction. ☐
4. The first time she asks her brother to change channels she is patient. ☐
5. Pete gets angry because Lucy has borrowed his calculator. ☐
6. Lucy is angry because Pete refuses to change channels. ☐
7. Pete is not worried about Lucy not letting him use her computer. ☐
8. He gets nervous when she makes her last threat. ☐

5 🎧 Listen again. Classify the expressions in the Function File.

a) criticising b) contradicting c) refusing d) suggesting
e) threatening

Function File

Arguing

1. **Just stop** gett**ing** at me, will you?
2. **You're always** tell**ing** people about your exciting maths problems.
3. **No, I'm not**.
4. **I wish you wouldn't** interrupt me all the time.
5. **Why don't you** turn over and see if it's started?
6. No, **why should I** turn over?
7. **You never** let other people watch anything.
8. **Why do you always have to** twist the truth?
9. **I did give** it back to you.
10. **I do tidy** it.
11. **I don't see why** I should.
12. **If you don't, I'll** never let you use my computer again.
13. And **if you do that, I'll** stop giving you a lift to school in the mornings.

---

6 🎧 **Pronunciation.** Listen to ten sentences. Identify the mood.

angry, annoyed, confident, happy, impatient, patient, sarcastic, triumphant, upset

Speaking

7 Work in pairs. Act out situations 2 and 4 from the questionnaire in Exercise 1. Use the expressions from the Function File.

Example
A: *Hey, you know I'm going to a party on Saturday.*
B: *Yes, what about it?*
A: *Well, can I borrow your blue T-shirt?*

Listening

8 🎧 Listen to a radio programme about how to resolve conflicts. Complete the sentences with the correct ending – a, b or c.

1. The worst thing to do when someone is aggressive is to
   a) say nothing at all. b) be aggressive back.
   c) go away from the situation.
2. Withdrawal is not a very useful strategy because
   a) it bottles up both people's feelings.
   b) the person leaving feels angry.
   c) the situation can become violent.
3. Mediation is a good strategy when
   a) the conflict is very serious.
   b) you have a good mediator.
   c) someone from outside decides.
4. When negotiating you should
   a) be prepared to speak for a long time.
   b) repeat your reasons again and again.
   c) find out what the other person wants.
5. You should propose solutions which
   a) everybody agrees with. b) do not threaten the other person. c) suggest you take turns.
6. When you are in conflict situations you should
   a) be aware of your body language.
   b) speak firmly and loudly.
   c) use strong body language.

Speaking

9 Work in pairs. Act out situations 2 and 4 from Exercise 1 again. Use the advice from the radio programme to resolve the conflict.

10 How were the roleplays in Exercises 7 and 9 different? How useful was the advice? Tell the class.

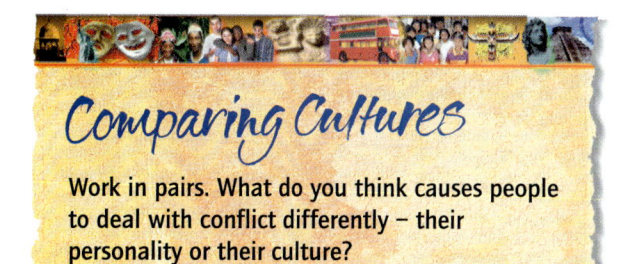

Comparing Cultures

Work in pairs. What do you think causes people to deal with conflict differently – their personality or their culture?

QUOTE .... UNQUOTE
'You raise your voice when you should reinforce your argument.'
Samuel Johnson (1709–84), British poet, essayist and lexicographer.

Communication Workshop

Writing: A Letter of Complaint

Before you start

1 Read the letter. Match the titles (1–6) with the paragraphs (A–E). There is one extra title you don't need.

1 poor service
2 false claims
3 the product
4 money back
5 diet programme
6 poor quality

2 Linking Review. Read the letter again. Classify the underlined linking words and expressions according to the following groups:

manner, condition, contrast, purpose, reason, result, time, addition, relative pronoun

---

45 Milton Street,
Cambridge.
25 October, 2002.

Fitness Products Ltd,
St Helier,
Jersey JE6 9NJ.

Dear Sir/Madam,

A I am writing to you about a Tour de France exercise bike (serial number 39879) <u>which</u> I bought from Mogul Megastores on 29th September for £499.99. I enclose copies of the guarantee and receipt.

B In your advertising you claim that, by using the exercise bike for ten minutes a day, you would lose at least two kilos a week. I have been using the bike for a month now and it is <u>as though</u> I have done no exercise at all. In fact, the more I use the bike, the more weight I seem to put on, <u>despite</u> following the instruction manual carefully.

C Even worse than that, the bike is extremely badly made. The speedometer stopped working <u>after</u> a week and the machine <u>that</u> measures heartbeats must also have broken <u>since</u> it gave readings of over two hundred beats per minute when I was cycling at full speed! I was <u>so</u> worried <u>that</u> I went to the doctor, who told me <u>not to</u> worry <u>as</u> my heartbeat was perfectly normal. <u>However</u>, the final straw came when the pedals broke <u>just as</u> I was cycling at full speed. <u>As well as</u> falling off the bike and nearly breaking my arm, I pulled a muscle in my thigh, which has caused me considerable pain and meant that I have had to take three days off work.

D <u>When</u> I took the exercise bike back to Mogul Megastores, <u>not only</u> did the manager refuse to refund my money, but said that he would not repair the bike <u>either</u>. He was <u>also</u> extremely rude and treated me <u>as if</u> I was stupid to have bought the bike in the first place.

E I would like you to refund my money <u>as soon as</u> possible and I suggest that you pay compensation for the injuries that I have received. <u>Unless</u> I receive a satisfactory reply within the next three weeks, I will have to take further action. I have already been in contact with my local consumer protection office <u>in order to</u> ask for advice and they have recommended me to take legal action, <u>if</u> I do not get full satisfaction.

I look forward to hearing from you.

Yours faithfully,

Jeffreys

A. N. Jeffreys (Mr)

3 Look at the examples, then use the cues (1–6) to write similar sentences.

Example
The more I use the bike, the more weight I seem to put on.
The earlier you leave, the sooner you will arrive.

1 get to know her / like her
2 sport play / fit / get
3 hard / study / good / marks be
4 sweets eat / bad / teeth be
5 dangerous sport / like it
6 old / get / difficult / work becomes

Write a letter of complaint. Follow the stages.

Stage 1
Match the products (1–6) with the Key Words.

1 a CD player 2 a pair of shoes or boots 3 a jacket
4 a mobile phone 5 a portable television 6 a digital watch

> **KEY WORDS: Complaints**
> • it won't open • the zip broke • it won't work indoors
> • the sound is distorted • the alarm doesn't work
> • the heel fell off • the headphones don't work
> • it's not waterproof • the picture is bad
> • the colour faded after one wash
> • it loses about five minutes every hour

Stage 2
Imagine you bought one of the products and something went wrong with it. Make notes about these things.

- What went wrong with the product?
- What false claims did the advertisement make?
- What happened when you took it back to the shop?

Stage 3
Organise your notes into four or five paragraphs.

⇨ *Writing Help 10 (layout), page 145.*

Stage 4
Use your plan to write the letter.

⇨ *Writing Help 10 (style, useful vocabulary, linking).*

Stage 5
Check your essay.

⇨ *Writing Help 10 (checking).*

Listening: A Filmscript

Before You Start

1 Look at the still from the film 'All Quiet on the Western Front'. Try to guess if these statements about the film are true (T) or false (F).

1) It cost a lot to make.
2) The film is set during the Second World War.
3) It's an anti-war film.

Listen to the film critic and an extract from the film. Answer the questions.

2 Listen to Part 1 and check your guesses for Exercise 1. Then listen to Parts 1 and 2. Answer these questions.

1 When was the film made?
2 How many Oscars did it win?
3 Who are the soldiers in the film fighting against?
4 How many soldiers are left in their unit after the attack?
5 How do the soldiers feel about the enemy?
6 What people do the soldiers think benefit from the war?

3 Listen to Part 2 again. Who do they think starts wars? Tick the correct boxes.

emperors and kings ☐   generals ☐
manufacturers ☐   soldiers ☐
nations of people ☐

4 Work in groups. Discuss these questions.

1 What do you think of the soldiers idea for kings and generals to fight wars themselves in a big field?
2 Why do you think wars start?
3 Can wars be avoided?

Speaking Workshop

Speaking: A Formal Telephone Conversation

Before you start

1 🎧 Listen to the telephone conversation between the manager of Fitness Products and the customer. Answer these questions:

1. How does the manager react at first?
   a) confidently b) nervously c) angrily
2. How does the manager try to resolve the conflict?
   a) she makes excuses b) she is rude to the customer c) she stays calm
3. How satisfied is the customer with the solution?
   a) very satisfied b) quite satisfied c) not satisfied

Chatroom

FORMAL EXPRESSIONS

2 Classify the sentences from the phone call (1–12) according to the following categories.

apologising, complaining, promising, starting or ending a call, threatening

1. Good morning. Fitness Products Ltd. Can I help you?
2. Good morning. I'd like to speak to the customer service manager, please.
3. I still haven't had a reply.
4. I'm very sorry about that.
5. I'm extremely sorry to hear that.
6. On top of that, when I took the bike back to the shop, the manager was extremely rude.
7. Unless I receive it, I'll have to take legal action.
8. Well, let me apologise for your experiences.
9. Well, I can assure you personally that you will receive a full refund.
10. And we will look into the subject of compensation for your injury.
11. Thank you. I'll be in touch.
12. Goodbye, and thank you very much for calling.

Have a telephone conversation about a faulty product. Follow the stages.

Stage 1
Look at your notes about your product from Stage 2 in the Writing Workshop. Decide what you want the company to do.

Stage 2
Work in pairs. One student is the manager and the other is the customer. Look at the expressions in the Chatroom and decide which ones you will use.

Stage 3
Act out the situation and come to an agreement.

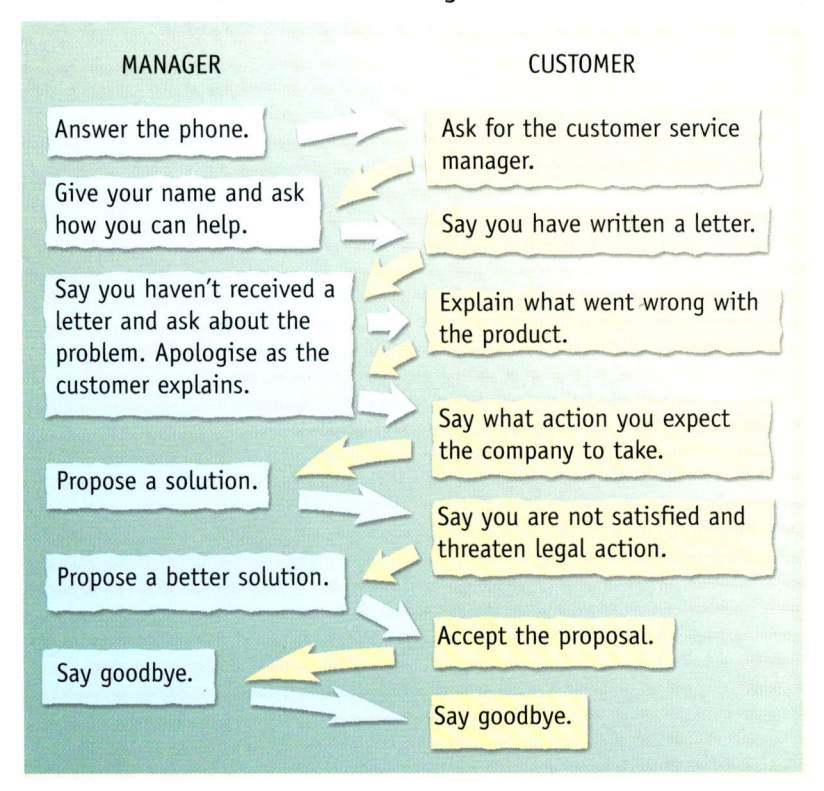

MANAGER	CUSTOMER
Answer the phone.	Ask for the customer service manager.
Give your name and ask how you can help.	Say you have written a letter.
Say you haven't received a letter and ask about the problem. Apologise as the customer explains.	Explain what went wrong with the product.
	Say what action you expect the company to take.
Propose a solution.	
	Say you are not satisfied and threaten legal action.
Propose a better solution.	
	Accept the proposal.
Say goodbye.	Say goodbye.

Stage 4
Now change roles and have another phone conversation.

Talkback
What agreements did you come to? Tell the class.

Language Awareness 6

1 Read the letter. What conflicts are mentioned? What are the reasons for them?

Example
Clare and her boyfriend - he spends too much time on his computer

2 What advice would you give Nick to help him resolve the conflicts?

Hi Clare,
How are things? Why haven't you got in touch? You've had my e-mail for ages!!! What have you been doing during the holidays? And how are you getting on with your boyfriend? I hope things are a bit better and he isn't still stuck in front of that awful computer all the time.
I expect you have been working hard for your exams! Hee hee. I've finished most of mine, so I can sit back and relax (a bit anyway). At least by the time I get back I will have read that awfully boring book that my History teacher has made me read over the holidays.
I've been staying with my family here on the coast. My grandfather's lived here for years and we come here every year. Unfortunately, my younger brother's been getting on my nerves. You know what he's like!
For example, yesterday, Damian and I went for a walk to the tower at the top of the cliff behind the town. Anyway, having walked all the way to the top, we were tired and stopped for a breather. I'd loved to have had a drink of water but my brother had finished it all!
Then he remembered once having been taken round the tower when we were younger, so he jumped the fence around it and went to the top. I refused to go up and I told Damian it was not safe. Well, he had been standing there for a minute or so when there was a noise. I jumped back. It must have been an instinctive reaction but it saved my life because a large stone crashed past me. If I had realised it was that dangerous I would never have stood so close!
When we got back home and I told Mum about it, she told me off for letting him go up the tower and we had a real row. I mean, I'm not responsible for Damian, am I? He's fifteen!
Apart from that it's great here. Having come here every summer means that most of the people in the village are really friendly. I suppose they must have known me since I was a baby. The only person I don't get on with is the woman in the supermarket. The other day she complained because I went in with no shoes on.
Well, I'd better stop. I should have been out helping Granpa with his fence. He's been having problems with the neighbouring farmer whose sheep have been getting into the garden and eating his plants.
Get in touch.
Nick

Perfective Verb Forms
➡ **Grammar Summary, page 150.**

3 Match the names of the verb forms with the structures in bold in the sentences below.

Present Perfect, Present Perfect Continuous, Past Perfect, Past Perfect Continuous, Future Perfect, perfect infinitive, perfective *-ing* form, passive perfective *-ing* form

1 By the time I get back I **will have read** that book.
2 I expect you **have been working** hard for your exams!
3 I**'ve finished** most of mine.
4 **Having come** here every summer means that all of the people in the village are really friendly.
5 My brother remembered once **having been taken** round the tower.
6 I **had been standing** there for a minute or so when there was a noise.
7 I suppose they **must have known** me since I was a baby.
8 My brother **had finished** it all!

4 Read the sentences below from the text. Which of these (a–c) do the perfective verb forms refer to?

a) something happening before a time in the past
b) something happening before the present
c) something happening before a time in the future

1 I**'ve been staying** with my family here on the coast.
2 My grandfather**'s lived** here for years.
3 By the time I get back I **will have read** that book.
4 He **had been standing** there for a minute or so when there was a noise.

Read two more sentences from the text and decide what all perfective verb forms refer to:

1 **Having walked** all the way to the top, we were tired and stopped for a breather.
2 I **should have been** out helping Granpa with his fence.

a) something that happened in the past
b) something happening before a certain point in time
c) something that has clear consequences

☞ Find practice exercises in the Language Powerbook, page 130.

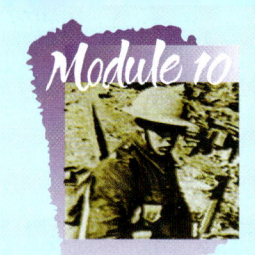

Review Modules 9 and 10

Grammar

1 Complete the second sentence so that it has a similar meaning to the first sentence.

1 I think you should spend less money on designer clothes.
   If _____ .
2 I wouldn't have gone there if I had known what it was like.
   Had _____ .
3 I'm very busy. Why don't you go and get the newspaper this time?
   I'd _____ .
4 We hardly ever get a chance to watch such a good film.
   Seldom _____ .
5 I think the government should do something to reduce crime.
   It's _____ .
6 People dropping litter in the streets make me very angry.
   What _____ .
7 We just need another five minutes to finish the job.
   All _____ .
8 They are always making a lot of noise late at night, which really irritates me.
   What _____ .
9 I cleaned the bathroom only last week.
   It _____ .
10 She always arrives late and then she does not even apologise.
   Not only _____ .
11 The local council really should prevent cars from going into the centre.
   It's _____ .
12 Could you not ring me up after 10 o'clock?
   I'd _____ .
13 It was the toughest decision he had ever had to make in his life.
   Never _____ .
14 Can't you talk about something else?
   I wish _____ .
15 He walked into the room and immediately started an argument.
   No sooner _____ .

2 Complete the conversation with a suitable auxiliary verb.

A: Hey, Mary, can you give me back my walkman?
B: I (1) _____ give it back to you.
A: No, you (2) _____ .
B: Yes, I (3) _____ . I left it on your desk.
A: Well, it isn't there now, (4) _____ it? I can't find it anywhere.
B: (5) _____ you? Someone else must have taken it, (6) _____ they? You (7) _____ ring Alan. He (8) _____ always going off with other people's things.
A: I (9) _____ . The battery's low on my mobile. (10) _____ you phone him?
B: Oh, all right, I (11) _____ do it. But it (12) _____ annoy me when people just take things.
A: Yes, what we (13) _____ to do is take something of his, (14) _____ you think?
B: Yes, I (15) _____ !

3 Use the cues to complete the sentences with perfective verb forms.

1 _____ (arrive) at the village, we went for a meal.
2 He _____ (stay) with some friends on the coast for a few days.
3 By next week, I _____ (finish) my diving course.
4 _____ (be trained) in first aid by my dad, I knew what to do in the accident.
5 We _____ (wait) for the bus about five minutes when we heard the explosion.
6 This afternoon I _____ (do) my homework, but people have just kept ringing me up on my mobile.
7 It _____ (be) terrible for you to lose your wallet in Paris.

Vocabulary

4 Complete the text with the correct words.

At the moment, I am having a (1 argument / feud / fight / quarrel) with the neighbours who live in the flat above me. What is most (2 annoying / offending / outstanding / worrying) is that they often make a lot of noise late at night. Sometimes they put on very loud music and other times they have arguments and (3 argue / complain / shout / whisper) at each other. At the weekends they have parties in their flat that (4 go on / last out / take / take up) until two in the morning. When I phone up and (5 complain / mention / recall / say) the noise they (6 apologise / promise / suggest / threaten) to be quiet but then it starts up again. Last night, I finally lost my (7 fear / mood / pride / temper) with them and called the police. When they came, the neighbours (8 claimed / denied / mentioned / refused) nobody else in the block had complained, which is not true. The police said they couldn't (9 do / give / make / take) any action unless they had (10 evidence / examples / proofs / signs) the neighbours made more than the legal level of noise.

Conflict

A painting by George Grosz

5 Complete each gap with one word.

The golden (1) _____ of Berlin was in the 1920s when there was an explosion of (2) _____ in the arts. The city was in a state of (3) _____ after the First World War and was (4) _____ through major social and economic changes. The most (5) _____ of the arts were the theatre and cinema with (6) _____ playwrights like Bertolt Brecht and film directors like Fritz Lang. There was also a (7) _____ of literary activity with novelists like Alfred Döblin and Thomas Mann. Both architecture and painting also (8) _____ with the influence of the Bauhaus school and expressionist painters like George Grosz. Why did this creative (9) _____ occur? For a very short time, before the rise of Hitler, Berlin acted as a (10) _____ for talented artists in Germany and Europe, such as the Czech film director Janowitz. Technology also had an important (11) _____ on both the theatre and cinema and there was a lot of cross-fertilisation between all of the (12) _____ , such as painting and cinema.

6 Complete each sentence with the correct word, a, b, c or d.

1 The number of cases of violent crime has _____ recently.
 a) expanded b) gained c) risen d) raised
2 The top 20 percent of the working population _____ more money than twenty years ago.
 a) achieve b) earn c) gain d) win
3 _____ people are generally better off, the gap between rich and poor has widened.
 a) Although b) Despite c) However d) Whereas
4 More people have a _____ than five years ago.
 a) employment b) job c) living d) work
5 There was a slight _____ between the two governments.
 a) argument b) clash c) disagreement d) quarrel

7 Match each of these words with two words from the box.

big, cold, hungry, laugh, look, rich, say, walk

chilly, chuckle, freezing, giggle, glance, huge, massive, peckish, shout, stare, starving, stroll, trudge, wealthy, well-off, whisper

Pronunciation

8 🔊 Listen and repeat these words. Which are difficult for you to say?

architecture, breathtaking, expenditure, explosion, fear, greed, negotiation, outstanding, pride, racism, sixteenth, soldier, suggestion, throughout, vicious, withdrawal

9 🔊 Listen and repeat these sentences.

1 He was an outstanding soldier throughout the war.
2 They agreed with our suggestion for increased expenditure.
3 There was an explosion of outstanding architecture in the sixteenth century.
4 They agreed to a withdrawal after negotiations.
5 Racism is often based on fear.

10 Look through the Lexicon and choose five words that are difficult for you to say. Then work in pairs. Compare your words with your partner's. Try to think of synonyms so you can avoid saying the words.

11 Can you say this proverb? Use the phonetic chart on the inside back cover to help you.

/ðə hɑːdə ðeɪ kʌm, ðə hɑːdə ðeɪ fɔːl/

What do you think the proverb means?

Check Your Progress

Look back at the Module Objectives on pages 101 and 111.

- Which activities did you enjoy most?
- Which activities did you have the most problems with?
- Which grammar area do you need to practise more?

Literature Spot 1

THE STRANGE CASE OF DR JEKYLL AND MR HYDE

BACKGROUND

Robert Louis Stevenson was born in Edinburgh, Scotland, in 1850. After studying law at university, he decided he wanted to be a writer. He travelled around France and Belgium and then went to California where he had many adventures, at one point coming close to death. He met and married his wife there. Over the next few years they moved between France, Scotland and England. Stevenson had health problems and in 1888 he and his wife sailed to the Pacific Islands. Stevenson never returned to Europe, but bought a house in Samoa where the weather was good for his health. He died suddenly in 1894 and was buried on the island, where he had been known as 'Tusitala' or 'The Storyteller'. His most famous works are *Treasure Island*, *The Strange Case of Dr Jekyll and Mr Hyde*, *Kidnapped*, *Catriona* and *The Master of Ballantrae*.

The personal struggle between good and evil is a theme that Stevenson returns to again and again in his writing, most famously in the story of Dr Jekyll and Mr Hyde, who each try to defeat the other's values. The other main theme of the book is that scientific experimentation can achieve almost anything, but needs to be done with great care since it can be used for evil purposes as well as good.

Before you start

1 Read the background notes and answer these questions.

1. What countries did Stevenson travel to?
2. Why did he decide to settle in Samoa?
3. What are the two main themes of *The Strange Case of Dr Jekyll and Mr Hyde*?

Reading and Listening

2 Read and listen to the story. Are the statements below true or false?

1. The butler asked Mr Utterson to come to Dr Jekyll's house.
2. Utterson and the butler heard Dr Jekyll's voice in the study.
3. They found Hyde's dead body wearing Dr Jekyll's clothes.
4. Dr Jekyll's will was made out to Edward Hyde.
5. In his note, Dr Jekyll explained how he changed identity.
6. His other personality was similar to his original one.
7. When he was Mr Hyde, Dr Jekyll committed crimes.
8. After some time, Dr Jekyll couldn't control the changes of identity.

3 Answer these questions.

1. Why did Mr Hyde have the key to Dr Jekyll's house?
2. Why did Utterson say 'Dr Jekyll would not be pleased'?
3. What did Poole mean when he said his master was 'got rid of'?
4. What do you think had been in the bottle next to the body of Mr Hyde?
5. Why were Mr Hyde's clothes 'far too big for him'?
6. After he had read the note, where did Utterson think Dr Jekyll was?
7. How did things get out of control for Dr Jekyll?
8. Why did Dr Jekyll say in his statement that it was 'my true hour of death'?

4 Complete the sentences with a word formed from the word in brackets.

1. Dr Jekyll was a respected and ____ man. (honour)
2. Dr Jekyll regained his ____ when he took the mixture again. (high)
3. Mr Hyde was completely _____ – nobody had heard of him (know).
4. The drugs began to have ____ effects. (predict)
5. The second time Utterson asks to enter, he won't accept Mr Hyde's ____ . (refuse)
6. Before he reads the statement, Utterson cannot explain the ____ of Dr Jekyll. (disappear)

Speaking

5 In groups, or with the whole class, discuss the following.

1. What do you think the servants were talking about when they were together in the hall?
2. How do you think Dr Jekyll was feeling when he wrote his final note?
3. What questions do you imagine that Mr Utterson would like to ask Dr Jekyll if Jekyll were alive to answer them?

Dr Henry Jekyll is a successful and well-known London doctor who is liked for his pleasant character and respected for his work. The mysterious Mr Edward Hyde, on the other hand, appears to be a thoroughly bad man, although he is completely unknown in London society. A well-known man is murdered, and Edward Hyde seems to be responsible. So how does Mr Hyde come to have the key of Dr Jekyll's house? And why does Dr Jekyll give his lawyer, Mr Utterson, a new will in which he leaves everything to Mr Hyde? One night, Poole, Dr Jekyll's butler, visits Mr Utterson and asks him to come quickly to Dr Jekyll's house.

When they arrived the butler knocked gently on the door, and a voice inside asked: 'Is that you, Poole?'
'Yes, it's all right,' said Poole. 'Open the door.'
They entered the brightly lit hall. All the servants were crowded together there like frightened sheep.
'Why are you all here?' asked Utterson. 'Dr Jekyll would not be pleased.'
'They're all afraid,' said Poole. 'And now,' he said, addressing a kitchen boy, 'bring me a candle, and we'll get this done immediately.' Then he begged Mr Utterson to follow him to Dr Jekyll's study.
Poole knocked on the study door and said: 'Mr Utterson is here, sir.'
'Tell him I can't see anyone,' said a voice from inside.
Poole led Utterson in silence back to the kitchen. 'Sir,' he said, looking Mr Utterson in the eyes, 'was that my master's voice?'
'It seems much changed,' replied the lawyer, very pale.
'Changed? No, sir. That is *not* my master. He was got rid of eight days ago when we heard him cry out in the name of God. And who's there instead of him?'
'This is a strange story, Poole,' said Mr Utterson, biting his finger. 'Suppose Dr Jekyll was murdered. What could persuade the murderer to stay? That doesn't make sense.'

Eventually, Utterson returns to the study and demands to enter. The voice from inside refuses and Utterson realises it is Mr Hyde's voice. Poole and Utterson decide to break into the study.

They looked into the room. There it lay in the quiet lamplight, a good fire burning, papers set neatly on the desk, and things arranged for tea. Right in the middle there lay the body of a man, horribly twisted and not yet quite still. They went towards it carefully and recognised the face of Edward Hyde. He was dressed in clothes that were far too big for him, clothes of the doctor's size. The muscles of his face still moved, but life was quite gone; there was a broken bottle in his hand.

The two men turned to the desk. On it they found an envelope addressed to Mr Utterson. The lawyer opened it and several papers fell to the floor, including a new will from Dr Jekyll - but in place of the name of Edward Hyde, the lawyer read his own name.
'I don't understand,' said Utterson. 'Hyde has been here for days. He must have been angry to see my name instead of his, but he didn't destroy this paper.'
'Why don't you read that note, sir?' asked Poole.
'Because I'm afraid to,' replied the lawyer. And with that he fixed his eyes on the paper and read the note.

My dear Utterson,
When this comes into your hands, I shall have disappeared. I cannot be certain as to how that will happen, but my feelings tell me that the end is sure and must come soon. If you wish to hear more, turn to the story of,
Your ashamed and unhappy friend,
HENRY JEKYLL.

'We'd better say nothing about this,' said Utterson, putting all the papers in his pocket. 'If your master has run away or is dead, we may at least save his good name. I must go home and read these papers, but I shall be back before midnight, when we shall send for the police.'

When Utterson returned home, he read Henry Jekyll's full statement of the case.

I was born into a rich family and was gifted with excellent abilities; so I was certain, you might have thought, to become a respected and honourable man. But I began to lead a double life. I did experiments with a mixture of drugs that would change my body and mind and would reshape them in a new way.

The first time I drank the mixture I experienced terrible pain, and I lost height; but then I felt younger and happier. I also felt the desire to do evil. When I looked in the mirror, I saw for the first time the appearance of Mr Hyde. When I took the mixture again, I became Henry Jekyll once more. So now I had two identities; my original self; and a completely evil identity. This new identity was the clear expression of the lowest qualities of my soul.

I repeated the experiment many times and as Mr Hyde I did unthinkable crimes. Even now, I can hardly believe I did them. But the drugs began to have unpredictable effects. Once I went to bed as Dr Jekyll and woke up as Mr Hyde! My hands became bony and covered in hair. Things were getting out of control, and everyone was on my track; I was hunted, a known murderer, with a sure end on a hangman's rope.

I have been a prisoner in my own study, more often in the shape of Mr Hyde. The mixture of drugs doesn't seem to work anymore. I have become seriously weak and feverish in body and mind. Nobody has ever suffered in such a terrible way. I am now finishing this statement. It is probably the last time that Henry Jekyll can think his own thoughts or see his own face. I must hurry. If Hyde finds this statement, he will tear it to pieces. Half an hour from now, I know how Hyde will sit shaking and crying in my chair, or march endlessly up and down this room listening in terror for any sound of danger. Will Hyde be hanged on the hangman's rope? Or will he find the courage to take his own life?
I do not care. This is my true hour of death, and what follows concerns a person who is not myself. Here then, as I lay down the pen, I bring the life of that unhappy Henry Jekyll to an end.

Literature Spot 2

Four Love Poems

BACKGROUND

Alliteration: A technique where two or more words begin with the same sound, e.g. 'one white winter's day'.

Bathos: A technique which contrasts something very serious with something much less important for comical effect, e.g. 'In the accident she lost her husband, her children and her earrings.'

Cliché: An idea or expression that is very common or overused, e.g. 'There's no smoke without fire'.

Image: A picture created in words.

Irony: The amusing use of words which are clearly the opposite of what you mean *or* an event which has the opposite result of what you expect.

Metaphor: A kind of image where you compare one thing to another by saying it is the other thing, e.g. 'He searched the dark room of his mind for an idea'.

Rhyme: A technique where two words end with a similar sound, usually at the end of lines. Verses can have rhyme patterns or *schemes*, e.g. a four-line verse could have the rhyme scheme AABB, ABAB, ABCB, etc.

Simile: A kind of image where you say that one thing is similar to another, e.g. 'the dead trees were *like* bony hands' or 'his muscles were *as* hard *as* iron'.

Stanza or **Verse:** A group of lines which forms part of a poem.

Symbol: An object which represents something else, e.g. 'this ring is a symbol of our love'.

Theme: The subject of a piece of writing, e.g. love, war, jealousy.

Tone: The mood of a poem - imagine what tone of voice you would use if you read the poem, e.g. sad, joyful.

Before you start

1 Read the explanations of words in the background information and check you understand them. Do poets use similar techniques in your language?

Reading

2 Read the Strategies again in Lesson 10. Read the poems on the opposite page. Match the poems with these themes:

the first touch of two lovers, a lover leaving, a description of a lover, a lifelong love

3 Read each poem again and answer these questions.

Declaration of Intent

1 'I'll love you for eternity' is a romantic cliché. Find three more expressions of this kind.
2 What is normally reduced for 'good behaviour'?
3 What does 'such accessories' refer to?
4 What technique does the poet use to make the poem funny?
5 What is ironic about the last three lines?

Love Song for Alex

6 How old do you think the poet was when she wrote this? Give reasons.
7 Walker's husband was an interior decorator. What mention is there to this?
8 What images are used for passion?
9 What image is used to show how the past unites the poet and her lover?

I wish I could remember that first day

10 Why do you think the poet couldn't remember the meeting?
11 What metaphor does she use for the development of her love?
12 What simile is used to show that there is no sign or trace of something?

My mistress' eyes are nothing like the sun

13 How would you describe the tone of the poem?
14 What is the rhyming scheme of the poem?
15 What things are used to compare with the woman's appearance?
16 Why does the poet think that his love is special?

Reading and Listening

4 🎧 Read and listen to the poems. Which one do you prefer? Tell the class.

Declaration of Intent by Steve Turner

Steve Turner is a British poet, biographer and music journalist. He has published books of poetry for both adults and children. He has also written books about rock music and biographies of pop musicians.

She said she'd
love me for eternity,
but managed to reduce
it to eight months
for good behaviour.
She said we fitted
like a hand in a glove,
but then the hot
weather came and such
accessories weren't needed.
She said the future
was ours, but the deeds *
were made out in
her name.
She said I was
the only one who
understood completely,

and then she left me
and said she knew
that I'd understand completely.

* deeds – written agreements

Love Song for Alex by Margaret Walker

Margaret Walker (1915–1998) was an African American poet from Birmingham, Alabama.
Many of her poems are about the experiences and struggles of African Americans in the Deep South of the USA.

My monkey-wrench[1] man is my sweet patootie[2];
the lover of my life, my youth and age.
My heart belongs to him and to him only;
the children of my flesh are his and bear his rage
Now grown to years advancing through the dozens
the honeyed kiss, the lips of wine and fire
fade blissfully into the distant years of yonder[3]
but all my days of Happiness and wonder
are cradled in his arms and eyes entire[4].
They carry us under the waters of the world
out past the starposts[5] of a distant planet
And creeping through the seaweed[6] of the ocean
they tangle[7] us with ropes and yarn[8] of memories
where we have been together, you and I.

1 monkey-wrench – adjustable spanner
2 sweet patootie – (American) sweetheart, darling
3 yonder – the past
4 entire – completely
5 starposts – invented word: mixing star and outpost
6 seaweed – plants growing in the sea
7 tangle – to join
8 yarn – material to make rope

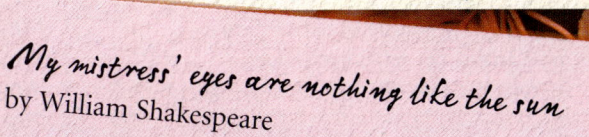

I wish I could remember that first day by Christina Rossetti

Christina Rossetti (1830–1874) was born in London. She was a prolific writer and poet and her most famous collection is 'Goblin Market and Other Poems' (1862). Her brother, Dante Gabriel, was a famous Pre-Raphaelite painter.

I wish I could remember that first day,
First hour, first moment of you meeting me,
If bright or dim the season, it might be
Summer or winter for aught[1] I can say;
So unrecorded did it slip away,
So blind was I to see and to foresee,
So dull to mark the budding[2] of my tree
That would not blossom[3] yet for many a May.
If only I could recollect it, such
A day of days! I let it come and go
As traceless[4] as thaw[5] of bygone[6] snow;
It seemed to mean so little, meant so much;
If only now I could recall that touch,
First touch of hand in hand - Did one but know!

1 aught – anything (poetic)
2 budding – to start growing leaves
3 blossom – to flower
4 traceless – without any sign
5 thaw – to melt
6 bygone – past

My mistress' eyes are nothing like the sun by William Shakespeare

William Shakespeare (1564–1616) is universally recognised as the greatest English writer. In his twenties he left his native Stratford upon Avon and moved to London where he became an actor. As well as writing over forty plays, Shakspeare wrote poetry (Sonnets, 1609) about the themes of love and friendship.

My mistress' eyes are nothing like the sun;
Coral is far more red than her lips' red;
If snow be white, why then her breasts are dun[1];
If hairs be wires, black wires grow on her head.
I have seen roses damask'd[2], red and white,
But no such roses see I in her cheeks;
And in some perfumes is there more delight
Than in the breath that from my mistress reeks[3].
I love to hear her speak, yet well I know
That music hath[4] a far more pleasing sound;
I grant[5] I never saw a goddess go;
My mistress, when she walks, treads on the ground:
And yet, by heaven, I think my love as rare
As any she belied[6] with false compare[7].

1 dun – dull brown colour
2 damask'd roses – an old variety of rose
3 reeks – smells
4 hath – has (16th century)
5 grant – to admit/confess
6 belied – failed to fulfill expectations
7 compare – comparison (16th century)

Literature Spot 3

BACKGROUND

Science fiction is a genre in which scientific knowledge is used as a basis for imaginative fiction. The 19th century French writer, Jules Verne, is often seen as the father of science fiction. He used his knowledge of engineering to write stories about trips to the moon or under the sea (*Journey to the Centre of the Earth* 1864). Later in the century, H.G. Wells explored the themes of time travel as well as space travel and wrote about an invasion from Mars (*The War of the Worlds* 1898). From the beginning of the 20th century, science fiction started to become popular and 'pulp' science fiction magazines sold widely. Serious authors also began to be interested in the genre, such as Aldous Huxley with his perceptive account of life in the future (*Brave New World* 1932). In the middle of the century a golden age for sci-fi began with outstanding writers such as the scientist Isaac Asimov, Arthur C. Clarke and Ray Bradbury. Their stories not only looked at life in the future but examined the possible destiny of the human race.

Ray Bradbury was born in Illinois in 1920. He began his career writing stories for sci-fi magazines in the 1940s. His most famous novels are *The Martian Chronicles*, which describes the colonisation of Mars by the Earth people, and *Fahrenheit 451* set in a future where the written word is forbidden.

Before you start

1 Read the background notes.

1 What is the difference between science fiction and other fiction?
2 Why do you think science fiction started to become popular in the early 20th century?
3 Which of the books mentioned would you most like to read? Why?

Reading and Listening

2 Read and listen to the story. Are these statements true or false?

1 Mr and Mrs K lived on Mars in a house near a red sea.
2 Mr K liked listening to old songs about Mars.
3 Martians were small with narrow yellow eyes.
4 Mrs K had a very long, strange dream.
5 She dreamt about a very large alien with blue eyes and brown skin.
6 The alien's spaceship looked quite strange to Mrs K.
7 Mrs K used telepathy to understand the alien.
8 Martian scientists said that life on Earth was possible.

3 Read the story again. Answer these questions.

1 Why were Mr and Mrs K not very happy?
2 Why did Mrs K look into the sky?
3 Why was Mr K irritated when his wife cried out in her dream?
4 How did Mr K react to her description of the man?
5 Why did Mr K think his wife had made up the man?
6 Why did Mrs K enjoy the dream?
7 How were Mr and Mrs K's reactions to the idea of alien life different?
8 Do you think it was a dream or did Mrs K really meet the man somehow?

What do you think happens next in the story?

Speaking

4 Work in pairs. List the differences mentioned in the story between Mars and Earth. Think of these things:

the houses, the people, the landscape, leisure activities, the food

Tell the class.

5 Work in pairs. Think of your own imaginary planet. Describe it to your partner.

MARTIAN CHRONICLES

They had a house of crystal pillars on the planet Mars by the edge of an empty sea, and every morning you could see Mrs K eating the golden fruits that grew from the crystal walls, or cleaning the house with handfuls of magnetic dust which, taking all dirt with it, blew away on the hot wind. Afternoons, when the fossil sea was warm and motionless, and the wine trees stood stiff in the yard, and the little Martian bone town was all enclosed, and no one drifted out their doors, you could see Mr K himself in his room, reading from a metal book with raised hieroglyphs over which he brushed his hand, as one might play a harp. And from the book, as his fingers stroked, a voice sang, a soft ancient voice, which told tales of when the sea was red steam on the shore and ancient men had carried clouds of metal insects and electric spiders into battle.

Mr and Mrs K had lived by the dead sea for twenty years and their ancestors had lived in the same house, which turned and followed the sun, flower-like, for ten centuries.

Mr and Mrs K were not old. They had the fair, brownish skin of the true Martian, the yellow coin eyes, the soft musical voices. Once they had liked painting pictures with chemical fire, swimming in the canals in the seasons when the wine trees filled them with green liquors, and talking into the dawn together by the blue phosphorous portraits in the speaking-room.

They were not happy now.

This morning Mrs K stood between the pillars, listening to the desert sands heat, melt into yellow wax, and seemingly run on the horizon.

Something great was going to happen.

She waited.

She watched the blue sky of Mars as if it might at any moment grip in on itself, contract, and expel a shining miracle down upon the sand.

Nothing happened.

Tired of waiting, she walked through the misting pillars. A gentle rain sprang from the fluted pillar-tops, cooling the scorching air, falling gently on her. On hot days it was like walking in a creek. The floors of the house glittered with cool streams. In the distance she heard her husband playing his book steadily, his fingers never tired of the old songs. Quietly she wished he might one day again spend as much time holding and touching her like a little harp as he did his incredible books.

But no. She shook her head, an imperceptible, forgiving shrug. Her eyelids closed softly down upon her golden eyes. Marriage made people old and familiar, while still young.

She lay back in a chair that moved to take her shape even as she moved. She closed her eyes tightly and nervously.

The dream occurred.

Her brown fingers trembled, came up, grasped at the air. A moment later she sat up, startled, gasping.

She glanced about swiftly, as if expecting someone there before her. She seemed disappointed; the space between the pillars was empty.

Her husband appeared in a triangular door. 'Did you call?' he asked irritably.

'No!' she cried.

'I thought I heard you cry out.'

'Did I? I was almost asleep and had a dream!'

'In the daytime? You don't often do that.'

'She sat as if struck in the face by the dream. 'How strange, how very strange,' she murmured. 'The dream.'

'Oh?' He evidently wished to return to his book.

'I dreamed about a man.'

'A man?'

'A tall man, six foot one inch tall.'

'How absurd; a giant, a misshapen giant.'

'Somehow' - she tried the words - 'he looked all right. In spite of being tall. And he had - oh, I know you'll think it silly - he had blue eyes!'

'Blue eyes! Gods!' cried Mr K. 'What'll you dream next? I suppose he had black hair?'

'How did you guess?' She was excited.

'I picked the most unlikely colour,' he replied coldly.

'Well black it was!' she cried. 'And he had a very white skin; oh, he was most unusual! He was dressed in a strange uniform and he came down out of the sky and spoke pleasantly to me.' She smiled.

'Out of the sky; what nonsense!'

'He came in a bright metal thing that glittered in the sun,' she remembered. She closed her eyes to shape it again. 'I dreamed there was the sky and something sparkled like a coin thrown into the air, and suddenly it grew large and fell down softly to land, a long silver craft, round and alien. And a door opened in the side of the silver object and this tall man stepped out.'

'If you worked harder you wouldn't have these silly dreams.'

'I rather enjoyed it,' she replied, lying back. 'I never suspected myself of such imagination. Black hair, blue eyes, and white skin! What a strange man, and yet - quite handsome.'

'Wishful thinking.'

'You're unkind. I didn't think him up on purpose; he just came in my mind while I drowsed. It wasn't like a dream. It was so unexpected and different. He looked at me and he said, "I've come from the third planet in my ship. My name is Nathaniel York."'

'A stupid name; it's no name at all,' objected the husband.

'Of course it's stupid, because it's a dream,' she explained softly. 'And he said, "This is the first trip across space. There are only two of us in our ship, myself and my friend Bert."'

'Another stupid name.'

'And he said, "We're from Earth; that's the name of our planet,"' continued Mrs K. 'That's what he said. "Earth." was the name he spoke. And he used another language. Somehow I understood him. With my mind. Telepathy, I suppose.'

Mr K turned away. She stopped him with a word 'Yll?' she called quietly. 'Do you ever wonder if - well, if there are people living on the third planet?'

'The third planet is incapable of supporting life,' stated the husband patiently. 'Our scientists have said there's far too much oxygen in their atmosphere.'

'But wouldn't it be fascinating if there were people? And they travelled through space in some sort of ship?'

'Really, Ylla, you know how I hate this emotional wailing. Let's get on with our work.'

Literature Spot 4

The Shepherd Andreas

BACKGROUND

There is a long tradition of travel writing in English, which dates back to the 14th century with Sir John Mandeville's *Travels*, an extraordinary mixture of fact and fantastic information about monsters and two-headed men. More serious was the collection by Richard Hakluyt of descriptions of the voyages made by English merchants and explorers in the 16th and early 17th century. In the 18th century, travel literature started to become a popular genre as great novelists like Henry Fielding and Laurence Sterne described their trips around Europe. In the following century, classic travel literature includes: the writings of the intrepid explorer Mary Kingsley describing her travels in West Africa; Charles Darwin's account of his trip around South America; the naturalist Henry Bates' description of his research in the Amazon. Among great travel writers of the 20th century were: Robert Byron who journeyed across Central Asia; Freya Stark who travelled widely in Arab countries; Bruce Chatwin whose travel books such as *In Patagonia* are a mixture of anthropology, philosophy and fiction. Famous contemporary travel writers include the Trinidadian novelist, V.S. Naipaul and the Americans, Paul Theroux and Bill Bryson whose books are major best-sellers.

Travel writing is now not only more popular than ever but is no longer regarded as a minor genre of literature. Good travel literature combines observation with imagination and can give profound insights into the human condition. However, as the great Doctor Johnson said: 'Books of travels will be good in proportion to what a man has previously in his mind; his knowing what to observe; his power of contrasting one mode of life with another. As the Spanish proverb says, 'He, who would bring home the wealth of the Indies, must carry the wealth of the Indies with him.'

Karen Connelly was born in Alberta in Canada. She has published award-winning travel books such as *Touch the Dragon: A Thai Journal* and *One Room in a Castle*. She is also the author of two works of poetry. When she is not travelling, Karen Connelly lives in Greece.

Before you start

1 Read the background notes and answer these questions.

1 Which of the travel writers mentioned would you most like to read about? Why?
2 Which two of the writers listed mixed fact and fiction?
3 When did travel literature first become popular?
4 What in Dr Johnson's opinion makes a good travel book?

Reading and Listening

2 Read and listen to the story. Order these events.

a) The writer gave the shepherd a cup of tea.
b) The shepherd started to talk louder.
c) The shepherd got a bit frustrated because she couldn't understand.
d) The writer made breakfast and went outside.
e) The shepherd tried to show that he wanted a cup of tea.
f) The writer asked the shepherd questions.
g) The shepherd used his cane to dismount from his donkey.
h) The shepherd started laughing a lot.
i) The shepherd and his donkey came into the garden.

3 Read the story again and answer these questions.

1 Why did the writer spill her tea?
2 Why did the shepherd use the cane to dismount?
3 What did the writer most notice about the islanders?
4 How did the shepherd finally explain what he wants?
5 How did the writer think you can learn a language?
6 Why did the shepherd laugh so much?

4 Match the objects with the writer's descriptions of them (a-f).

a cup of tea, a laugh, the sea, the land, a sound, the sky

a) like wide blue hands   b) bearish   c) cradled in my hands
d) lassoing the entire island   e) the curved and plummetting body
f) rumbles

Speaking

5 Work in pairs. Which of these things would you like to do? Why?

visit the Greek island, meet the islanders, live abroad for a while, write a travel book, learn another language (not English), know more words in English

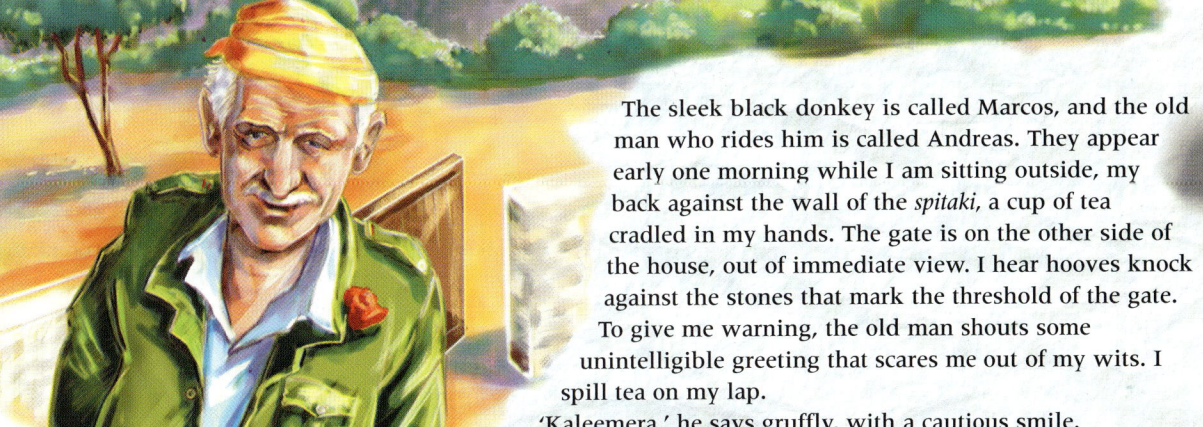

The sleek black donkey is called Marcos, and the old man who rides him is called Andreas. They appear early one morning while I am sitting outside, my back against the wall of the *spitaki*, a cup of tea cradled in my hands. The gate is on the other side of the house, out of immediate view. I hear hooves knock against the stones that mark the threshold of the gate. To give me warning, the old man shouts some unintelligible greeting that scares me out of my wits. I spill tea on my lap.

'Kaleemera,' he says gruffly, with a cautious smile.

'Kaleemera,' I return the greeting and reach for my dictionary.

He pulls his cane from its resting place in the ropes of the saddle, maneuvers Marcos to a stone, where he aims the cane, then slides off the donkey's back. His lower left leg and foot are deformed; the foot fits into a black boot cut open to accommodate its dimensions. How to describe Barba Andreas, the old shepherd? A yellow piece of cloth is wrapped around his head of white hair. He has a big white moustache, blue eyes, a dandy's flower stuck in the lapel of his green army jacket. Hands. What will I love most here, what will I dream about years later, to return me to this place? The hands of the islanders. Their thickness, their roughness, their ugliness. Nails broken below the quick. Scars. Missing fingertips and lines of dirt.

Barba Andreas names the plants for me, pointing with his cane and leaning down to pluck off the chamomile blooms. Sitting on a milk crate, he lifts his bad leg up to rest on a stone. I remain sitting against the house in the shade. We both take in the view before us: slender Marcos, eating my melon rinds and shifting in what is, effectively my front yard: poppies; olive trees; the curved and plummetting body of the land, its shapes of green, sage-green, yellow, almond; rose and purple and gray shadow. The sky opens over everything like wide blue hands. And all around us, lassoing the entire island, the sea.

A bearish sound comes from Barba Andreas' throat. As though bored with the view - how familiar it must be to him - he turns back to me and says something I don't understand. He points in my direction with his cane. Is he pointing to the low table between us? I look at the table. Is he pointing to my books on the table? I offer him a book, which he wisely refuses to touch. He pantomimes a motion, but I don't understand. Once more, he directly asks for something and pokes his finger against his chest. I don't understand. Finally, smiling but clearly frustrated, he grabs the tea-pot with one large hand, pours tea into the palm of the other, and raises it to his lips. 'Ena poteeri!' he cries, and bangs his cane on the ground, demanding a cup.

Embarrassed, I jump up and into the little house for another cup. I come out, pour tea, hand it to him. He waves away my apologies. He drinks the tea in one go. How many Greek words do I know now? How many? Not enough, never enough. To learn another language one must re-acquire the greedy hunger of a child. I want, I want, I want. Every desire begins and ends with a word. I want to ask a thousand questions. Where does the path behind the house lead and who lived here before and how do you make cheese and are the sheep in the neighboring field yours and what is this place, truly, and how do I go to the mountains behind the house? Because there is a gate closing off the field that leads to the mountains, and I am afraid to walk through it.

He understands my last, garbled question. 'How do you go to the mountains?' he parrots back to me, almost shouting. It is an international assumption that when people don't hear and understand our language, we think they can't hear at all. 'How do you go up to the mountains?' Now a slow laugh rumbles in his throat. 'Me ta podia!' he cries. Every line of his face proclaims laughter. He slaps his knees, guffawing.

How do you go to the mountains?

Me ta podia. With your *feet*.

Open the gate, go through it, close it behind you. And walk to the mountains.

spitaki – is the Greek word for a one-roomed shepherd's house

Literature Spot 5

No Crime in the Mountains

BACKGROUND

Raymond Chandler (1888-1959) was born in California and educated in England. After returning to the USA he went into business. Chandler only started writing detective novels in the 1930s when he was in his forties. His most famous novels are *The Big Sleep* (1939), *Farewell My Lovely* (1940) and *The Long Goodbye* (1954) but he also wrote other novels and short stories including *No Crime in the Mountains*. The work of Chandler and that of Dashiel Hammet helped to give crime fiction the status of 'serious' literature for the first time. Above all, Chandler had great powers of observation and he knew his subject well, the society of Southern California from the 1930s to the 1950s. Chandler's work also shows a total mastery of plot and his style is highly distinctive, full of humour and irony. Some of his books, such as *The Big Sleep*, were made into extremely successful Hollywood films.

Before you start

1 Read about Raymond Chandler. Have you ever read or would you like to read one of his books? Why or why not?

Listening and Reading

2 Listen and read the extracts from the story. Order these events.

a) Evans spoke to Mrs Lacey on the telephone.
b) He arrived in Puma Point and went to the hotel.
c) He drove round the lake and stopped.
d) He found the body of Mr Lacey under a tree.
e) He spoke to the girl in the phone office.
f) He smoked his pipe and watched the boats in the lake.
g) He had lunch and drove to the mountains.
h) A letter arrived at Evans' office from Mr Lacey.

3 Read the story again and choose the best answer to these questions.

1 How did Evans feel when he got the letter?
   a) worried   b) relieved   c) suspicious
2 How did he feel by the time he got to the hotel.
   a) hot and tired   b) hungry   c) nervous
3 What sort of a hotel was it?
   a) luxurious   b) basic   c) cheap
4 How did Mrs Lacey react to Evans?
   a) angrily   b) suspiciously   c) coldly
5 What was the girl in the phone office like?
   a) suspicious   b) friendly   c) bored
6 How did Evans feel when he was smoking his pipe?
   a) worried   b) relaxed   c) thoughtful
7 How did he find the body?
   a) by accident   b) by being observant   c) by looking under the tree
8 What did the dead man look like?
   a) kind   b) quite young   c) prosperous

4 Which of these adjectives would you use to describe the detective?

anxious, tough, observant, friendly, direct, decisive, independent, polite, ironic, weak

5 Find examples of Chandler's style in the text.

- his use of irony
- his use of metaphor and simile
- his detailed description
- his natural dialogues

6 Listen to the rest of the story and find out what happens in the end.

The letter came just before noon, special delivery, a dime-store envelope with the return address F.S. Lacey, Puma Point, California. Inside was a check for a hundred dollars, made out to cash and signed Frederick S. Lacy, and a sheet of plain white bond paper typed with a number of strikeovers. It said:

```
Mr John Evans,
Dear Sir,
    I have your name from Len Esterwald. My business is urgent and extremely confidential. I inclose a retainer. Please come to Puma Point Thursday afternoon or evening, if at all possible, register at the Indian Head Hotel, and call me at 2306.
```

There hadn't been any business in a week, but this made it a nice day. The bank on which the check was drawn was about six blocks away. I went over and cashed it, ate lunch, and got the car out and started off.

It was hot in the valley, hotter still in San Bernadino, and it was still hot at five thousand feet, fifteen miles up the high-gear road to Puma Lake. I had done forty of the fifty miles of curving twisting highway before it started to cool off, but it didn't really get cool until I reached the dam and started along the south shore of the lake past the piled-up granite boulders and the sprawled camps in the flats beyond. It was early evening when I reached Puma Point and I was as empty as a gutted fish.

The Indian Head Hotel was a brown building on a corner, opposite a dance hall. I registered, carried my suitcase upstairs and dropped it in a bleak, hard-looking room with an oval rug on the floor, a double bed in the corner, and nothing on the bare pine wall but a hardware-store calendar all curled up from the dry mountain summer. I washed my face and hands and went downstairs to eat ...

I gobbled down what they called the regular dinner, drank a brandy to sit on it, and went out ...

The phone office was a log cabin, and there was a booth in the corner with a coin-in-the-slot telephone. I shut myself inside and dropped my nickel and dialled 2306. A woman's voice answered.

I said: 'Is Mr Fred Lacey there?'

'Who is calling, please?'

'Evans is the name.'

'Mr Lacey is not here right now, Mr Evans. Is he expecting you?'

That gave her two questions to my one. I didn't like it. I said: 'Are you Mrs Lacey?'

'Yes. I am Mrs Lacey.' I thought her voice sounded taut and over-strung, but some voices are like that all the time.

'It's a business matter,' I said. 'When will he be back.'

'I don't know exactly. Sometime this evening, I suppose. What did you ...'

'Where is your cabin, Mrs Lacey?'

'It's ... it's on Ball Sage Point, about two miles west of the village. Are you calling from the village? Did you ...?'

'I'll call back in an hour, Mrs Lacey,' I said, and hung up. I stepped out of the booth. In the other corner of the room a dark girl in slacks was writing in some kind of account book at a little desk. She looked up and smiled and said: 'How do you like the mountains?'

I said: 'Fine.'

'It's very quiet up here,' she said. 'Very restful.'

'Yeah. Do you know anybody named Fred Lacey?'

'Lacey? Oh, yes, they just had a phone put in. They bought the Baldwin cabin. It was vacant for two years, and they just bought it. It's out at the end of Ball Sage Point, a big cabin on high ground, looking out over the lake. It has a marvelous view. Do you know Mr Lacey?'

'No,' I said, and went out of there. I walked back to the Indian Head and got into my car ...

I stopped the car on the tip of the point and walked over to a huge tree fallen with its roots twelve feet in the air. I sat down against it on the bone-dry ground and lit a pipe. It was peaceful and quiet and far from everything. On the far side of the lake a couple of speedboats played tag, but on my side there was nothing but silent water, very slowly getting dark in the mountain dusk. I wondered who the hell Fred Lacey was and what he wanted and why he didn't want to stay home or leave a message if his business was so urgent ...

At the end of half an hour I got up and dug a hole in the soft ground with my heel and knocked my pipe out and stamped down the dirt over the ashes. For no reason at all, I walked a few steps toward the lake, and that brought me to the end of the tree. So I saw the foot ...

The man was middle-aged, half bald, had a good coat of tan and a line mustache shaved up from the lip. His lips were thick, and his mouth, a little open as they usually are, showed big strong teeth. He had the kind of face that goes with plenty of food and not too much worry. His eyes were looking at the sky. I couldn't seem to meet them.

The left side of the green sport shirt was sodden with blood in a patch as big as a dinner plate. In the middle of the patch there might have been a scorched hole. I couldn't be sure. The light was getting a little tricky ...

There was twelve dollars in his wallet and some cards, but what interested me was the name on his photostat driver's license. I lit a match to make sure I read it right in the fading light.

The name on the license was Frederick Shield Lacey.

Pairwork / Answer Key

MODULE 2, LESSON 6, EXERCISE 8

Student A

Read the cues below and check vocabulary. Then, tell the joke to your partner.

- an old couple go into a café for a cup of tea; they sit down; a chimpanzee walks in
- the chimpanzee is wearing a suit and carrying a newspaper
- the chimpanzee sits down and orders a cup of tea and a cheese sandwich
- the chimpanzee finishes his tea and sandwich, pays and walks out
- the couple go to a waiter; the woman says 'I've never seen anything like that before!'
- the waiter replies 'Yes, very strange. He normally has a salad sandwich.'

MODULE 5, LESSON 13, EXERCISE 8, A SCIENCE QUIZ

Student A

Ask your partner these questions. The correct answer is underlined.

1. Who discovered the three laws of motion in the 17th century?
   a) Copernicus   b) <u>Newton</u>   c) Galileo
2. Who developed the periodic table of elements in chemistry?
   a) Mendel   b) <u>Mendeleyev</u>   c) Mendelssohn
3. Who discovered the practical uses of radio waves?
   a) Sony   b) <u>Marconi</u>   c) Hertz
4. Who discovered that electricity existed as a current?
   a) Ampere   b) <u>Volta</u>   c) Faraday
5. Who proposed the existence of the atom?
   a) Rutherford   b) Einstein   c) <u>Democritus</u>

Can you add a question of your own?

MODULE 5, LESSON 15, EXERCISE 4

Student A

A robot guard dog

- quite small (80 cm high / weight 25 kilos)
- made of metal (steel and aluminium)
- moves fast (moves at 40 kph on flat surfaces)
- uses wheels (ten small wheels at the bottom)
- goes up stairs (uses spring action like a kangaroo)
- recognises people and friends (can recognise people's voices)
- detects intruders to a house (uses 3 high-resolution cameras and noise sensors on its 'head')
- 'bites' intruders or burglars (uses two metallic claws to immobilise intruders)
- useful for guarding the home (cheaper and more reliable than a real guard dog; doesn't need to be fed)
- makes a loud noise (a loud bark or siren depending on options)
- if problems, calls for help (directly phones the police)
- is it intelligent? (not really – it relies on programming but cleverer than the average Rotweiler)

MODULE 10, LESSON 28, EXERCISE 1, A QUIZ

Answer Key: 1 b, 2 a, 3 b, 4 c, 5 b, 6 a, 7 c, 8 b, 9 a

MODULE 7, LESSON 21, EXERCISE 7

Student A

Use the Speaking Strategies on page 83 and take turns to be the tourist and the hotel receptionist. When you are the receptionist, refuse some of the requests politely. Think of other (more difficult) requests to make.

You are checking into a hotel. Prepare to ask for these things politely.

- a double room on the first floor
- a wake-up call at 7.30
- a full English breakfast in your room at 8.15
- a map of the city
- a taxi at 9.00

LANGUAGE AWARENESS 1

End of Story

After that, Holmes explained all the clues about the hat to Watson. Then Peterson came into the room carrying an enormous diamond which his wife had found inside the goose. Holmes realised that this was the famous diamond stolen from a countess when she was staying at a London hotel. Two hotel servants had been involved. One was the butler, James Ryder, and the other was John Horner, a plumber. Horner had been working in the countess's room when Ryder noticed that the diamond had been stolen. Since then, Horner had been in prison for several days. Sherlock Holmes decided to advertise for the goose and hat in the newspapers. That evening a man appeared; it was Baker. Baker did not know anything about the diamond but he told Holmes and Watson where he had bought the goose. They went there and saw a man, who turned out to be Ryder the hotel butler, asking about the goose. Holmes invited him back to his house and when Holmes mentioned the diamond Ryder confessed that he had stolen it. After Horner's arrest, Ryder had gone to his sister's house to hide the diamond. There had been some geese in the garden and Ryder had put the diamond into its mouth and then asked his sister for this goose for Christmas. Later, he had taken the goose away and killed it but there was no diamond as he had chosen the wrong goose! Holmes had enough proof to put Ryder into prison, but he decided to let the man go. In the end, Horner was released from prison and the diamond returned to the countess.

MODULE 1, LESSON 1

Background information about the texts in Lesson 1.

Anne Frank (1929–1945) Anne's Jewish family moved from Germany to Holland when Hitler came to power. Then in 1942 the Germans began interning Jews and the Franks went into hiding at the top of the house where Mr Frank had his office. They were helped by some Dutch friends and employees of Mr Frank. The entrance to their 'Secret Annexe' was hidden by a moving bookshelf. They were joined by another family with their son Peter. Anne was thirteen at the time and stayed there for over two years where she wrote her diary. In August 1944, they were found by the Germans. Anne and her family were deported to Auschwitz and then to Bergen-Belsen, where she died shortly before her 16th birthday.

Helen Keller (1880–1967) was deaf, blind and severely speech-impaired when she met her teacher Anne Sullivan. Sullivan taught her to communicate by finger-spelling words. Helen Keller learnt French, German and Latin and graduated from Radcliffe College in the USA. As an adult, Helen Keller wrote and lectured for the deaf and blind. Her autobiography *The Story of My Life* was published while she was at university.

MODULE 1, LESSON 2, EXERCISE 2

Answer Key: a – Text 2, b – Text 3, c – Text 1

MODULE 1, LESSON 2, EXERCISE 3

Handwriting analysis

connected letters = logical, rational
unconnected letters = not very cooperative, individualistic
break after 1st letter in a word = a good observer of people
large writing = ambitious, idealistic
writing of average size = conventional
small writing = accurate, a perfectionist
narrow writing = shy

(Information from the British Institute of Graphology)

MODULE 5, LESSON 15, EXERCISE 1

Answer Key

Computers and robots can do these things:

- robots and computers can work in factories;
- robots can play football (though not very well); every year a robot World Cup is held;
- computers can control cars and planes;
- computers can beat us at chess: the world champion Gary Kasparov was beaten by the computer *Deep Blue*.
- computers can compose music (see Exercise 4 in Lesson 15): a programme enabling computers to compose music, has been developed by the American composer, William Cope;
- computers can give us the news (see Exercise 2 in Lesson 15);
- computers can speak to us: computers can now simulate the sounds of human speech.

However, robots and computers <u>cannot</u> have a real conversation and do not have feelings (yet!).

MODULE 6, WARM-UP, EXERCISE 4

Check your answers to the questionnaire.

1 a) You probably aren't getting enough sleep.
1 b) Seven or eight hours per night is sufficient for most people.
1 c) You *are* a sleepy head, aren't you!

2 a) Once a day is not enough!
2 b) Once in the morning and once at night is probably OK.
2 c) Very good. Dentists recommend cleaning teeth after *every* meal.

3 a) You should take up some kind of sport!
3 b) Good – once a week is better than never!
3 c) Excellent! You must be very fit.

4 a) Well done! You probably save lots of money on dentist bills.
4 b) Well, every now and then is OK.
4 c) You should cut down!

5 a) Good. As they say – an apple a day keeps the doctor away!
5 b) Very good. Doctors recommend several pieces of fruit per day.
5 c) You really should try to eat more fresh fruit.

MODULE 6, LESSON 16, EXERCISE 2

All the statements are, unfortunately, true.

MODULE 6, CULTURE CORNER 3, EXERCISE 4, A QUIZ

Answer Key: 1 d, 2 c, 3 a, 4 e, 5 b

MODULE 8, CULTURE CORNER 4, EXERCISE 4, A MUSIC QUIZ

Answer Key:
1 Madonna – USA; 2 Eric Clapton – UK; 3 Robbie Williams – UK;
4 Britney Spears – USA; 5 Ricky Martin – Puerto Rico;
6 Enrique Iglesias – Spain; 7 Cher – USA;
8 George Michael – UK; 9 Laura Pausini – Italy;
10 Jon Bon Jovi – USA

MODULE 9, LESSON 25, EXERCISE 1

Answer Key:
1 Rome = 50 BC–150 AD (the imperial capital)
2 Manchester = 1760–1830 (the industrial revolution)
3 Paris = 1870–1910 (a revolution in painting)
4 Los Angeles = 1910–1950 (the golden age of Hollywood)
5 San Francisco = 1950–2000 (the information revolution)

MODULE 9, LESSON 25, EXERCISE 4

So what was the key to the creative outbursts of these cities? First of all, Athens, Florence and London were all important trading centres with surplus money to be spent on culture. They all acted as cultural magnets, attracting talented individuals from far and wide. Above all, they were not stable or conservative societies. All three were dynamic places living through major changes, bursting with new opportunities and new ideas.

Pairwork / Answer Key

MODULE 10, LESSON 28, EXERCISE 1, A QUIZ

Decide if the War Facts below refer to:
a) World War I (1914–18)
b) World War II (1939–45)
c) The Vietnam War (1954–75)

War Facts
1. The USA ended the war in the Far East by dropping two atomic bombs on Japan.
2. The main countries involved were: Britain, France and Russia against Germany, Austria, Hungary and Turkey.
3. The war began when Germany invaded Poland.
4. The country was divided into the communist North, supported by Russia and China, and the South, supported by the USA.
5. The main countries involved were: Britain, Russia and the USA against Germany, Italy and Japan.
6. Most of the battles were fought in Belgium and France.
7. The USA secretly bombed Cambodia during the war.
8. More civilians died than soldiers in this war, including 6 million Jews in concentration camps.
9. Poison gas was first used in this war.

Check your answers on page 134.

MODULE 10, LESSON 30, EXERCISE 2

Answer Key

Answers 'a' show you are assertive. You are self-confident and try to resolve conflict situations in a sensible and constructive way.

Answers 'b' show that you are very assertive but you probably react too aggressively to conflict situations.

Answers 'c' show you are not assertive. You perhaps lack self-confidence; look at the 'a' answers for some ideas on how to react to conflict situations.

MODULE 2, LESSON 6, EXERCISE 8

Student B

Read the cues below and check vocabulary. Then, tell the joke to your partner.

- scientists in a laboratory are testing the effects of cigarette smoke on rabbits
- two rabbits escape from the laboratory; have a great time in fields, eat lovely carrots and lettuce; they meet lots of rabbit friends
- one of the rabbits says 'I'm going back to the laboratory'
- the other rabbit says 'Why? Are you crazy?'
- the first rabbit says 'No, it's just that I really need a cigarette!'

MODULE 5, LESSON 13, EXERCISE 8, A SCIENCE QUIZ

Student B

Ask your partner these questions. The correct answer is underlined.

1. Who discovered the fundamental principles of genetics?
   a) Darwin   b) Lamark   c) <u>Mendel</u>
2. Who discovered that light is made up of a mixture of coloured light?
   a) Maxwell   b) Einstein   c) <u>Newton</u>
3. Who discovered the existence of radioactivity?
   a) <u>Bequerel</u>   b) Pierre Curie   c) Marie Curie
4. Who established the principles for naming and classifying plants?
   a) Lamarck   b) Darwin   c) <u>Linnaeus</u>
5. Who discovered that the Earth orbits the Sun?
   a) <u>Copernicus</u>   b) Newton   c) Galileo

Can you add a question of your own?

MODULE 5, LESSON 15, EXERCISE 4

Student B

A robot friend

- size is variable (you can choose three options: basketball player, normal, child-size)
- made of metal (looks like a traditional robot, with metal head, arms and legs)
- recognises its owner's moods (uses cameras and sensors to see facial expressions and body language)
- talks to people (has a choice of ten languages)
- talks about anything (list of options are supplied, e.g. sport, pop music, films)
- reacts to people (its conversation depends on the owner's mood)
- is a good listener (sympathetic and gives the advice its owner wants to hear)
- tells jokes to cheer people up (has 1,000 jokes programmed)
- does personalised homework (teachers can't tell the difference)
- does small domestic chores (e.g. makes your bed, takes the dog out)
- accompanies owner (enjoys the cinema, football matches, etc.)
- can lose to the owner at a variety of games (e.g. chess, draughts, Monopoly)
- is it intelligent? (probably more so than us)

MODULE 7, LESSON 21, EXERCISE 7

Student B

Use the Speaking Strategies on page 83 and take turns to be the tourist and the hotel receptionist. When you are the receptionist, refuse some of the requests politely. Think of other (more difficult) requests to make.

You are checking into a hotel. Prepare to ask for these things politely.

- a room with an en suite bathroom
- a table for twelve in the hotel restaurant at 8.30
- some stamps for postcards
- a morning newspaper with your breakfast
- information about museums

WRITING HELP

1 A Letter (page 12)

Layout

A Formal Letter (to a language school)

	Your address and the date
School's name and address	

Greeting
Dear Ms Dutton, (when you know the person's name)
Dear Sir / Madam, (when you don't know the person's name)

Paragraph 1: Introduction
Thank you for your letter of …
I am writing with reference to your letter of …
I would definitely like to go on the course.

Paragraph 2: Personal information
basic information about yourself and your family: where you live and who you live with, school you go to, your interests

Paragraph 3: Experience as learner
years studied, current level, exams passed, areas you have most problems with

Formal ending
I look forward to hearing from you soon.
Yours sincerely, (if you started your letter Dear Ms Dutton)
Yours faithfully, (if you started your letter Dear Sir / Madam)
Your signature
Print your name clearly.

An Informal Letter (to a pen friend / relative)

Greeting
Dear … , / Hi … , / Hi there!

Paragraphs 1/2/3
information about yourself, your family and your friends

Informal ending
That's all for now. / I hope to hear from you soon. /
Get in touch soon. / Look forward to hearing all about you. /
Write soon. / Give my regards to … / Please keep in touch.
All the best, / Yours, / With love, / Love, / Cheers,
Your name

Style

Requests
Formal style: _I would be grateful if you could_ write us a letter. _Could you please_ tell us about yourself?
Informal style: _Can you_ do me a favour? _It'd be great if you could_ …

Punctuation
Informal style:
- use of contractions – _I'm_ a cousin of yours.
- use of exclamation marks – Get in touch soon_!_

Grammar
Informal style: dropping of the subject in very informal correspondence (e.g. postcards, e-mails, very informal letters) – _(I) Don't_ know if you got my first message.

Vocabulary
Formal style: formal language – _teaching staff_ (= teachers) / _I enclose_ (= here is … with the letter)
Informal style:
- vague language – I'm _kind of_ interested … / What _sort of thing_ are you interested in?
- colloquial expressions – _our folks_ (= family) back in the _old country_ (= our country of origin)
- abbreviations – _info_ (= information), _grandad_ (= grandfather)

Linking words
Formal style: It is a small school. _However_, we have good facilities. _In addition_, we have an excellent teaching staff.
Informal style: It's a nice place to visit. _But_ it's expensive. / _Well_, how are you? / _So_, everyone's well here. / _Anyway_, I must be going. / She's getting on well _too_.

Useful Vocabulary

Family: members of the family; relatives (people in your family you don't live with, e.g. uncles, aunts, cousins); in-laws (family by marriage); stepmother, stepfather, stepbrother, stepsister (related not by birth but because your parent has remarried); ancestor (someone in your family who lived a long time ago)

Language school: class size (number of students in a class); excursions; general courses, exam courses, business English courses; facilities, e.g. language laboratory, self-access centre (a place where you can study on your own)

Free time: stay in; go out, go to a gig / concert, go clubbing, go to a club (a place to dance); go shopping; go for a jog; meet up with friends

Linking

Time: _When_ he arrived, there were very few people. / _After_ he arrived, some people came. / _After_ lunch we went out.

Addition: I am _also_ interested in music. / I am interested in music _too_. / _As well as_ that there are excursions to London. / There are excursions to London _as well_. / _As well as_ organising excursions to London we organise them to Oxford and Cambridge. / _In addition_, there are excursions to Oxford and Cambridge. / There is a self-access centre _plus_ a language laboratory.

Contrast: _Although_ the school is small, the atmosphere is friendly. / The school is small. _However_, the atmosphere is friendly. / _Despite_ being small, the school has good facilities.

Reason: Can you complete the test, _so that_ we can judge your level? / Bring an umbrella _in case_ it rains.

Cause: I'm late _because_ of the traffic. / _Because of that_, I arrived late.

Example: We organise activities _such as_ horse-riding.

Checking

Style: Have you used formal or informal style?
Have you used formal or informal words and expressions?
Have you used formal or informal greetings or endings?

Writing Help

2 A Personal Anecdote *(pages 22–23)*

Layout

> **1 Introduction**
> Introduce your anecdote.
> *Probably the worst day I have ever had was when I went to the zoo with my five-year-old nephew.*
> Set the scene – give information about what you were doing, who you were with, what had happened earlier.
> *We had left home very early to get to the zoo before the crowds. There we were at 8 o'clock in the morning waiting for the bus. I was carrying a bag with our packed lunches and Jack had his camera with him. It was a beautiful day, the sun was shining and the birds were singing.*

> **2 Beginning of the narrative**
> Describe what happened to you – what things started to go wrong.
> *As I was waiting for the bus, a lorry went past and splashed water all over me. Then …*

> **3 Development of the narrative**
> Write about what happened next – what else went wrong.
> *We finally got to the zoo at about ten. There was an enormous queue to get in and Jack started to get very bored.*

> **4 Development of the narrative**
> Add more things that happened to you.
> *I was taking a photo of one of the penguins, when I heard a splash. I looked round and saw that Jack had fallen into the pond. Luckily, just at that moment …*

> **5 Conclusion**
> Write how the story finished and how you and everyone else felt at the end.
> *In the end, the keeper took us to the office and we dried out Jack's clothes. He wasn't at all upset and thought it was all a great adventure, but I must admit that I had a real fright and I was worried about what my sister would think. However, when we finally got home, my sister saw the funny side and we all had a laugh about it.*

Style

A written personal anecdote has similarities with a spoken anecdote:
- it is told in the first person:
  The funniest thing that happened to me was when I tried to cross the river.
- very formal expressions are not used:
  ~~I expressed our concern to the teacher about the state of repair of the bus.~~
  I had a chat with the teacher and told her that we were worried that the bus was unsafe.

However, there are important differences between a written and a spoken anecdote:
- do not use vague language or as many contractions as in spoken language:
  ~~It was sort of dark and we hadn't got a clue where they'd gone.~~
  It was just beginning to get dark and we hadn't a clue where they had gone.
- use a variety of time linking expressions (see Linking); do not repeat linking expressions or use 'but' at the start of a sentence:
  ~~And so we got there late and it was already dark. Then we left the train and then started looking for her. But she must have left before us.~~
  We got there late so it was already dark. After leaving the train, we started looking for her but she must have already left.

Useful Vocabulary

Verbs: scream, shout, run into (something/somebody), clutch hold of (something/somebody), collide with (something/somebody), faint, get lost, get stuck, get into trouble, get out of trouble, take the wrong turning, fall down, keep (doing something)

Feelings:
afraid: to be scared stiff, to be really scared, to turn pale, to tremble/shake (violently)
happy: delighted, relieved, over the moon (very happy)
angry: annoyed, irritated, furious (very angry)
nervous: on edge, worried, anxious

Expressions:
*I had no idea how to …, I had not got / didn't have a clue what to do.
There was absolutely nothing I could do about it.
I tried to put up a fight but … / I did my best to …
It went totally out of control.
I had a nasty shock when …
I started to get the feeling that …
It was a real shame that …
I had a nasty shock when I saw who it was.
He was only kidding. / He was only pulling my leg.
They all burst out laughing.
The funniest thing about it was that …
To our relief, we found her sleeping peacefully …
Everything worked out all right in the end.*

Linking: Time Linkers

Time adverbials:
*I was standing there. <u>Suddenly</u>, I heard a noise.
I was standing there when <u>all of a sudden</u> I heard a noise.
I heard a strange noise outside. <u>Immediately</u>, I reached for the phone.
<u>In the end</u>, I got back home in the middle of the night.
<u>Eventually</u>, I got back home after a really long journey.
I saw my dad coming. <u>At last</u>, I started to feel a bit more relaxed.*

Conjunctions:
*<u>As soon as</u> we finished, we went outside and waited until he came.
<u>Just as</u> we were finishing, there was a terrible storm.
<u>When</u> we were finishing, there was a terrible storm.
It started <u>while</u> I was having lunch.
He arrived <u>just before</u> I got home.*

Prepositions:
*<u>Just after</u> lunch … / <u>Before</u> lunch …
<u>Following</u> the accident there was an investigation.* (formal)

Participles:
*<u>After</u> leaving home, I bought the newspaper.
<u>Before</u> leaving, I had a good breakfast.
<u>Having left</u> home, I bought a newspaper.*

Checking

Grammar: Have you included examples of different past tenses? Have you used tenses correctly?
Linking: Have you included linking words and expressions? Have you used participle linkers (e.g. *having done/after doing*)?
Content and style: How can you make your anecdote more interesting? How could you make it more dramatic? Have you included any dialogue?

Writing Help

3 A Description Of A Person And Place
(pages 36–37)

Layout

Paragraph 1
Introduce the person and the place.
Pamela is my cousin. She is in her mid thirties.

Paragraph 2
Give a general description of the house.
It's quite old and has got three spacious bedrooms.

Paragraph 3
Focus on one room in more detail.
It has got a very relaxed atmosphere and has a …

Paragraph 4
Give a final comment on the person.
She is very independent. She is one of the most likeable …

Style
For this type of composition, you should write in a neutral style. Below are examples of different styles.
Formal style: *The house, with numerous rooms and an extensive garden, is situated in the country. The spacious living room is ideal for entertaining guests.*
Neutral style: *She has just moved into a big house in the country with a huge garden. It's such a big house that she has lots of room for parties.*
Colloquial style: *Her new house is massive with a great big garden and loads of room for parties.*

Useful Vocabulary
Personality: → Lexicon, page 151
House features: armchair, bookshelf, carpet, clock, coffee table, curtains, cushions, fireplace, lamp, lampshade, mantelpiece, mirror, painting, rug, sideboard, sofa, stove, tiles
Describing a place/object: cluttered (with), comfortable, cosy, covered (with), enormous, fair-sized, huge, marvellous, massive, old-fashioned, relaxing, spacious, tasteless, warm, wooden

Linking
Result: *She is so untidy that she cannot find her computer mouse.* (so + adjective + 'that' clause)
It has got such lovely views of the countryside that it is a lovely place to be in. (such + adjective + noun + 'that' clause)
It is too big for one person to live in. (too + adjective + 'to' infinitive)
The kitchen is big enough to eat in. (adjective + enough + 'to' infinitive)
Comparison: *It is not as big as other rooms.*
The living room is a bit smaller.
It is a lot bigger than her previous house.
One of her biggest hobbies is gardening.
Giving examples: *Pamela writes for magazines, such as Vogue.*
She likes Romantic composers like Chopin, Brahms and Liszt.
She is reckless, particularly with her money!
She is sociable. For example, she often invites people round.

Checking
Layout: Have you followed the paragraph plans?
Linking: Have you included linking words and expressions?
Useful vocabulary: Have you included examples of behaviour to illustrate the personality adjectives?

4 A Film Review (pages 46–47)

Layout

Paragraph 1
Give some basic information about the film.
'Dances With Wolves' won an Oscar in 1990. It was directed by Kevin Costner.

Paragraph 2
Give a brief summary of the plot.
He is sent by the army to live on the edge of Indian territory.

Paragraph 3
Give your opinions – good and bad things about the film.
The film is very realistic in the way it shows us the everyday life of the Indians.

Paragraph 4
Conclusion and recommendation.
It is a historical film with an obvious message. It speaks to people of all ages.

Style
Most of your review should be written using present tenses:
It is set in the nineteenth century.
One day he meets an Indian.
You should aim for a neutral style, not too formal and not too colloquial.
Despite being very long, there isn't a dull moment. (neutral style)

Useful Vocabulary
It is set in the 1920s / in the sixteenth century / during the French Revolution.
It is based on a story/play/book by …
The special effects are impressive/disappointing.
The scenery is often breathtaking with wonderful photography.
The dialogue is often excellent/weak.
X plays the part of … / X is magnificent/unconvincing in the role of …

Linking
Summarising the plot:
One day, Costner finds himself being watched by …
After that, the plot begins to get complicated.
Eventually, he manages to convince the chief he is not dangerous.
In the end, they move north to Canada.
Giving examples:
There are some sad moments, especially when …
The director pays great attention to details, such as the authentic costumes.
Contrasting:
Despite being very long, there isn't a dull moment.
I'd recommend the film for everyone, although some scenes are quite violent.
Adding points:
Their family life is very realistic. The hunting scenes are also very convincing.
The scenery is beautiful. Moreover, the background music is perfect.
Concluding:
All things considered, this is a real masterpiece.

Checking
Layout: Have you followed the suggestions for paragraphs?
Linking: Have you included a variety of linking words?

5 An Article (pages 60–61)

Layout

Paragraph 1: Introduction
Introduce the topic. Say why it is important or interesting.
Since earliest times, people have always enjoyed dancing. Dancing has formed an important part of social and religious events.

Paragraph 2: Background or history
Provide some background about when it started and major developments up to now.
The folk dances of the middle ages developed into classical ballet in the eighteenth century.

Paragraph 3: Now
Say what is happening at the moment? Who is the best?
*The best dancers today are probably …
Many modern ballets do not tell a story.*

Paragraph 4: The future
Say how things will develop in the future.
In my opinion, there will be a return to more traditional ballet. The suggestion that one day robots will dance is ridiculous. They could never …

Paragraph 5: Conclusion
Summarise the main points and say again why you think your subject will continue to be important.
*To sum up, ballet has its roots in …
As long as people feel the need to dance, there will be a place for ballet.*

Style

Articles in English newspapers vary in style considerably, from tabloids to quality newspapers. However, the journalistic style focussed on here is fairly formal and has the following features:
- the use of formal linking expressions:
  <u>Nevertheless</u>, space probes continued to be sent.
  <u>In conclusion</u>, space exploration …
- the use of time adverbials:
  By the beginning of the century, … / After this, … / Recently, … / Later in the century, …
- the use of formal vocabulary and phrases:
  the age of space exploration / culminating in the moon landing
- the use of formal idiomatic expressions:
  We have <u>left our mark</u>. / There has been <u>a burst of interest</u> in … / Space travel is still <u>in its infancy</u>.
- the use of passive structures (see Module 4, Lesson 11):
  … all of Planet Earth <u>has been visited, photoed, described, mapped</u> / space probes continued <u>to be sent out</u> … / the space station <u>is now being built</u> …

Useful Vocabulary

Writing about origins:
Since earliest times, … / Ballet has its roots back in … / The age of ballet began in … / The history of ballet goes back to … / The first performance of modern ballet took place in … / Over … years ago, …

Writing about the present:
Recently, there has been renewed interest in … / Recent developments in the field include … / Other exciting developments have been … / One of the most ground-breaking … / State of the art technology has been used … / Cutting edge techniques have been introduced …

Writing about the future:
The outlook is bright. / The outlook is gloomy. / The future looks rosy. / The future looks grim. / Who knows what will happen in the future, but … / Many experts predict that … / Some forecasts predict … / The field of … has enormous potential / The sky's the limit.

Linking

Purpose:
The new probe is <u>for</u> looking at the climate of the planet. (*for* + '-ing')
The new probe has been developed <u>to</u> examine the climate of the planet. (*to* + infinitive)
The new probe has been developed <u>in order to</u> examine the climate of the planet. (*in order to* + infinitive)
NASA has launched the new probe <u>so that</u> they can examine the climate of the planet. (*so that* + modal verb)
NASA has launched the probe <u>so as to</u> examine the climate of the new planet. (*so as to* + infinitive)
NASA has launched the probe <u>in order that</u> they might examine the climate of the planet. (*in order that* + modal verb)
NASA has changed the launching procedures <u>so as not to</u> use so much energy. (*so as not to* + infinitive)

Reason:
There were a lot of accidents <u>as a result</u> of the rain.
There were a lot of accidents <u>because of</u> the heavy rain.
There were a lot of accidents <u>because</u> it had rained heavily.
There were a lot of accidents <u>due to</u> the heavy rain.
There were a lot of accidents <u>caused by</u> the heavy rain.
Take an umbrella <u>in case</u> it rains.

Checking

Layout: Have you written clear paragraphs? Is there any information that you can add?
Style: Check your article for style. Make sure you have not used any informal vocabulary or expressions.
Grammar and useful vocabulary: Check your work again for grammar or spelling mistakes.

6 A Discursive Essay (1)
(pages 70–71)

Layout

1 Introduction
A short paragraph to introduce the topic. Give some background. This may be historical or personal.
Tobacco was introduced to Europe after the discovery of America.
My parents smoke and they have both tried to give up many times.

Note that if you are 'for' something, put the arguments 'against' first.
If you are 'against' something, put the arguments 'for' first.

2 A list of arguments 'for'
Choose two or three main points. Give examples where possible.
Firstly, it costs a lot of money to treat smokers who get diseases, such as heart disease or lung cancer. Secondly, ...

3 A list of arguments 'against'
Choose two or three main points. Back up your arguments with examples.
On the other hand, if they banned smoking, the government would lose a lot of money from taxes on cigarettes.

4 Conclusion
Give your own personal opinion about the topic.
In my opinion, ...
All things considered, I believe that ...

Style

Most essays are written in a formal or neutral style:
- use formal linkers for listing arguments 'for' and 'against' the title:
  A smoke-filled room is also bad for non-smokers who have to breathe in the smoke. Moreover, the smell of smoke ... / Furthermore, people who smoke ... / Finally, ...
- use formal vocabulary and phrases:
  ~~Cigarette smoke stinks the place out.~~ (too colloquial)
  It is unpleasant to be in a smoke-filled room.
  ~~Some people smoke like a chimney.~~ (too colloquial)
  Some people chain-smoke.
- use passives when appropriate (see also Module 4):
  ~~They introduced tobacco to Europe after they discovered America.~~
  Tobacco was introduced to Europe after the discovery of America.

Useful Vocabulary

Adjectives: addictive, anti-social, dangerous, dirty, glamorous, unhealthy
Nouns: ashtray, bronchitis, cigarette, heart disease, lung cancer, nicotine, no-smoking areas, public places, tobacco
Issues: cost of health treatment, dangers in pregnancy, individual freedom of choice, passive smoking, smell on clothing and furniture, sports sponsors, starting fires, tax revenue

Linking: Contrast linkers

Although/Even though they know the dangers, many people still smoke. (Although/Even though + clause, + main clause)
* Note: ~~Even although~~

Despite/In spite of knowing the dangers, many people still smoke. (Despite/In spite of + '-ing', + main clause)
Despite/In spite of the dangers, many people still smoke. (Despite/In spite of + noun, + main clause)
Despite the fact that / In spite of the fact that they know the dangers, many people still smoke. (Despite the fact that / In spite of the fact that + clause, + main clause)

'However' and 'On the other hand' are used to begin a new sentence that contrasts what came before.
Many people know the dangers of cigarettes. However, they still smoke.
Many people know the dangers of cigarettes. On the other hand, they still smoke.

'Whereas' is used to contrast two examples which are closely linked.
My parents both smoke, whereas none of their children does.
You can't smoke in hospitals, whereas you can smoke in other public places, such as ...
Some people spend all their money on cigarettes, whereas I prefer to spend my money on CDs.

Checking

Layout: How well does your essay flow? Look at the paragraphs again and check the structure of your argument.
Style: Have you used words or expressions that are too colloquial? If so, try to express the same ideas in a more formal way.
Linkers: Have you used linkers and linking expressions? Can you add any linkers to join sentences or link ideas?
Grammar and spelling: Check your essay for mistakes of grammar and spelling.

Writing Help

7 A Formal Letter *(pages 84–85)*

Layout and Style

> **Your address and the date**
> 17 Orchard Rise,
> London, NW12.
> January 15, 2002.

> **Greeting**
> *Dear Mrs Smith,* (if you know the person's name)
> *Dear Sir / Madam,* (if you don't know the person's name)

> **Paragraph 1**
> Give your reason for writing the letter. Say where you saw the advertisement. Give some information about you and other people interested in the holiday.
> *I am writing to ask for more information about the 'Amazonian Adventure' holiday which I saw advertised in The Mirror. My sister and I are both university students. We are interested in the holiday, but I would like some more details.*

> Divide your queries about the holiday into two or three paragraphs, e.g. conditions on holiday, health and safety, price.

> **Paragraph 2**
> *Firstly, I would like to know more about the sort of conditions on the holiday. Could you tell me more about the accommodation provided …*

> **Paragraph 3**
> *Secondly, I am slightly worried as I have never been on this sort of holiday before. Could you please send me information about the diseases and health risks in the Amazon area? I would also be grateful if you could give me information about health and accident insurance.*

> **Paragraph 4**
> *Thirdly, you say that the price includes everything except certain extras. Could you possibly give me details about what extras there might be?*

> **Formal ending**
> Most formal letters end with this sentence. Learn it!
> *I look forward to hearing from you.*

> **Signing off**
> *Yours sincerely,* (if your letter starts with *Dear Mrs Smith*)
> *Yours faithfully,* (if your letter starts with *Dear Sir / Madam*)
> Sign your name and print it clearly.
> *R. S. Wilson*
> R.S. WILSON (MS)

Style

Formal written requests for information:
<u>I would be grateful if you could</u> give me more information about the accommodation.
<u>Could you please</u> send me information about the accommodation?
<u>Could you possibly</u> tell me what …
<u>I wonder whether you could possibly</u> send me details about health insurance.
You mention the need for vaccinations. <u>Does this mean that</u> you organise them?

Stating preferences:
<u>I would prefer to</u> have a single room, <u>if possible</u>.
<u>I would also like to</u> stay on for another two days, <u>if that is at all possible</u>.

Useful Vocabulary

Reservations:
I would like to reserve a place / to make a reservation / to confirm a reservation / to cancel a reservation / make a group booking

Price:
What is included in the price? / Do you offer discounts for groups? / Do you give reductions for students? / Are there any special offers?

Accommodation:
What sort of accommodation do you provide?
What kind of facilities has the hotel got?
Types of accommodation: *cabin, campsite, tent, hotel rooms (single/double room, suite), self-catering flat*

Food:
What is the local food like? / Is the water drinkable? / Do you offer full or half board? / Are there any facilities for self-catering?

Transport:
Kinds of transport: *balloon, boat, camel, canoe, cruise, excursion, tour, transport/shuttle service to and from the airport, trek, trip*

Baggage / Luggage:
What is the weight limit? How much does excess baggage cost?
Kinds of baggage/luggage: *backpack, holdall, overnight bag, rucksack, suitcase, pack*

Clothes:
anorak, diving suit, swimsuit, trainers, walking boots, waterproof jacket

Linking

Conditions:
It is not clear <u>if</u>/<u>whether</u> your company only arranges flights from London.
I would like to reserve a room, <u>as long as</u>/<u>provided that</u> it has a modern shower and toilet facilities.
I would prefer not to share a cabin <u>unless</u>/<u>except if</u> I have to.

Listing:
<u>Firstly</u>, I would like to … / <u>Secondly</u>, could you … /
<u>Thirdly</u>, I would be … / <u>Finally</u>, I would like to …
<u>In addition to that</u>, could you …
<u>Another query</u> I have is about …
<u>Something else</u> I would like to ask about is transport from the airport.

Checking

Style: Check your letter for style, e.g. starting, finishing the letter, polite requests.
Grammar: Check whether all your questions are grammatically correct.

8 A Report (pages 94–95)

Layout

Heading
Subject:
Date:

1 Aim of the report
Introduce the report with your aim and background information.
The aim of this report is to ...
This report aims to ...

2 Negative comments
List all the negative findings.
There are several disappointing facts and figures.
a) There are ...
b) Only twenty percent of women ...

3 Positive comments
List any positive findings.
On the other hand, there were some encouraging things.
a) Some women ...
b) The majority of women ...

4 Conclusion and recommendations
Write a simple conclusion and make a couple of recommendations.
To sum up, most women in the world are ...
Governments should ...
People need to ...

Style

A report is normally written in a formal style:
- avoid giving personal opinions:
  ~~I think women are treated unfairly.~~ (too personal)
  This suggests women are treated unfairly. (sounds more objective)
- use formal linking words and expressions:
  ~~If you look at the figures, lots of animals are in danger of extinction.~~ (too informal)
  According to recent figures, many animals are in danger of extinction. (more formal)

Useful Vocabulary

General: developed countries, developing countries (the Third World), figures, majority, percent, politicians, poverty, statistics, successful, victims
Women: discrimination, to earn, equality of opportunity, executive positions, housework, job opportunities, qualifications, underpaid, unpaid work, wages
Environment: crime, noise, pollution, traffic jams, stress
Global warming: burning of fossil fuels, carbon emissions, floods, greenhouse effect, harmful gases, hurricanes, melting of the ice caps, rising water levels
Disasters: aid programmes, avalanches, cyclones, droughts, earthquakes, floods, forest fires, hurricanes, landslides, volcanic eruptions, windstorms
Animals: deforestation, elephants, endangered species, natural habitats, pandas, rhinos, tigers
Rich and poor: illiteracy, qualifications, GNP (gross national product), poverty, Third World debt, vicious circle, wealth
Refugees and immigration: civil war, homeless, neighbouring countries, refugee camps, war

Linking

Listing points:
There are _also_ problems caused by wars.
Furthermore, there are the problems caused by wars.
In addition, there are the problems caused by wars.
Moreover, there are the problems caused by wars.

Contrasting points:
However, things have improved recently.
On the other hand, things have improved recently.
Although these figures are depressing, things have improved recently.
Despite these depressing figures, things have improved recently.

Giving examples:
For example, the US government has recently decided to ...
In this way, they hope to ...
They have introduced things _such as_ ...
This is bad, _particularly/especially_ in the area of ...

Showing effects:
As a result of this, people now expect ...
What this means is people now expect ...

Concluding:
To sum up, the situation is ...
All things considered, there seems to be ...

Checking

Layout: Have you followed the layout above? Are all your points clearly lettered and numbered?
Linking: Have you used a selection of linking words and expressions?
Content and style: Have you included a couple of recommendations in the conclusion?

Writing Help

9 A Discursive Essay (2) *(pages 108–109)*

Layout

> **1 Introduction**
> Introduce the topic. Give some background about the situation in your country/area. Then mention the possible reasons for the situation.
> *Crime is one of the most important issues …*
> *In the last few years, crime has been going up/down.*
> *The most common crimes are …*
> *The most worrying trend is the increase in …*
> *One of the reasons for this is possibly the fact that unemployment has risen …*
> *Another reason is that …*

Note that if you are 'for' something, put the arguments 'against' first.
If you are 'against' something, put the arguments 'for' first.

> **2 A list of arguments 'for'**
> Express the attitudes and reasons to support this point of view. Provide examples and facts where possible.
> (see Style below)

> **3 A list of arguments 'against'**
> Express the attitudes and reasons to support this point of view. Provide examples and facts where possible.
> (see Style below)

> **4 Conclusion**
> Finally, give your own personal opinion about the topic.
> *In my opinion, … / All things considered, I believe that …*

Style

In a discursive essay it is important to list the points of view of both sides of an argument as objectively as possible. Only in the conclusion can you express your own point of view. Notice the use of report structures (e.g. *feel that*), passives and formal linkers (e.g. *moreover, furthermore*) in the sentences below.

Listing arguments:
Many people feel that harder sentences should be brought back.
The American system of 'three strikes and out' *has supporters* in Britain.
Moreover, some people say that conditions in prisons are too soft.
There are arguments for the restoration of the death penalty.
The wishes of victims' family and friends *possibly need to be taken into account*.
There are arguments against harder sentences and capital punishment.
One of the arguments against longer prison sentence *is that* the prisons are already full.
Other people disagree and think that prisons should reform offenders.
It is strongly felt by many people that capital punishment is the equivalent of judicial murder.
Others point to the possibility of judicial errors and the risks of executing innocent people.
Furthermore, the death penalty *is seen as* savage and an affront to human dignity.

Giving reasons, examples and facts:
Some people think that *one of the benefits of* harder sentences *would be to* keep more dangerous criminals off the street.
Another advantage would be to give people a greater feeling of personal security.
This would be the best way of reducing crime caused by a small group of professional criminals.

For example, many crimes are committed by people leaving prison.
Other people feel that *there would be many disadvantages to giving* harder sentences, *because there would be* less chance of integrating prisoners into society afterwards.
Research *has shown that* …
Describing statistics and figures: → Lexicon 9, page 155

Useful Vocabulary

Crime and punishment (also see Lexicon 9, page 155):
crimes: *burglary – burglar, drug dealing – drug dealer, mugging – mugger, murder – murderer, rape – rapist, shoplifting – shoplifter; to commit a crime, to be arrested, to be sentenced, to be given a soft/hard sentence, to be locked up, to be let off with a fine, to be let out of prison, to deter young people, to take into account the wishes of the victims, to restore (bring back) capital punishment, to commit judicial murder*
the law: *the courts, the judges, the judicial system / the legal system, the law, judicial mistakes*

Linking

Cause / Result:
The consumption of drugs has gone up. *Consequently*, there has been an increase in violent crime.
The amount of violent crime has gone up *due to* an increase in consumption of drugs.
The number of cases of violent crime has increased *as a result of* the rising consumption of drugs.
The consumption of drugs has risen. *Because of this*, there has been an increase in violent crime.
Because of the rise in consumption of drugs, there has been an increase in violent crime.
The increase in violent crime is *just because of* the rising consumption of drugs.
So much money has been spent on prisons that they are now like luxury hotels.

Reason:
We need to reform prisoners *so that* they can go back into society.
We need to reform prisoners *in order to* help them go back into society.

as / like:
It was a very interesting article *as* it was about the arrest of a group of drug dealers. (*as* = because)
My father *works as* a prison officer. (works as = is)
Capital punishment is *like* any other kind of murder. (like = similar to)
Because of his record he was treated *as* a dangerous criminal. (*as* = in the same way as)
It is due to social problems, *like* poverty and unemployment. (*like* = for example)
It is due to social problems *such as* poverty and unemployment. (*such as* = for example)
It is not *as* easy *as* people think. (comparison)

Checking

Layout: How well does your essay flow? Use the paragraph diagram above to check the structure of your argument.
Linking: Have you used linking expressions? Can you add any linking words to join sentences or link ideas?
Style: Check the style of the essay. Make sure you have only put personal opinions in your conclusion.
Grammar and spelling: Check your essay for mistakes of grammar, vocabulary and spelling.

Writing Help

10 A Letter Of Complaint
(pages 118–119)

Layout

Your address and the date
Write your address with correct punctuation. Do not write your name here.
24 Market Street,
Middleton,
Manchester, M24 6HD.

June 16, 2003.

The company's name and address
Computer World,
17 Tower Road,
London, SW12.

Greeting
Dear Mr Scott, (if you know the person's name)
Dear Sir / Madam, (if you don't know the person's name)

1 Introduction
Give your reason for writing and specific information about the product or service, including where and when you bought it.
I am writing to you about ... which I bought from ... on ...
I enclose copies of the guarantee and the receipt.

2 Reasons for the complaint
Write one or two paragraphs saying:
a) why the advertising for the product was misleading,
In your advert you claim that the watch is waterproof. /
The advert gave the impression that the jacket would last a lifetime.
b) what went wrong with the product.
However, the first time I went swimming, the watch stopped working. /
However, after only one wash, the colour had faded.

3 Reactions to your complaint
Say what happened when you took the product back or complained about it the first time.
When I took the ... back to the shop, the assistant said it was my fault and I hadn't read the instructions carefully.

4 Your demands
Say clearly what you want the company to do. State further action that you will take if your demands are not met.
I would like you to refund my money.
Unless I receive a satisfactory reply, I will write to the Consumer Association.

5 Formal ending
The most common ending for a formal letter is:
I look forward to hearing from you.

Signing off
Yours sincerely, (if your letter starts with *Dear Mr Scott*)
Yours faithfully, (if your letter starts with *Dear Sir / Madam*)
Sign your name and print it clearly.
P. Lowe
P. LOWE (MR)

Style
Write a letter in a formal style:
- do not use contractions:
  ~~I'm writing to complain about~~ ...
  I am writing to complain about ...
- use formal linking words:
  Moreover, the picture was not clear.
  However, the first time I used it ...

Useful Vocabulary
Products: *guarantee, receipt, serial number, date of purchase*
Criticisms: *arrived late, poor quality, poor service, poor workmanship, rude employees, it was so ... that I ... / it was not ... enough / it was too ...*
Demands: *pay compensation, refund money, replace the product*
Threats: *go to court, go to the Consumer Association, take legal action, write a letters to the local newspaper*

Linking
He spoke to me <u>as if</u>/<u>as though</u> I knew nothing about it.
<u>However</u>, it didn't work.
<u>Despite</u> following the instructions, it didn't work.
<u>Although</u> I followed the instructions, it didn't work.
<u>Not only</u> did it lose time, <u>but also</u> the alarm didn't work.
<u>As well as</u> the zip breaking, the heel fell off!
<u>Just as</u>/<u>As soon as</u>/<u>When</u> I switched it on, it made a funny noise.
<u>Unless</u> you refund my money, I will take legal action.

Checking
Style: Check your letter for style. Make sure that it is not too informal or does not sound too aggressive.
Linking: Have you used linking expressions? Can you add any linking words to join sentences or link ideas?
Grammar and spelling: Check your essay for mistakes of grammar, vocabulary and spelling.
Check this:
I look forward to hearing from you.
~~I look forward to hear from you.~~

Grammar Summary

1 Tenses (pages 8–9)

Present Simple
We use the Present Simple to talk about:
- general truths and rules: Most bears **hibernate** in winter.
- routines and habits: **Do** you **swim** every weekend?
- permanent situations and states: We **live** in Gilbert Street.
- future facts: The train **leaves** in twenty minutes.

Present Continuous
We use the Present Continuous to:
- talk about activities in progress at the time of speaking:
  Where's Joe? He's **having** a shower.
- talk about temporary activities and habits:
  I'm **looking** after Peter's dog while he's away.
- talk about personal arrangements for the future:
  We're **flying** back on Saturday.
- show irritation about a person's bad habit:
  You **are** always **loosing** the keys.

Present Perfect
We use the Present Perfect to talk about:
- past events and activities with consequences in the present:
  Oh no! The house **has been burgled**. Phone the police.
- single or repeated events in the past when it doesn't matter when they happened:
  Have you ever **tried** Thai food?
- situations that started in the past and continue up till now:
  She's **been** ill since Thursday.

Present Perfect Continuous
We use the Present Perfect Continuous to talk about:
- continuous or repeated activities that started in the past and aren't finished:
  I've **been doing** a lot of overtime recently to save money for a holiday.
- continuous or repeated activities from the recent past which have consequences in the present:
  You look exhausted!
  What **have** you **been doing**?

Past Simple
We use the Past Simple to talk about single or repeated events in the past when we know when they happened:
I **bought** some nice things at the market at the weekend.
I **ate** a lot of chocolate when I was a student.

Past Continuous
We use the Past Continuous to talk about:
- activities that continued for some time in the past, especially to show a longer activity that was interrupted by a shorter one: I **was making** dinner when the phone rang.
- activities that form the background, especially to set a scene:
  We **were walking** along the beach chatting to one another.
  Suddenly, we heard a call for help.

Past Perfect
We use the Past Perfect to talk about events or situations in the past which happened before other past events:
When we got home, Jane **had** already **left** so we didn't manage to say goodbye to her.

will
We use *will* + infinitive without 'to' when we want to make:
- a decision at the moment of speaking: I'**ll go** there at once.
- a prediction based on our opinions or beliefs:
  We'**ll** probably **get** home after midnight.
- a request: **Will** you **wait** for me?

to be going to
We use *to be going to* + infinitive without 'to' to express:
- an intention: I'm **going to do** an English summer course.
- a prediction based on something we can observe:
  It's **going to be** hot today.

2 Past Tenses (pages 18–19)

Apart from the Past Simple, Past Continuous and Past Perfect (see 1 Tenses), we use the following verb forms to talk about the past:
- *would* and *used to* + infinitive without 'to' to talk about regular events in the past which no longer happen; we use *used to* to talk about states and activities and *would* to talk only about activities:
  Erica **used to be** a champion. (state)
  We **would** (or **used to**) always **celebrate** together. (activity)
- **Past Perfect Continuous** to talk about longer activities in the past that happened before other past events:
  She was rescued by a man who **had been working** in a nearby garage.

3 Relative And Participle Clauses (pages 32–33)

Relative clauses
There are two types of relative clauses: defining and non-defining. We use:
- **defining relative clauses** to identify the person or thing we are talking about:
  I only pierce young people **who come with their parents**.
  (Note that we do <u>not</u> put a comma before the defining relative clause.)
- **non-defining relative clauses** to give extra information about the person or thing, which is not necessary to identify this person or thing and can be left out:
  Mick Shannon, **who is a qualified body piercer**, took me to his salon.
  Mick showed me his certificate, **which was on the wall**.
  (Note that we <u>always</u> put a comma before a non-defining relative clause.)

We cannot not use the pronoun *that* or omit the relative pronoun in non-defining relative clauses.

We use a special type of non-defining relative clauses to add a comment to what was said in the first part of the sentence:
They don't clean their equipment, **which shows they don't know what they're doing**.
In these clauses, we always use a comma and the relative pronoun **which** (<u>not</u> **what**).

Participle clauses

Instead of a full relative clause we can sometimes use a participle clause. We use:
- a present participle to say what the person/thing is doing:
  *You can see many people **wearing rings everywhere**.*
- a past participle to say what is/was done to the person/thing mentioned:
  *I was looking at the walls, **covered with photos of clients**.*

4 THE PASSIVE (pages 42–43)

We use the Passive when:
- the doer of the action is unknown:
  *The bus stop **has been vandalised**.*
- we want to focus attention on the action rather than the doer:
  *The whole gang **was arrested** yesterday.*
- we want to put special attention on the doer:
  *All these projects **have been managed** by <u>the Bulgarian artist Christo</u>.*
- we want to avoid a very long subject of the sentence:
  *His projects **are financed** by the sale of his drawings through galleries and the Internet.*

The Passive is used mainly in formal and written language. It is very typical of the language used in newspapers and by journalists.

Apart from passive forms of tenses, we can use some other passive forms:
- passive infinitive: *It's nice **to be taken** seriously.*
- passive gerund: *We all enjoyed **being praised** by the teacher.*
- passive perfect infinitive:
  *The train may **have been delayed** by the storm.*

5 THE FUTURE (pages 56–57)

Apart from *will / may / might* + infinitive without 'to', the Present Continuous, *to be going to* and the Present Simple, we use the following tenses and verb forms to talk about the future:

- **Future Continuous**
  We use the Future Continuous to talk about activities that will be in progress at a certain time in the future:
  *At 9 a.m. on Saturday, I'**ll be listening** to Duke Willard.*
  *I'**ll be working** all evening so I won't be able to see you.*

- **Future Perfect**
  We use the Future Perfect to talk about actions that will be completed before a certain time in the future:
  *By the end of the century, we **will have colonised** our solar system.*
  *He **will have written** two books by next summer.*

- **Time clauses**
  When we refer to the future in time clauses, after *when, as soon as, until, before* and *after* we do not use *will*. We use the Present Simple:
  *When you **get** home, you'll receive good news.*
  If we want to emphasise the fact that an activity will be finished before the other one happens, we use the Present Perfect instead of the Present Simple:
  *After you'**ve done** the shopping, you'll have a pleasant surprise.*
  *I'll help you as soon as I'**ve finished** the washing up.*

6 CONDITIONALS AND MIXED CONDITIONALS (pages 66–67)

There are four basic types of conditional sentences: the Zero Conditional, First Conditional, Second Conditional and the Third Conditional.
(For more information about these types of conditional sentences see the Mini-Grammar in the Language Powerbook.)

The term 'mixed conditionals' comes from the fact that the mixed conditional sentences combine different conditional structures.

We use **mixed conditionals** to talk about:
- imaginary past events that could have some consequences in the present:
  *If he **had broken** the record, he **would be** famous now.* (but he didn't break the record in the past so he isn't famous now)
  *If they **hadn't invited** me to the party, I **wouldn't be** here.* (but they invited me to the party so I'm here now)

  Form: *If* + Past Perfect, *would* + infinitive without 'to'
  ↓ ↓
  (as in 3rd conditional) (as in 2nd conditional)

- unreal present situations, usually imaginary states, which could have had some consequences in the past:
  *If he **was/were** a more skilful player, he **would have scored** more points.* (but he isn't a skilful player so he didn't score points)
  *If she **didn't speak** a few languages, she **wouldn't have got** that job.* (but she speaks a few languages so she got the job)

  Form: *If* + Past Simple, *would* + perfect infinitive
  ↓ ↓
  (as in 2nd conditional) (as in 3rd conditional)

7 VERB PATTERNS: '-ing' FORM AND INFINITIVE (pages 80–81)

used to, be used to and *get used to*

We use:
- **used to** + infinitive without 'to' to talk about states or activities that happened regularly in the past but they are no longer true:
  *We **used to go** camping a lot.*
  *He **used to be** a doctor.*
- **be used to** + '-ing' form of the verb or a noun to say that we are very familiar with something:
  *We'**re used to getting** up early.*
  *She'**s not used to** the cold climate.*
- **get used to** + '-ing' form of the verb or a noun to describe the process of getting familiar with something:
  *We **got used to eating** rice when we lived in Asia.*
  *How long did it take you to **get used to** the food here?*

Grammar Summary

Verbs of senses
With verbs of senses such as *see, hear, watch, notice* we can use two patterns. We use:
- **see / hear / watch / notice somebody do something** when we want to say that we observed the whole action (and we know how it ends):
  I **watched** the children **cross** the street. (I saw them as they reached the other side.)
  We **heard** John **sing** our national anthem. (We heard the whole song.)
- **see / hear / watch / notice somebody doing something** when we want to say that we observed the action in progress:
  We **watched** the whales **swimming** off the coast of Patagonia.
  I **saw** them **sunbathing** on the balcony.

8 Reporting (pages 90–91)
We can use the following verbs (with the patterns given) to report what a person has said:

- **verb + *that*:**
  He **complained that** he was paid too little.
  The following verbs can be used with this pattern:
  add, admit, agree, announce, believe, boast, claim, complain, deny, declare, explain, insist, remind, suggest, warn.

- **verb + *somebody* + *that*:**
  They **warned us that** we might be stopped at the gate.
  The following verbs can be used with this pattern: *warn, remind.*

- **verb + *somebody to do something*:**
  We **advised him to change** the bank.
  The following verbs can be used with this pattern:
  advise, beg, order, promise.

- **verb + *to do something*:**
  He **threatened to take** legal action.
  The following verbs can be used with this pattern:
  agree, offer, refuse, threaten.

- **verb + '-ing' form:**
  I **suggested going** to the presentation.
  The following verbs can be used with this pattern:
  admit, deny, suggest.

- **verb + *if/whether*:**
  She **asked if** it was possible to see the patient.
  The following verbs can be used with this pattern: *inquire, ask.*

- **verb + preposition + '-ing' form:**
  He has been **accused of pick-pocketing**.
  The following verb can be used with this pattern: *accuse of.*

We do not change the tense in the reported sentence when:
- the reporting verb is in the present:
  '*I feel feverish.*' → She **says** she **feels** feverish.
- we report something which is still true, e.g. a general truth:
  '*Kangaroos live in Australia.*' → The teacher **said** that kangaroos **live** in Australia.
- we report something which is still in the future at the moment of reporting:
  '*The documents will be published in 2020.*' → The ministry spokesperson **announced** that the documents **will be published** in 2020.

9 Complex Sentences (1): Persuasion (pages 104–105)
We usually use different forms in written formal English and spoken informal English to tell people what we think they should do.

Written English
We use the following expressions to make strong suggestions when we write in a formal style:
- **should + infinitive without 'to':**
  We **should remember** that 'being' is more important that 'having'.
- **ought to + infinitive without 'to':**
  The government **ought to do** something about unemployment.
- **demand / insist / suggest** + *(that)* + subject + **should**
            do something
  + *(that)* + subject + **present tense**
  + *(that)* + subject + **subjunctive**
     (same form as infinitive)
  They **are suggesting** that a new school **should be built** in this area.
  I **insist** that the money **is transferred** into my account immediately.
  The protesters **demanded** that the supermarket **be** closed.
- **It's high time** *(that)* + subject + **past tense**
  It's high time the council **started** to think about local businesses.

Spoken English
We use the following expressions to make weak, tentative suggestions when we talk to someone we know:
- **If I were you, I'd + infinitive without 'to':**
  If I were you, I'd stop using so much make-up.

To make a slightly stronger suggestion, we use:
- **I think you should + infinitive without 'to':**
  I think you should take up some evening classes.
- **I think you ought to + infinitive without 'to':**
  I think you ought to give away your old school books.

We use the following expressions to criticise, reproach or advise somebody in a strong way. These expressions are often used by a person in authority, e.g. teacher talking to a student, parent talking to a child.
- **It's about time** + subject + **past tense:**
  It's about time you **got** down to work.
- **I'd (= I would) rather** + subject + **past tense:**
  I'd rather you **didn't go** there.
  ('I'd rather you' is usually followed by a negative verb form)
- **You'd (= You had) better + infinitive without 'to':**
  You'd better start thinking about your exams.
  'You'd better' could also be used to a friend to encourage or to persuade:
  You'd better hurry up or you'll be late.

The expression **I'd sooner you** + **past tense** is not used very much any more; we use **I'd rather** instead. Both structures are usually followed by a negative form:
I'd sooner you didn't tell anyone about it.

10 Complex Sentences (2): Emphasis
(pages 114–115)

To make something sound stronger and more emphatic, we use a negative word (e.g. *seldom, rarely, never, neither, no sooner (than), not only*) at the beginning of the sentence plus inversion, i.e. the word order of a question. We usually use this kind of inversion in formal written English:

He has never known anything like it. → **Never** *has he* **known** *anything like it.*
The police arrived just after the robbers had left. → **No sooner** *had the robbers* **left than** *the police arrived.*
Snakes are not only unpleasant but they are dangerous as well. → **Not only** *are snakes unpleasant* **but** *they are dangerous as well.*

We can also use emphatic inversion in third conditional sentences. Note that we drop *if* in the inverted form. This structure is common in both formal and informal language:
If I had known they were in town, I would have phoned them.
→ **Had** *I* **known** *they were in town, I would have phoned them.*

In both formal and informal language, we can use these structures to put more emphasis on some words:
He is interested in money. → **It's** *money* **that** *he's interested in.* (we put emphasis on 'money')
I'm really upset about the noise you're making. → **What** *I'm upset* **about is** *the noise you're making.* (we put emphasis on 'noise')
I only need some rest. → **All** *I need* **is** *some rest.* (we put emphasis on 'rest')

Language Awareness 1 (page 14)
Reference (1): Determiners

We use the following determiners in front of:
- singular countable nouns: *a/an, the, another, the other*.
- uncountable nouns: *the, some, any, no, a lot of, much, all (of the)*.
- plural countable nouns: *the, some, any, no, many, several, a lot of, all (of the), (the) other*.

We use *a/an* when:
- we mention something for the first time:
  There is **a** *new shop assistant in the bakery.*
- it does not matter which particular person/thing we are talking about, e.g. when we mention this person/thing as an example of a group or category:
  Can I have **an** *orange?*

We use *the* when the person we are talking to knows precisely which person/thing we are talking about and can easily identify them/it:
Let's have breakfast outside on **the** *terrace.*

Language Awareness 2 (page 25)
Continuous and Simple Tenses

We use continuous rather than simple tenses when:
- we want to say that an activity is not finished:
  The doctor **was writing** *a note.* (she was in the process of writing it)
  The doctor **wrote** *a note.* (the note was ready)
  I've been reading this book for weeks. (I'm still reading it)
  I've read this book. (I've finished reading it)

- we want to suggest that an activity is temporary rather than permanent:
  You're breathing quite heavily. (for some time only, because you're exhausted or ill)
  People with heart condition often breath quite heavily. (that's a common characteristic)
  My aunt was living here. (for some time only)
  My aunt lived here. (permanently)

- we refer to a prolonged or repeated action rather than a single event:
  The man was looking at his watch. (continuously or repeatedly)
  The man looked at his watch. (once)
  She dived into the pool. (once)
  She's been diving into the pool. (many times)

The following verbs are not used in continuous tenses: *know, like, understand, belong, resemble, realise.*

Language Awareness 3 (page 49)
Reference (2): Pronouns

Pronouns are words that we can use instead of a noun in a sentence so that we do not repeat the noun too often. English has the following pronouns:
- **personal pronouns:**
  a) subject pronouns: *I, you, he, she, it, we, they.*
  b) object pronouns: *me, you, him, her, it, us, them.*
- **indefinite pronouns:** *someone, something, anywhere, nobody, nothing,* etc.
- **possessive pronouns:** *mine, yours, his, hers, ours, theirs.*
- **demonstrative pronouns:** *this, that, these, those.*
- **reflexive pronouns:** *myself, yourself, himself, herself, itself, ourselves, yourselves, themselves.*
- **relative pronouns:** *who, which, that, whose, whom.*

Possessive adjectives (*my, your, his, her, its, our, their*) are not pronouns because they cannot replace a noun.

one vs. *you*
We use the pronouns *one* and *you* when we make statements about people in general, and they mean 'anyone, at any time'. *One* is used in formal language, whereas *you* is informal:
One *has got (or You have got) more chance of finding an interesting job abroad nowadays.*
How do **you** *get to Wembley from here?*

Grammar Summary

LANGUAGE AWARENESS 4 (page 73)
Modal Verbs and Expressions

We use modal verbs and expressions to:
- talk about obligations and necessity:
  You **must** clean your teeth after every meal.
  We **have to** leave earlier to arrive on time.
  I **had to** walk ten miles to get home.
  Did you **have to** pay to go in?

- talk about permission and prohibition:
  You **can** go in now.
  We **mustn't** disturb them.
  They **can't** tell me what to do.

- talk about lack of obligation:
  We **didn't have to** pay for the beer, it was free.
  We **don't have to** think about anything, the tour operator does it all.
  You **needn't** worry, everything will be all right.
  You **don't need to** bring any food, there'll be enough.

- talk about abilities:
  My little daughter **can** sing and dance.
  I **can't** speak French.
  I **could** talk when I was two.
  Can you roller blade?

- talk about possibility:
  I **can't** get through to them, the line is busy.
  I **could** go there and tell them what I think.
  John **couldn't** see us in the crowd.

- make a guess and to speculate:
  He **will** be cooking lunch now.
  They **must** have found out about the article.
  She **might** be Russian.
  He **could** be at the library.
  What **could** I have done?

- make predictions:
  He'**ll** be late, as usual.
  They **may** win if they try hard.
  They **won't** come.

- make decisions:
  I'**ll** talk to Jim about it.
  I **won't** go there.

didn't need to vs. needn't

We use didn't need to + infinitive without 'to' to say that someone did not do something because it was not necessary:
She **didn't need to play** because the match was cancelled.
He was so rich he **didn't need to worry** about money.

We use needn't + perfect infinitive to say that someone did something although it was unnecessary:
We **needn't have brought** any food to the party – there was plenty already.

LANGUAGE AWARENESS 5 (page 97)
Impersonal Report Structures

When we report what people generally believe or say we can use the subject **It + the passive** of verbs like say, know, believe, claim, suppose, think, fear, predict:
It is said that dolphins are very friendly animals.
It was feared that the plane would crash into a skyscraper.

We can also start the sentence from the person/thing that the information concerns and use the structure
subject + the passive + infinitive:
It is known that storks live in a clean environment. → **Storks are known to live** in a clean environment.

We use an ordinary infinitive if the action reported is parallel with the time of reporting:
It was said that Elvis Presley was the king of rock and roll. →
Elvis Presley was said to be the king of rock and roll.
It is claimed that police officer accept bribes. → **Police officers are claimed to accept** bribes.

We use a perfect infinitive if the action happened before the time of reporting:
It is supposed that the plane was hijacked. → **The plane is supposed to have been hijacked**.
It was said that the minister had been involved in organised crime → **The minister was said to have been involved** in organised crime.

LANGUAGE AWARENESS 6 (page 121)
Perfective Verb Forms

We use perfective verb forms to say that something happened <u>before</u> a certain time:
I'**ve been staying** with my family on the coast. (before / until now)
They **had finished** dinner when we came. (before a point in the past)
Jim **will have written** the essay by 10 p.m. (before a point in the future)
Having spent every summer there, I knew everyone in the village. (before a time in the past)
They may **have eaten** lunch at school and aren't hungry. (before a time in the present)

We can use the following perfective verb forms:
- Present Perfect: I'**ve seen** the Mona Lisa twice.
- Present Perfect Continuous: I'**ve been repairing** my bike.
- Past Perfect: She died after she **had contracted** tuberculosis.
- Past Perfect Continuous: They were very dirty because they'**d been playing** football in mud.
- Future Perfect: We **will have moved out** by the end of next year.
- perfect infinitive: They may **have lost** their way.
  She must **have been invited** by Jonathan.
- perfective '-ing' form:
  I remembered **having met** the man a long time ago.
  Having parked the car on the side of the road, he went to sleep for an hour.

Lexicon

The Lexicon contains important words and vocabulary areas in *Opportunities Upper Intermediate*. To find other words that are not in this Lexicon, use *The Longman Active Study Dictionary* or *The Longman Essential Activator*.

Contents

Module words	pages 151-155
Wordbuilding (prefixes, suffixes, compunds, etc.)	pages 156-160
Collocation bank	pages 160-161
Expressions with *do, get, have, make*	page 162
Word pairs	page 162
Word families	page 163
Idiomatic Language	page 164
Prepositions bank	pages 165-169
Multi-part verbs	pages 170-176
Pronunciation symbols/Abbreviations	inside back cover

Module words

Module 1 – Identity
Personality adjectives

positive

adventurous /ədˈventʃərəs/: *an **adventurous** traveller.*
ambitious /æmˈbɪʃəs/: *She's an **ambitious** girl and will go far.*
careful /ˈkeəfl/: *He's **careful** and thinks before doing anything.*
cheerful /ˈtʃɪəfl/: *She's **cheerful** – even on Monday mornings!*
communicative /kəˈmjuːnɪkətɪv/ *A **communicative** person gives opinions and talks a lot.*
competitive /kəmˈpetətɪv/: *He's **competitive** and does his best.*
considerate /kənˈsɪdrət/: *She's **considerate** – she thinks about other people's feelings.*
co-operative /kəʊˈɒprətɪv/: *They're **co-operative** and willing to help.*
creative /kriˈeɪtɪv/: *He's a **creative** student – full of ideas.*
decisive /dɪˈsaɪsɪv/: *A **decisive** boss makes decisions quickly.*
easy-going /ˌiːzi ˈɡəʊɪŋ/: *She's **easy-going** and everybody likes her.*
hard-working /ˌhɑːd ˈwɜːkɪŋ/: *He's **hard-working** and gives 100%.*
helpful /ˈhelpfl/: *She's **helpful** and willing to lend a hand.*
imaginative /ɪˈmædʒɪnətɪv/: *She's a very **imaginative** pupil and writes fantastic stories.*
independent /ˌɪndɪˈpendənt/: ***Independent** people prefer to make their own decisions.*
inventive /ɪnˈventɪv/: *an **inventive** writer.*
kind /kaɪnd/: *He's **kind** and friendly to others.*
liberal /ˈlɪbrəl/: ***Liberal** people respect other people's ideas and behaviour, especially new ideas.*
likeable /ˈlaɪkəbl/: *She's **likeable** – people find her friendly.*
logical /ˈlɒdʒɪkl/: *He's **logical** and makes careful decisions.*
natural /ˈnætʃrəl/: *He's a **natural** athlete and doesn't need to try hard.*
outgoing /ˌaʊtˈɡəʊɪŋ/: *She's **outgoing** and makes friends easily.*
polite /pəˈlaɪt/: *She's **polite** and always says 'Thanks'.*
practical /ˈpræktɪkl/: *He's **practical** and makes sensible decisions.*
realistic /rɪəˈlɪstɪk/: *She's **realistic** – not trying the impossible.*
reasonable /ˈriːzənəbl/: *A **reasonable** parent is fair and sensible.*
relaxed /rɪˈlækst/: *She's **relaxed** and doesn't get angry easily.*
reliable /rɪˈlaɪəbl/: *I like **reliable** people who do what they say they're going to do.*
sensible /ˈsensɪbl/: *She's **sensible** and never does anything silly.*
sensitive /ˈsensətɪv/: *A **sensitive** person shows sympathy towards people who have difficulties.*
sociable /ˈsəʊʃəbl/: *He's **sociable** and enjoys being with others.*
sympathetic /ˌsɪmpəˈθetɪk/: *She was **sympathetic** when I told her my dog had died – she listened and said she was sorry.*
tolerant /ˈtɒlərənt/: *Their behaviour was terrible but he was **tolerant** and didn't complain.*
unselfish /ʌnˈselfɪʃ/: *He's **unselfish** and puts other people first.*

negative

ambitious /æmˈbɪʃəs/: *He's **ambitious** and will do anything to get what he wants.*
boring /ˈbɔːrɪŋ/: *She's dull and **boring** and never does anything exciting.*
careless /ˈkeəlɪs/: *He's **careless** and his work is full of unnecessary mistakes.*
childish /ˈtʃaɪldɪʃ/: *She's **childish** and behaves like a ten-year-old at times.*
cold /kəʊld/: *He's **cold** and so unfriendly.*
excitable /ɪkˈsaɪtəbl/ *She's **excitable** and gets excited far too easily.*
impatient /ɪmˈpeɪʃnt/: *You're so **impatient** – can't you wait even a few minutes?*
individualistic /ˌɪndɪvɪdʒuəˈlɪstɪk/: *He's rather **individualistic** and doesn't work very well with other people.*
insensitive /ɪnˈsensətɪv/: *She's quite **insensitive** and doesn't think about other people's feelings.*
intolerant /ɪnˈtɒlərənt/: *An **intolerant** person doesn't accept the way other people live. Don't be **intolerant of** others.*
moody /ˈmuːdi/: *You're so **moody**! One minute you're cheerful, the next minute you're miserable.*
nasty /ˈnɑːsti/: *She's such a **nasty** and unpleasant person.*
reckless /ˈrekləs/: *He's **reckless** and doesn't care about danger.*
selfish /ˈselfɪʃ/: *You're **selfish** – you only think about yourself.*
suspicious /səˈspɪʃəs/: *He's **suspicious of** foreigners and unwilling to accept their ways of living.*
unreliable /ˌʌnrɪˈlaɪəbl/: *She's **unreliable** – never doing what she says she'll do.*
vain /veɪn/: *He's so **vain** – he thinks he's handsome and very intelligent.*

neutral

chatty /ˈtʃæti/: *She's very **chatty** in fact she talks all the time.*
competitive /kəmˈpetətɪv/: *He's very **competitive**, even with his friends.*
conservative /kənˈsɜːvətɪv/: *She's **conservative** and doesn't approve of young people who go clubbing.*
conventional /kənˈvenʃnəl/: *He's **conventional** and hates new ideas.*
emotional /ɪˈməʊʃənəl/: *She's **emotional** and cries when she watches romantic films.*
idealistic /ˌaɪdɪəˈlɪstɪk/: *He's **idealistic** - and his ideas are not practical.*
proud /praʊd/: *My dad is **proud of** my success.*
reserved /rɪˈzɜːvd/: *He's **reserved** and doesn't express his opinions.*
romantic /rəˈmæntɪk/: *She's **romantic** and loves getting flowers.*
serious /ˈsɪəriəs/: *He's a **serious** student and works hard.*
sentimental /ˌsentɪˈmentl/: *He's **sentimental** and shows his gentle and loving side easily.*
shy /ʃaɪ/: *She's **shy** and sometimes feels uncomfortable with other people.*

Module 2 – Laughter
Humour

burst out laughing /ˌbɜːst aʊt ˈlɑːfɪŋ/ *to laugh suddenly and loudly: I **burst out laughing** when I saw her new haircut.*
cackle /ˈkækl/ *verb to laugh loudly and unpleasantly: She **cackles** like a witch.*
chuckle /ˈtʃʌkl/ *verb to laugh quietly: I **chuckled** to myself when I was reading that book.*
comedy /ˈkɒmədi/ **1** *noun a funny film, play or TV programme: He stars in **comedies**.* **2** *adjective amusing: I watched a good **comedy** programme last night.*

Lexicon

comic /ˈkɒmɪk/ *adjective* funny: I like reading **comic** novels.
crack (someone) up /kræk ˈʌp/ *verb* to make someone laugh a lot: Her jokes **crack** me **up**.
fall about laughing /fɔːl əbaʊt ˈlɑːfɪŋ/ *verb* to laugh a lot: We **fell about laughing** when he dressed up as Superman.
funny /ˈfʌni/ *adjective* **1** amusing: That programme is really **funny**. **2** strange: There's something **funny** about that man.
giggle /ˈɡɪɡl/ *verb* to laugh in a silly way: The teacher was angry because some students couldn't stop **giggling**.
hilarious /hɪˈleəriəs/ *adjective* very funny: The new Woody Allen film is **hilarious**.
humorous /ˈhjuːmərəs/ *adjective* quite funny: My grandad often tells **humorous** anecdotes about his childhood.
ironic /aɪˈrɒnɪk/ *adjective* amusing because something happens that is the opposite of what should happen: It was **ironic** that he fell over while telling me to be careful!
irony /ˈaɪərəni/ *noun* the use of words that are the opposite of what you really mean: 'Oh, that was just brilliant,' he said with **irony** after his team missed a penalty.
keep a straight face /kiːp ə ˌstreɪt ˈfeɪs/ *verb* to hide your amusement: When he dropped his papers during the speech, I couldn't **keep a straight face**.
kid /kɪd/ *verb* to make someone believe something that isn't true: The dinner's burnt. No, I'm only **kidding**!
laugh your head off /ˌlɑːf jɔː ˈhed ɒf/ *verb* to laugh loudly
make someone laugh /ˌmeɪk sʌmwʌn ˈlɑːf/ *verb* to do or say something so that someone laughs: Her jokes **make** me **laugh**.
make/pull a face /ˌmeɪk/pʊl ə ˈfeɪs/ *verb* to make your face look odd or funny: He **made faces** at me and I laughed so much.
play a practical joke /ˌpleɪ ə ˌpræktɪkl ˈdʒəʊk/ *verb* to do something funny to make someone look silly: We **played a practical joke** on him. We put a spider in his bed!
play around /ˌpleɪ əˈraʊnd/ *verb* to do something funny: Don't **play around** during lessons.
pull someone's leg /ˌpʊl sʌmwʌnz ˈleɡ/ *verb* to make someone believe something that isn't true: Have I really won ten pounds? Or, are you **pulling my leg**?
sarcastic /sɑːˈkæstɪk/ *adjective* saying the opposite of what you mean in order to be unkind: She's so **sarcastic**. She's always saying how clever Sue is, but she doesn't mean it.
sense of humour /ˌsens əv ˈhjuːmə/ *noun* the ability to laugh or make people laugh: He has a good **sense of humour**.
tell (someone) a joke /ˌtel sʌmwʌn ə ˈdʒəʊk/ *verb* to tell a funny story: She **tells** excellent **jokes**.
witty /ˈwɪti/ *adjective* expressing yourself in a clever and amusing way: My history teacher is always making **witty** remarks.

MODULE 3 - STYLE

Expressing opinions

clothes/decoration
Negative: a **cheap** dress; **tacky** wallpaper; **tasteless** paintings; the colours are **over the top**
Positive: a **classy** dress – very **smart**, very **chic**!
I think that baseball hat's really **cool**. She wore a very **stylish**, **elegant** suit. His house has very **sophisticated** décor.
Modern: **contemporary** architecture; a **trendy** blouse; a **fashionable** jacket; **up-to-date** furniture
Not modern: **dated** furniture; an **old-fashioned** hairstyle; **unfashionable** earrings

places
Negative: That ugly building's an **eyesore**. His room's so **messy**. That area's **unsightly** because of all the litter.
Positive: In the winter, my bedroom's really warm and **cosy**. It's not very **stylish** but it's a very **comfy** sofa. Her home has a **relaxed atmosphere**. There are some **nice views** from my bedroom window.

people (→ PERSONALITY ADJECTIVES, PAGE 151)
Positive: I think he's really **attractive**. My cousin's very **bright** and always does well in exams. I am quite **independent** and don't like being told what to do. I like people who are **laid-back** and relaxed.

Negative: She's very **scatty** and **absent-minded** and always forgets things. I'm totally **useless** at singing. She's so **witty** and makes everybody laugh with her remarks.
→ COLLOCATION BANK, PAGE 160.

Personal appearance

mid-thirties / **late twenties** / **early forties**
He's **a bit on the thin side**. She always **dresses casually**. I don't like **dressing formally**. He has just **dyed** his hair blonde. Young people often have a **pierced ear**. Some **pierce** their **eyebrows** or **nose** and even their **tongue**, **lips** or **navel**! **Tattoos** are hard to get off your **skin**.
She has got **varnished nails**.

Fashion

brand /brænd/ *noun* a product made by one particular company
craze or fad /fæd/ *noun* a very temporary fashion or interest
designer label /dɪˌzaɪnə ˈleɪbl/ *noun* a label on clothes showing a fashionable manufacturer
logo /ˈləʊɡəʊ/ *noun* a drawing or symbol of a company
chart /tʃɑːt/ *noun* a list of the most popular songs or CDs
trend /trend/ *noun* a style, colour, etc. that more and more people prefer

Street art

billboard /ˈbɪlbɔːd/ *noun* (also **advertising billboard**) a large picture in a street, etc. that advertises something
fireworks display /ˈfaɪəwɜːks dɪˌspleɪ/ *noun* a show of bright colours and noises at night using objects that burn or explode
graffiti /ɡrəˈfiːti/ *noun* writing or drawings on walls
live statue /ˌlaɪv ˈstætʃuː/ *noun* someone who keeps still like a statue for money
pavement artist /ˈpeɪvmənt ˌɑːtɪst/ *noun* an artist who draws pictures on the pavement in chalk for money

MODULE 4 - BEAUTY

Describing beauty

people
In a general sense: an **attractive** person; a **good-looking** person; a **handsome** man or boy; a **pretty** woman or girl; she and he are absolutely **gorgeous**.
About a person who is extremely attractive: A very **striking** man or woman. That model is **stunning**.
About the way a person dresses: an **elegant** man/woman

buildings
It's a **magnificent** church. That bridge is really **impressive**.

places/scenes
The sunset was **breathtaking**. The whole area is very **scenic**. We saw some **picturesque** countryside.

paintings/sculpture
I think Van Gogh's paintings have such **powerful** colours.
'Sunflowers' is **a masterpiece**. He painted in **striking** colours.
That statue is **beautiful**. It is **a thing of great beauty**.

movement
She makes gymnastics seem **effortless**. He's an **elegant** and **graceful** dancer.

Describing music

Her voice is **beautiful**.
That song has a **catchy** tune – I can't stop singing it!
His new symphony is **dramatic** and **lively**.
I think 'rock and roll' is **exciting** music – and good to dance to.
The film music was **haunting** – I can't get it out of my mind.
The song is quite **boring**, even **tedious**, and the words are very **repetitive** and **monotonous**, the same tune over and over again.
That music is very **sad** and **moving** – it makes me want to cry!

Lexicon

He writes a lot of **romantic** and **sentimental** love songs with **tear-jerking** words – I think they're all very **soppy**, actually.
The music in the frightening part of the film was **scary** and **sinister**, quite **terrifying**!
I find this music very **soothing** and **thoughtful**.
I don't like it – it's **not my** (**kind of**) **thing**.

MODULE 5 – NEW FRONTIERS

Biology/Medicine
antibiotic /ˌæntɪbaɪˈɒtɪk/ noun a drug like penicillin used to destroy dangerous bacteria
bacteria /bækˈtɪəriə/ plural noun small living things that cause diseases
DNA molecule /ˌdiː en ˈeɪ ˌmɒləkjuːl/ noun a molecule that contains genetic information
gene /dʒiːn/ noun a part of a cell inherited from the parents of a living thing that controls development
human genome /ˌhjuːmən ˈdʒiːnəʊm/ noun the collection of genetic information of a living thing
molecule /ˈmɒləkjuːl/ noun a group of atoms

Information technology
artificial intelligence /ˌɑːtɪfɪʃl ɪnˈtelɪdʒəns/ noun the ability of computers and robots to do things without humans
data-processing /ˈdeɪtə ˈprəʊsesɪŋ/ noun the use of computers to organise and store information
microchip /ˈmaɪkrəʊtʃɪp/ noun a very small electric circuit made of silicon
online /ˈɒnlaɪn/ adjective on the Internet
search engine /ˈsɜːtʃ ˌendʒɪn/ noun a programme that you use to look for particular information on the Internet

Physics
atom /ˈætəm/ noun the smallest piece of a substance that can exist on its own
electric current /ɪˌlektrɪk ˈkʌrənt/ noun a flow of electricity
equation /ɪˈkweɪʒən/ noun a mathematical statement that shows two equal quantities
gravity /ˈgrævəti/ noun the force that attracts things to the ground
mass /mæs/ noun the amount of physical material in something
matter /ˈmætə/ noun physical material
particle /ˈpɑːtɪkl/ noun a very small piece or the part of an atom, e.g. an **electron** or **neutron**
radioactivity /ˌreɪdiəʊækˈtɪvəti/ noun the energy produced by some elements, e.g. radium and polonium

Astronomy/Space travel
black hole /ˌblæk ˈhəʊl/ noun a dark part of outer space that attracts light and energy
deep space /ˌdiːp ˈspeɪs/ noun space outside our own solar system
galaxy /ˈgæləksi/ noun a huge collection of stars
light year /ˈlaɪt jɪə/ noun how far light travels in space in one year
manned mission /ˌmænd ˈmɪʃn/ noun a space journey in which humans travel
meteorite /ˈmiːtiəraɪt/ noun a piece of rock from outer space that lands on the earth
orbit /ˈɔːbɪt/ verb to move round a planet or a star
solar system /ˈsəʊlə ˌsɪstəm/ noun the sun with the planets, etc. that move round it
space probe /ˈspeɪs prəʊb/ noun a space ship without humans

Science (general)
data /ˈdeɪtə/ noun information or facts
field /fiːld/ noun an area of study
principle /ˈprɪnsəpl/ noun a general rule that explains a natural force or how something works
procedure /prəˈsiːdʒə/ noun a method for doing something
process /ˈprəʊses/ noun a sequence of actions to get a result
research /rɪˈsɜːtʃ/ noun the scientific study of a subject
study /ˈstʌdi/ noun a piece of research

MODULE 6 – SOFT MACHINE

Parts of the body
ankle /ˈæŋkl/ noun the part of your body where your leg joins your foot
brain /breɪn/ noun the organ in your head that controls your thoughts, feelings and movements
heart /hɑːt/ noun the organ in your chest that sends blood round your body
kidney /ˈkɪdni/ noun one of a pair of organs in your body that takes away waste materials from your blood
liver /ˈlɪvə/ noun the large organ that cleans your blood
lung /lʌŋ/ noun one of a pair of organs in your chest that you use to breathe
muscle /ˈmʌsl/ noun a part of your body that joins your bones and helps you to move
neuron /ˈnjʊərɒn/ noun a nerve cell that sends messages about movement or feeling
organ /ˈɔːgən/ noun one of the parts in your body with a particular function, e.g. heart, liver
rib /rɪb/ noun one of twelve pairs of bones round your chest
skin /skɪn/ noun the outer covering of your body
spine /spaɪn/ noun the row of bones down the centre of your back
stomach /ˈstʌmək/ noun the organ in your body that digests your food
tissue /ˈtɪʃuː/ noun one of the groups of cells that form plants or animals, e.g. muscular, nervous
wrist /rɪst/ noun the part of your body where your arm joins your hand

Medicine
chemotherapy /ˌkiːməʊˈθerəpi/ noun the form of treatment of diseases that uses chemical substances
clone /kləʊn/ **1** noun a group of cells or a living thing produced using one ancestor **2** verb to make a clone
cure /kjʊə/ noun a medicine or treatment that makes you better when you are ill
gene therapy /ˈdʒiːn ˌθerəpi/ noun medical treatment using genes from cells
genetic engineering /dʒɪˌnetɪk ˌendʒɪˈnɪərɪŋ/ noun the deliberate changing of the form of a living thing using its genes
immune /ɪˈmjuːn/ adjective not able to be harmed by a disease or infection
infusion /ɪnˈfjuːʒn/ noun a slow injection of a substance to treat a disease or infection
medication /ˌmedɪˈkeɪʃn/ noun any drug used to treat someone who is ill
therapy /ˈθerəpi/ noun a particular way of treating illnesses
treatment /ˈtriːtmənt/ noun a method or medicine used to cure an illness
vaccine /ˈvæksiːn/ noun a substance used to protect people from a particular disease

Illness/Disease
Aids /eɪdz/ noun (abbreviation of **Acquired Immune Deficiency Syndrome**) a very serious disease that destroys your defence against infection
blotches /ˈblɒtʃɪz/ plural noun irregular red or brown shapes on your skin caused by a disease or infection
bronchitis /brɒŋˈkaɪtɪs/ noun an illness of the lungs causing severe coughing
cancer /ˈkænsə/ noun a disease in which cells grow too fast, producing a growth that can cause death
complications /ˌkɒmplɪˈkeɪʃənz/ plural noun new medical problems that happen during another illness
contract /kənˈtrækt/ verb to begin to suffer from an illness
diarrhoea /ˌdaɪəˈrɪə/ noun a medical condition that makes you go to the toilet too often
disorder /dɪsˈɔːdə/ noun a disease or illness
epidemic /ˌepɪˈdemɪk/ noun a large number of cases of an infectious disease occurring at the same time
heart disease /ˈhɑːt dɪˌziːz/ noun a disease of the heart

153

Lexicon

immune system /ɪˈmjuːn ˌsɪstəm/ *noun* the system in your blood that fights diseases
infect /ɪnˈfekt/ *verb* to give someone a disease
influenza /ˌɪnfluˈenzə/ *noun* (also **flu**) an illness that causes a very bad cold and a very high temperature
malaria /məˈleəriə/ *noun* a serious tropical disease caused by the bite of a mosquito
measles /ˈmiːzəlz/ *noun* an illness that gives you a high temperature and small red spots on your skin
pneumonia /njuːˈməʊniə/ *noun* a serious disease of the lungs causing great difficulty in breathing
polio /ˈpəʊliəʊ/ *noun* a serious disease of the nerves in the spine that can cause you to lose the ability to move your muscles
tetanus /ˈtetnəs/ *noun* a serious disease caused by an infection in a cut that makes muscles, especially in the jaw, go stiff
tuberculosis /tjʊˌbɜːkjʊˈləʊsɪs/ *noun* (also **TB**) a serious infectious disease that attacks the lungs

Module 7 - Journeys

Describing places

bustling /ˈbʌslɪŋ/ *adjective* very busy and with many people
cultural melting pot /ˌkʌltʃrəl ˈmeltɪŋ pɒt/ *noun* a place with an exciting mixture of cultures
dramatic /drəˈmætɪk/ *adjective* very beautiful or unusual: **dramatic** scenery.
exotic /ɪɡˈzɒtɪk/ *adjective* from another part of the world: **exotic** birds.
historic /hɪˈstɒrɪk/ *adjective* important in history: **historic** buildings.
flora and fauna /ˌflɔːrə ən ˈfɔːnə/ *plural noun* plants and animals
lively /ˈlaɪvli/ *adjective* busy and exciting: an **exciting** place.
nightlife /ˈnaɪt laɪf/ *noun* entertainment at night: an exotic **night life**.
romantic /rəʊˈmæntɪk/ *adjective* that makes you think of love: a **romantic** atmosphere.
snow-capped /ˈsnəʊ kæpt/ *adjective* covered with snow: **snow-capped** mountains.
spectacular /spekˈtækjʊlə/ very impressive and beautiful: **spectacular** scenery.
teeming /ˈtiːmɪŋ/ (usually **teeming with**) *adjective* crowded: The river was **teeming with** salmon.
unspoilt /ʌnˈspɔɪlt/ *adjective* in its natural state: **unspoilt** countryside.
wide open /ˌwaɪd ˈəʊpən/ *adjective* very large with no buildings: **wide open** spaces.
world-class /ˌwɜːld ˈklɑːs/ *adjective* of the highest quality: **world-class** art.

Travel

cruise /kruːz/: They went on a **cruise** round the Mediterranean.
excursion /ɪkˈskɜːʃn/: While I was on holiday on the Spanish coast, we **went on an excursion** to Granada.
flight /flaɪt/: The **flight** home was terrible – we had to wait four hours in the airport.
hitchhiking /ˈhɪtʃhaɪkɪŋ/: I'd never go **hitchhiking** because I'd worry about getting lifts in strangers' cars.
journey /ˈdʒɜːni/: The **journey** took five hours by train.
outing /ˈaʊtɪŋ/: The last school **outing** I went on was to a wildlife park.
package tour /ˈpækɪdʒ tʊə/: She **went on a package tour** with a group of other people.
tour guide /ˈtʊə ɡaɪd/: Everything during the trip was organised by our **tour guide**.
travel /ˈtrævl/: Many people say that **travel** broadens the mind.
trip /trɪp/: I **went on a trip** to Paris over the weekend.
voyage /ˈvɔɪ-ɪdʒ/: She got back from a **voyage** around the world in her yacht.

Baggage/luggage

holdall /ˈhəʊldɔːl/ *noun* a large bag for carrying clothes
overnight bag /ˌəʊvənaɪt ˈbæɡ/ *noun* a small bag for clothes
rucksack /ˈrʌksæk/, **backpack** /ˈbækpæk/, **pack** /pæk/ *noun* a bag used for carrying things on your back

saddle bag /ˈsædl bæɡ/ *noun* a bag you put on a bicycle or horse
sleeping bag /ˈsliːpɪŋ bæɡ/ *noun* a bag for sleeping in, especially when camping
spare /speə/ *adjective* extra: I've packed a **spare** pair of shoes in case these get dirty.
washbag /ˈwɒʃbæɡ/ *noun* a small bag for soap, toothbrush, toothpaste, etc. when you travel

Module 8 - Global Issues

Environmental issues

acid rain /ˌæsɪd ˈreɪn/ *noun* rain that contains acid from industrial waste
deforestation /diːˌfɒrəˈsteɪʃn/ *noun* the act of cutting down large areas of forest
destruction of habitats /dɪˌstrʌkʃn əv ˈhæbɪtæts/ *noun* the destruction of where wildlife lives as a result of deforestation
drought /draʊt/ *noun* a long period of dry weather so that there isn't enough water
global warming /ˌɡləʊbl ˈwɔːmɪŋ/ *noun* the raising of the temperature of the earth's atmosphere caused by the burning of fossil fuels and increased amount of gases such as carbon dioxide
greenhouse effect /ˈɡriːnhaʊs ɪˌfekt/ *noun* the warming of the earth's atmosphere → GLOBAL WARMING
ozone layer /ˈəʊzəʊn ˌleɪə/ *noun* a layer of the chemical ozone in the earth's atmosphere that blocks harmful rays from the sun
pollution /pəˈluːʃn/ *noun* the damage done to air, water or soil by the addition of harmful chemicals
recycling /ˌriːˈsaɪklɪŋ/ *noun* the process of treating paper, plastic and metals so that they can be used again
verge /vɜːdʒ/ *noun* a position near the end of something: Some species of animals are **on the verge of extinction** and there are very few left alive.

Disasters

avalanche /ˈævəlɑːnʃ/ *noun* a large amount of snow, rocks or soil that falls down a mountain
cyclone /ˈsaɪkləʊn/ *noun* a violent tropical wind that moves in circles round a calm area
earthquake /ˈɜːθkweɪk/ *noun* a sudden, violent shaking of the earth's surface
flood /flʌd/ *noun* a great overflow of water onto a place that is usually dry
forest fire /ˌfɒrɪst ˈfaɪə/ *noun* the burning of a forest, sometimes accidental in times of extreme heat
hurricane /ˈhʌrɪkən/ *noun* a storm with a very strong and fast wind
landslide /ˈlændslaɪd/ *noun* a sudden large fall of rocks or soil down a hillside
volcanic eruption /vɒlˌkænɪk ɪˈrʌpʃn/ *noun* the situation when steam or lava escapes from a volcano
windstorm /ˈwɪndstɔːm/ *noun* a very violent wind → CYCLONE, HURRICANE

Economic and social issues

discrimination /dɪˌskrɪmɪˈneɪʃn/ *noun* the treatment of someone or group of people differently from others: There is **racial discrimination** in some societies.
exploitation /ˌeksplɔɪˈteɪʃn/ *noun* a situation in which certain people are treated unfairly and have fewer advantages: **the exploitation of** women.
famine /ˈfæmɪn/ *noun* a serious situation when there is very little food
GNP /ˌdʒiː en ˈpiː/ *noun* (abbreviation of **gross national product**) the total amount of money earned by a country
malnutrition /ˌmælnjʊˈtrɪʃn/ *noun* bad health resulting from lack of food or eating the wrong sorts of food
overpopulation /ˌəʊvəpɒpjʊˈleɪʃn/ *noun* the situation in which there are too many people living in a place
per capita /pə ˈkæpɪtə/ = per person: The average income **per capita** is $25,000 per year.
poverty /ˈpɒvəti/ *noun* the state of being very poor

Lexicon

shanty town /ˈʃænti taʊn/ *noun* a part of a town with homes made of waste materials where very poor people live
Third World /ˌθɜːd ˈwɜːld/ *noun* the developing countries

MODULE 9 - SOCIETY
Social problems

begging /ˈbegɪŋ/ *noun* the act of asking people to give you money because you are very poor
discrimination /dɪˌskrɪmɪˈneɪʃn/ *noun* the unfair treatment of particular groups of society: **discrimination against** immigrants.
domestic violence /dəˌmestɪk ˈvaɪələns/ *noun* violence within the home mainly against women and children
drug abuse /ˈdrʌg əˌbjuːs/ *noun* the use of drugs for pleasure and not for medical reasons
homeless people /ˌhəʊmlɪs ˈpiːpl/ *noun* people who do not have somewhere to live
inequality /ˌɪnɪˈkwɒləti/ *noun* an unfair situation in which some people have more opportunities than others
poverty /ˈpɒvəti/ *noun* the situation of people who are extremely poor
racism /ˈreɪsɪzm/ *noun* discrimination against people because of their colour or race
unemployment /ˌʌnɪmˈplɔɪmənt/ *noun* the situation of people who do not have a job
vandalism /ˈvændəlɪzm/ *noun* the deliberate destruction of property
violent crime /ˌvaɪələnt ˈkraɪm/ *noun* crime that involves violence, e.g. mugging or rape. → CRIME below

Statistics

decline /dɪˈklaɪn/ *verb* to decrease: The amount of people working in industry **has declined**.
on the decrease /ɒn ðə ˈdiːkriːs/ to be decreasing: Crime is **on the decrease**.
double /ˈdʌbl/ *verb* to increase by 100%: The number of students in full-time further education **has doubled**.
fall /fɔːl/ *verb* to decrease: The share of wealth of the bottom 20% of society **has fallen**.
fluctuate /ˈflʌktʃueɪt/ *verb* to increase and decrease: The number of people in work **has fluctuated** recently.
on the increase /ɒn ði ˈɪnkriːs/ *verb* to be increasing: The life expectancy of women is **on the increase**.
plunge /plʌndʒ/ *verb* to decrease very fast: The amount of airlines making a profit **has plunged** recently.
rise /raɪz/ *verb* to increase: The income of British families **has risen**.
rocket /ˈrɒkɪt/ *verb* to increase very fast: The amount of crime **has rocketed** recently.

Crime

break the law /ˌbreɪk ðə ˈlɔː/ *verb* to do something illegal
burglary /ˈbɜːgləri/ *noun* the crime of breaking into someone's house and stealing things
commit a crime /kəˌmɪt ə ˈkraɪm/ *verb* to do something that is illegal
drug dealing /ˈdrʌg ˌdiːlɪŋ/ *noun* the crime of buying and selling illegal drugs
fraud /frɔːd/ *noun* the crime of getting money illegally
mugging /ˈmʌgɪŋ/ *noun* the crime of demanding money with violence or threats
murder /ˈmɜːdə/ *noun* the deliberate killing of someone
offence /əˈfens/ *noun* an illegal action
rape /reɪp/ *noun* a crime of forcing someone to have sex
robbery /ˈrɒbəri/ *noun* the crime of stealing things from a bank or other place
shoplifting /ˈʃɒpˌlɪftɪŋ/ *noun* the crime of stealing something from a shop
steal /stiːl/ *verb* to take something that belongs to someone else
theft /θeft/ *noun* the crime of stealing
thief /θiːf/ *noun* someone who steals

Punishment

capital punishment /ˌkæpɪtl ˈpʌnɪʃmənt/ *noun* the killing of someone by the state when they are found guilty of a serious crime
death penalty /ˈdeθ ˌpenlti/ *noun* the punishment by killing someone
fine /faɪn/ *noun* an amount of money paid as a punishment
prison sentence /ˈprɪzn ˌsentəns/ *noun* the time that someone has to spend in prison as a punishment

MODULE 10 - CONFLICT
Reasons for conflict

ambition /æmˈbɪʃn/ *noun* the desire to get power or success
fear /fɪə/ *noun* the strong unpleasant feeling you have when you are in danger
greed /griːd/ *noun* the desire to have more money or food
hatred /ˈheɪtrɪd/ *noun* a very strong feeling of dislike
intolerance /ɪnˈtɒlərəns/ *noun* the refusal to accept ideas and behaviour that is different from your own
jealousy /ˈdʒeləsi/ *noun* the angry and unhappy feeling you have because someone has something that you want
revenge /rɪˈvendʒ/ *noun* something you do to punish someone who has harmed you

Types of conflict

argument /ˈɑːgjʊmənt/ *noun* a disagreement between two people: They **have** many **arguments about** politics.
battle /ˈbætl/ *noun* a fight between two groups or armies
civil war /ˌsɪvl ˈwɔː/ *noun* a war between two groups in the same country
clash /klæʃ/ *noun* a fight between opposing groups, smaller than a battle: There were violent **clashes between** opposing groups.
feud /fjuːd/ *noun* a quarrel between two people or groups for a long time: There has been **a feud between** those families for years.
fight /faɪt/ *noun* an attempt by two or more people to hurt each other: There was **a fight between** two boys outside the school.
friction /ˈfrɪkʃn/ *noun* strong unfriendliness and disagreement between two people or groups: There was **friction** at first **between** the workers and the new boss.
quarrel /ˈkwɒrəl/ *noun* an angry argument: They **had a quarrel about** money.
row /raʊ/ *noun* an angry, noisy argument: We could hear the neighbours **having a row** last night.
war /wɔː/ *noun* a period of armed fighting between countries: The Second World **War** lasted six years.
warfare /ˈwɔːfeə/ *noun* violent activity: Tension on the streets has led to gang **warfare**.

War

concentration camp /ˌkɒnsənˈtreɪʃn kæmp/ *noun* a prison camp for large numbers of people
invade /ɪnˈveɪd/ *verb* to attack and enter another country with an army
no-man's-land /ˌnəʊ mænz ˈlænd/ *noun* the area between two opposing armies that neither side controls
trench /trentʃ/ *noun* a long narrow hole in the ground for soldiers to shelter in
truce /truːs/ *noun* an agreement between enemies to stop fighting for a short period of time
withdrawal /wɪðˈdrɔːəl/ *noun* the act of moving away troops from an area of fighting

Lexicon

WORDBUILDING

1 PREFIXES

Prefixes **change the meaning of a word** because each prefix has a meaning. They do not change the word to a different part of speech. Some words use different prefixes for different parts of speech: **dis**belief (noun); **un**believable (adjective). Prefixes to express 'not' are very common: **dis-** dishonest, **in-** incorrect, **non-** non-violent, **un-** unlucky.

Another common use is to form words with the opposite meaning or action: **anti-** anti-climax, **dis-** disconnect, **in-** invisible
Note: For words beginning with *l*, *m* (or *p*) and *r*, **in-** changes to **il-** illegal, **im-** immobile, impossible, **ir-** irregular, **un-** undress

MEANING	PREFIX	EXAMPLES
afterwards	after-	aftertaste; afterthought
against	anti-	anti-war; anti-capitalist
opposite	anti-	anti-clockwise; anti-globalisation; antisocial
by yourself/itself	auto-	autobiography; autobiographical; automatic
two or twice	bi-	bicycle; bilingual; bimonthly (twice a month)
together	co-	co-operate; co-author
reduce	de-	degenerate; defuse; devalue
remove	de-	decode; deforestation; deregulate
not	dis-	disagree; disbelief; dishonest; disloyal; dissimilar
opposite	dis-	disappear; disconnect; disqualify
to a lower level	down-	downgrade; downhill; downstairs; downstream
former	ex-	ex-husband; ex-president; ex-student
before	fore-	forecast; foresee
in front	fore-	foreground; forename
not	il-; im- in- ir-	illegal; illiterate; illogical; immoral; impatient; impossible inability; inconvenient; incorrect; inefficient; insensitive; intolerant; invisible irrelevant; irregular; irresponsible
between	inter-	international; interact
badly or wrongly	mal-	malfunction; malnourised; malpractice
huge	mega-	megarich; megastar
extremely small	micro-	microchip; microscope; microscopic
small or short	mini-	minibus; miniskirt
bad/badly or wrong/wrongly	mis-	misbehave; misplace; misunderstand; mismanagement
one or alone	mono-	monolingual; monotonous
many	multi-	multinational; multi-purpose; multi-racial
not	non-	non-smoker; non-violent; non-profit-making
more/more than	out-	outgrow; outnumber
outside	out-	outdoors; outskirts
too much or too long	over-	over-estimate; overgrown; overpopulation; oversleep; overwork
above/on top	over-	overcoat; overhead; overlap
across	over-	overland; overseas
after	post-	postgraduate; post-war; postscript
before	pre-	pre-historic; pre-school; pre-war
in favour of	pro-	pro-European; pro-war
not real	pseudo-	pseudo-intellectual; pseudonym
again	re-	rebuild; re-examine; re-unite; rewind
in another way	re-	replace; rearrange; replant
half	semi-	semi-circle; semi-final
partly	semi-	semi-active
below	sub-	submarine; substandard; subway
less or less important	sub-	subnormal; sub-committee; subplot
large, great or powerful	super-	supermarket; superstar; superpower
across	trans-	trans-continental; trans-Atlantic; transport
showing change	trans-	transform; translation
three	tri-	triangle; trilogy
not	un-	uncomfortable; uncommon; uncrowded; unfriendly; unhelpful; uninteresting; unlikely; unlucky; unreliable; unspoilt; unstable; unusual
opposite action	un-	undo; undress; unlock; unpack; unzip
not enough	under-	undercooked; undernourished; underpaid
underneath	under-	underclothes; underline; underpass
too little/too small	under-	under-estimate; undersized
to a higher level	up-	upgrade; uplift; upstairs

Remember: You can add a prefix as well as a suffix: **dis**appear**ance**; **ill**egal**ly**; **mis**understand**ing**

Lexicon

2 SUFFIXES

Most suffixes **change a word to a different part of speech**. When we add a suffix, we sometimes change the spelling of the original word (*silent > silence; glamour > glamorous*). The stress or pronunciation often changes (*communicate > communication; produce /prəˈdjuːs/ > production /prəˈdʌkʃn/*).

The table below shows some key words from *Opportunities*; check word stress and pronunciation in a good dictionary.
→ page 158 for suffixes that change words to particular parts of speech.

NOUN	VERB	ADJECTIVE	ADVERB
ambition	-	ambitious	ambitiously
attraction	attract	attractive	attractively
beauty	-	beautiful	beautifully
breadth	broaden	broad	broadly
care	care	careful, careless	carefully, carelessly
chat	chat	chatty	chattily
child	-	childish, childlike	childishly
communication	communicate	communicative	communicatively
competition	compete	competitive	competitively
consideration	consider	considerate	considerately
creation, creativity	create	creative	creatively
critic, criticism	criticise	critical	critically
danger	-	dangerous	dangerously
decision	decide	decisive	decisively
depth	deepen	deep	deeply
difference	differ	different	differently
disaster	-	disastrous	disastrously
elegance	-	elegant	elegantly
enjoyment	enjoy	enjoyable	enjoyably
fame	-	famous	famously
fashion	-	fashionable	fashionably
glamour	glamorise	glamorous	glamorously
grace	-	graceful	gracefully
happiness	-	happy	happily
help	help	helpful, helpless	helpfully, helplessly
height	heighten	high	highly
hope	hope	hopeful	hopefully
imagination	imagine	imaginative	imaginatively
importance	-	important	importantly
impression	impress	impressive	impressively
interest	interest	interesting, interested	interestingly, interestedly
introduction	introduce	introductory	-
length	lengthen	long, lengthy	lengthily
logic	-	logical	logically
mood	-	moody	moodily
mystery	-	mysterious	misteriously
nation	-	national, nationalistic	nationally, nationalistically
nature	-	natural	naturally
obsession	obsess	obsessive	obsessively
perfection, perfectionist	perfect	perfect	perfectly
pleasant, pleasure	please	pleasing	pleasingly
politeness		polite	politely
popularity	-	popular	popularly
poverty	-	poor	poorly
practice	practise	practical	practically
pride	-	proud	proudly
production	produce	productive	productively
rarity	-	rare	rarely
reality	realize	real	really
reliability	rely	reliable	reliably
satisfaction	satisfy	satisfactory, satisfied, satisfying	satisfactorily, satisfyingly
sense	-	sensible	sensibly
silence	-	silent	silently
spectacle, spectator	-	spectacular	spectacularly
suspicion	suspect	suspicious	suspiciously
sympathy	sympathise	sympathetic	sympathetically
thought	think	thoughtful	thoughtfully
threat	threaten	threatened, threatening	threateningly
tolerance	tolerate	tolerant	tolerantly
width	widen	wide	widely

Lexicon

Forming nouns from verbs
–ance (accept > accept**ance**); **–ence** (exist > exist**ence**)
–tion (produce > produc**tion**); **–sion** (divert > diver**sion**)
–ation (inspire > inspir**ation**); **–ication** (qualify > quali**fication**)
–isation (privatise > privat**isation**); **–ition** (add > add**ition**)
–er (teach > teach**er**); **–or** (act > act**or**); **–r** (bake > bake**r**)
–ing (paint > paint**ing**); **–ment** (judge > judge**ment**)
–ist (type > typ**ist**); **–ure** (please > pleas**ure**)
–y (discover > discover**y**)

Forming nouns from adjectives
–ability (suitable > suit**ability**)
–ibility (responsible > respons**ibility**)
–ance (important > import**ance**); **–ence** (silent > sil**ence**)
–ness (ill > ill**ness**); **–iness** (happy > happ**iness**)
–ity (human > human**ity**)
–ty/ieth (six > six**ty**/six**tieth**)

Forming nouns from nouns
–ian (music > music**ian**)
–ist (science > scient**ist**)

Forming adjectives/adverbs from nouns
–al/–ally (magic > magic**al**/magic**ally**), **–ial/–ially** (industry > industr**ial**/industr**ially**)
–ate/–ately (affection > affection**ate**/affection**ately**)
–ic/–ically (artist > artist**ic**/artist**ically**), **–ical/–ically** (economy > econom**ical**/econom**ically**)
–ful/–fully (peace > peace**ful**/peace**fully**), **–iful/–ifully** (beauty > beaut**iful**/beaut**ifully**)
–ing/–ingly (interest > interest**ing**/interest**ingly**)
–ised (computer > computer**ised**)
–ive/–ively (expense > expens**ive**/expens**ively**), **–itive/–itively** (sense > sens**itive**/sens**itively**)
–less/–lessly (harm > harm**less**/harm**lessly**)
–ous/–ously (glamour > glamor**ous**/glamor**ously**), **–ious/iously** (industry > industr**ious**/indusctr**iously**)
–th/–ieth (sixty > six**th**/six**tieth**),
–ular/–ularly (spectacle > spectac**ular**/spectact**ularly**)

Forming adjectives and adverbs from verbs
–able/–ably (fashion > fashion**able**/fashion**ably**); **–ible/–ibly** (flex > flex**ible**/flex**ibly**)
–ed (worry > worri**ed**)
–ing/–ingly (annoy > annoy**ing**/annoy**ingly**)
–ive/–ively (attract > attract**ive**/attract**ively**)

Forming verbs from adjectives
–ate (active > activ**ate**)
–en (sweet > sweet**en**)
–ify (simple > simpl**ify**)
–ise/–ize (legal > legal**ise**/legal**ize**)

Unusual suffixes
long (adj.) > length (noun) > lengthy (adj.) > lengthen (verb)
belief (noun) believe (verb) > believable (adj.)

Suffixes with meanings
–dom (star > star**dom**)
–hold (house > house**hold**)
–hood (mother > mother**hood**)
–ish/–ishly (child > child**ish**/child**ishly**)
–less/–lessly (end > end**less**/end**lessly**)
–like (life > life**like**)
–ship (friend > friend**ship**)

Remember: You can add a suffix as well as a prefix: **dis**agree**ment**; **il**leg**ally**; **un**accept**able**.
Some words use different prefixes for different parts of speech:
believe (verb) > **dis**belief (noun) > **un**believable (adj.) > **un**believable (adv.)

3 Confusing words

childish immature: *That was a **childish** thing to say.*
childlike like a child: *He has an attractive, **childlike** innocence.*

different not the same: *These shirts are **different** sizes.*
indifferent 1 not caring about something: *He's **indifferent to** my problems.* 2 not noticing something: *There was a loud party next door, but I was **indifferent to** the noise.*

dissatisfied not happy with the quality of something: *I was **dissatisfied** with my exam result.*
unsatisfied not happy with the quantity of something: *He ate a big meal but was still **unsatisfied**.*

helpful willing to help or be useful: *That's a **helpful** suggestion.*
helpless unable to do things for yourself: *He is totally **helpless** in difficult situations.*

hopeful feeling optimistic: *I'm **hopeful** we can find a solution.*
hopeless 1 having no signs of hope: *This is a **hopeless** situation.* 2 very bad at something: *She's **hopeless at** playing chess.*

senseless illogical, or with no reason or purpose: *It's **senseless** to try and change things now.*
sensible reasonable and practical: *She's a very **sensible** girl and you can rely on her.*
sensitive being easily hurt or offended: *He's very **sensitive to** criticism about his work.*

4 Compounds

Compounds are two or more words together that act as a single word. They usually represent an action or description in a short form ('a game played using a computer' becomes a *computer game*; someone with fair hair is described as *fair-haired*). Compounds can be written as one word (*hairstyle*), two words joined by a hyphen (*old-fashioned*) or two separate words (*rain forest*). There are no rules for this.

Compound adjectives

We can form compound adjectives by combining:
1 an adjective or noun with a word ending in *–ing* or *–ed*: *good-looking, old-fashioned* **2** a past participle or adverb with a preposition: *fed-up, grown-up* **3** a noun with an adjective: *duty-free*

absent-minded forgetful
airtight not allowing air to pass in or out
antisocial showing no concern for other people
brand-new new and unused
class-conscious aware of the social class that people come from
family-orientated believing the family is very important
fair-sized fairly big
far-reaching having a great influence
firsthand learnt directly and not from other people
full-time working the usual hours in a job → PART-TIME
good-looking handsome or pretty
grown-up like an adult behaves
ground-breaking making important discoveries or using completely new methods
high-powered very powerful
homesick missing home very much
law-abiding who never does anything illegal
life-size of the same size as a real person or thing
long-standing existing for a long time
long-term for a long period into the future
long-term (effects)
mass-produced made in large quantities in a factory
mould breaking = ground-breaking
old-fashioned no longer fashionable or popular
one-year-old being one year old
open-air outdoor
part-time working only part of the usual hours → FULL-TIME
performance-enhancing that improves physical performance
ready-made cooked and ready for eating
real-time describes a virtual reality game that takes as long as the real game
record-breaking better than the existing record
run-down in bad condition
second-hand not new and already used
short-lived lasting only a short time
time-consuming using up a lot of time
ultra-smart very clever
user-friendly easy to use and understand
well-behaved behaving in an acceptable and polite way
well-known famous
well-off rich
world-class among the best in the world
world-famous famous in all parts of the world
worn-out very tired or in a poor condition

Compound nouns

In compound nouns, the first part usually describes the type of the second part. We can form compound nouns by combining:
1 two nouns: *sunglasses* **2** an adjective and a noun: *popstar* **3** a verb and a preposition or adverb: *breakthrough* **4** a noun and a word ending with *–ing*: *water-skiing*

blood pressure the force with which your blood moves through your body
body-piercing the act of putting jewellery into the skin in a part of your body
carbon emissions gases produced as a waste product of burning fuels such as coal or oil
civil war a war between two groups in the same country
common sense good sense and judgement
consumer society a modern society in which advertising encourages people to buy things
designer label a label on clothes showing a fashionable manufacturer
eyesore something ugly (often a building)
fossil fuel coal or oil
gang warfare fighting between groups of people
gene therapy medical treatment using genes from cells
genetic code the arrangement of genes that makes a living thing like its parents
genetic engineering the deliberate changing of the form of a living thing using its genes
human being a man, woman or child
hydro-electric power electricity produced by moving water
ice skating moving on ice for fun or sport using special boots
immune system the system in your blood that fights diseases
information technology technology using computers
jigsaw puzzle a picture cut into pieces that you try to fit together
job security the condition of feeling safe in a job
junk food bad quality ready-made food
laptop a small, portable computer
legal action the use of the law to punish someone for doing something illegal
lifetime the usual period of time of someone's life
long-term that last into the future
living-room a place in a house for relaxing, watching TV, etc.
machine gun a gun that shoots many bullets
neuroscientist a scientist who is an expert in the body's nervous system
nightlife entertainment at night
no-man's land the area between two opposing armies that neither side controls
organ donor someone who gives a body organ for medical use, especially after they have died
package tour a holiday with everything organised for you
passive smoking breathing in smoke from other people's cigarettes
rain forest a hot and wet forest in a tropical region
road rage violent behaviour by drivers towards other drivers
room service the service in a hotel of providing food and drinks in your room
science-fiction describes stories about future scientific and technical developments and their effects on life
self-defence the skill of defending yourself when attacked
sightseeing visiting places of interest as a tourist
slow motion movement on television that is much slower than in real life
so-called having the description or name that you think is wrong
software computer programs
solar power electricity produced by heat and light from the sun
solar system the sun with the planets, etc. that move round it
stepping stone an act or event that helps you achieve something else
telephone directory a book that contains the telephone numbers of all the people in a particular area
test tube a thin glass bottle used in scientific experiments
trading centre a place that imports and exports goods
wake-up call a phone call in a hotel to wake you up
washbag a small bag for soap, toothpaste, etc. when you travel
working week the hours you work in a week
zero-gravity the state or situation of having no gravity

Compound verbs

We can form compound verbs by combining:
1 a preposition or adverb and a verb: *overtake* **2** a noun and a verb: *mass-produce* **3** an adjective and a verb: *double-check*

bypass to avoid something: *Can we bypass this part of the tour?*
double-check to examine something again to make sure it is correct: *I double-checked that I had turned the gas off.*
mass-produce to make large quantities of products in a factory

Lexicon

Compounds using prepositions or adverbs

adjectives

follow-up something that follows something else: *The group's **follow-up** album to their first hit was not a success.*
in-depth very detailed: *an **in-depth** report.*
laid-back very relaxed: *He never gets excited – he's **laid-back**.*
oncoming coming towards you: ***oncoming** traffic.*
outgoing 1 friendly and easy to get on with. 2 leaving a job: *The **outgoing** manager gave a press conference.*
out-of-date not popular or valid any more
outspoken giving your opinions freely
overloaded having too much to carry
rundown 1 tired or ill: *I feel pretty **rundown**.* 2 in bad condition: *It's a very **rundown** area.*
underpaid not paid enough
understaffed with not enough workers: *Many hospitals are **understaffed** at the moment.*
underweight too thin or light
up-to-date modern or popular

nouns

after-shave: *I love the smell of his **after-shave** (lotion).*
breakthrough an important discovery: *The discovery of penicillin was a major **breakthrough** in medicine.*
bypass 1 a road round a town. 2 an operation to send blood round a part of your heart with a problem: *a heart **bypass**.*
downfall something you do that makes you lose success: *Gambling led to his **downfall**.*
follow-up something you do to make sure an earlier action is successful: *This lesson is **a follow-up to** last week's.*
getaway an escape: *The thieves made **a quick getaway**.*
outbreak a sudden appearance of something (usually bad): *There was **a serious outbreak** of flu.*
outcome the result: *What was **the outcome of** the election?*
outlook a developing situation: ***The outlook for** tomorrow's weather is fine.*
rundown a summary of events: *Give me **a rundown of** what happened.*
setback something that prevents progress or makes something worse: *Peace negotiations have suffered **a setback**.*
upkeep the cost of keeping something in order: *We can't afford **the upkeep of** such a big house.*

verbs

off-load to take things out of a car, lorry, train, etc.
outgrow to grow bigger than the size or space provided: *He has already **outgrown** his shoes.*
overhear to hear what other people are saying to each other
oversleep to sleep longer than you wanted to
undercook to not cook something for enough time
underestimate to think that a quantity, skill, etc. is less than it really is: *I **underestimated** her ability.*
update to provide the latest information: *After the attack, there were radio broadcasts **updating** the news every half hour.*
upgrade 1 to make something, e.g. a computer, more powerful. 2 to give someone a more important job

Multi-word compound nouns and adjectives

We can make compound nouns and adjectives with more than two words. There are always hyphens between the words.

*an **eighteen-year-old** boy*
*a **heart-to-heart** talk*
*my **mother-in-law***
*a **one-in-a-thousand** chance*
*an **out-of-work** actor*
*an **up-to-date** dictionary*

COLLOCATION BANK

verb + noun or adjective

break the record to do something better than the best achievement so far
catch a cold to get a cold
close the gap to do something that brings two extremes closer together, e.g ***closing the gap between** rich and poor.*
contract an illness/disease to get an illness/disease
drive someone mad to make someone feel upset or angry
express your concern/worry/horror/shock/an opinion about something to say what you feel or think
express your thanks (to someone) (for something) to say thank you
feel part of something to feel you are a member of a group
give someone/something a bad name to harm the reputation of someone or something
give someone permission (to do something) to say someone can do something
give someone a warning (about something) to warn someone
go mad 1 to get very angry. 2 to become insane
last a lifetime to last a very long time
miss home to feel unhappy because you are not at home
pack your bags to pack your things before you travel
play a joke on someone to play a trick on someone
play a role to take part in a play, project, etc.
put on weight to gain weight and become fatter
reach an agreement (with) to agree on something after a discussion
receive acclaim for something to receive compliments and admiration
spend money/time (on something) to spend money on/give time to something
take it easy to stop doing so much work
turn cold (weather)/ **nasty** (person or animal)/ **pale** (person)
turn red to show you feel embarrassed

adjective + noun

anti-social behaviour bad behaviour
developed country a country with an advanced economy
developing country a country without an advanced economy, often called a 'Third World' country
dry climate/clothes/land without rain/water
dry sense of humour humour when someone pretends to be serious when they are not
fatal disease a disease that often causes death
fresh air clean and pleasant air
heavy fighting/rain a lot of fighting/rain
latest fashion/style the most popular fashion/style now
petty argument a minor argument
renewable energy natural energy from such sources as the wind or the sun: *Solar power is a source of **renewable energy**.*
severe punishment very hard and strict punishment
social benefit something that will help society
social mobility movement between levels of society
urban decay the decline in living conditions in big cities
vast majority nearly all of a large group
violent crime a crime that hurts or kills someone
working conditions the conditions for workers in a factory, etc.

verb + adverb

fall down heavily to fall and hurt yourself badly
rain/spend heavily to rain/spend a lot
sleep heavily to sleep deeply and be hard to wake up
take someone/something seriously to value someone or something: *Graffiti is often not **taken seriously** in the art world.*

For expressions with *do, get, have, make* → PAGE 162
For prepositions in phrases → PAGE 166

Lexicon

Adjectives for describing appearance

This table tells you which adjectives you can use (✓) with a variety of nouns. The choice of a word depends on the context.

Example: You CAN say '*I saw a **breathtaking** view*', but you CAN'T say '*I saw a **breathtaking** man*'.
For adjectives describing music → MODULE 4, PAGE 152.

	people	clothes	hairstyles	movement, e.g. of a dancer, animal	buildings, e.g. church, bridge	rooms	furniture	views, e.g. sunset	works of art, e.g. paintings, sculptures	decoration, e.g. wallpaper
attractive	✓	✓	✓	✓	✓	✓	✓	✓	✓	✓
beautiful	✓	✓	✓	✓	✓	✓	✓	✓	✓	✓
breathtaking				✓				✓	✓	
cheap		✓					✓			✓
chic		✓					✓			✓
classy	✓	✓				✓	✓			✓
comfortable		✓				✓	✓			
contemporary		✓	✓		✓	✓	✓		✓	✓
cosy		✓				✓				
dated		✓	✓				✓			✓
dramatic			✓	✓	✓			✓		
effortless				✓						
elegant	✓	✓	✓	✓	✓	✓	✓			✓
enormous	✓	✓			✓	✓	✓		✓	
exotic		✓	✓						✓	✓
fashionable	✓	✓	✓			✓	✓			✓
good-looking	✓	✓								
gorgeous	✓	✓			✓	✓	✓	✓	✓	✓
graceful	✓			✓			✓			
handsome	✓(men)				✓					
impressive	✓			✓	✓	✓		✓	✓	
magnificent		✓		✓	✓	✓	✓	✓	✓	✓
messy	✓	✓	✓			✓				
old-fashioned	✓	✓	✓			✓	✓			✓
picturesque								✓		
powerful	✓			✓					✓	
pretty	✓(women)	✓				✓		✓		
relaxed	✓			✓						
scenic								✓		
smart	✓	✓	✓			✓	✓			✓
sophisticated	✓	✓				✓				
spacious					✓	✓				
spectacular		✓	✓		✓	✓		✓		
striking	✓	✓	✓		✓					✓
stunning	✓	✓	✓		✓	✓	✓	✓	✓	✓
stylish	✓	✓	✓	✓	✓	✓	✓			✓
tacky		✓				✓	✓		✓	✓
tasteless		✓				✓	✓		✓	✓
trendy	✓	✓	✓			✓	✓		✓	
unsightly				✓		✓	✓	✓		✓
unspoilt								✓		

Lexicon

EXPRESSIONS WITH DO, GET, HAVE AND MAKE

do

1 tasks and work:
Can you **do** me **a favour** and help me with this maths problem?
I hate **doing the garden** – it's such hard work!
I like to **do my homework** as soon as I get home.
Who **does the housework** in your home?
My parents **do the shopping** on Saturday mornings.
Don't **do the washing-up** – we've got a dishwasher.
She has **done** some useful **research** into the causes of Aids.

2 activities:
I **do athletics/gymnastics/tennis/horse riding** every Tuesday after school.
My sister is **doing English/history/science** at university.
Don't just sit there **doing nothing** - **do something**!

3 actions:
This isn't working – I think I **did something wrong**.
Don't worry about the exam; just **do your best**.
The storm **did a lot of damage**.
It'll **do you no harm** to visit your grandparents now and again.
Did you **do well** in your test?

get

1 to obtain or receive:
I really must **get a haircut** before the wedding.
I **got a letter/email/message** from Brigit this morning.
He **got** a lot of **money** from his weekend job.
After two years with the company, he **got a promotion**.
I **got a shock/surprise** when he arrived – I didn't expect him.
Get some sleep! You look like you need it!
I think I'm **getting a cold**! I feel awful.

2 to become or achieve:
I have **got attached to** our neighbours puppy.
That's a terrible cold – I hope you **get better** soon.
These instructions are awful – I can't **get beyond** the first step.
I'd better go; it's **getting dark**.
Hurry and **get dressed** or you'll be late.
She can't concentrate for long. She **gets fed up** quickly.
I **get the feeling** you don't agree with the government.
Don't leave when it's dark – you could easily **get lost**.
Our car **got stuck** in the mud after the heavy rain.
She's very ambitious. I'm sure she'll **get to the top**.
I'd like to **get in touch with** Jim, but I've lost his phone number.
I was just beginning to **get worried** when he phoned.

have

1 experiences:
I **had a cold/fever/headache**, so I took an aspirin.
Last night, I **had** a terrible **dream** about being lost.
Have fun at the party!
I'm **having a haircut** this afternoon.
We always **have a laugh** when we get together.
She's going to **have an operation** on her bad leg next week.
I'm tired. Let's **have a rest**.
You'll **have a surprise/shock** when you see him – he's really changed.

2 actions:
We **had an argument about** football.
I **have a bath/shower** every morning.
I **had breakfast/lunch/dinner** with Charlie.
Can I **have a look at** your holiday photos?
At weekends I **have a lie-in** till about ten.
I'm going to **have a party** on my birthday.
I think the neighbours are **having a row**.
They're **having a swim** in the hotel pool.

3 to possess something (also **have got**):
How many brothers and sisters do you **have**?
You must accept the decision – you really **have no choice**.
I don't know the answer. I **haven't a clue**!
We both like music and reading – we **have a lot in common**.
I **have an idea** – why don't we go swimming?
I **have a good/bad** memory.
He **has a lot of patience** with children.
I've tried to give up sweets, but I **have no willpower**.

4 to produce an effect:
The war will **have a bad effect on** the economy.
The weather **had an influence on** the result of the match.

make

1 actions:
They **made an agreement with** us **to** meet at 6 o'clock.
You should **make an appointment** at the dentist's.
I **make my bed** as soon as I get up.
We'd like to **make a complaint** about the bad service.
I had to **make a decision** before six o'clock.
We **made an effort** to finish on time.
He **made an excuse for** not doing his homework.
Don't **make fun of** him – it's not fair.
Keep calm. There's no need to **make a fuss**.
He's so funny. He always **makes me laugh**.
I'm going to **make** you **an offer** you can't refuse!
Can I **make a phone call**, please?
She's **making progress** at school.
I'd like to **make a reservation** at the hotel for Friday night.
I think she'll **make a success of** her business.

2 to create, or produce:
Make me **a cup of tea**, please.
He invested well and **made a fortune**.
He **makes a living** selling his own vegetables.
Don't **make a mess** in your bedroom – try to keep it tidy!
I think you've **made a mistake** – Mr Smith doesn't live here.
He **made** a lot of **money** selling his paintings.
Our neighbours often **make a** lot of **noise** at weekends.
You **made a good point** at the meeting.
Could I **make a suggestion**, please?

WORD PAIRS

I love watching old **black and white** films from the 1930s.
I've got lots of **bits and pieces** to take to school tomorrow including my pen, pencil, paper, and books.
Italian merchants travelled **far and wide** buying and selling goods.
The **flora and fauna** in the region is very interesting, particularly the trees, flowers, birds and a rare breed monkeys.
There is a million people in the city, **give or take** a few thousand.
More and more people joined the protest march.
There were **loads and loads** of people there – over 20,000!
I found **odds and ends**, like my racket and some books.
I've been learning French **on and off** for years.
He's feeling better and I've seen him **out and about** again.
I hate all this traffic noise. I'd like to go to the country for some **peace and quiet**.
You must take this one – you can't **pick and choose**.
A hundred years ago, both **rich and poor** suffered from polio.
I'm **sick and tired** of getting up at six o'clock. I'd love a lie-in!
Sooner or later you're going to have to tell her.
He made a real **song and dance** about going to the doctor.
I expected them to post my passport later but they gave it to me **then and there**.
The price of petrol has been going **up and down** this year.
I've had my **ups and downs** this past year, but it's good experience!
Prices keep on going **up and up**. They don't stop.

Lexicon

Word families

This list gives you words for saying similar things. It is a good idea to make your own lists as you find new words for each group.

Verbs

laugh
cackle /ˈkækl/ to laugh loudly
chuckle /ˈtʃʌkl/ to laugh quietly
giggle /ˈgɪgl/ to laugh in a silly way
smile /smaɪl/ to move the corners of your mouth up to show you are happy
snigger /ˈsnɪgə/ to laugh to yourself in a disrespectful way

hold
cling /klɪŋ/ to hold something tightly: *The little boy was clinging to his mother because he was frightened.*
clutch /klʌtʃ/ to hold something tightly because you are frightened: *She clutched at the police officer's hand.*
cuddle /ˈkʌdl/ to hold someone close to you in a loving way: *He cuddled his young son in his arms.*
grab /græb/ to take something suddenly and quickly: *The thief grabbed my bag and ran off.*
grasp /grɑːsp/ to take hold of something strongly: *He grasped my hand and led me through the crowd.*
handle /ˈhændl/ to hold or move an object in your hands in order to examine it: *Please handle the glass with care.*
hug /hʌg/ to hold someone in your arms because you like them a lot: *She hugged her mother when they met at the airport.*
take hold of /ˌteɪk ˈhəʊld əv/ to take something in your hands: *The captain took hold of the trophy and held it up to the fans.*
touch /tʌtʃ/ to make contact, usually with your hand: *She touched her arm to show me where it hurt.*

say/speak
beg /beg/ to ask someone for something in an eager way: *He begged me not to leave him.*
chat /tʃæt/ to talk to someone in a relaxed, informal way: *I met an old friend and we chatted about our schooldays.*
claim /kleɪm/ to state that something is true, although you may not be able to prove it: *He claimed he hadn't received the letter.*
exclaim /ɪkˈskleɪm/ to say something loudly and suddenly, usually when you are shocked or surprised: *'Hey, look at the time!' he exclaimed, 'We're late!'*
howl /haʊl/ to make a loud cry: *He howled in pain when he fell over.*
inquire /ɪnˈkwaɪə/ to ask in a polite and formal way for information: *'What time does the plane land?' she inquired.*
mention /ˈmenʃn/ to say something without giving details: *During our chat, he mentioned that Sue had had a baby.*
mutter /ˈmʌtə/ to say something in a quiet voice, usually when you are not happy about something: *Jim muttered something about not wanting to go shopping.*
recall /rɪˈkɔːl/ to remember something and tell it: *Do you recall seeing anything unusual?*
reply /rɪˈplaɪ/ to answer: *I asked him to help me. He replied that he was busy.*
scream /skriːm/ to shout in a high voice: *When I fell into the water, I screamed for help.*
shout /ʃaʊt/ to say something very loudly: *I heard someone shouting for help.*
shriek /ʃriːk/ to shout in a high voice: *They shrieked with laughter.*
whisper /ˈwɪspə/ to say something in a very quiet voice: *He whispered the answer so no one else could hear.*
yell /jel/ to shout very loudly: *Stop yelling – come here and tell me what you want.*

look
gaze /geɪz/ to look at something or someone for a long time: *He gazed out of the window.*
glance /glɑːns/ (often **glance around, at**, etc.) to look at something or someone very quickly: *She glanced at herself in the mirror.*
glimpse /glɪmps/ to see something quickly and without a complete view: *I only glimpsed him – I wouldn't recognise him again.*
observe /əbˈzɜːv/ to look and pay careful attention: *Observe the change in colour as I add the acid.*
spot /spɒt/ to identify or notice someone or something when it is not easy: *Can you spot me in this old photo?*
stare /steə/ (often **stare at someone/something**) to look at someone or something for a long time: *Who are you staring at?*
watch /wɒtʃ/ to look carefully: *We watched Arsenal beat United.*
witness /ˈwɪtnɪs/ to see something happen: *Did anyone witness the accident?*

walk
limp /lɪmp/ to walk slowly and with difficulty, often because of an injury: *He limped home after the long match.*
march /mɑːtʃ/ to walk with regular steps: *The band marched through the streets in the parade.*
shuffle /ˈʃʌfl/ to walk slowly without lifting your feet: *I could hear the old woman next door shuffling around.*
stagger /ˈstægə/ to walk unsteadily: *She staggered away from her car after the accident.*
stride /straɪd/ to walk with long steps: *The teacher strode across the playground to stop the fight.*
stroll /strəʊl/ to walk slowly in a place for pleasure: *They strolled around the park.*
strut /strʌt/ to walk in a proud way, with your chest forward: *Male birds strut in front of female birds to attract their attention.*
trudge /trʌdʒ/ to walk slowly with a lot of effort: *The soldiers trudged through the mud.*
wander /ˈwɒndə/ to walk slowly in a place without a particular purpose: *We wandered round the shops for an hour.*

Adjectives

big
1 describing very large and impressive buildings, animals or organisations: colossal; enormous; gigantic; huge; massive
2 describing very large places, areas or distances: enormous; huge; immense; vast

happy
cheerful /ˈtʃɪəfl/ showing you are happy: *a cheerful smile.*
contented /kənˈtentɪd/ satisfied and happy: *He sat looking contented after the meal.*
delighted /dɪˈlaɪtɪd/ very pleased and happy: *I'm delighted to see you.*
elated /ɪˈleɪtɪd/ happy because you have been successful: *We left the stadium elated by our team's victory.*
glad /glæd/ pleased and happy: *I'm glad you came.*
pleased /pliːzd/ happy and satisfied: *He's pleased with your work.*
thrilled /θrɪld/ very happy or excited: *I was thrilled to see her.*

rich
affluent /ˈæfluənt/ having money for expensive clothes, meals, etc.
loaded /ˈləʊdɪd/ extremely rich.
prosperous /ˈprɒspərəs/ successful and rich
wealthy /ˈwelθi/ very rich and with valuable property
well-heeled /ˌwelˈhiːld/ rich and often from a high social class
well-off /ˌwelˈɒf/ having more than enough money to live well
well-to-do /ˌweltəˈduː/ rich and with a high social position

sad
dejected /dɪˈdʒektɪd/ unhappy because you feeling disappointed
depressed /dɪˈprest/ very unhappy and not hopeful
down /daʊn/ (colloquial) unhappy and sad
gloomy /ˈgluːmi/ unhappy and not at all hopeful
glum /glʌm/ sad and not willing to talk
miserable /ˈmɪzrəbl/ very unhappy because you're poor, ill, etc.

Lexicon

IDIOMATIC LANGUAGE

animals
have a bee in your bonnet to have a fixed idea: *He's got **a bee in his bonnet about** graffiti.*
a bookworm a very keen reader: *She's always reading – she's a real **bookworm**.*
let the cat out of the bag to tell a secret, often without intending to: *He **let the cat out of the bag about** the surprise party.*
as sick as a dog very ill: *I was **as sick as a dog** after I ate that seafood.*
like a fish out of water uncomfortable because you are not in your usual surroundings: *He lives in the city and when he goes to the countryside he's **like a fish out of water**.*
be a fly on the wall to be a secret observer: *I'd love **to be a fly on the wall** when those two are arguing.*
a/the rat race a competitive and stressful lifestyle: *Working in marketing is **a rat race**.*
the black sheep of the family someone in a family or group who doesn't behave like the rest: *The Smiths are all very nice, except for Jim – he's **the black sheep of the family**.*

body
before their very eyes in front of something so they can't avoid it: *She slapped him **before my very eyes**.*
face (up to) something, face it to accept something: *I had to **face (up to)** the fact that I was never going to be a famous football player. Let's **face it**, it's not going to be easy.*
face death to be in a very dangerous situation: *Racing drivers **face death** whenever they race.*
be knee deep in something to have a lot of things to do: *He's **knee-deep in** work at the moment.*
not make head or tail of something to not understand something: *I can't **make head or tail** of these instructions.*
pull someone's leg to do or say something as a joke to make someone worry: *Don't be upset, I'm only **pulling your leg about** your girlfriend!*
fed up to the (back) teeth to be very angry or bored: *I'm **fed up to the back teeth** with getting up so early every day.*

food/cooking
eat humble pie to admit that you were wrong: *When I discovered I had made a mistake, I had to **eat humble pie** and apologise for my behaviour.*
a melting pot a place with an exciting mixture of cultures: *London is **a melting pot** with people from every part of the world.*
for starters to begin with: ***For starters** he's selfish and he's also rude.*
be starving to be extremely hungry: *Isn't it time for lunch? We're **starving to death**!*

life/death
the birth of something the beginning: ***The birth of** English theatre was in the 16th century.*
be the cradle of something the place where something began: *Greece was **the cradle of** western civilisation.*
be bored to death extremely bored: *I'm **bored to death of** your complaints.*
be dying for something to want something very much: *I'm **dying for** a sandwich.*
be in its infancy to be in the early stages: *In the 1960s, space travel was still **in its infancy**.*

money/work
bet to say you are sure about something: *I **bet** she's late again.*
(all) the betting is that it is fairly certain that: ***All the betting is that** he fails his exams.*
take its toll on someone/something to have a bad effect: *All that hard work **has taken its toll on** her health.*

movement
go downhill to get worse: *His health **went downhill** after the accident.*
kick up a fuss to complain a lot: *He **kicked up a fuss** because the soup was cold.*
be within reach to be able to be achieved: *A cure for AIDS **is within** our **reach**.*
be a major step forward to be an important advance: *Landing on the moon was **a major step forward** for space exploration.*
a stepping stone something you can use to achieve a long-term goal: *I want to be a chef but I work in a restaurant as **a stepping stone** for the future.*
not touch something with a bargepole to not get involved or use something because you think it is bad: *That new sports club sounds awful. I wouldn't **touch it with a bargepole**.*

nature
be a breath of fresh air to be something new or different that encourages you: *My new school **is a breath of fresh air** – we have lots of different subjects.*
put someone out to grass to make someone leave a job because they are too old: *They've **put him out to grass** and given him the job of making the coffee.*
be (skating/walking) on thin ice to be in a situation when you may make someone angry: *When you regularly arrive late at work, you're **skating on thin** ice.*
the last straw something that happens that, added to other problems, makes a situation impossible: *I had one problem after another. The **last straw** was when the car broke down.*

places
a vicious circle a bad situation that affects other things: *He is **in a vicious circle**. He's homeless. This means that he can't get a good job and so he stays poor.*
to the four corners of the globe all over the world: *He has travelled **to the four corners of the globe**.*
be home and dry to have succeeded in doing something
be right up your street to be in your area of interest or activity: *Science fiction **is right up my street**.*
off the beaten track a long way from anywhere: *We went to a little cottage in the countryside right **off the beaten track**.*
be in the middle of nowhere to be in a place far from a town: *It's **in the middle of nowhere**. The town is miles away.*

others
set the ball rolling to begin something: *Let's **set the ball rolling**. Who wants to talk first?*
not have a clue to not have any idea about something: *I **haven't got a clue** how to repair my computer.*
be on a short fuse easily made angry: *She was tired and **on a very short fuse**.*
from the word go from the start: *We fought **from the word go**.*
not care two hoots (about someone/something) to not care at all: *I don't **care two hoots** if they come or not.*
(get/give someone/something) a bad name to get or give someone or something a bad reputation: *That club's **got a bad name**. The police have closed it down twice.*
a nightmare something very unpleasant: *The exam was **a complete nightmare**. Everything went wrong.*
be not (all) plain sailing not easy: *The job **wasn't all plain sailing**.*
give it to somebody straight to say something directly: *I'm going to **give it you straight**. I don't love you any more.*
make a song and dance (about something) to complain too much: *Don't **make a song and dance** about your homework.*

Lexicon

PREPOSITION BANK

1 PREPOSITIONS OF TIME

at shows a particular point in time: **at** night; **at** lunchtime; **at** five o'clock; **at** Christmas; **at** sixteen years of age; **at** the age of sixteen; **at** my age; **at** the beginning/end of the year; **at** the moment

by no later than a particular in the future: **by** Friday; **by** next week, year, etc.; **by** ten o'clock; **by** the end; **by** the time (that)...

during throughout a period of time: **during** the afternoon, evening, etc.; **during** the exam; **during** the holidays; **during** the past month, year, etc.; **during** (the) winter, spring, etc.

for shows a length of time: **for** ages; **for** a couple of months; **for** a few minutes, days, etc.; **for** a long time; **for** almost a week; **for** the weekend; **for** twenty years

from starting at a particular time: **from** one o'clock; **from** about seven in the evening; **from** March **to** July; **from** morning till night; **from** now on

in
1 during a period of time: **in** the afternoon, morning, etc.; **in** the middle of the night; **in** the 1990s; **in** (the) spring; **in** my spare time; **in** the last hundred years
2 at the end of a period of time: **in** the end; **in** the future; **in** a minute; **in** a month or two; **in** five years; **in** half an hour; **in** an hour's time
3 shows the month, year, etc. when: **in** May; **in** 2005; at five **in** the morning; **in** future

into (usually **late into** or **well into**) during a particular time or age: **late into** the night; **well into** her twenties

on at a time during a particular day: **on** Christmas morning; **on** Tuesday; **on** 5 November; **on** the right/wrong day

since from a particular time or date in the past up to now: **since** 5 o'clock; **since** Tuesday; **since** January; **since** 2001; **since** her birthday; **since** then; **since** last year; ever **since** she arrived

throughout during a period of time until the end: **throughout** March; **throughout** the afternoon; **throughout** the exam; **throughout** the holidays; **throughout** her life; **throughout** the past month, year, etc.; **throughout** (the) winter, spring, etc.

until (also **till**) shows when something stops happening: **until** Friday; **until** 9 o'clock; **until** the end of the month; **until** now; **until** the 1980s; **until** next week

up to (also **up until**) until an exact time: **up to** ten o'clock; **up until** the time they got married

within before a period of time has passed: **within** a year, week, etc.; **within** a few days

2 PREPOSITIONS OF POSITION/ORDER

above: There's a mark on the wall just **above** the door.
across: There is a tree **across** the road and we can't get past.
against: The bike was leaning **against** the tree.
along: There are trees **along** the side of the street.
among: She was standing **among** a group of people.
around (also **round**): They were standing **around** the statue.
at → THE END OF THIS SECTION
back to front: You've got your vest on **back to front**.
behind: I heard a voice **behind** me. I turned round and saw Pete.
below: From the top you could see the whole city **below** you.
between: I was sitting **between** two people – Tom on my left and Sue on my right.
in front (of): He stood **in front of** the students and started to give his lecture.
in the front/middle (of): Who's that **in the middle of** the picture?
inside out: He's got his socks on **inside out**.
near to: My house is quite **near to** the city centre.
next to: I sit **next to** her in class and we do pairwork together.
on → THE END OF THIS SECTION
on top of: There's a church **on top of** the hill.
opposite: There's a café directly **opposite** my house.
over: We put a cloth **over** the parrot's cage at night.
under (also **underneath**, **beneath**): My case is **under** my bed.
upside down: The picture is **upside down** – put it the right way up.
within → THE END OF THIS SECTION

at
1 shows the position or general area: **at** the cinema, bank, etc.; **at** the corner; **at** the end; **at** the entrance; **at** dinner; **at** home; **at** Anna's house; **at** the station; **at** work
2 shows sequence: **at** last; **at** my second attempt; **at** the end

in
1 inside containers or vehicles: **in** a bottle, box, etc; **in** a taxi
2 inside a place: **in** Africa; **in** class; **in** bed; **in** London; **in** town; **in** a book; **in** a spaceship; **in** her car; **in** the street; **in** the world
3 part of a group: **in** a pop group; **in** the school football team
4 with a particular arrangement: **in** alphabetical order; **in** groups of ten; **in** a line, row, queue, etc.; **in** the right order

on
1 inside a vehicle, etc., or on a vehicle, animal: **on** a boat; **on** a bus; **on** a cruise; **on** horseback
2 in a particular area or place: **on** a farm; **on** the beach; **on** the coast; **on** page 52; **on** the pavement; **on** the planet; **on** the road; **on** the Underground
3 in a particular position: **on** the left/right; **on** the edge, side, etc.; **on** the inside/outside; **on** the top (of)
4 shows travelling, etc. in a place: **on** a cruise; **on** holiday, journey, trip, etc.; **on** the way to work

within inside an area: **within** range; **within** reach; **within** sight of

3 PREPOSITIONS OF DIRECTION

across: He walked **across** the street to the other side.
along: We drove **along** the road until we came to the village.
around: I ran **around** the house three times.
away: He stole the apple and ran **away**.
behind: It went cold when the sun went **behind** some clouds.
down: We followed the path **down** the hill.
from: I ran home **from** the station **to** my house.
into: I put the papers **into** my case. He jumped **into** the water. I got **into** bed. He has to go **into** hospital for an operation.
on (also **onto**): I got **on/onto** the bus outside my house.
out of: I went **out of** the house to get some fresh air.
over: The gate was closed so I had to jump **over** the fence.
towards: The fans ran **towards** the stadium.
through: The thieves came into the house **through** one of the windows.
to: I walked **to** the end of the street to meet a friend.
round: He drove **round** the corner much too fast.
under: The mouse ran **under** a cupboard to escape the cat.
up: I ran **up** the stairs and rested when I got to the top.
up to: I went **up to** a policeman to ask the way to the museum. Fill the kettle **up to** the top.

Lexicon

4 PREPOSITIONS IN PHRASES

above all: Be kind and polite but **above all** be helpful.
ahead of: There was a long queue **ahead of** us.
along with: I passed the piano exam **along with** three other people in the class.
apart from: Your essay is very good, **apart from** a few spelling mistakes.
as for me, you, etc: My family is moving to Canada. But **as for me**, I don't want to go. → FOR ME, TO ME
at the end of: Let's meet up **at the end of** the month when we are less busy.
at first: I was angry **at first** but then I realised she was very sorry.
at home: I **stayed at home** because of the awful weather.
at (long) last: I've found a good tennis coach **at (long) last**.
at the moment: **At the moment** I'm living in Athens.
at that very moment: I was turning the corner and **at that very moment** a child ran into the road.
at any rate: I think they are coming – **at any rate** that's what they told me.
at risk: Your health is **at risk** if you smoke.
because of: We can't go for a walk **because of** the rain.
by accident: I knocked over the display **by accident**.
by chance: We planned to meet on Sunday but we met **by chance** on the bus this morning.
by mistake: I'm sorry but I took your dictionary **by mistake**.
by the time: **By the time** we arrived, they had already gone.
for a while: We waited **for a while** and then left without her.
for me, her, you etc.: I don't like that disco – **for me** it's too noisy! → AS FOR ME, TO ME
for now: We have enough tea **for now** but we might need more later.
for sale, rent, etc: Is your old computer **for sale**?
from bad to worse: Your behaviour **is going from bad to worse**.
from memory: I can play the whole tune **from memory**.
from now on: **From now on** you must all show your membership cards.
in addition to: She works in the café **in addition to** her job at the cinema.
in aid of: We're collecting money **in aid of** the refugees.
in case: Let's take an umbrella (**just**) **in case** it rains.
in charge of: Who's **in charge of** the tickets on the door?
in comparison to/with: She is much taller **in comparison to** (or **with**) most of us here.
in contact with: Are you **in contact with** anyone we met in London?
in danger of: You're **in** great **danger of** failing all your exams.
in demand: Are those electronic pets still **in demand**?
in the end: **In the end** all of us agreed with her plan.
in front of: She stood **in front of** the mirror admiring herself.
in a hurry: Sorry, I can't stop. I'm **in a hurry** to get work.
in a mess: Your room is **in a terrible mess**.
in my opinion: **In my opinion**, bus fares should be cheaper.
in need of: The house is very old and **in need of** major repairs.
in order that: I did it **in order that** you would notice me.
in order to: I shouted **in order to** get help.
in reality: She said she was rich but **in reality** her parents are very poor.
in return for: I lent her a couple of CDs **in return for** using her bike.
in search of: They've gone **in search of** a cheap restaurant.
in spite of: We enjoyed our walk **in spite of** the rain.
instead of: Why don't you go to the match **instead of** me?
in terms of: **In terms of** their recent successes, the team is a good one.
in good time: Please be there **in good time** because we still have to buy the tickets.
in time: I arrived **just in time** for the start of the film.
in no time: Work hard and you'll finish **in no time** (**at all**).
in touch: Goodbye – keep **in touch** and email me.
in a way: You're right **in a way** but I still don't agree with you.
not at all: I'm **not at all** happy with my essay.
of course: 'Can I come?' '**Of course** you can.' 'Do you mind?' '**Of course** not.'

on a diet: She has been **on a diet** for the last month.
on fire: Oh, look! The shed is **on fire**!
on the grounds of: He was expelled from school **on the grounds of** cheating in the exam.
on the increase: Sadly, street muggings are **on the increase** in major cities.
on the Internet: I found a way to buy books cheaply **on the Internet**.
on the lottery: Have you ever won any money **on the lottery**?
on his own: Did Sol really go to the cinema **on his own**?
on my mobile: Leave a text message **on my mobile**.
on the phone: She's **on the phone** at the moment.
on purpose: I think you lost my pen **on purpose**.
on a huge, large, small, etc. **scale**: In the 1980s, there was unemployment **on a large scale**.
on time: The train arrived exactly **on time**.
on top of that: She refused to help and **on top of that** she called me a liar.
on the whole: **On the whole** I prefer swimming to playing tennis.
on the verge of: Scientists are **on the verge of** finding a cure for some cancers.
out of breath: I was **out of breath** when I reached the top of the hill.
out of control: Your younger brother is completely **out of control**.
out of order: 1 The phones at the station are always **out of order**. 2 not polite or acceptable: Her behaviour was completely **out of order**!
out of the ordinary: Nothing **out of the ordinary** happens in our town.
out of practice: I'd love to play chess with you but I'm **out of practice**.
over a million, etc: There are **over two million** refugees in the camps.
over the top: Don't you think your anger was **over the top**? He wasn't that bad!
to me, her, us, etc.: **To me**, that picture is terrible! → AS FOR ME, FOR ME
together with: I went to the museum **together with** most of our group.
under control: The situation is now **under control** and things are back to normal.
under your breath: 'I'll prove that you are wrong,' she muttered **under her breath**.
under way: Plans are **under way** to build a new stadium.
up to you: It's **up to you** to decide – I can't make the decision for you.
ups and downs: Every family has its **ups and downs**.

5 THE PASSIVE

We use **by** to show the 'agent' (WHO is responsible for the action):
'Hamlet' was written **by** Shakespeare.
The website was designed **by** a young computer programmer.

We use **with** to say HOW the action was done:
The winning team was greeted **with** cheers.
It was covered **with** water. It was made **with** flour and eggs.

6 PREPOSITIONS AT THE END OF SENTENCES

I know the man you are working **for**. (with a relative clause)
I asked him who he was talking **to**. (reported speech)
What are you getting **at**? (questions with multi-part verbs)
I don't like being laughed **at**. (passives with multi-part verbs)

7 Prepositions after nouns, adjectives, and verbs

Index

about
nouns: *argument; article; complaint; decision; discussion; opinion; protest; question; reminder*
adjectives: *angry; annoyed; anxious; curious; disappointed; enthusiastic; nervous; optimistic; passionate; pleased; sad; worried*
verbs: *care; complain; hear; know; talk; think; worry*
against nouns: *campaign; complaint; protest*
among noun: *competition*
at
nouns: *look*
adjectives: *amazed; angry; bad; clever; good; pleased; sad; shocked; surprised; useless*
verbs: *laugh; look; smile*
between noun: *competition*
by
adjectives etc.: *annoyed; close; disgusted; impressed; shocked; surprised* → THE PASSIVE above
for
nouns: *affection; application; campaign; cause; competition; demand; excuse; hope; look; need; opportunity; punishment; reason; request; respect; reward; suggestion; sympathy*
adjectives, etc: *bad; enough; essential; except; famous; good; ready; responsible; sorry; unfit; well-known*
verbs: *admire; apologise; pay; play; wait*
from
nouns: *distance; extract; view*
adjectives, etc: *absent; different; far*
verb: *suffer*
in
noun: *confidence; fall; growth; interest; rise; taste; trust*
adjectives: *experienced; interested; involved*
verbs: *believe; invest; take part*
into noun: *research; study; translate*
of
nouns: *advantage; approval; beginning; cause; collection; cradle; end; enough; evidence; feat; hope; importance; loss; masses; member; mention; number; opinion; packet; percentage; period; piece; portion; question; range; reminder; risk; series; slice; study; suggestion; threat; turnout; victim; view*
adjectives, etc: *afraid; ashamed; aware; fond; full; made; nervous; plenty; proud; short; typical; unaware*
verbs: *consist; remind; think*
on
nouns: *agreement; article; attack; effect; impact; influence; lecture; opinion; view*
adjectives: *dependent; keen*
verbs: *comment; concentrate; decide; depend; focus; insist; operate; rely; spend; work*
out of
adjective: *made*
verb: *make*
over noun: *victory*
to
nouns: *attention; attitude; damage; entrance; injury; reaction; relation; reply; solution; thanks; threat*
adjectives, etc.: *according; bad; close; due; kind; next door; owing; polite; related; rude; similar*
verbs: *apologise; belong; complain; emigrate; listen; refer; talk*
towards noun: *attitude*
with
nouns: *appointment; argument; chat; contact; interview; relationship; sympathy; talk; trouble* → THE PASSIVE above
adjectives: *angry; annoyed; bored; busy; delighted; disappointed; disgusted; familiar; happy; impressed; infected; pleased; satisfied*
verbs: *argue; chat; deal; fall in love; get in touch; play*
upon
adjective: *dependent*
verb: *insist; rely*

Examples with adjectives and nouns

absent from: She was **absent from** class for two weeks because of her illness.
according to: **According to** our records, you haven't paid your fees.
advantage of: Surely, I don't need to explain **the advantages of** a good education.
affection for: After our holiday, I felt **a strong affection for** everyone in our group.
afraid of: I'm still afraid of the dark.
agreement on: They couldn't **reach an agreement on** how much the car was worth.
amazed at: I was **amazed at** how easy it was to get a ticket for the match.
angry about, at/with: He'll **be angry about** your decision to cancel the party. She was **angry at** (or **with**) me for being late.
annoyed about/by, with: She was annoyed **about** (or **by**) their loud music. I'm **annoyed with** him for making me wait.
anxious about: Are you **anxious about** your exams?
application for: Have you filled in your **application for** the job?
appointment with: I have an appointment with my dentist on Monday.
approval of: You need **the approval of** your manager before you can leave early.
argument with, about: He had an **argument with** his parents **about** the mess in his bedroom.
article about/on: Did you read **the article about** (or **on**) Afghanistan?
ashamed of: You ought to **be ashamed of** yourself **for** being so unkind.
attack on: The speech was **an attack on** the government's immigration policy.
attention to: No-one seemed to **pay** any **attention to** what he was saying.
attitude to/towards: Their **attitude to** (or **towards**) foreigners is unacceptable.
aware of: I'm sure you're **aware of** the dangers of smoking.
bad at, for: She's **bad at** tennis and even I can beat her. Sweets are **bad for** your teeth.
beginning of: Please give me your essay **at the beginning of** next week.
bored with: I'm **bored with** watching television all the time.
busy with: He was too **busy with** his homework to go to the cinema.
campaign against, for: We took part in **the campaign against** the war. We need **a strong campaign for** cheaper public transport.
cause of, for: No-one knew the **cause of** the fire. There's no **cause for** alarm.
chat with: Why don't you **have a chat with** your parents about your problem?
clever at: My sister is very **clever at** maths and always gets good marks.
close by, to: Is there a bank **close by**? Do you live **close to** the school? He moved **closer to** the fire. I'm very **close to** my sister and we tell each other everything.
collection of: He has **a superb collection of** stamps.
competition among/between, for: There is a lot of **competition among** (or **between**) the banks **for** new customers.
complaint about, against: We've received a few **complaints about** the quality of some of our toys. We investigate all **complaints against** our staff.
concerned about: I'm **concerned about** you walking home alone.
confidence in: I **have** complete **confidence in** your ability to do the job.
contact with: I'm still **in contact with** several people from my primary school.
cradle of: Is Greece **the cradle of** democracy?
curious about: I'm **curious about** how you managed to get a ticket to the game.
damage to: The floods did a lot of **damage to** the village.
decision about: We haven't yet made **a decision about** who will have the lead role in the school play.
delighted with: Dad's **delighted with** his new car.

Lexicon

demand for: There has been **a** strong **demand for** an end to Third World Debt.
dependent on/upon: Your place at university is **dependent on** (or **upon**) your exam results.
different from: My idea of a perfect holiday is very **different from** yours.
disappointed about, with: I'm **disappointed about** not being allowed to go out tonight. We were **disappointed with** the players during the second half.
discussion about: They were having **a discussion about** what to do at the weekend.
disgusted by/with: We were **disgusted by** (or **with**) his obscene language.
distance from: The hotel is **a** short **distance from** the airport.
due to: The game has been cancelled **due to** the bad weather.
effect on: Smoking will have **a** very bad **effect on** your health.
end of: Nearly everyone was crying **at the end of** the film.
enough for, of: There is **enough** food **for** everyone. I've **had enough of** your bad behaviour.
enthusiastic about: She didn't seem very **enthusiastic about** my idea.
entrance to: We agreed to meet **at the entrance to** the cinema.
essential for: Vegetables and fruit are **essential for** your health.
evidence of: Your exam result shows no **evidence of** having done any revision.
except for: Everyone arrived on time **except for** Ben.
excuse for: Losing your shoes is **a** poor **excuse for** being late.
experienced in: I'm not very **experienced in** using the Internet.
extract from: Let me read you **a** short **extract from** his letter.
fall in: There's been a dramatic **fall in** tourists in London.
familiar with: Are you **familiar with** the rules of tennis?
far from: Is the station **far from** here?
famous for: She's **famous for** writing excellent detective novels.
feat of: The bridge is **a** marvellous **feat of** engineering.
fond of: I'm **fond of** chocolate.
full of: The café was **full of** people last night.
good at, for: I'm no **good at** remembering names. Exercise is **good for** you.
growth in: There has been **a** significant **growth in** the number of women playing football.
happy with: I'm not very **happy with** my peformance.
hope for, of: Until the war is over we have no **hope for** the future. We had no **hope of** escape.
impact on: Computers have had **an** enormous **impact on** education.
importance of: Don't underestimate **the importance of** eating a good breakfast.
impressed by/with: Everyone was **impressed by** (or **with**) her piano playing.
infected with: Millions of people are **infected with** Aids throughout the world.
influence on: Which of your teachers has had the most **influence on** you?
injury to: He suffered serious **injuries to** both legs in the accident.
interest in: I have no **interest in** sport whatsoever.
interested in: I am not at all **interested in** sport.
interview with: She has **an interview with** a journalist on Thursday.
involved in: Don't **get involved in** any arguments about politics or religion.
keen on: I'm not very **keen on** swimming in the sea because it's too cold.
kind to: Be **kind to** her – she is only trying to be helpful.
lecture on: He gave **an** interesting **lecture on** the latest theories about how life began.
look at, for: When you are in London; **have a look at** the Tate Modern building. I'll **have a look for** a postcard of it if you like.
loss of: She never recovered from **the loss of** her parents in the car crash.
made (out) of: My jacket is **made of** leather. What's this table **made out** of?
masses of: He was surrounded by **masses of** fans.
member of: You're **a member of** the sports centre, aren't you?

mention of: There was **no mention of** his latest film in the newspaper. Was there any **mention of** the match on TV last night?
need for: I think there's **a need for** international co-operation to stop global warming.
nervous about, of: I'm very **nervous about** my exams. She's **nervous of** dogs because she was once badly bitten.
next door to: We live **next door to** the stadium.
number of: **A** large **number of** countries signed the treaty to reduce greenhouse gases.
opinion about, of, on: I don't have any **opinion about** who to blame. What's your **opinion of** his latest film? I'd like to hear your **opinion on** capital punishment.
opportunity for: A visit to London would be a great **opportunity for** improving your English.
optimistic about: I don't feel very **optimistic about** world peace.
owing to: The motorway was closed **owing to** a serious accident.
packet of: Can you get me **a packet of** cornflakes, please.
passionate about: He's **passionate about** football.
percentage of: A large **percentage of** women voted against the government.
period of: We are expecting **a** long **period of** hot weather.
piece of: Can I have another **piece of** cake; please?
pleased about, at, with: Mum was very **pleased about** my exam results. We were so **pleased at** the news of your success. Dad is very **pleased with** his new car.
plenty of: There will be **plenty of** food at the party.
polite to: Most children are **polite to** their parents.
portion of: I'd like two **portions of** ice-cream, please?
protest about, against: What is your **protest about**? It's a **protest against** the war.
proud of: You can be very **proud of** what you have achieved.
punishment for: What is **the punishment for** murder?
question about, of: They asked me lots of **questions about** my hobbies. It's **a question of** who will be our representative.
range of: Have you seen their new **range of** clothes? The plane was **in** (or **within**) **range of** airport control.
reaction to: What's your **reaction to** the news that the fees will be increased?
ready for: Hurry up and **get ready for** school.
reason for: What is your **reason for** being late this time?
request for: There has been **a request for** more blood donors.
related to: I think ill health is definitely **related to** poverty.
relation to: Opportunities for women are small **in relation to** men.
relationship with: Practically everyone has **a** good **relationship with** our teacher.
reminder about/of: Do you need more **reminders about** (or **of**) the dangers of smoking?
reply to: Have you written **a reply to** your uncle yet?
research into: They are doing lots of **research into** a vaccine for malaria.
respect for: I have great **respect for** people who work for charities.
responsible for: Who is **responsible for** all this mess?
reward for: You can stay up late tonight **as a reward for** your good behaviour.
rise in: There has been **a rise in** crime over the past year.
risk of: There is always **a risk of** failure but we must try.
rude to: He is never **rude to** his parents in front of other people.
sad about/at: We were **sad about** leaving London. Everyone was **sad at** (or **about**) the news of the air crash.
satisfied with: I'm not **satisfied with** your reason for being late.
series of: After **a series of** failures, we finally won a match.
short of: We're **short of** volunteers to help with the school play.
shocked at/by: I was **shocked at** (or **by**) the way he spoke to his father.
similar to: Her taste in music is **similar to** mine.
slice of: Can I have another **slice of** cake; please?
sorry for: I'm **sorry for** all the trouble I caused you.
solution to: I'm afraid I can't think of **a solution to** your problem.
study of, into: He's making **a study of** birds in tropical forests. It will be **a study into** how birds survive in smaller forests.
suggestion for, of: Do you have **a suggestion for** what to do this weekend? I thought I heard **a suggestion of** doubt in his voice.

Lexicon

surprised at/by: He was not **surprised at** (or **by**) her success.
sympathy for, with: I've no **sympathy for** students who never do their homework. Do you have any **sympathy with** their views on world poverty?
talk with: Have a **talk with** your parents and see what they say.
taste in: She has no **taste in** clothes.
thanks to: **Thanks to** your help, I passed my exams.
threat of, to: There's a **threat of** colder weather later this week. The conflict is a serious **threat to** world peace.
trouble with: The **trouble with** you is that you don't listen to good advice.
trust in: Have **trust in** your own opinions.
turnout of: We expect a good **turnout of** fans in spite of the rain.
typical of: It's so **typical of** you to say 'no' at first when you mean 'yes'.
unaware of: I'm **unaware of** any opposition to our plans.
unfit for: After his lies, he's obviously **unfit for** any job in government.
useless at: I'm **useless at** learning languages.
victim of: Many **victims of** crime never get any support.
victory over: The treaty is a **victory over** those who prefer to fight than to talk.
view from, of, on: The **view** across London **from** the London Eye is outstanding. The **view of** Paris in his last painting is the best I've seen. Do you have any **view on** how to solve global warming?
well-known for: London is **well-known for** its museums and galleries.
worried about: I was so **worried about** waking up in time that I couldn't get to sleep.

Examples with verbs

Many verbs have more than one part that include prepositions. Sometimes the preposition is optional and depends on meaning: She's **working** hard. She's **working on** a project.
→ MULTI-PART VERBS, PAGES 170–176 Some of these have prepositions and usually have an idiomatic meaning: get in touch **with** someone, make up **for** something, come **across** something.

Remember: Verbs with more than two parts take the object at the end: I **got in touch with** an old school friend.

admire someone for something: I **admired** him **for** showing his true feelings.
agree with someone/something: I don't **agree with** the report on the match.
apologise to someone (for): I **apologised for** my behaviour at the party. I **apologised to** the teacher **for** arriving late.
argue with someone (about): I hate **arguing with** my neighbours **about** noise.
believe in something: I'm afraid I don't **believe in** ghosts. I think it's all in people's imagination.
belong to someone: This bag **belongs to** a friend of mine.
care about someone/something: Do you **care** at all **about** what is happening in the world?
chat with someone (about): He's **chatting with** my mum **about** his family.
comment on something: It's still too early to **comment on** the success of the project.
concentrate on something: **Concentrate on** getting the spelling right.
complain to someone (about): We **complained to** the manager **about** the quality of the service in the restaurant.
consist of something: Air **consists of** oxygen and hydrogen.
deal with someone/something: The dentist **dealt with** my tooth and the pain stopped.
decide on something: I've **decided on** a career in computers.
depend on/upon someone/something: Your exam results will **depend on** the amount of work you do. (also **rely on/upon someone/something**) Can I **depend on** you to be there on time?
emigrate to somewhere: They **emigrated to** Australia last year.
fall in love with someone/something: 1 I've **fallen in love with** you. 2 We've completely **fallen in love with** Mozart's music.

focus on something: We use the passive form to **focus on** the action and not the person who does it.
get in touch (with): She promised **to get in touch with us** as soon as she gets back from her holiday.
hear something about something: Have you **heard** the joke **about** the elephant and the ant?
insist on/upon something: Our sports teacher **insisted on** us training three days a week. My mother **insists that** I eat breakfast before I go to school.
invest something in something: We need to **invest** more **in** solar energy.
know something (about): I don't **know** a lot **about** politics.
laugh at someone/something: It's not very nice to **laugh at** other people.
listen to someone/something: I love **listening to** music on the radio.
look at someone/something: Everybody **looked at** me when I got onto the bus.
make something out of something: She **made** a dress **out of** pure silk.
operate on someone: They **operated on** her after her heart attack.
pay for something: I **paid for** the newspaper and left the shop.
play for, with someone/something: The Portuguese footballer, Luis Figo, used to **play for** Barcelona. The children are very bored here because they have no one to **play with**.
refer to someone/something: You'll need to **refer to** your notes before you do the exercises.
rely on/upon someone/something → DEPEND ON/UPON
remind someone of someone/something: She **reminds** me **of** my own sister. Seeing him **reminded** me **of** a great holiday in the Lakes.
smile at someone/something: The bus driver **smiled at** me when I paid him.
spend (money) on something: I've **spent** a lot (of money) **on** clothes this month.
suffer from something: Do you **suffer from** headaches?
take part in something: I **took part in** a demonstration last week **about** the new power station.
talk about someone/something: Hi. We **were** just **talking about** you.
talk to someone (about): We met at a party and **talked about** music for two hours. I often **talk to** my friend Susan in the evenings.
think about, of someone/something: What do you **think about** that new CD by Prince? I often **think of** my family when I am away from home.
translate something into something: The novel **has been translated into** several languages.
wait for someone/something: I'm **waiting for** the post. We **waited for** someone to begin dancing. I've been **waiting for** the bus for ages.
work on something: Scientists have been **working on** a new drug to cure Parkinson's disease.
worry about someone/something: I wouldn't **worry about** that exam if I were you.

Lexicon

MULTI-PART VERBS

Most multi-part verbs have an object and we can usually put it after the verb or after the preposition: *Please **turn** the TV **on**. Please **turn on** the TV*. The list shows this by putting 'something' or 'someone' in the middle and using an example with it at the end: → BACK SOMETHING UP.
When the object can only go after the preposition, the list has 'something' or 'someone' at the end: → BE ABOVE SOMETHING.
If the object is a pronoun, it usually goes before the preposition: *Please **put** it **on***.
Some multi-part verbs do not have an object: *Please **go in** and **sit down***.
Other multi-part verbs have an adverb + preposition and the object goes at the end. → BE IN FOR SOMETHING.
Brackets show that an object or a preposition is optional.
→ CHEER (SOMEONE) UP.

back out (of something/doing something) to not do something you have promised: *She **backed out of** her promise to help.*
back something up to be proof or evidence to support an idea, explanation, etc: *Find more information to **back up** your theory.*
be above something 1 to be so important that you needn't do particular things: *She think she's **above** doing housework.* 2 to be so good that no one can think you did something wrong: *He's **above** suspicion.*
be about something (also **be to do with something**) to explain, describe or give facts on a particular subject: *It's a book **about** information technology.*
be about to do something to be ready to start to do something very soon: *I was **about to** close the door when the phone rang.*
be after someone to be trying to catch someone: *The police had been **after** the robber for months.* → GO AFTER SOMEONE/SOMETHING
be against something/someone to disagree with or not support someone or something: *I'm **against** every kind of racism.* → TURN AGAINST SOMEONE
be getting at something to be explaining or saying something important: *What I'm **getting at** is that computers can never express human emotions.*
be behind (with) to not have done as much as you should: *You're **behind** with your homework.* → FALL BEHIND (WITH)
be down to feel very sad: *He's been so **down** since he failed his exam.* → GET SOMEONE DOWN
be (all) for something/someone to support an idea, plan, person, etc. very strongly: *I'm all **for** nurses being paid more.*
be dying for something to want something very much: *I'm **dying for** a cup of coffee.*
be in 1 to be at home: *Is your mother **in**?* → STAY, STOP IN 2 to be popular: *Very short hair is definitely **in** these days.* → FIT IN
be in for something to be likely to experience something uncomfortable or difficult: *I'm afraid we're **in for** another very cold night.* → COME IN FOR SOMETHING
be taken in (by) to be made to believe something that isn't true: *He was completely **taken in by** the girl's sad story.*
be into something to enjoy doing a particular activity very much: *I'm not really **into** stamp collecting.*
be off 1 to not be going to happen: *The match is **off** because of the rain.* → CALL SOMETHING OFF 2 to smell or be bad: *This fish is **off**.* → GO OFF
be let off to be allowed to go without being punished: *Luckily we were **let off** by the manager.* → LET SOMEONE OFF
be on to be going to happen: *The tennis match is **on** again because the rain has stopped.*
be not on to not be acceptable: *It's just **not on** to change the date of the meeting so late.*
be out 1 to not be at home: *I'm sorry, my mother's **out**.* → GO, WALK OUT 2 to not be in fashion any more: *Hats are **out**.*
be out of something to not have something in your home or shop: *We're **out of** brown bread.* → RUN OUT OF SOMETHING
be over to have finished: *The play will be **over** by ten o'clock.* → GET OVER SOMETHING

be through (with) to be tired or bored with someone or an activity and so determined to leave: *I can't bear any more lies – we're **through**. I'm **through with** gambling, I promise.*
be up 1 to be out of bed: *It's very late – are you still **up**?* → GET, WAIT UP 2 to have increased in price: *Bus fares are **up** again.* → GO UP
be up to something to be doing something wrong or bad: *What have you been **up to**?*
be caught up (in) to be in a difficult or dangerous situation: *Sadly, many women and children **are caught up in** the war.*
be made up of something to include as its parts: *The population is **made up of** several nationalities.*
blow something up to use a bomb to destroy something: *The bridge has been **blown up**.*
break out to start to happen: *Most of us hope that peace will soon **break out**.* Noun: OUTBREAK
brighten something up to make something more colourful or interesting: *Orange sheets will **brighten up** your bedroom.*
bring something back 1 to return with something: *Please **bring back** my pen tomorrow.* → GET, GIVE, TAKE SOMETHING BACK 2 to make you remember something or someone: *The photograph **brought** it all **back** to me.* → COME BACK (TO)
bring something down to cause a business, etc. to collapse: *The union strikes **brought down** the government.* → FALL DOWN
bring someone on to help or encourage someone to make progress: *Her new piano teacher is **bringing** her **on** nicely.*
bring something on to cause ill health: *Rain **brought on** my cold.*
bring something over (to) to hold something and go near to someone: *He **brought over** another cup of coffee **to** us.*
bring someone up to have a child in your home to live and grow: *My parents **brought** us **up** to be polite and friendly.* → GROW UP
bring something up to mention a topic or piece of information: *I hate to **bring** it **up**, but you owe me ten pounds, don't you?* → COME UP
bump into someone to meet someone by chance: *Guess who I **bumped into** in the supermarket!*
button (something) up to fasten clothes using buttons: ***Button up** your coat – it's very cold.* → DO, ZIP (SOMETHING) UP
call something off to cancel or stop something: *It's raining – shall we **call off** the picnic? The strike was **called off**.* → BE OFF
call on someone to visit someone as a routine: *The nurse will **call on** your mother later.*
call something out to say something in a loud voice: *They **called out** my name.*
can/could do with something/someone to need or want: *I **can do with** someone to help me. He **could do with** a bath.*
carry on (with) to continue a particular activity: *They **carried on** playing in the rain. Be quiet and **carry on with** your work.*
carry something out 1 to take action and complete an examination, research, etc: *The police are **carrying out** a full investigation into the car crash.* 2 to do something planned, promised, threatened, etc: *They are **carrying out** essential repairs to the bridge. She said she'd report us and now she has **carried out** her threat.*
catch up (with) 1 to move and reach the same position as someone else: *You start cycling and I'll you **catch up**.* → KEEP UP 2 to reach the same standard or level as someone else: *You'll need to work harder if you want to **catch up with** the others.* → KEEP UP
chat with someone (about) *He's **chatting with** my mum **about** his family.*
check in to go to the desk of a hotel or airport and say you have arrived: *Please **check in** two hours before your flight.* Noun: CHECK-IN
cheer (someone) up to make yourself (or someone) happier: ***Cheer up**, this rain will stop soon. He did his best to **cheer** me **up**.*
clean something up to make a dirty or untidy place clean: *I must **clean up** my bedroom every Saturday.* Noun: CLEAN-UP
clear (something) up to make a place clean and tidy again: *You can have a party if you promise to **clear up** afterwards.*

Lexicon

click on something to press a key so that an icon on a computer screen works: *Click on that icon to make the email file open.*
come about to happen: *How did it come about that everyone knows my decision?*
come across (as someone) to seem to be a particular kind of person: *He comes across as an idiot but he's really very intelligent. How did I come across at the interview?*
come across something to find something by chance: *I came across this old jacket in my cupboard.*
come apart to fall into pieces: *Honestly, your dictionary just came apart when I opened it.* → FALL APART
come back (from) to return to a place from another place: *Please come back soon. I was coming back from the supermarket when I saw her.* → BRING, GET, GIVE, TAKE SOMETHING BACK, TURN BACK
come back (into fashion) to become fashionable again: *Long coats came back during that cold winter last year.* Noun: **COMEBACK**
come back (to) to return to your memory: *Wait a minute – her name is coming back to me.* → BRING SOMETHING BACK
come between someone and someone to cause a quarrel between two or more people: *Nothing can ever come between me and my girlfriend.*
come down to decrease: *Prices have come down since the summer.* → CUT, GO, SLOW DOWN
come down with something to become ill with a particular infection: *I think I'm coming down with flu.*
come from somewhere 1 to be born or live in a place: *He comes from Istanbul.* 2 to have started or developed from a particular animal, plant or substance: *Do humans come from apes?*
come on 1 to move more quickly: *Come on, let's go.* 2 to begin gradually: *I've got a cold coming on.* 3 to arrive somewhere after others: *You go and I'll come on when I've finished working.*
come out to arrive in the shops, etc: *When will their new CD come out?*
come round 1 to visit someone's home: *Can you come round this evening?* → GO ROUND 2 to become conscious again after fainting: *She's coming round, thank goodness.*
come through to become known: *News came through that they had arrived safely.*
come through something to survive a difficult event or period: *He has come through the operation but he's still sleeping.*
come to to become conscious again after fainting: *She came to and found herself lying on the floor.*
come up 1 to rise in the sky: *The sun was coming up as we began our walk.* 2 to be mentioned: *Whenever there is trouble, her name comes up.* → BRING SOMETHING UP 3 to be used in a test, etc: *I hope that comes up in the exam.* 4 to become available: *A summer job has come up in the café.*
come up against someone/something to have to deal with a difficulty, opposition, etc: *We came up against several problems in the beginning.*
come up to something 1 to reach a particular level: *The water came up to our knees* 2 to be as good as the level people expect: *Your homework doesn't come up to your usual high standard.* → LIVE UP TO SOMETHING
come up with something to produce an excuse, a suggestion, the correct answer, etc: *He came up with a brilliant idea for her birthday present.*
copy something down to write facts, etc. in your notebook: *Copy down these words.* → GET, TAKE, WRITE SOMETHING DOWN
crack (someone) up to begin to laugh a lot, or make someone laugh a lot: *His jokes make me crack up.*
cry out (for) to shout loudly: *She cried out for help but no one heard her.* → CALL, SHOUT, YELL OUT (FOR)
cut down (on) to use much less of something: *Try to cut down on using your mobile phone.*
do (something) up 1 to fasten a piece of clothing, shoes, etc: *Do up your laces. The dress does up at the back.* → BUTTON, ZIP (SOMETHING) UP 2 to decorate a room, etc: *He's doing up the kitchen.*
do with something (always **to do with**) to have something as the topic, reason, etc: *Their rows are to do with money.*
do without to manage without something: *I haven't got any more sweets so you'll have to do without.*

dress up (as someone) (for something) to put on particular clothes so that you look like someone: *Liz dressed up as Tina Turner for the party.*
drop in (on) to visit someone when you are passing: *I'll drop in on you this evening if you like.*
drop off 1 to fall asleep: *I always drop off on the train.* 2 to become fewer: *The number of people who go to restaurants is dropping off.* Noun: **DROP-OFF** → FALL OFF
drop someone off to let a passenger leave a car, bus, etc: *Drop me off at the next corner, please.* → LET SOMEONE OFF
drop out (of) 1 to leave a course of study: *Many students drop out of university at the end of the first year.* 2 to abandon the usual lifestyle of most people in society and live apart: *The twins dropped out of society and went to live with others in the mountains.* Noun: **DROP-OUT**
eat out to eat a meal in a restaurant: *Shall we eat out tonight?*
eat up (something) to eat the whole amount: *He's eaten up all his dinner.*
fade away to become weaker gradually: *The voice under the heap of bricks was fading away.*
fall apart to fall into pieces: *It fell apart in my hands.* → COME APART
fall back on something to use money you kept because you need it: *Do you have money to fall back on if you lose your job?*
fall behind (with) 1 to move more slowly so that others are further ahead: *We fell behind cycling uphill and lost the others.* 2 to make slower progress than others: *Your son has fallen behind with his schoolwork.* 3 to not make the necessary regular payments: *You have fallen behind with your rent.*
fall for someone to feel strong romantic feelings for someone: *I've fallen for her in a big way.*
fall for something to be tricked into believing something that isn't true: *You didn't fall for his excuse about being busy at in the library, did you?*
fall off 1 to become separated from an object: *The handle has fallen off.* → COME OFF 2 to become less gradually: *Sales are falling off.* → DROP OFF
fall out (of) to fall from a high place: *Her favourite toy has fallen out of the window.*
fall out (with) (over) to have a quarrel and end a friendship: *He's fallen out with his girlfriend over the fact that he's often late.* Noun: **FALL-OUT**
fall over to fall onto the ground: *He fell over and hurt his leg.*
fall through to not be agreed, completed, etc. successfully: *At the last minute, the negotiations fell through.*
fill something in/out to complete a questionnaire, application form, etc: *Please fill in the card and give it to Passport Control.* → MAKE SOMETHING OUT
fill (something) up to put liquid in a container, especially petrol into a car: *Let's fill up at the next petrol station. We filled up the car before we drove to Germany.*
find (something) out to learn information about something: *Phone and find out when the film starts.*
find out about something to find facts about something: *What did you find out about dinosaurs at the museum?*
finish something off to eat or drink the last parts: *Hey, you've finished off all the ice-cream!*
fish something out to find and take out something: *The police fished out two bicycles before they found the body in the canal.*
fit in to live easily with your neighbours, friends, family, etc: *For some reason she doesn't fit in and she has few friends.*
fit something in to put something or many things in a container: *I couldn't fit in all my things.*
fix something up 1 to arrange a meeting, etc: *My best friend fixed up a date for me with her brother.* 2 to repair a home and make it attractive: *My dad fixed up the flat for us.*
flood something out to cover a place with deep water: *The whole area was completely flooded out, wasn't it?*
follow something up (with) to take action to deal with something: *The doctors suggested I follow up the operation with a period of complete rest.* Noun: **FOLLOW-UP**
get something across (to) to be successful in explaining your idea, plan, etc: *His speech got across to the audience the reasons for the need to raise interest rates.*

Lexicon

get ahead to have success in your life: *You need a good education in order to **get ahead**.* → GET ON IN LIFE
get around to → GET ROUND TO DOING SOMETHING
get at someone to criticise someone all the time and upset them: *You're always **getting at** me.*
get at something → BE GETTING AT SOMETHING
get away (from/to) 1 to be successful in going on holiday: *We are hoping to **get away to** Berlin for the weekend.* 2 to go from a place, sometimes because it is difficult to stay: *I really must **get away from** this town.* Noun: **GET-AWAY**
get away with something to not be punished for doing something wrong or bad: *He always **gets away with** being late.*
get back (from) to return to a place: *What time will you **get back from** school?* → COME, TURN BACK
get something back to manage to have something you own returned to you: *I'll never **get** my lost watch **back**.* → BRING, TAKE SOMETHING BACK
get your own back (on someone) to punish or harm someone who has done something bad to you: *I'll **get** my own **back** on you one day.*
get by to have enough money or food: *She finds it hard to **get by** on her pension.*
get someone down to cause someone to feel very sad: *All these bills **are getting** me **down**.* → BE DOWN
get something down to write something: *I wasn't able to **get down** her phone number from the answer phone.* → COPY, PUT, TAKE, WRITE SOMETHING DOWN
get down to something to start doing something: *Stop talking and **get down to** your work!*
get in touch (with someone) to phone, email, etc. someone: *I'll **get in touch with** you when I know the exact date.*
get into something 1 to manage to enter a place after an effort: *How did you **get into** the stadium without a ticket?* 2 to start a conversation, fight, etc with someone: *He's always **getting into** rows **with** his parents.*
get (someone) into trouble (with) to do something that makes yourself deserve punishment (or someone): *Staying out late **will** only **get** you **into trouble with** your parents.* → GET (SOMEONE) OUT OF TROUBLE (WITH)
get off 1 to leave a bus, train, etc: *I **got off** at the train station.* → DROP, LET SOMEONE OFF. 2 to start a journey: *We **got off** at eight o'clock.*
get on (in life) to have success in your life: *You need a good education in order to **get on (in life)**.* → GET AHEAD
get on (with) to have a friendly relationship with someone: *I **get on** very badly **with** my cousin. We don't **get on**. Really? I **get on** fine/well **with** her.*
getting on (for) → BE GETTING ON (FOR)
get (someone) out of trouble (with) to do something so that you avoid (or someone avoids) punishment: *Saying you were tired won't **get** you **out of trouble with** your teacher for being late.* → GET (SOMEONE) INTO TROUBLE (WITH)
get out of (doing) something to manage to avoid doing a job you don't like: *I tried to **get out of (doing)** the washing up.*
get something out of something to enjoy an activity, a course of study, etc. and learn many things: *We got a lot **out of** our visit to London.*
get over someone to become happier after the end of a romantic relationship: *How can ever **get over** Jana?*
get over something 1 to become well after being ill with a particular illness: *It takes time to **get over** a bad cold.* 2 to become happier after being sad, frightened, etc: *I'll never **get over** my mother's death.*
get round to doing something (also **get around to**) to do something you have planned or wanted to do for a long time: *When will you **get round to** painting the table?*
get through 1 to be successful when you try to phone someone: *I waited for a long time but I finally **got through to** the ticket office.* 2 to pass a test or exam: *I'm sure you'll **get through**.*
get through something 1 to pass a test or exam: *You'll **get through** your driving test this time.* 2 to survive an unpleasant or difficult period: *If I can **get through** this week, I can **get through** anything!*

get (something) through to someone 1 to manage to reach someone by telephone: *I can't **get through to** the manager.* → PUT SOMEONE THROUGH (TO) 2 to manage to make someone understand something: *I don't seem able to **get through to** you all that this test is very important.*
get to someone to make you feel very angry or upset: *Her criticism of my clothes **is getting to** me.*
get to somewhere to arrive at a place: *When will you **get to** Madrid?*
get together (with) to join other people for a party, meeting, etc: *Let's **get together with** the others after school.* Noun: **GET-TOGETHER**
get (someone) up to wake (someone) up and get (them) out of bed: *What time do you **get up** on Sundays?* → BE, STAY, WAIT UP
get up to something to do something naughty: *What are those boys **getting up to**?*
give something away 1 to give something to someone because you don't want it or because you want them to have it: *Why don't you **give away** that racket since you never use it now?* Noun: **GIVE-AWAY** 2 to tell a secret or give information: someone did not want to know: *Please don't **give away** the ending – we're seeing the film tomorrow.*
give (someone) something back to give something to someone who had it before you: *Please **give** me **back** my dictionary. I'll **give** it **back** to you tomorrow.*
give in (to) to agree to something but not because you want to: *You mustn't **give in to** your children all the time.*
give something out 1 to give copies of the same thing to many people: *Julia **will give out** the books.* → SHARE SOMETHING OUT (AMONG) 2 to tell people something: *The news **was given out** that the attacker had been found.*
give up 1 to admit that you don't know: *I don't know the answer – I **give up**.* 2 to stop doing something because you think you can't make progress: *Don't **give up** – if you practise more, you'll be a good tennis player.*
give something up 1 to stop doing something you have done regularly, especially something bad: *I'm trying to **give up** smoking.* 2 to leave your job: *She **gave up** her job in the bank and travelled round the world, didn't she?*
go after something/someone 1 to try to catch someone: *The police **have gone after** the thieves.* → BE AFTER SOMEONE 2 to try to get something: *He's **gone after** a job in Paris.*
go along with someone/something 1 to go with someone to a place: *I've decided **to go along with** the others to the cinema.* 2 to agree with someone or support something: *We **went along with** all her suggestions.*
go around (also **go about/round**) → GO ABOUT
go away 1 to travel and stay somewhere: *She's **gone away** to France for a holiday.* 2 to stop being present: *I told you – **go away**! Will this cold ever **go away**?*
go down 1 to move to a lower place: *The sun **went down** behind the clouds.* 2 to change to a lower, amount, price, etc: *Do taxes ever **go down**?* → COME, CUT DOWN
go down with something to become ill with a particular disease, etc: *I'm afraid she's **gone down with** flu.*
go for something to make an effort to get or achieve something because you want to: *She's **gone for** a job in the new factory. If you want to win, **go for it**!*
go in 1 to enter: *We can **go in** at seven o'clock.* 2 to be understood: *I try to learn English grammar but it just won't **go in**.*
go in for something 1 to do a particular activity, exam or course of study: *I'm thinking of **going in for** a career in television.* 2 to do something because you enjoy it: *I never did **go in for** watching football on TV.*
go into something 1 to enter a building or room: *He **went into** hospital for three days.* 2 to examine the details of something: *We **will have to go into** all the details of your application.*
go off 1 to move away to another place: *He **went off** on holiday to Spain. Don't **go off** on your own – wait for us.* 2 to become bad: *I think this milk **has gone off**.* → BE OFF 3 to burst into pieces and cause damage: *A bomb **went off** in the street.*
go off something/someone to stop liking someone or something: *I've **gone off** Brad Pitt.*

Lexicon

go off with someone/something to leave a place with someone or something: *My brother **has gone off with** my football shirt.*

go on 1 to happen: *Read newspapers if you want to know what's going on in the world.* 2 to continue doing something: *She was so tired climbing the hill that she thought she couldn't **go on**.* → BE OUT

go on something to be used to pay for something: *This money will **go on** the books I need.*

go on about someone/something 1 to complain about someone or something: *Stop **going on about** how awful your parents are.* 2 to talk about something or someone all the time: *She **goes on and on about** her new boyfriend.*

go out 1 to leave a place: *He's **gone out** to the coffee bar.* 2 to go away from home and enjoy yourself: *I don't **go out** a lot during the week.* → BE OUT 3 to stop burning or producing light: *The fire's **gone out** again. Suddenly, the light **went out**.* 4 (also **go out of fashion**) to stop being fashionable: *High heels **went out** ages ago.* → BE OUT

go out with someone 1 to leave a place with someone: *He's **gone out with** Max to the coffee bar.* 2 to have someone as your girlfriend or boyfriend: *Are you **going out with** anyone at the moment?*

go over (to) to move near someone: *I **went over** (**to**) her and shook her hand.*

go over something to read something or practise something again and check your knowledge: *I need to **go over** the grammar we learned yesterday.*

go round 1 to walk, drive, etc. round the outside of a place: *Trucks must **go round** (the city centre).* 2 to visit a place: *Let's **go round** to Charlotte's house.* → COME ROUND 3 to be enough for everyone or everything: *Is there enough food to **go round**?* 4 (also **go about/around**) → GO ABOUT

go through 1 to pass from one side to the other: *The bed won't **go through** (the door).* 2 to search somewhere: *I've been **through** all the drawers but I can't find it.* 3 to experience pain or difficulty: *He's **gone through** a lot of pain.* 4 to do a set of tasks: ***Go through** the exercises at home.*

go through with something to do something you have threatened to do: *He said he'd tell my mum but he didn't **go through with** it.*

go together 1 to go somewhere with someone: *Let's **go together** to the meeting, shall we?* 2 to look attractive together: *Do you think this blouse and that skirt **go together**?*

go under to go below the surface of water: *The boy **went under** for the third time.*

go up 1 to move to a higher place: *They've **gone up** that hill over there.* 2 to increase: *Prices **have gone up** again.* 3 to be built: *New office blocks **are going up** all over the town.*

go with someone/something 1 to travel with someone: *She's **gone** to London **with** her parents.* 2 to look attractive with something: *I don't think this blouse **goes with** that skirt.* 3 to be part of something: *Does crime always **go with** poverty?*

grow out of something 1 to become too big for clothing or shoes: *You've **grown out of** that jacket.* Noun: OUTGROW 2 to become too old for an activity: *She'll never **grow out of** biting her nails.*

grow into someone to become a particular kind of person as you grow: *He's **grown into** a such a polite young man.*

grow up 1 to become an adult: *What will you do when you **grow up**?* → BRING SOMEONE UP Noun: GROWNUP 2 to behave as an adult: *Will that young man ever **grow up**?*

hang on 1 to hold something: *We **hung on** as the car suddenly turned the corner.* 2 to stay on the phone: ***Hang on**, I'll see if she's still here.* 3 to be patient or wait: ***Hang on** – the ambulance will be here soon.*

hang up to end a phone call by putting down the phone: *If you shout, I'll **hang up**.*

have (got) something on 1 to be wearing particular clothes: *He **had on** blue jeans and a white shirt.* → PUT, TRY SOMETHING ON 2 to have arranged to do something: ***Have** you **got** anything **on** this evening?*

hold on to something 1 to keep you hands on something as support: ***Hold on to** that chair.* 2 to keep something: *May I **hold on to** your dictionary for the weekend?*

hold someone up to prevent someone from leaving or doing something: *The customer was arguing and **held up** everyone in the queue.* → BE HELD UP Noun: HOLDUP

hurry up to move, finish a job, etc. faster: ***Hurry up** or we'll be late.*

join in to be one a group doing something: *Now, I'll sing and I'd like everyone to **join in**.*

keep on (doing something) to continue doing something: *I warned her but she **keeps on smoking**.*

keep someone/something out to prevent someone, a vehicle, etc. from going in or through a place: *How can we **keep out** so many cars in the city centre?*

keep out of something to not be active in something: *I try to **keep out of** discussions about politics.*

keep to something 1 to stay on a particular road, stay with a schedule, etc: ***Keep to** the motorway all the way to Manchester. **Keep to** the left. We must **keep to** the agreed timetable.* 2 to do something you promised or agreed to: *You said you would pay and you must **keep to** that.*

keep up (with) to move at the same speed or level: *You can't come if you don't **keep up with** us.* → CATCH UP (WITH)

keep someone up to stop someone from going to bed: *Everyone was **kept up** by the noise. The party next door **kept** everyone **up** all night.* → BE, STAY, WAIT UP

keep something up to maintain the same high level: ***Keep up** the good work!*

kick off (with) 1 to start playing football: *The match **kicks off** at seven thirty tonight.* Noun: KICK-OFF 2 to start taking part in a discussion, meeting, etc: *Let's **kick off with** a report from the sales manager.* → START OFF (WITH)

kick up a fuss to complain very loudly because you are angry: *She **kicked up a** terrible **fuss** just because the bus was ten minutes late.*

kneel down to rest yourself on your knee: *We all **knelt down** on the floor to look for her contact lens.* → LIE, SIT DOWN

know something about something *I don't **know** a lot **about** science.*

leave for somewhere to start a journey to a place: *The train will be **leaving for** Madrid in one hour.*

leave something on to let a light or machine continue working: *You **left** the lights **on** all night.* → PUT, SWITCH, TURN SOMETHING ON

leave someone/something out (of) to not include someone or something in a group, list, etc: *My name **has been left out of** the list. Did you **leave** anyone **out**?*

let someone down to make someone feel disappointed because you didn't do something you promised: *You've agreed to feed the cat while I'm away – don't **let** me **down**.*

let someone off 1 to let someone leave a bus, train, car, etc: *You can **let** me **off** at the corner.* → GET OFF; PUT SOMEONE DOWN. 2 to allow someone to go without being punished: *I'll **let you off** this time but don't do it again.* → BE LET OFF Noun: LET-OFF

lie down to put yourself in a position with your body flat on a bed, the floor, etc: *I've got a headache so I'll **lie down** for a while.* → KNEEL, SIT DOWN. Noun: LIE-DOWN

lie in to stay in bed after your usual time for getting up: *He **lies in** all morning on Sundays.* Noun: LIE-IN

listen to someone/something *I love **listening to** music on the radio.*

live it up to enjoy yourself, especially while you spend money: *He's **living it up** in London.*

live up to something to do something to the excellent level people expect: *It's hard to **live up to** your parents' expectations.* → COME UP TO SOMETHING

log on/off to do the actions that turn a computer on or off: *Click on 'Shut down' to **log off**.*

look after someone to take care of someone and give them what they need: *There was no one to **look after** Margery when she was ill.*

look after something to watch something so that it isn't stolen or broken: *Can you **look after** my bag while I go and buy my ticket?*

look around (also **look round**) to look in every direction: *I **looked around** for an empty seat.*

look at someone/something 1 to look in the direction of someone or something: ***Look at** that lovely garden.* 2 to examine something: *The doctor will need to **look at** that cut.*

173

Lexicon

look back on something to think about a period when you did something in your past: *I'll **look back on** my school days with a lot of pleasure.*

look for something/someone to try to find someone or something: *We've been **looking for** you for ages.* → SEARCH FOR SOMEONE/SOMETHING

look forward to something to be excited about something that will happen: *I'm **looking forward to** meeting you.*

look into something to try to find the truth about something: *The police **are looking into** what happened.*

look out 1 to look through a window, etc: *I **looked out** and saw it was raining.* Noun: LOOKOUT; OUTLOOK 2 (also **watch out**) to be careful: ***Look out** – there's a car coming.*

look out for someone (also **watch out for**) to take care of someone by making sure they don't get into difficulties: *I've promised to **look out for** the younger members of the group.*

look round → LOOK AROUND

look through something to search papers, list, etc. to try to find something: *I've **looked through** the magazines but I can't find that photograph.*

look something up to find information in a dictionary, on the Internet, etc: *If you have problems, **look up** the words in your dictionary.*

look up to someone (for) to like and respect someone, especially someone in authority: *I've always **looked up to** my mum **for** her patience and encouragement.*

make something out 1 to manage to see something through bad light, a telescope, etc: *We could just **make out** a dark shape moving across the field.* 2 to understand something: *We couldn't **make out** his handwriting.* 3 to claim that you are someone that you aren't or you can do something you can't do: *He **made out** that he could swim to the island but he couldn't.*

make up to become friendly with someone after a quarrel: *After a quarrel that lasted more than a week, we decided to **make up**.*

make something up 1 to say or write something that is not true: *She **made up** a ridiculous excuse. You didn't see her – you **made** it all **up**.* 2 to put cosmetics on your face: *Your face **is made up** before you go on television.* Noun: MAKE-UP 3 to put things together to make something: *Young men **make up** most of United's supporters.* Noun: MAKE-UP

make up for something 1 to do something nice to make a disappointment, a bad experience, etc. better: *I'm sorry I couldn't come with you but I'll **make up for** it next weekend.* 2 to have a good quality so that bad qualities are less important: *He may not be good-looking but he **makes up for** that by being very caring.*

meet up (with) to meet someone you arranged to meet: *You all go ahead and I'll **meet up with** you later.*

miss someone/something out to not include someone or something: *My name **was missed out** from the list.*

mix something up (with) 1 to change the order or arrangement of something: *Please don't **mix up** the CDs **with** the tapes.* 2 (also **muddle something up (with)**) to put two or more things together so that you don't know which is which: *The agent has **mixed up** our flight tickets.* Noun: MIX-UP

move in to take possession of a home: *When did your new neighbours **move in**?*

move on 1 to move further along a road, etc: *The police told us to **move on**.* 2 to get a better job, home, etc: *You've worked here for several years and it's time you **moved on**.*

move out to leave a home: *They **are moving out** next week.*

muddle something up (with) → MIX SOMETHING UP (WITH)

open up 1 to open the door and let people in: *What time does the supermarket **open up**?* 2 to feel relaxed and talk: *After a few kind words from her teacher, she began to **open up**.*

part with something to give something to someone else: *I'll never **part with** your ring.*

pass away to die: *His mother **passed away** last week.*

pass by to move past someone or something: *I saw her smile as she **was passing by**.* Noun: PASSER-BY Plural: PASSERS-BY

pass through something to come into a building, town, etc. and then leave: *Thousands of refugees **have passed through** this port.* → COME THROUGH SOMETHING

pass out to suddenly become unconscious: *She **passed out** in the heat.*

pay someone/something back to return money you owe: *I must **pay back** a large loan from the bank.*

pay up to pay the money you owe: ***Pay up** or I'll tell your parents.*

perk (someone) up to become (or make someone) happier, more active, etc: *A coffee should **perk** me **up**.*

pick something out to choose something from many: *She **picked out** a small blue T-shirt.* → POINT SOMETHING OUT

pick someone up 1 to collect someone and let them ride in your car or taxi: *I'll **pick** you **up** at seven o'clock.* Noun: PICK-UP 2 to make someone feel better: *A cup of tea will soon **pick** you **up**.* 3 to talk to and get a boyfriend or girlfriend: *He tried to **pick** me **up** at the party.*

pick something up 1 to take something from the ground, etc: *You dropped the books so you must **pick** them **up**.* 2 to collect something: *I've come to **pick up** my post.* 3 to buy something: *I **picked up** a cheap coat in the market.* 4 to become affected by a disease: *She **picked up** malaria in Zimbabwe.*

point something out 1 to show something by pointing: *He **pointed out** the large size T-shirts.* → PICK SOMETHING OUT. 2 to tell someone something they did not know: *I **pointed out** that night flights are cheaper.*

pop off to die: *Do more exercise or you'll **pop off** before you're fifty!*

press ahead (with) (also **press on (with)**) to continue to make an effort to do something: *In spite of the bad report we decided to **press ahead with** our plans.*

pull into somewhere to drive into a place: *We **pulled into** the petrol station and bought a road map.*

pull out (of) to drive away from a place: *We didn't see the van as we **pulled out of** the petrol station.*

pull over to drive towards the side of the road: *The police asked us to **pull over** and stop.*

pull through to recover from a serious illness: *Suddenly she opened her eyes – she **had pulled through**.*

pull up to stop driving, running, etc: *We **pulled up** and looked at the map.*

put something aside 1 (also **put something away/by**) to save money regularly: *We're **putting aside** a few pounds each month to buy a camera.* 2 to keep a period free for a particular activity: ***Put aside** two hours every evening for your homework.*

put someone down 1 (also **put someone off**) to stop and let someone leave a taxi, etc: *Please **put** me **down** at the corner.* → LET SOMEONE OFF 2 to criticise someone: *He always **puts** her **down** in front of the children.* Noun: PUT-DOWN

put something down to write something: *Where did you **put down** her phone number?* → COPY, GET, TAKE, WRITE SOMETHING DOWN

put something forward to suggest an idea, plan, etc: *He **put forward** some interesting ideas.*

put someone off to make someone not like something or not want to do something: *The dirty knife **put** me **off** my meal.* Adj: OFF-PUTTING

put something off to delay doing something: *He **put off** telling her about it until the next morning.*

put something on 1 to dress in a piece of clothing: ***Put on** a clean shirt.* 2 to make a light, etc. start working: *Please **put** the television **on**.* 3 to become heavier: *He's **put on** a kilo since November.* 4 to perform a play, show, etc: *Which play is the National Theatre **putting on**?* 5 to pretend to have something: *She **put on** a posh accent.*

put it on to pretend to have a particular feeling: *He's not upset – he's **putting it on**.*

put someone up to let someone stay in your home: *I can **put** you **up** for a few nights.*

put something up 1 to increase an amount: *I hope they don't **put up** the rent.* 2 to build something: *They've **put up** a statue in the main square.*

put up with someone/something to accept an unpleasant person or situation: *I don't think I can **put up with** this job for much longer.*

reach for something to put your hand out in order to get something: *I saw her **reaching for** the chocolate on the shelf.*

read something over to read something and check it: *I **read over** my notes before the exam.* → GO OVER SOMETHING

Lexicon

ring (someone) up to make a phone call: *Ring me up when you get home.* → GET ON TO SOMEONE

round something off (with) to complete or end a meal, speech, etc. with something: *We rounded off dinner with a fruit salad.*

run off (with) to steal something and run: *The dog ran off with the cooked meat.* → MAKE OFF (WITH)

run away to run far away to avoid being caught, punished, etc: *The dog took the meat and ran away.*

run into someone to meet someone by chance: *Guess who I ran into in the supermarket.*

run out (of) to have no more supplies of something: *We haven't run out of milk again, have we? Yes, the milk's run out.*

run over someone/something to drive a car, etc. over someone, an animal, etc: *The dog was run over by a bus.*

saddle up to get a horse ready for you to go on a journey: *When we were saddling up, he said we had too much luggage.*

search for someone/something to look carefully for someone or something: *We searched everywhere for a cheap café.* → LOOK FOR SOMEONE/SOMETHING

send away for (also **send off for**) to order something by post: *I've sent off for an application form.*

send someone on something to arrange for someone to go on a journey, etc: *My parents sent me on a trip to London.*

send something out to distribute a notice, etc: *A letter has been sent out to all our members.*

set something aside to save an amount money: *I set aside a few pounds each month for my trip to London.*

set in to begin or appear and continue: *Cold weather has set in.*

set off (on) to start to move: *We set off on a walk to the lake.*

set out to start a journey: *We must set out early tomorrow.*

set out (to do something) to start or plan to achieve something: *We had set out to win but were pleased to come second.*

set something up 1 to put something in a particular position: *The refugees set up homes on poor soil.* 2 to arrange a meeting, etc: *I'll set up another meeting for next week.* Noun: **SET-UP**

settle down 1 to make yourself comfortable in a seat, bed, new home, etc: *How are you settling down in England?* 2 to start living a responsible life with a job, etc: *Isn't it time you settled down and got a decent job?*

shout out (for) to shout loudly: *She shouted out for help but no one heard her.* → CALL, CRY, YELL OUT

show someone in to lead someone into a room: *When the next applicant arrives, show her in, please.*

show off to show or describe your own abilities in order to make people admire you: *Stop showing off!* Noun: **SHOW–OFF**

shut up to stop talking: *Shut up and sit down.*

sidle up to someone to move slowly and carefully towards someone as if you don't want to be seen: *He sidled up to me and asked me for money.*

sit back 1 to sit comfortably: *Sit back in your chairs.* 2 to make no effort: *He sat back while others did the work.*

sit down to rest yourself in a chair, on the floor, etc: *We sat down on the nearest seat.*

sit up to sit with your back straight: *He's able to sit up in bed.*

slow down 1 to drive, develop, increase, etc. more slowly: *You should slow down in a busy street. Sales in supermarkets show no sign of slowing down, do they?* Noun: **SLOWDOWN**

sort something out 1 to arrange things in groups or a particular order: *I must sort out my old photographs.* 2 to settle disagreements, etc: *The prime minister had to sort the chaos out between the two politicians.* 3 to deal with a bad situation: *When will this mess be sorted out?*

speak out (also **speak up**) to say in public what you think or fell: *If people spoke out, the war might end.*

speak up 1 to speak more loudly: *Speak up – we can't hear you.* 2 → SPEAK OUT

speed up 1 to move faster: *We speeded up but the car was still behind us.* 2 to happen more quickly: *Changes in climate will speed up over the next ten years.*

split up (with) to no longer be someone's girlfriend or boyfriend: *I split up with my girlfriend a few months ago.*

spread out to move apart and cover or fill a larger area: *I suggest everyone spreads out and looks for her.*

stand by to not do anything to help: *He just stood by while others helped us.*

stand out to be obvious: *Her intelligence stood out.*

stand up to rise to your feet with your body upright: *We stood up as the visitor entered the room.*

stand up for someone/something to support someone, an idea, etc. that is being attacked: *You never stand up for me when dad blames me. Stand up for your rights!*

stand up to someone to refuse to accept unfair treatment from someone: *Don't let your brother tell you who to be friends with – stand up to him.*

start off (with) to start an activity: *Let's start off with a vocabulary game.* KICK, SET OFF

start out 1 to start a journey: *They started out at six o'clock.* 2 to begin your career: *He started out as a lorry driver but became a famous judge.* 3 to begin to be heard, done, etc: *Jazz started out in New Orleans.*

start something up to begin a business, group, etc: *Helen has started up a walking group.*

stay in (also **stop in**) to be at home and not go out: *I can't come to the cinema – I'm staying in tonight.* → BE IN

stay up (late) to not go to bed at the usual time: *You can stay up on Friday.* → WAIT UP (FOR)

stick something up to attach a notice, etc. on a wall, etc: *I've stuck up a poster of Madonna.*

stop in → STAY IN

stop off (at) to break your journey: *We stopped off at the motorway café for a meal.*

stroll over (to) → WALK OVER (TO)

sum up to give a short statement at the end that shows the main point: *To sum up, computers can do many tasks.*

switch off to stop paying attention: *He switches off when I ask him a question.*

switch something off to use a switch to stop a light, machine, etc. working: *Don't forget to switch off the lights.* → TURN SOMETHING OFF

switch something on to use a switch to make a light, machine, etc. work: *Switch on the kettle and let's have tea.* → TURN SOMETHING ON

take after someone to look or behave like someone: *He takes after his mother.*

take something back 1 to return with something to a shop: *This jacket doesn't fit and I'm taking it back.* → BRING, GET, GIVE SOMETHING BACK 2 to admit that you were wrong to say something: *How dare you call me a liar – take that back.*

take something down to write something: *Take down this message.* → COPY, GET, PUT, WRITE SOMETHING DOWN

take something in to understand and remember something: *I didn't take in much of what she said.* → BE TAKEN IN (BY)

take off to leave the ground: *The plane took off at seven.* Noun: **TAKE-OFF**

take someone in to make someone believe something that is not true: *We were taken in by her expensive clothes.*

take something off 1 to remove clothing: *I took off my coat.* 2 to remove something from a list: *Beef has been taken off the menu.* 3 to reduce a price: *They took ten percent off the price. I'll take off another pound from the price.* 4 to use a period of time to have a holiday, etc: *I'm taking off Friday.*

take someone on to give someone a job: *They've taken on several more men.*

take something on 1 to accept work: *You've taken on too much work.* 2 to do something about a problem: *The government must take on the problem of homelessness.*

take someone out to invite someone to go to a cinema, restaurant, etc: *I'm taking her out for a meal this evening.*

take something/it out on someone to make someone suffer because you are angry: *Just because he won't phone you – don't take your disappointment out on me! You may be angry with him, but don't take it out on me.*

take over (from) to take control from someone else: *Diana is ill and she has asked me to take over. I've taken over from Diana.*

take over something to take responsibility for something: *The government took over management of the railways.* Noun: **TAKE-OVER**

175

Lexicon

take to someone/something to form a liking for someone or something: *We took to our new teacher immediately.*
take something up to do an activity: *Paul has taken up swimming.*
take up something to use an amount of space: *The sofa is nice but it takes up too much space.*
take someone up on something to accept something that someone offers: *If he offers you the job, will you take him up on it?*
talk something over (with) to discuss something before making a decision: *Talk things over with your parents before you decide.*
talk (to someone) about something *We met at a party and talked about music for hours. I often talk to Susan in the evenings.*
think about someone/something to think carefully: *Think about what failing the exam could mean.*
think of something to invent an excuse, etc: *Can you think of one good reason why I shouldn't punish you?*
throw something away (also **throw something out**) to get rid of something because you don't want or need it: *I'm throwing out my old clothes.* → GIVE SOMETHING AWAY
throw something off to take off clothes quickly: *I threw off my coat and sat down.*
throw someone/something out (of) to make someone go, or take rubbish, etc. out, of a place: *He was thrown out of college because he didn't do any work.*
tidy (something) up to make an untidy place tidy: *Tidy up your room before you go out.*
trigger something off to cause something to start or happen: *The changes in climate have triggered off floods in many countries.*
try for something to try to get a place at a college or university, a job, a record: *He is trying for the world record. A place at university is worth trying for.*
try something on to put on clothing and see if it fits or that you like it: *Why not try on this coat?*
try something out (on) 1 to use something and find out if it works well: *I haven't tried out my new dictionary yet.* Noun: **TRY-OUT** 2 to test a skill: *Have you tried out your English on your penfriend yet?*
turn against someone to become unfriendly towards someone: *After he came out of prison, everyone had turned against him.* → BE AGAINST SOMETHING/SOMEONE
turn away to turn round and look in another direction: *He turned away and put his hands in his pockets.*
turn someone away to not allow someone into a place: *They are turning away everyone without a ticket.*
turn back to return the way you had come: *Let's turn back because the we can't see our path in this bad weather.*
turn down something to turn round and move along a street, etc: *The car turned down the road and went into the car park.*
turn someone down to refuse to allow someone to have a job, place at university, etc: *I applied for a place on the computer course but they turned me down.*
turn something down 1 to make noise, a light, heat, etc. less strong: *Turn down that television!* 2 to decide not to take a job, offer, etc: *He turned down the chance to play professional football.*
turn into someone/something to change or develop into someone or something else: *Her daughter has turned into a beautiful young woman. The caterpillar turned into a beautiful butterfly.*
turn off to drive off a road and join another one: *Turn off at the next exit.*
turn someone off to be unpleasant, not funny, etc. so that you do not like the person responsible: *His silly jokes about women really turn me off.*
turn something off to stop a light, machine, tap, etc. from giving you light, power, water, etc: *Please turn the television off. Turn it off. The street lights are turned off at dawn.* → SWITCH SOMETHING OFF
turn off something to leave one road and be in another: *We turned off the High Street into a narrow road.* Noun: **TURN OFF**

turn on someone to attack someone or treat them badly: *Why did she turn on you like that?*
turn something on to make a light, machine, tap, etc. give you light, power, water, etc: *Please turn on the radio. Turn it on.* → PUT, SWITCH SOMETHING ON
turn out 1 to appear and be present: *A large crowd turned out to greet the President.* Noun: **TURN-OUT** 2 to have a particular result: *Luckily, her treatment has turned out well. It turned out that Max had my ticket.*
turn someone out (of) to make someone leave a place: *We were all turned out of the classroom.*
turn something out 1 to stop a lamp, etc. from giving you light: *Turn out the light and go to sleep. Turn it out.* → SWITCH SOMETHING OUT. 2 to produce a piece of work: *She's been turning out some good essays this term.* 3 to take everything out of a bag, pocket, etc: *I turned out my handbag but I couldn't find my address book.*
turn over to move so that you face the other way when you are lying down: *I turned over and faced the wall.*
turn round to face the opposite direction: *I turned round to see who was behind me.*
turn to someone (for) 1 to turn round and look towards someone: *He turned to me and smiled.* 2 to ask someone for help or advice: *I don't know who to turn to. He turned to his father for advice.*
turn up to appear somewhere, especially as a surprise or after a delay: *When did Peter turn up? Don't worry – your camera will turn up.*
turn something up 1 to increase the amount of sound in a radio, etc: *I can't hear – please turn up the volume.* 2 to shorten trousers, etc: *I'll turn up your trousers.* Noun: **TURN–UP**
use something up to use all of something: *You've used up all the milk.*
walk out of somewhere to leave a place, usually because you are disappointed: *Have you ever walked out of a film?*
wake up (from) to stop sleeping: *He woke up from the anaesthetic with a bad headache.*
wake someone up to stop someone from sleeping: *The sound of the window breaking woke up the whole family.*
walk in to enter: *Look who's just walked in!*
walk out (of) 1 to leave a meeting, job, etc: *They have walked out of the talks.* Noun: **WALK-OUT**
walk over (to) (also **stroll over**) to walk towards someone: *She calmly walked over to him and pushed his arm.*
watch out → LOOK OUT
watch out for someone 1 → LOOK OUT FOR SOMEONE 2 to pay careful attention: *The owners were watching out for shoplifters.*
wear off to become less strong gradually: *The pain will soon wear off.*
wind someone up to do something so that you annoy someone: *Don't respond – he said that to wind you up.* Noun: **WIND-UP**
wipe something out to destroy something: *The disease wiped out half the population.*
work at something to try hard to do something: *He won't talk to me but I'm working at becoming friends again.*
work on something 1 to study something in order to find a solution: *Scientists have been working on a cure for leukaemia.* 2 to do work on a building, etc: *He's been working on his paintings for several weeks.*
work out 1 to happen successfully: *If things work out, we'll be home by six o'clock.* 2 to do lots of exercise: *We worked out hard at the gym.* Noun: **WORK-OUT**
work something out 1 to manage to find a solution to a problem: *I've worked out a way to get there.* → MAKE SOMETHING OUT. 2 to find the reason why: *Try to work out why you made mistakes.*
wrap up to put on warm clothes: *Wrap up well – it's cold outside.*
wrap something up to cover something: *Have you wrapped up the presents yet?*
write something down to write information: *I wrote down her phone number.* → COPY, GET, PUT, TAKE SOMETHING DOWN
zip (something) up to fasten clothes, etc. using a zip: *Zip up the tent – it's very cold.* → BUTTON, DO (SOMETHING) UP